WORKING DEMOCRACIES

WORKING DEMOCRACIES

Managing Inequality in Worker Cooperatives

Joan S. M. Meyers

ILR PRESS

AN IMPRINT OF CORNELL UNIVERSITY PRESS   ITHACA AND LONDON

First published 2022 by Cornell University Press

Library of Congress Cataloging-in-Publication Data

Names: Meyers, Joan S. M., author.
Title: Working democracies : managing inequality in worker cooperatives / Joan S. M. Meyers.
Description: Ithaca : Cornell University Press, 2022. | Includes bibliographical references and index.
Identifiers: LCCN 2021042181 (print) | LCCN 2021042182 (ebook) | ISBN 9781501763687 (hardcover) | ISBN 9781501763700 (pdf) | ISBN 9781501763694 (epub)
Subjects: LCSH: Producer cooperatives—Management. | Producer cooperatives—California—Case studies. | Equality. | Management—Employee participation.
Classification: LCC HD3444 .M48 2022 (print) | LCC HD3444 (ebook) | DDC 334.068—dc23
LC record available at https://lccn.loc.gov/2021042181
LC ebook record available at https://lccn.loc.gov/2021042182

For Bob Meyers: more than salt

Contents

Figures

Tables

Acknowledgments

An undertaking of this scope and duration is never completed alone. I am very grateful for the varied support over the years that made this work possible. My biggest debt of gratitude is to the workers at the businesses I call One World Natural Grocery and People's Daily Bread Bakery for their welcome, insight, critical feedback, teasing, and tasty food. This work would not have been as rich as it is without the generosity of those I encountered, and particularly the fifty-three current and former workers who consented to be interviewed and/or shadowed by me. This book has benefited from their collective wisdom, although of course all responsibility for accuracy and all conclusions drawn are mine alone. I am also grateful to the participating worker-owners at the Western Worker Cooperative Conferences in 2001, 2002, and 2003 for their input, and to the members of two formerly cooperative large West Coast firms who allowed me to visit and interview them.

No research can be completed without money for materials, travel, and food, California rent, and utilities while in the field, analyzing data, or writing. My early investigations were made possible by travel and research grants from the University of California, Davis's Consortium for Women and Research, Department of Sociology, Institute for Governmental Affairs, and Letters and Sciences Dean's Office. Much of my work was facilitated by early- and late-stage fellowships from the University of California Institute for Labor and Employment and its later incarnation as the University of California Labor and Education Research Fund. I was able to transform my fieldwork and research into a book manuscript thanks to a Michael W. Huber Fellowship in Democratic Capitalism from the School of Management and Labor Relations at Rutgers, the State University of New Jersey.

At the University of California, Davis, Vicki Smith gave me patient and regular counsel and excellent feedback (even years after I had left). Her interest, care, and enduring friendship have been precious beyond words. My understanding of what I was observing also benefited from the incisive critique and helpful suggestions of Fred Block, Ming-Cheng Lo, and Miriam Wells, who pointed out significant theoretical holes and often helped me find my way out of them, pushed for more empirical evidence and responsible ethnography, and helped me see the light at the end of the tunnel. Although he returned to Ireland before my research really got under way, Seán Ó Riain's initial intellectual guidance and enthusiasm allowed me to frame my initial questions. My data analysis was sustained by the insights, rewrites, questions, and camaraderie of my Davis writing group: Alison Alkon Simon, Julie Collins Dogrul, Lori Freeman, Jennifer Gregson, Julie Setele, Magdalena Vanya, and Makiko Yamaguchi, and the late and sorely missed Dina Biscotti, whose many contributions to this book include conceptualizing the grocery's distributed earnings as support for distributed management. At the wonderful and too-brief University of California Institute for Labor and Employment conference, Kim Voss offered a kind and critical reading of an early version of a chapter of the manuscript, and Richard P. Applebaum offered useful warnings.

As a postdoctoral associate at the Rutgers University School of Management and Labor Relations, I was fortunate to be drawn into the "shared capitalism" galaxy of accomplished and committed scholars and practitioners orbiting around Joseph Blasi and Doug Kruse at the annual (and insanely paced) Mid-Year Kelso Fellows Workshop and Beyster Fellowship Symposium generously funded by the Beyster Family Foundation and others. The workshopping of beginning and advanced projects have created a deep camaraderie and opened space to rethink some cherished beliefs. Through this association I have benefited from Joseph and Doug's feedback and advice, but also that of Daphne Berry, Mary Ann Beyster, Craig Borowiac, Alfredo Carlos, Adrienne Eaton, Charles Heckscher, Melissa Hoover, Mark Kaswan, Chris Mackin, Tricia McTague, Phil Melizzo, Chris Michael, Erik Olsen, Sanjay Pinto, Joyce Rothschild, Laura Hansen Schlachter, Lisa Schur, Vernon Woodward, Eric Olin Wright, Jackie Yates, and Trevor Young-Hyman. Many of their findings and insights have informed this book as we struggled together to think through questions of worker ownership, inequality, and what we can hope for in the future.

Navigation through the complexities of university procedures and forms would not have been possible without the competent and caring academic staff. I am particularly grateful to Mary Reid, Ben Timmons, and Heidi Williams at the University of California, Davis Department of Sociology; Judy Woods Lugo, Eugene McElroy, and Laura Walkoviak at the School of Management and Labor Relations at Rutgers, Department of Labor Studies and Employment Relations; Sharon Donahue and Susan Mitchell at the University of the Pacific Department of Sociology; and Christina Casillas and Dejana Fiorenza at California Polytechnic State University, San Luis Obispo Department of Social Sciences. Universities survive only by the too-often undervalued labor of their staff.

It was my great good luck to have my manuscript catch the eye of the brilliant Fran Benson before her retirement from ILR Press, and to see it steered to completion by Ellen Labbate and Mary Kate Murphy. My warmest thanks to Christine Williams and the two anonymous reviewers whose astute feedback greatly improved the book's theoretical focus and the scope of its aims. Mary Gendron and Brian Bendlin at Westchester Publishing Services provided laser-focused line editing. In.Site Collaborative's design prowess allowed the complexity of workplace democracy to take visual shape. Maneesha Kanukuntla's eagle eyes kept key errors out of print. The delightful worker-owners of Twin Oaks Indexing offered further proof of the power of worker cooperatives.

One of the best parts of being an academic is the informal sharing of ideas and work. In all the years since our Davis writing group, Alison Alkon Simon has been my most consistent cheerleader, big-picture visionary, and on-call editor—this book would be significantly less readable without her. My long-distance writing buddy, Alexandre Frenette, has kept me going when I feel demoralized or lost. Steve Vallas took me under his wing when I was struggling and provided canny counsel and super-smart editing along with his friendship. I was also the beneficiary of wise and sharp-eyed feedback on various drafts from Rachel Berger, Daphne Berry, Craig Borowiac, Dana Britton, Ed Carberry, Veronica Davidov, John-Paul Ferguson, Elizabeth Jones, Nick Mamatas, Tricia McTague, Anna Muraco, Ethel Nicdao, Eileen Otis, Kylie Parrotta, Jennifer Pierce, Sanjay Pinto, Vicki Smith, Katie Sobering, Clare L. Stacey, Lesley J. Wood, and Andrew Zitzer. Thank you for this true fellowship.

The fieldwork for a book like this is full of joy and the excitement of meeting new people. But the years of analysis and writing can be lonely, and I can't imagine how I could have got through it without the loving support of friends and family in the form of meals, drinks, desserts, a bed to sleep in on a research trip, talks, walks, dance parties, motorcycle rides, trips to the desert, and babysitting (or baby loaning). Many thanks for these and other sanity-preservation measures to Richard Aranow, Martin Battle, Toby Beauchamp, Amy Beinart, Shirley Broussard, Ed Carberry, Julie Collins-Dogrul, Julie Cowles, Cynthia Degnan, Sarah Dentan, Christina Drum, Can Dogrul, Jenny Glazer, David Gruen, Paul Hays, Elizabeth Jones, Laura Kemp, David Kimball, Sabine Kittel, Peggy Lee, Gary Mangus, Ethel Nicdao, Cyndi Perry, Greg Pullman, Gabriella Sandoval, Karyn Schwartz, Ellen Scott, Sean Streiff, R. E. Szego, Juan Carlos and Sandra Vargas, Amy Wollman, and the departed but never forgotten Mary Brown, Jonny Kaplan, and Helen Rosenfield. My mother and stepfather, Mimi Meyers and Gary Mangus, provided weeks of joyful childcare in addition to significant financial assistance in the lean years of non-tenure-track employment as a solo parent: I am so grateful to you both. Being adopted into the encouraging writing group of Coleen Carrigan and Jenny Denbow made for a very soft landing here at Cal Poly. The final stretch during the pandemic year was made bearable by the near-daily texts from wonderful colleague-friends Martine Lappé and Sara Lopus. I owe all of you some part of this book.

This project has been a constant throughout the life of my beloved kiddo, Bob Meyers, and he has accommodated my research trips, weeks-long writing binges, and deadline crankiness with a surprising degree of grace and good humor. Now a shockingly delightful teenager who takes on essential household chores and offers love and wisdom often beyond his years, Bob inspires me to keep trying to imagine and realize another world.

WORKING DEMOCRACIES

WORKER COOPERATIVES
What Workers Want

Working-class people . . . want to come in, do their job, and get home to their families. They don't want to sit through endless meetings.

—Herbert Gubbins, People's Daily Bread Bakery

Everyone knows . . . their boss is an asshole who doesn't know anything, and if the boss would just go away they could get the job done more efficiently.

—Jan Bridges, One World Natural Grocery

The 2001 annual meeting of the Western Worker Cooperative Conference has occupied the whole of Breitenbush Hot Springs, a health spa and rustic resort of cabins and a lodge scattered around a geothermal hot springs along a tributary of the North Santiam River in the Cascadian Range in Oregon. Its soothing beauty is appealing to conference organizers, but at least equally important is that it is a *worker cooperative*: a company collectively owned and run by its workers. That is, rather than investors extracting profit by paying below what the scheduling, housekeeping, grounds maintenance, cooking, and administrative labor of running a resort generates, the Breitenbush Hot Springs workers make up the collective entity that owns the business, and they share profits among themselves. In choosing this site as a place for worker-owners to share practices and insights, the international principle of "cooperation among cooperatives" (International Cooperative Alliance, n.d.) is brought to life.

In October, the thick surrounding forest is starting to flare into oranges, reds, and yellows; trails through them to the many natural saunas and hot tubs that dot the property are tempting. Nevertheless, the cheery central lodge room—its floors strewn with pillows used by most conference-goers to sit on, its walls hung with tapestries and the sort of batiked fabric that proclaims an alternative vibe—is warm and full of West Coast worker cooperative members gathered for a presentation on coordinating power between cooperative teams. Like the attendees, the presenters are almost entirely also members of worker cooperatives, although a few are members of nonprofits that provide development services, and occasionally an academic researcher like me is present. Two white women and one white man from One World Natural Grocery are explaining how their fourteen work groups choose their own method of democratic control (consensus, majority rule, or two-thirds rule) and how this affects the decisions the grocery makes together in its monthly meetings. During the question and answer period that makes up half the session, conference-goers probe members of this cooperative grocery about personal dynamics and managing conflicts. There are many approving nods when the presenters describe their system of communication notebooks and policy manuals, but it seems like half the room gasps and the other half giggles when, after being asked how they manage so many books of rules, a grocery presenter claims that any rules that do not work get "buried and forgotten." He shrugs off their reaction: "That's how it works!"[1]

A worker-owner from People's Daily Bread Bakery, Herbert Gubbins, is frown-ing. He, I know, is the bakery's CEO, although here he tends to use the title more commonly used within the bakery of "lead coordinator." A tall, severely thin white man in his fifties with neatly cropped hair, he's dressed in crisp khakis and a forest green button-down shirt embroidered with the bakery's logo, a long earring dan-gling incongruously from one ear. When called on, he compliments the grocery on its innovations, but then quickly shifts into a critique of the conference. All the workshops on management, he asserts, are about participative self-management, a deeply democratic version of the team-based management style that seems to be all the rage in the corporate world at the turn of this new century (Appelbaum et al. 2000). Herbert's voice gets harder when he says that's all well and good for young people ready to practice skills developed in their college seminars, but it is not efficient or useful for workers at his bakery. "These are working-class people who want to come in, do their job, and get home to their families. They don't want to sit through endless meetings." He says the bakery's managers—most of whom, I will later discover, were raised with little family wealth, little family or commu-nity experience of higher education, and a local culture commonly described as working-class (see, e.g., Bettie 1995; Bourdieu 1984; Halle 1984; Lareau 2002; Skeggs 2011; Willis 1977)—did not want to post a "no boss"-focused conference advertisement in the bakery because they were insulted by the insinuation that real cooperatives do not have managers. Herbert proclaims that if worker coopera-tives are to truly address the material and cultural needs of working people "who have never even heard of democratic employee ownership," the conference needs to include workshops on how to reconcile hierarchical management with worker ownership. That we need to accept the reality of management.

I was unsettled by Herbert's argument about class and worker control. Back in the Golden Valley region of Northern California, where the worker-owned cooperatives I call One World Natural Grocery and People's Daily Bread Bakery are located,[2] I had been a customer of the cooperative grocery for many years and was friends with a few of its worker-owners. I had been highly impressed by what I saw as the grocery's ability to combine individual autonomy, organizational democracy, and good, regular paychecks. The grocery appeared to give its workers flexibility but also protect the business. Workers could create their own weekly schedules or take time off work to care for family members or create art projects, but from the stories I heard, it seemed the grocery still fired shirking workers and required work groups to meet the needs of the store as a whole. Now I wondered if this balance of flexibility and financial stability was just another unfair advantage of being "elite," something only available to members of a group who, using ethnoracial and class privilege, have an outsize opportunity to wield power. It seemed true that the earlier generation of 1970s worker-owned cooperatives were composed primarily of white, college-educated youth from economically privileged homes. And the whiteness and youth of participants at the Oregon conference was unrepresentative of the US workforce. I initially took their nonconformist clothes, tattoos, facial piercings, and multicolored and unkempt hair as the sartorial markers of labor market elites, workers with physically safe and economically advantaged and secure jobs who did not need a boss's approval to guarantee an income. Herbert's explicit class criticism made me look at this a different way: Were worker cooperatives simply creating a boutique labor market, fulfilling but only open to those who had the social skills of a privileged class? I decided to pursue my curiosity about the social class, democratic control, and worker ownership.

Members of the grocery themselves would later challenge this pessimistic assessment. I interviewed grocery members during the pilot phase of my project (see appendix A), but when I asked how they felt about the required levels of participation, only one person—herself from an economically and educationally privileged family background—agreed with Herbert's assessment of people from culturally working-class backgrounds as only wanting to do routine tasks and improve their paychecks. Others, almost all of whom were raised with little economic privilege, rejected this claim and instead described the personal appeal of not having a boss and therefore having more control over their business. Jan Bridges, a white woman from an economically marginalized background with a high school diploma and a few years of college, said, "Everyone knows when they have a boss that their boss is an asshole who doesn't know anything, and if the boss would just go away they could get the job done more efficiently. So that's how it works in our work group. We just do it, get it done." She offered an empirical counter to Herbert's characterization of lower-class people being unskilled in business administration. Sweeping her arm out towards the numerous family-owned stores in the economically marginal neighborhood around us, she said, "All kinds of working-class people run their own businesses every day.... Every liquor store in every street corner is a small business owned by working-class people." As she saw it, economically marginalized people did their best to exert entrepreneurial decision-making in small groups whenever they possibly could.

These, then, are two strikingly different views of what workers want, and two different ideas about democratic employee ownership and working-class options. On the one hand is Herbert's claim regarding participatory democracy's exclusion of people who have been called *the working class*: those who must labor most of their lives for a wage in order to purchase food, shelter, clothing, and other necessities for survival; who tend to live and play and create culture with others in similar economic relations; and whose opportunities—for work, education, material goods, and political power—are actively constrained for the benefit of the upper classes. In his eyes, the insistence of most worker cooperatives on participatory self-management reproduces an organizational structure that not only saps the energies of working people but also subtly transfers power to other members, those whose class culture develops in them the skills and training to manipulate organizational processes. On the other hand is Jan's assertion that people Herbert would consider "working class" can and do run their own businesses quite well, and that top-down management hinders productivity and profitability. This book explores how working people manage these different ideas about democracy, organization, and economic life.

What Do Workers Want?

The worker-owned cooperative essentially poses the question, "What do workers want?" and attempts to address perceived worker needs and desires. As with organized labor, this answer has rarely focused on the entire spectrum of "workers' interests." Stable and economically supportive jobs have been at the forefront of all worker demands, yes, but less consistent have been those for respect and dignity, safety, workplace voice, the expression of human creativity, control over what is created and how it is made, or ethnoracial and gender equality. Indeed, the labor movement of the first half of the twentieth century primarily (but not uniformly) pursued only the first (Lipset, Trow, and Coleman 1956; Lipsitz 1994).

Yet workers have made claims on far more than jobs and pay. The postwar period has seen increasing demands in and out of unions for more "say/influence/representation/participation/voice (call it what you will)" (Freeman and Rogers 2006, 32), even if top-down management and a lack of shared ownership are accepted as givens (Appelbaum et al. 2000; Blauner 1966). Furthermore, although most people will opt for choices that seem in the realm of the possible—for instance, the *voice rights* of what organizational theorist Catherine Turco (2016) describes as the "conversational firm" rather than the *resource rights* of worker ownership—a strain of labor organizing dating back to the turn of the last century has repeatedly proposed the "unimaginable": shorter workweeks and compensation for domestic labor (Federici 1975; Roediger and Foner 1989; Weeks 2011). Some union traditions have insisted on ethnoracial or gender egalitarianism (Milkman 2007; Roediger 1999). Some clearly labor-focused, if not strictly union, organizing has demanded democratic worker associations to determine labor and production (Comisso 1979; Fung and Wright 2001; Gordon Nembhard 2014; Pateman 1970; Polletta 2002). And, either as revolutionary social movements (Brenner, Brenner, and Winslow 2010; Lenin 2012; Shafer 2005; Taylor 2010) or as the "recovery" of formerly investor-owned factories (Larrabure, Vieta, and Schugurensky 2011; Vieta 2009), one strain of worker demand has long focused on worker ownership.

A Tale of Two Worker Cooperatives

Understanding the difference between what the workers of One World Natural Grocery and People's Daily Bread Bakery wanted was, it turned out, much more complicated than identifying class differences or acknowledging managers' inefficiency. Indeed, through interviews, observation that was both intensive and intermittent, and a review of financial and historical records between the fall of 2001 and the spring of 2005 (see appendix A), I discovered that almost all of the members of both cooperatives shared similar levels of personal and family education, family wealth and occupational prestige, and "class culture," as I discuss in this chapter. At both sites the people I met had almost all stopped their education at high school, had little to no family wealth as a fallback, and were working in the kinds of manual production or service jobs that are usually considered low-skill and low-pay. They were what some might call working-class people doing working-class jobs. While there was a great deal of variation between how the bakery and grocery workers "got it done"—that is, in how day-to-day working conditions were structured through managerial authority at the bakery and through democratic processes at the grocery—there was also a great deal of overlap in how these authority structures were codified, documented, and formally implemented. Indeed, although I initially saw myself as studying the difference between bureaucratic and antibureaucratic organizations, over time I came to see each as embodying a distinct but nonetheless equally bureaucratic form.

There were, however, areas of divergence. While the grocery had preserved its gender balance, bakery women were a small minority, and power and authority mapped onto race/ethnicity at the bakery in a way not found at the grocery.

I began to wonder about how a shared vision of social and economic justice had produced such different levels of opportunity by race/ethnicity and gender. I strongly suspected that organizational practices were an important part of this story of divergence, but did not yet understand how or why these practices mattered. Although the worker cooperative community was not yet talking about "scale" in a way it does now (Abell 2014), it seemed likely to me that worker cooperatives would be like other small businesses: likely to fail unless they grew. I therefore focused my original pilot interviews on members of cooperatives with at least one hundred workers, eventually settling on the grocery and the bakery. As I spent more time with members of the two cooperatives—shadowing the daily activities of more than thirty bakery and grocery cooperative members in their workplaces, interviewing members in their homes or in cafés and bars, sitting in on large and small meetings, and attending a variety of social events— I came to better understand what was at stake and how practices shaped (and were shaped by) the way each organization interpreted its workers' interests.

Most of the countercultural cooperatives evaporated before the mid-1980s. This was due in part to the ebb of their customers' sociopolitical commitments. And in part the expectations and needs of the typically college-educated collective members grew: as they discovered other, more profitable, job opportunities, their withdrawal often left their organizations strapped for cash and expertise. Yet by the time I arrived to study these companies in 2001, both One World Natural Grocery and People's Daily Bread Bakery had not merely survived but had transformed demographically, economically, and organizationally.

Both companies were still owned by a majority of their workers, but these workers were different from the founders. As table 1.1 shows, both were ethnoracially diverse, particularly compared to noncooperative bakeries and retail stores. Further, most members described family backgrounds with little disposable income or wealth, and little education for themselves or their parents beyond high school. As Dutch Henry, a white seven-year veteran of the sales and delivery work group who described himself as working-class, observed, "There's not many silver-spoon people there." Both companies had grown: the bakery's varied line of organic baked goods was available fresh and frozen in mainstream supermarket chains throughout North America; the grocery had made a series of expansion moves until it settled into a former car showroom covering almost half a city block. In 2003 the bakery had over a hundred employees and net revenues of $17.5 million, and the grocery over two hundred employees and net revenues just shy of $25 million.[3] Both companies were in the process of

TABLE 1.1 Bakery and grocery worker demographics in 2003

WORKFORCE DEMOGRAPHICS	BAKERY SAMPLE: 95 (100)	GROCERY SAMPLE: 185 (234)	CALIFORNIA NONRETAIL BAKERY WORKERS (INDUSTRY)	CALIFORNIA GROCERY WORKERS (INDUSTRY)
People of color	44% (42)	39% (72)	20%	18%
Whites	56% (53)	61% (113)	80%	82%
Transgender/ nonbinary	—	1% (2)	—	—
Women	15% (14)	53% (99)	30%	50%
Men	85% (81)	46% (85)	70%	50%
Women of color	2% (2)	23% (43)		
Men of color	42% (40)	15% (28)		
White women	13% (12)	30% (56)		
White men	43% (41)	31% (57)		

Sources: Bakery and grocery data from the two cooperatives' own reporting; state-level California worker data from Hirsch and Macpherson (2004).

Notes: Neither sample includes employees who worked on average less than five hours per week, had not been employed long enough to be eligible for membership, or were hired more than six months or terminated less than six months into the fiscal year. Total population for the cooperatives follows sample size (in parentheses); neither sample fully captures employment at either cooperative. An em dash (—) indicates no data reported. Only the grocery reported more than two genders; grocery gender numbers do not entirely add up, as one of the two grocery transgender workers identified as both transgender and as a man. The grocery permitted established workers to become "special members" (working fewer than the twenty-four-hour threshold for health benefits), and this option was taken by more women than men, and more whites than Black or Brown members. The bakery strongly discouraged part-time employment (only two part-time members were on the payroll), but hired a steady stream of contracted workers in production who were not tracked by the bakery's personnel accounting but were anecdotally and visually identified as entirely composed of men and almost entirely of Latinx men.

expanding their spaces and workforces. Both provided employees with generous health, education, and vacation benefits, and both paid well above nonunion and union wages for food production and retail work in the region (see table 1.2). In short, both the bakery and grocery were economically stable businesses providing what Arne Kalleberg (2011) has identified as increasingly rare "good jobs" to an ethnoracially diverse group of people whose educational and economic backgrounds offered few other such options.

There were, however, visible and significant differences in the two organizations. The grocery maintained its slight majority of women (54 percent), and there were only very small ethnoracial or gender differences in earnings, job distribution, decision-making authority, or job autonomy.[4] In contrast, things at the bakery were generally less egalitarian. Although bakery women had higher average earnings than did bakery men (see table 1.2), this was largely because they were a small minority (15 percent) of the workforce, and concentrated in white-collar positions in the all-women office. Eighty-three percent of the Black

TABLE 1.2 Bakery and grocery worker earnings in 2003

	BAKERY	GROCERY	CALIFORNIA UNIONIZED BAKERS (OCCUPATION)	CALIFORNIA NONUNIONIZED BAKERS (OCCUPATION)	CALIFORNIA UNIONIZED RETAIL SALES (OCCUPATION)	CALIFORNIA NONUNIONIZED RETAIL SALES (OCCUPATION)
Mean Annual Earnings						
All employees	$61,374	$40,155	$48,100	$39,700	$45,600	$46,700
Whites	$67,955	$40,134				
People of color	$54,080	$41,227				
Men	$60,999	$43,400				
Women	$68,104	$38,623				
White men	$67,461	$43,409				
White women	$69,687	$37,030				
Men of color	$53,854	$43,382				
Women of color	$58,606	$40,721				
2003 metropolitan area median annual earnings	$31,660	$39,320				
Mean Hourly Earnings						
All employees	$32.46	$28.28	$12.38	$10.73	$11.03	$12.59
Whites	$35.93	$28.97				
People of color	$27.83	$27.17				

Men	$31.80	$28.62
Women	$36.67	$28.08
White men	$35.59	$29.20
White women	$37.10	$28.76
Men of color	$27.53	$27.34
Women of color	$34.06	$27.19
2003 metropolitan area mean hourly wage	$19.12	$24.15

Sources: Bakery and grocery data from the two cooperatives' own reporting; occupation-level data are from Hirsch and Macpherson (2004); metropolitan area median annual earnings and mean hourly earnings data are from the Bureau of Labor Statistics 2003.

Notes: Descriptive statistics of annual earnings include wages or salaries, profit sharing (in cash and value shared of the company), and dividends paid on accrued noncash shares; the comparison is somewhat incomplete, as grocery employees also received a 20 percent discount on food, and their health care benefits were more generous than those of bakery workers. Hourly earnings are derived by dividing each worker's annual earnings by recorded hours; as required for profit sharing as an outcome of hours worked, even salaried bakery managers recorded their hours. Note that the data for women of color at the bakery is based on only two such workers, both in white-collar jobs. While occupation-level data for the categories of bakers and retail sales are not entirely comparable for all workers at the bakery or the grocery—some of whom worked in white-collar or other blue-collar jobs—it is the only level at which union/nonunion earnings data are available.

and Latinx bakery workers were in the all-men production division, doing the hottest, dirtiest, least autonomous, and lowest-paid jobs.[5] While bakery women were overrepresented as managers (30 percent), Latinx workers were underrepresented (20 percent of managers, but 40 percent of the bakery workforce), and there were only two Latinx women in any areas.[6] That is, while power, jobs, and earnings at the bakery were largely segregated and stratified by race/ethnicity and gender, at the grocery such segregation and stratification were minimal.

Just as clearly different was how each organization structured authority and the coordination of work. After financial crises in the 1980s, each organization had hired consultants to help restructure but had gone in opposite directions from their collectivist origins: the bakery to permanent and positional management supervised by a board of directors elected from the membership, and the grocery to the formalization and increased coordination of highly decentralized work group self-management. While there was pushback at both cooperatives—some bakery workers decried management as against the spirit of cooperation, and some grocery workers repeatedly proposed adding managerial positions for greater efficiency and profitability—there had been no change in structure for over ten years by the time I first began my study and, indeed, these remain the organizational structures of these cooperatives as this book goes to press.

But if I thought the presence or absence of managers meant I was going to be studying the difference between bureaucratic and antibureaucratic organizations, I was mistaken. Indeed, the bakery was typically bureaucratic, as I discovered when I asked a bakery driver, Leslie Johnson, if I could interview her to get my first sense of the bakery. She strongly urged me to wait and start "at the top" by contacting Herbert, the "lead coordinator," and letting him connect me to managers who could then help solicit nonmanager interviews for me. Her stated belief that my study would go more smoothly if I showed respect to the organizational hierarchy may not have been accurate, but Herbert certainly did facilitate my entrée to the bakery. After our first formal interview in November 2001, he directed the board of directors, managers, and every cooperative member I asked about to talk to me and made it clear that, as long as I did not interfere with the operation of machinery or client interactions, all time spent with me would be part of the worker-owners' paid hours. Yet when I thanked him for taking nearly two hours out of his day for that first interview, he dismissed my interpretation of his time as kindness and claimed that he could now tell the board of directors—whom he described as his "bosses" despite directly supervising most of them—that he had fulfilled the part of his job description that required dissemination of information about worker cooperatives to a broader public. As I pondered the complexity of being formally accountable to a group of people over whom one also held hiring and firing power, I also began to realize that cooperative worker ownership changed bureaucratic hierarchies in significant ways.

I would, however, learn much more when I approached the grocery. I expected my social ties with members—including a former board member—to ease my way into the grocery, but I was entirely wrong about that. Acting on the recommendation of this former board member, I wrote the board a letter requesting permission to approach workers for interviews and on-site observation. I then heard nothing for weeks while the board reviewed my letter at a weekly meeting, deemed itself to be the wrong authority for this matter, shuttled the letter to the Intracooperative Coordinating Committee (ICC), and considered the matter over. The ICC tabled my request for a few weeks while addressing more immediate issues, but finally—after soliciting a signed two-stage confidentiality agreement and a personal liability waiver—approved my application with a formal permission letter that I would be required to present upon demand. Indeed, when an ICC member called to let me know I had been given the green light and I immediately went to a membership meeting, I was turned away by the meeting's facilitator—a man who was himself a member of the ICC and had met me at least once socially—because I did not yet have the mailed physical copy of the document approving my research. Grocery members' insistence on following formal rules, adhering to stated organizational policies, and relying on written documents to designate roles and boundaries continued throughout my period of study, and made it clear to me that this was no antibureaucratic organization.

One of the surprising discoveries to me of this research process was the *variation of bureaucracy* and what I came to see as the centrality of these differences to workplace. Similar to the variations identified by other social scientists (Adler and Borys 1996; Ashcraft 2001; Gouldner 1954; Hales 2002), my study of the grocery helped me to identify what I came to call *participatory bureaucracy* (which I examine more fully in chapter 7). Indeed, I came to see bureaucracy and its variations as a critical part of worker cooperative survival and the part played by worker cooperatives in the disruption or reproduction of social inequality.

While no comparison of only two organizations can answer—or even raise—all possible questions, the study of these two worker-owned cooperatives helps to address questions in three areas of inquiry: (1) the potential and limitations of democratic worker ownership; (2) the relationship between organizational structure and workplace inequality, particularly as crystallized in locally specific ideas about what it means to be a "worker" within a worker cooperative; and (3) the relationship between the reconfiguration of workplaces through worker ownership and the potential reconfiguration of labor more generally. In this chapter, I clarify the types, potentials, and limitations of *worker ownership* and particularly the worker cooperative. But I also raise the key themes of the rest of the book: How does *worker control* change (or not change) workplace inequality? What is the relationship between organizational structure and organizational inequality? Why did two initially similar organizations develop into ones that were very different from each other and from most other cooperatives of their era? Particularly given their proximity to each other, the similarly privileged demographics of their founders, and the similarity of the external pressures they faced as they stabilized and grew between the mid-1970s and today, what explains the difference in degree and type of inequality—again, between each other and compared to their founding cohort? Can organizational structure significantly minimize or eliminate inequalities of class, race/ethnicity, and/or gender within an economic system built on differentiation and exclusion? How do conditions of worker ownership change the meaning of the term *worker* itself? How are *worker identities* produced in organizations owned by the workers? How do worker cooperatives conceive of those who labor together within them? How can these conceptions interrupt or facilitate the reproduction of the inequality found in the larger labor market?

Finally, I ask what worker cooperatives might offer beyond their own boundaries. What futures do worker cooperatives *prefigure*, or attempt to enact even in an unsatisfying present (Breines 1989; Dinerstein 2015)? Is prefiguration even possible, or do the constraints of capitalism in the United States in the early decades of the twenty-first century make that impossible? Can worker cooperatives act as bridges between other economic actors (corporate firms and labor movements), developing worker-centered practices to aid members of non-worker-owned enterprises, and supplying a new generation of members to the labor movement (Pinto 2018)? Is there a danger of inadvertent co-optation, transforming potentially oppositional workers into owners and directors of others' labor? Or do worker cooperatives help to enrich just and sustainable economic alternatives like consumer or housing cooperatives, B Corporations (benefit corporations), nonprofits, and other "real utopian" projects (Wright 2011) in a broader *solidarity economy* (Dacheux and Goujon 2011; Utting et al. 2015)?

Worker Ownership

When Jan said that "all kinds of working-class people run their own businesses every day," she was right. People who are paid low wages and whose jobs are labeled "unskilled" and thoroughly managed by others regularly and repeatedly find ways to opt out, setting up their own small businesses that are at least initially staffed only by themselves and perhaps family members. Usually, however, they move on to some small employment of others, and many hope to eventually convert entirely from being a worker to simply being an owner.

Types of Worker Ownership

Other forms of worker ownership are less transitory, instead intended to be a stable form of ownership. A common form in the United States—covering an estimated nearly 14.5 million workers (National Center for Employee Ownership 2020)—is the employee stock ownership plan (ESOP). An ESOP is a trust that holds a part or all of an existing firm's ownership, and benefits the firm's permanent workers as retirement funds payable in proportion to the firm's financial health, the worker's length of employment, and (usually) individual wages or salary (Blasi, Kruse, and Bernstein 2003). Such plans typically do not include profit sharing or payment of dividends, and despite the intentions of the plan's "inventor," Louis Kelso, many allow workers to riskily invest savings from their wages back into their company (Blasi, Freeman, and Kruse 2013). Furthermore, most current ESOPs do not include nonmanagerial workers on their boards of directors, although the trend is changing following research suggesting that such inclusion improves several measures of business health (Blasi, Freeman, and Kruse 2013; Rosen, Case, and Staubus 2005).

Other forms of what has been called shared capitalism include stock options programs that reward performance or length of tenure with grants of corporate stock (although they are more commonly aimed at managerial employees) or 401(k) matching (Kruse, Freeman, and Blasi 2010). Thus, in the United States, the only form of worker ownership that does not discriminate by occupation, does not defer realization of profitability until retirement, and demands a voice for workers in how the company is run is the *worker cooperative*.

Worker cooperatives are formed when people choose to pool their resources and create a new entity that collectively owns what Karl Marx (1976) called "the means of production": factories, tools, performance spaces, and so on. Due to a long history of US laws and social practices that limited the ability of men and women of color and white women to accumulate resources to pool in the way white men could (Chang 2006; Oliver and Shapiro 1997), it is easier for worker cooperatives to be formed by white men. By the same token of institutional racism and sexism, however, the capital necessary to start a private noncooperative enterprise is more easily achieved by white men. That is, worker cooperative formation is simultaneously harder to achieve and potentially more attractive to entrepreneurial people marginalized by the structuring of economies.

Worker cooperatives have been and continue to be highly varied in industry and structure. They can range from complex firms with multiple levels of management and wage differentials, to small groups of co-managers distributing tasks and wealth equally, to individual professionals having little more contact than a shared front office and advertising. It has been possible to turn to a worker cooperative to acquire almost anything one could ask for at different points in history, whether goods (food, clothing, shoes, dry goods, lumber, furniture, bicycles, technological machinery, or adult sex aids) or services (computing, domestic, educational, exotic dancing, legal, or massage; Curl 2009; Gregor 2013; Hoover, Harris, and Johnson 2012; Leikin 2004).

In the United States, workers have formed cooperatives more often in times of economic crisis than prosperity (Dickstein 1991), often in concert with or reaction to larger social movements of the time. As chapter 2 outlines, most worker cooperative activity in the United States occurred in three periods marked by both economic crisis and social movement activity: the late 1800s, the 1930s, and the 1970s. During these periods, reduced competition in the mainstream labor market and widespread social discourses addressing inequality supported worker cooperatives. It seems that we are currently witnessing a new period of worker cooperative proliferation (Hoover, Harris, and Johnson 2012; Monaco and Pastorelli 2013; Palmer 2014, 2017; Witherell 2013). Yet while worker cooperatives are no more likely to fail than other small businesses (Pinto 2018), they have tended to convert to noncooperative firms as labor markets and social movements themselves reconfigure and as cooperative logics are undermined by social discourses valorizing individual financial gain.

What Is a Worker Cooperative?

Despite being a regular part of an economics curriculum a hundred years ago, the disappearance of cooperative structure from financial education (Kalmi 2007) makes a review of worker cooperatives necessary. Worker cooperatives are firms in which (1) there are no private, external investor owners (all owners are also employees); (2) ownership is available to all workers, and the majority of workers are member-owners; and (3) the membership as a whole has ultimate authority over any elected officers or managers.[7] As sociologist and labor activist Sanjay Pinto (2018) has noted in his exhaustive review, worker cooperatives are located at the nexus of multiple forms of economic action and organization: cooperative associations, for-profit firms, ESOPs and nondemocratic forms of worker ownership, the solidarity economy, and worker movements. Worker cooperatives operate under internationally established cooperative principles that include education about and training in cooperative practice and history, broad availability of membership, collaboration with other cooperatives where possible, and the support of local communities (International Cooperative Alliance, n.d.). Although worker cooperatives share these characteristics with other kinds of cooperatives, what sets them apart is that their only shareholders are their workers rather than their residents, their consumers, or their neighbors.[8] And although they share certain characteristics with corporate firms and nondemocratic employee-owned firms (see table 1.3),[9] what sets worker cooperatives apart is that, unlike most businesses where the power to make long-range decisions about the company is allocated in proportion to a person's share of invested capital, cooperative power is distributed equally on the principle of one person, one vote.

While democratic decision-making is not exclusive to cooperative enterprises, the allocation of voting power by person rather than by number of shares held distinguishes worker cooperatives from both private partnerships (where partners may have unequal voting rights corresponding to unequal ownership shares of the firm) and ESOPs (where workers as a whole are given some proportion of the company's stock and proportional voting power, but the vote is cast as a single block by a trustee who is typically appointed by senior management or a small committee; Blasi, Freeman, and Kruse 2013).[10] Where traditional capitalist firms presume control over work derives from ownership of capital, and communist enterprises have allocated that control to state actors based on a diffuse people's mandate, such control in democratic firms is given directly to a firm's workers: the newest and perhaps most lowly paid member of a cooperative has the same formalized voice as that of the most senior and/or highly paid member.

Attempting to balance democratic commitment with the efficiency demands of contemporary capitalism, worker cooperatives have experimented with *organizational structure*, or the set of formal and informal rules, policies, and practices that distribute power within a particular firm. A membership is the source of organizational power in all democratic firms, but a firm's *governance* can vary along a continuum from entirely participatory (all workers discuss and make decisions as a group) to entirely representative (all decisions are made by a range of elected leaders). For instance, a worker cooperative may elect a representative committee to research and invest for the cooperative's future, but may vote or come to unanimous or near-unanimous consensus on the annual budget. Although cooperative scholar Frances Viggiani finds that self-described "democratic" work organizations are more likely than conventional firms to problematize issues of "accountability, ownership, or authority" (1997, 256), she and others (Pateman 1970; Polletta 2002) also note that "democracy" contains a number of different meanings in terms of reward, responsibility, and, critically, the delegation of authority.

This is because, in addition to different forms of democratic governance, there are also different forms of democratic *management* practices. Authority may be arranged in a steeply *hierarchical managerial structure*, with hired or appointed

TABLE 1.3 Comparison of worker cooperatives with other common forms of economic organization

		CORPORATION	ESOP	WORKER COOPERATIVE	NONWORKER COOPERATIVE
Ownership	Who owns	Those who buy shares; top management	Retirement trust administered on behalf of workers	Workers	Users
	Basis of ownership	Capital	Employment, or mix of employment and capital	Labor	Consumption of goods/services
Organizational structure	Governance	Voting by share of firm value (often by proxy)	Voting by share of firm value (usually by proxy)	One person, one vote (members); may require consensus	One person, one vote (members); may require consensus
	Management	Managerial, ranging from very steeply to gradually hierarchical	Managerial, ranging from very steeply to gradually hierarchical	Varied: collectivist-democratic (may require consensus); managerial; hybrid democratic/managerial	Varied: collectivist-democratic (may require consensus); managerial; hybrid democratic/managerial
Profits	Who benefits and how	Owners: immediate share of profits based on ownership share Workers: highly differentiated salaries and wages	Workers: deferred share of profits using formula based on hours, wages/salary, and/or seniority; highly differentiated salaries and wages Owners, if they exist outside ESOP: immediate share of profits based on ownership share	Worker-owners: mix of immediate and deferred share of profits based on hours; moderately differentiated to nondifferentiated salaries and/or wages	Consumers: share of profits, discounts, access to goods and services Workers: typically differentiated salaries and wages

directors, managers, and supervisors making decisions for employees. Or it may be an entirely flat *distributed managerial system*, with big decisions made by the whole group and small decisions delegated to individual initiative. Most cooperatives, however, operate somewhere in between, using a *hybrid managerial structure* of elected or appointed committees and work groups that have some discretionary power but are accountable to the membership as a whole. As chapter 2 will explore, cooperatives have a long history of internal debate over the value of different organizational structures, not only for their effects on worker autonomy and creativity but also for their economic benefits, and the result has been a diversity of workplace structures that at least nominally preserve the final word for the worker membership.

Worker cooperatives exist within a larger universe of economic and community cooperation. *Consumer* cooperatives—in North America, many of which are grocery stores—hire labor like typical businesses but coordinate the purchasing power of local residents to reduce costs, provide access to particular goods, and socially connect community members (Cotterill 1978; Viggiani 1999). *Agricultural* cooperatives involve neighboring farmers sharing machinery, distribution, and advertising (Cook 1995; Schneiberg, King, and Smith 2008). *Housing* cooperatives allow residents to collectively choose their neighbors and, to some extent, regulate their actions (Sazama 2000; Sousa 2015). *Financial* cooperatives (chiefly credit unions and insurance agencies) reduce costs for members of a particular community—defined geographically, by profession, or by institutional affiliation—and reinvest the savings in that community (Schneiberg 2011). *Utility* cooperatives coordinate the purchase of energy or water, often in areas where entirely profit-oriented corporations will not do business (Parker 1956; Selznick 1949). *Childcare* cooperatives often mix worker and consumer modes, allowing parents to learn parenting practices from each other and to save money on quality day care by providing all or most of the labor (Lindquist, Restakis, and Institute of Public Administration of Canada 2001).

Worker cooperatives share some goals with these other types: like consumer, agricultural, and childcare cooperatives, they seek to build community through mutual aid; like financial and utility cooperatives, they seek to return value to those who produce it rather than to investor-owners (Cheney et al. 2014). But they have critical differences from them as well. Worker cooperatives have attempted to reduce labor market inequalities and to create spaces where autonomous, creative, and financially supportive human activity can flourish. Sometimes these projects have overlapped; at other times they have been distinct, as worker-owners struggled over the meanings of worker ownership and democratic control within the context of business organizations operating in capitalist economies.

Worker cooperatives in capitalist economies thus face three inherent tensions. First, the ownership orientation of members to preserve working capital conflicts with their worker orientation to the just rewards for the value they create as they attempt to *economically empower* their members. Second, the democratic ethos of self-rule quickly comes up against the collective need for delegation and coordination of authority in order to compete successfully with nondemocratic firms, and this forces cooperatives to make hard choices regarding the *social empowerment* of their members. Third, the different market values of members' skills—particularly as shaped by market valuation of demographic characteristics—conflicts with the equity orientation of the worker cooperative project and produces cooperative struggles over the *egalitarian allocation* of power and resources.

Both cooperatives in this study were once prototypical cooperatives of the 1970s: they were both founded and initially staffed by entirely or almost entirely white, privileged youth from the "hippie" counterculture, a loosely connected subculture of psychedelic drug enthusiasts, peace and social justice activists, and cultural revolutionaries experimenting with alternative social institutions, including the workplace (Epstein 1991; Howard 1969; Miller 1991). In keeping with the "antiestablishment" ethos of this subculture, the cooperatives had few formal rules and little official leadership. Unlike most of the other thousand or so collectives of the 1970s (Jackall and Levin 1984), the bakery and the grocery continued as worker cooperatives, although their structures and cultures changed over time. Typical of worker cooperatives in the present moment, the bakery and the grocery have minimized a "peace and love" rhetoric and practice and have heightened their focus on the administration and organization of labor and other resources critical to their survival. Both cooperatives now have clearly delineated divisions of labor; extensive employee manuals specifying expected and acceptable actions, disciplinary policies, and grounds for termination; long-standing relationships with traditional lenders; and widely used cultural practices helping them distinguish personal from workplace relationships.

The makeover of the contemporary cohort of worker cooperatives has produced an ongoing conflict between the bureaucratic promise of efficiency and financial solvency on one hand and the human promise of protecting workers' creativity and autonomy on the other. The current period of worker cooperative expansion sits uneasily with cooperatives' desire to meet their workers' needs, particularly given the US reconfiguration of so-called working-class (manual and service) jobs as far more Black, Brown, and women.

On one hand, worker cooperative growth is drawing in many more labor market actors. In Argentina, Brazil, and Venezuela, urban workers have been occupying and running factories abandoned by their former owners (Dinerstein 2007; Larrabure, Vieta, and Schugurensky 2011; Lima 2007; Sobering 2016). The

United States saw the 2013 election of a "solidarity economy" mayor in Jackson, Mississippi (Bell et al. 2018), and the inclusion of a $1.2 million cooperative development fund in the 2014 New York City budget (Ifateyo 2014). In Cleveland the international cooperative Mondragón Corporation collaborated with the United Steelworkers to develop an "anchor institution" model of private, state, and community partnership that now operates three worker-owned cooperatives in low-income communities (Alperovitz, Howard, and Williamson 2010; Schlachter 2017). More than twenty immigrant cleaning and landscaping cooperatives now exist across the United States, many of them developed in the wake of the 2008 financial crisis (Hoover, Harris, and Johnson 2012). But because these cooperatives are drawing on more diverse and less "countercultural" labor populations, they face an urgent need to find solutions to manage diversity and create egalitarian outcomes. This raises the question of what role organizational structure itself plays.

Worker Control

"The decisive reason for the advance of bureaucratic organization," writes Max Weber, "has always been its purely technical superiority over any other form of organization" (Weber 1946, 214). Bureaucracies delegate authority permanently, classify job responsibility and authority on the basis of skill and ability rather than social status or kinship structures, organize the labor process in terms of rational efficiency rather than personal preference or social standing, and formalize procedures and policies to create specific ways of accomplishing tasks "precisely, unambiguously, continuously, and with as much speed as possible" (Weber 1946, 215). When Herbert interpreted the desires of People's Daily Bread Bakery workers to reduce time at work in favor of time at home, he was articulating a bureaucratic vision of efficiency: decision-making streamlined in the interest of maximized earnings. For these reasons, bureaucracy has been the vehicle through which capitalism spread. It is all but impossible to imagine a successful business that does not use basic bureaucratic principles; even "post-bureaucratic" firms (Heckscher and Donnellon 1994) such as Google have fairly traditional divisions of administrative and manual labor, meritocratic recruitment and promotion policies, and formalized work processes—presumably to maximize efficiency and profit.

Yet for most people the term *bureaucracy* does not imply productive ease or sustainability. Bureaucracy is associated with "red tape": the molasses pace and drudgery of excessive formal documentation, unending rules, and dehumanizing routine. The earliest cooperative movements opposed not only the exploitation of workers in the interests of profit but also the disruption of their autonomy and creativity, which external management was seen as inevitably producing. Managerial disruption of workers' abilities is precisely what Jan complained about and contrasted with the self-management process at One World Natural Grocery. In the present moment, bureaucracy is most clearly associated with all that reduces speed and nimbleness.

And the drag of red tape is not bureaucracy's only problem. Its seemingly depersonalized rational efficiency conceals enduring social beliefs, processes, and meanings that are very human—very *social* indeed. Joan Acker has argued that capitalist bureaucracy is at the heart of "inequality regimes" (2006b, 443): where job knowledge is preserved within classed, raced, and gendered cliques to unequally affect progress up career ladders; where specific jobs are defined in terms that privilege the socialization of men, whites, and those from the middle and upper classes; where restrictive policies and rules can be ignored by those with greater social power but limit the options of those with less; and where social advantage congeals into hierarchical organizational power. These inequality regimes, Acker notes, rely on and—more insidiously—reinforce social beliefs about race, class, and gender.

These critiques of bureaucracy inspired the 1970s countercultural collectivist era of worker cooperatives, organizations often formed by members of the 1960s counterculture that ran the gamut from hard-core political activists in social justice—for example, in the Civil Rights and Women's Liberation Movements (Mellor, Hannah, and Stirling 1988)—to those focused on "lifestyle," such as yogis and natural foods advocates (Gitlin 1993; McMillian and Buhle 2003). Unlike the earlier labor republican and self-help generations of worker cooperatives I describe in chapter 2, these were what Joyce Rothschild describes as "collectivist-democratic" organizations (Rothschild-Whitt 1979). Characterized by their consensus-based flat authority, task rotation to minimize problematic specialization, and commitment to shared human connections between equals in the workplace (Rothschild and Whitt 1986), these cooperatives were also relatively homogeneous organizations, sharing not only political or social values but also a narrow range of age, race/ethnicity, and class demographic attributes: they were young, white, economically privileged, and often college-educated (Davis 2017; Jackall and Crain 1984).

The bakery and the grocery were in many ways typical countercultural collectivist cooperatives at their inception. When I asked the most senior bakery employee, Adam Delaney, a white man with a long graying ponytail, what drew him to the bakery in 1982, he simply replied, "Hippies." When I asked what he meant, he explained, "It [was] a hippie bakery," and went on to explain that it was comforting to find a workplace full of people he regarded as holding values similar to his. These countercultural values were articulated in both bakery and grocery mission statement goals to treat each other "lovingly" in order to maintain "a sense of openness and unity" (in the case of People's Daily Bread Bakery) or to base their working relationships on "mutual esteem and cooperation" (in the case of One World Natural Grocery). In those early days—from their founding in the late 1970s through at least the mid-1980s—both bakery and grocery decisions were made in face-to-face meetings of all employees, and most job responsibilities rotated among the workers (fewer than twenty at each company).

Wages and benefits were described as fairly low at both cooperatives during this period, perhaps due to the lower efficiency of these collectivist practices, and certainly to the scant capital available. This did not necessarily bother employees at the time. The most senior grocery employee, a white man named Burgundy Levine, explained by pointing to gaps in his mouth where he had lost teeth when he could not afford to see a dentist: "We were poor! We had no cars. We had very low expectations. We were hippies! This was Edgefield in the 1970s. We only expected to make enough to survive. . . . And remember, we were young. There were very few children." In those days, neither grocery nor bakery workers seemed to have responsibilities—such as the levels of educational debt people have today—that might demand higher incomes. At both sites, workers were at least as ideologically committed to the countercultural organizational goals of creating new and better ways to relate to others as they were to their own personal financial goals.

Despite social justice goals of eliminating inequality, studies of cooperatives by scholars of the time (e.g., Jackall and Crain 1984; Kleinman 1996; Mansbridge 1980; Mellor, Hannah, and Stirling 1988; Rothschild and Whitt 1986) describe organizations in which it was clear that whiteness, family wealth, and being a man advantaged members in terms of job access and access to power and influence. These advantages emerged in relation to three typical organizational features of countercultural collectivist worker cooperatives.

First, small, impoverished organizations could only recruit or retain people who did not need to rely on their jobs for short-term needs or long-term wealth accumulation. The scale and process of collectivist-democratic control affected the cooperatives' ability to be financially stable or compete with intrusion into their niche markets. The size limits of face-to-face group decision-making reduced the ability to develop profitable economies of scale. The lengthy process of coming to group consensus also put collectivist-democratic worker cooperatives at a competitive disadvantage with traditionally managed firms, making it much less likely for these cooperatives to take quick advantage of opportunities in real estate, product discounts, or joint ventures. Organizational scale and process limited profitability, so the cooperatives typically generated only poverty wages, effectively excluding people who were unable to fall back on loans or gifts of family wealth for things like vacations, medical bills, or down payments on homes.

Second, the foregrounding of human connection and shared values inevitably favored members' social networks as sites for job recruitment and as social capital in making claims about member value. As sociologists have discovered, people from dominant racial/ethnic and class demographic groups typically make friends within those groups (Bonilla-Silva 2014; Kao, Joyner, and Balistreri 2019; McPherson, Smith-Lovin, and Cook 2001). Therefore, reliance on personal networks for recruitment first reduced the diversity of the available labor pool and then implicitly advantaged those who were most similar to the white, economically privileged founding members. Despite earnest social justice ambitions, very few of these cooperatives managed to attract or keep a workforce that was diverse in terms of class and race/ethnicity.

Third, a factor contributing to inequality in the countercultural collectivist worker cooperatives, as identified by political scientist Jo Freeman (1984), a scholar of the women's movement in the United States, is the collectivist ideal of "structureless" organizations. In privileging interpersonal relationships within these organizations and in replacing formal positions and explicit rules with consensus decision-making, these organizations did not become "leaderless" but instead developed informal leaders. With no formal criteria for their selection, those who seemed more confident, articulate, and skilled were more likely to be granted authority. The problem, as Freeman points out, is that confidence, articulateness, and financial and organizational skills are typical benefits of being raised white, a man, and within the culture of the middle and upper middle classes. Imbued with what French sociologist Pierre Bourdieu (1986) describes as "cultural capital"— the most socially valued skills, tastes, habits, and mannerisms—elite members of structureless organizations have a covert advantage over nonelite members in gaining authority. Herbert's criticism of the Western Worker Cooperative Conference's focus on participative management to the exclusion of formal, hierarchical management was rooted in a similar understanding of how such organizational practices disadvantage people from marginalized communities and families. Equally important, without explicit policies and procedures defining and delimiting the scope of power or conditions for removing someone from leadership, informal leaders had access to almost limitless authority. As scholars such as Jane Mansbridge (1980) have observed, this kind of structurelessness allows elites to dominate the goals and day-to-day activities of collectivist-democratic organizations.

Worker Identity

In addition to initially misreading the bureaucracy of the grocery and the democracy of the bakery, I also initially misunderstood the reasons why two very similar cooperatives—in founding date, alternative organizational structure, member demographics, and industrial niche—should evolve into such different organizations. I hypothesized that the choice of consultants had shaped each cooperative's bureaucratic development; I thought the dearth of empirical studies of large, successful collectivist-democratic organizations had affected options the consultants presented to the bakery. But when I met with Herbert in late 2003 to discuss some of these early conclusions I had drawn and presented at an academic conference, he was quick to correct my interpretation. Sardonically, he told me, "You're saying [*in a higher voice to approximate mine*], 'Oh, poor People's, if only they'd had good consultants they wouldn't be the hierarchical, straight white men they are now!' But we *fired* [the first consultant], the one who was trying to get us to retain management by committee. We went out and found consultants who would do what we wanted: help us bring management to our bakery." Sensitized to this issue, I reinterviewed long-term grocery members and found that the grocery, too, had been careful to interview and select consultants who shared their organizational orientation.

This left my question about the divergence of collectivist groups unanswered, and it indicated that organizational structure was not the whole story. While each company's organizational structure affected hiring and shaped the distribution of wealth, power, and job autonomy, it was not clear why such different structures would not only be tolerated but sought out by such demographically and culturally similar groups. If "working people" really wanted to avoid meetings, why were the grocery's working people happy to attend them? If "everyone" knows the boss is "an asshole," why were bakery members keen to hire bosses? What I came to find were very different formulations of what it meant to be a cooperative *worker*—a member role that at times overlapped and at others contrasted with that of the worker-owner. As I have noted, worker-owned cooperatives take their reason for being as embodying "workers' interests" through the provision of stable, remunerative, creative, dignified, and fulfilling jobs. Buried in that mandate are often unexamined ideas about who a worker is and how that might affect what counts as workers' interests. The worker-owned cooperative obviously views those interests as existing beyond the shop floor—increasing workers' wealth asserts that their interests exist in the larger community where spending occurs—but where do worker interests end and other types of interests (consumer, family member, community participant, etc.) begin?

Worker identity, like other forms of identity, is complex. Against a tradition of seeing identity as unique, fixed, and essential, another strain of social science has long asserted that individual and collective practices of identification shift over time and space (Foucault 1973; Goffman 1999; Rose 1992; Somers 1994). This strain has at times embraced and at others distanced itself from postmodern theorization of identities' fragmentation and "fictiveness" (Hall 1996; Scott 1991). Sociologists have increasingly focused on the material conditions that affect the particular shape this identity will take (Lamont 2000) and, most pertinent to this book, have contended that identities organized around workplace issues affect material outcomes on and off the shop floor (Bank Muñoz 2008; Hossfeld 1990; Lee 1998; Salzinger 2003; Skeggs 1997; Ward 2008; Weis 2004).

Focusing attention on the construction of the worker opens up questions regarding the meaning of the working class and social class more generally. Historically, the term *class* was monopolized by meanings that, as Lois Weis puts it, linked it "fundamentally to the male giving of labor power in a capitalist economy" (2004, 4): class as an outcome of an individual (man)'s relationship to the means of production. This conception of class is still dominant. Even though socialist feminists have demonstrated the centrality of the "reproduction of labor power"—the off-site and typically feminine domestic work that enables someone to be clean, fed, rested, and emotionally nourished enough to go out to a job—to the construction of the working class (Vogel 1983), class is mostly commonly used to refer to a set of social relations created *solely* within workplaces (Weeks 2011). The class of those absent from the work locale—women performing domestic labor, children, those too old to work, those not physically capable of working under available conditions—is assumed to be, by proxy, that of their source of financial support. But class relations are also produced at other sites and through other processes.

Acker attempts to shift thinking from the masculinized space of the shop floor to a broader social arena by defining it as "differing and unequal situations in access to and control over the means of provisioning and survival" (2006a, 55). By relocating class from the "mode of production" to the "means of provisioning and survival," Acker accounts for additional class sites and actors (for instance, women transforming groceries into meals). Yet her materialist definition problematically omits other, more interactional processes that have been tied to the (re)production of class, particularly in educational settings (Bettie 2003; Lareau 2003; Willis 1977). For this reason, social class is used in this book to refer to the social and cultural practices and processes that surround and include differing and unequal access to and control over the means of provisioning and survival. This means that the working class is defined not only through access to or control over material conditions but also through family and community cultural practices and processes that form a class habitus (Bourdieu 1984).

In addition, this gendered construction of working-class selfhood has been simultaneously raced due to the ethnoracially distinct experiences working people have had in the US labor market (as well those of many other nations). From Reconstruction on, the ethnoracially marginalized have faced both formal barriers (like Jim Crow and anti-Chinese laws) and informal barriers (like white worker hostility and violence) to better-paying jobs, unionized jobs, physically protected jobs, and durable jobs (Blauner 1972; Du Bois 1935; Ignatiev 1995; Omi and Winant 1994; Roediger 1999; Saxton 1995; Wells 1996). Such racial segmentation—ethnoracially distinct job options and pathways—narrowed the benefit of "working man" imagery and narrative to those able to project white masculinity.

The working class has thus been constructed in an ethnoracially and gender provincial manner: the construct relies on an employed white industrial working man as a measure of class, creating a metric that particularly fails to capture the lived working-class experiences of many white women and men and women of color in the United States. Work and the arrangements it produces have been transformed socially and economically: the working class is increasingly women, nonwhite, and nonindustrial (Kalleberg 2011; Smith 2001). Despite these transformations, however, both the dominant academic narratives and those of white, working-class subcultures reinforce the idea of the working class's whiteness, masculinity, and industrial employment in ways that benefit white men and undermine the legitimacy of others. For instance, service workers—most of whom are people of color and white women—are less likely to regard themselves through the valorized tropes of dignity (Hodson 2001) that have characterized working-class culture. This makes it harder to claim job and wage protections through these legitimated narratives. Women with primary family responsibilities come up against the provider narrative of working-class masculinity and are typically unable to reconcile the time commitments of provisioning and nurturance. The submerged but present whiteness and masculinity of the working-class narrative (Collinson 1992; Halle 1984) subtly undermines efforts of those outside its identity claims.

These notions of workers and the working class are critical to understanding the worker cooperatives in this book. Workers and their interests are interpreted through identities that promote certain aspects of their personhoods and minimize others; these identities thus legitimate different distributions of wealth and power and different organizational structures. As I will explore in chapter 7, despite the similar (white) ethnoracial and (middle-) class backgrounds of both the bakery and the grocery's founders, the bakery and grocery developed very different worker identities that were used to legitimate different organizational structures.

The Organization of This Book

Worker cooperatives have a lot to teach us about how democratic control can coexist with profitability and productivity, and how variation in organizational structure and organizational subjects affects opportunities for workers across class, race/ethnicity, and gender. The following chapters examine these concerns in the histories and lives of real worker-owners.

Chapter 2 defines and clarifies how worker cooperatives function and the different roles of worker cooperatives in American history. At times worker cooperatives have primarily been vehicles to transform relations of production; at other times they stabilized and supported local communities, and at others they reduced alienation by transforming day-to-day workplace relationships. This history and categorization provide the background for chapter 3, contextualizing the struggles of both cooperatives in this study as they matured from their mid-1970s origins as small collectives into the large companies they were in the early 2000s (and still are as this book goes to press).

The next two chapters offer case studies of People's Daily Bread Bakery and One World Natural Grocery. In chapter 4, I explore the ways in which democratic governance at the bakery tempers the inequality typical of managerial hierarchy in investor-owned firms while also creating a company that offers better jobs and job outcomes than could otherwise be expected by the bakery's worker-owners. Yet, as will become clear, these benefits are not equally available. Chapter 5 examines the grocery and its unusual hybrid of representative and participatory democratic control, in which a network of autonomous work groups and elected committees share responsibility for managing day-to-day and long-term operations. Unlike either the older collectivist-democratic cooperatives or the managerial bakery, the grocery's hybrid democracy is not coupled with unequal economic rewards or political power.

Chapter 6 focuses on how the two organizational structures affect the inequality outcomes at the bakery and the grocery. At the bakery, the formalization of hierarchical management obscures managerial biases in seemingly neutral hiring and promotion criteria to the detriment of white women and men and women of color. At the grocery, strong formalization coupled with distributed management undermines the most problematic "structurelessness" associated with the cooperatives of the countercultural collectivist era, creating more egalitarian outcomes. Both, I argue, are varieties of bureaucracy: a managerial version at the bakery and a participatory one at the grocery. Unpacking these different iterations reveals the significance and also flexibility of bureaucratic formalization, which can either subordinate or protect worker-owners.

Chapter 7 returns to the question of how such similar groups came to create such different organizational structures and different inequality regimes. The chapter explores how distinct worker identities were constructed between individuals and through organizational practices at each cooperative, and how those identities became something workers (and managers) could use to expand or limit workers' power. Worker identities became part of the organizations' "diversity regimes," or the formal mechanisms used by the cooperatives to address social differences among their workers. These diversity regimes further expanded or limited worker access to organizational resources, including wealth and power; they also legitimated each cooperative's organizational structure in important (but not inevitable) ways that seemed to render them "natural" at each site.

How did these cooperative "good jobs" fare after the financial crisis of 2008? In chapter 8, I return to the bakery and the grocery and describe what they faced, and what has changed or stayed the same. Compared to worker cooperation in earlier periods, these cooperatives have in many ways found greater success, but have also sharpened the contradictions of bureaucracy as a tool for working-class empowerment. The survival of these differently democratic bureaucracies offers important lessons about the possibilities of worker self-management, worker empowerment within more gender-diverse and ethnoracially diverse conditions, and the significance of organizational identities in sustaining democratic and egalitarian workplace control. In highlighting these issues this book provides a critical lens with which to view the relationship of worker cooperatives not only to other forms of worker ownership or cooperative organizations, but more broadly to the overlapping sets of economic arrangements practicing and prefiguring new and different economic and social relations of work.

Students and scholars of worker cooperatives in their many North American variations will be interested in chapters 2, 3, 4 and 5, which together provide a rich description of the various forms worker cooperatives have taken in this region. Those who are more historically minded will find that chapters 2 and 3 offer careful evaluation of the social and economic conditions producing different kinds of worker cooperation, while those who want to understand how democratic worker ownership can be used to run a business will want to spend more time on chapters 4 and 5. Organizational and feminist scholars will be most interested in chapter 6, which addresses a long-standing and overlapping concern regarding the effect of bureaucracy on gender inequality (conceived intersectionally), but will want to review chapters 4 and 5 in order to understand the empirical basis of the analysis in chapter 6. Similarly, those interested in workplace culture and in the situational production of identities will want to review chapters 4 and 5 before engaging with the discussion in chapter 7 regarding the importance of worker identity to the egalitarian potentials of workplace democracy. Finally, students and scholars of alternative organizations will hopefully find something of use throughout the book, but will be most interested in chapters 3, 4, 5, and 8, as these together not only flesh out the trajectory of two such organizations but also locate them within the wider universe of the labor movement and solidarity economy.

"BY DEED INSTEAD OF BY ARGUMENT"

Worker Ownership in the United States

> But there was in store a still greater victory of the political economy of labor over the political economy of property [than the first laws limiting work day length]. We speak of the co-operative movement, especially the co-operative factories raised by the unassisted efforts of a few bold "hands." The value of these great social experiments cannot be overrated. By deed, instead of by argument, they have shown that production on a large scale, and in accord with the behests of modern science, may be carried on without the existence of a class of masters employing a class of hands.

—Karl Marx, "Inaugural Address of the International Working Men's Association"

> Workers forming a co-operative in the field of production are . . . faced with the contradictory necessity of governing themselves with the utmost absolutism. They are obliged to take toward themselves the role of capitalist entrepreneur—a contradiction that accounts for the usual failure of production co-operatives which either become pure capitalist enterprises or, if the workers' interests continue to predominate, end by dissolving."

—Rosa Luxemburg, *Reform or Revolution?*

Why do worker cooperatives matter? Karl Marx and Rosa Luxemburg raise key concerns that worker cooperatives observers (Ellerman 1990; Gibson-Graham 2003; Paranque and Willmott 2014; Storey, Basterretxea, and Salaman 2014) and social theorists (Ali 1984; Gramsci 1971; Kautsky and Kerridge 1920; Trotsky 1922) have grappled with since: the tension between *economic* and *democratic* empowerment. Following Marx, questions emerge regarding the first: How can people truly imagine changing their economic conditions from ones of *exploitation* (in which owners of production facilities take possession of the value of what workers are compelled by economic necessity to produce) to ones of *mutual aid* (in which individuals enter into truly voluntary arrangements to produce for the egalitarian benefit of their collectivity) without living examples of alternative work arrangements? Are worker cooperatives therefore a *necessary* precondition to any transformation or revolution? But, as Luxemburg's criticism asks, is it possible for a financially sustainable firm to protect its workers from economic exploitation without first transforming the larger social and economic stage on which it plays out? Is worker cooperation a dead end, a limited arena in which workers' energy for transformation becomes trapped and squandered?

A second set of questions concerns the degree to which worker cooperatives are able to give workers control over how work gets done—what Marxists might call the conditions of production—and the extent to which democratic empowerment can transform the experience of work from one of alienation to more engaging and creative expressions of innate humanity. The contemporary mantra of young professional and technical workers to "do what you love," oversimplifies engagement (which may as easily be frustrating and enraging as love generating) but reminds us how seldom creativity has been prized in lower-paid manual and service jobs. Marx's praise of cooperatives recognizes the potential of workers to use their knowledge, imagination, and initiative to democratically establish productive enterprise. But Luxemburg suggests that there is no separate peace with capitalism and that, without an actual boss, workers' democracy is corrupted by the external pressures of capitalist markets, their firms' interests elevated over those of the working class, and even their own working selves.

These debates have practical implications for workers, both when a business faces obstacles and when it is successful. When workers try to protect a new or struggling enterprise by reducing wages or donating labor, does it undermine the wages of noncooperative workers in similar industries, eventually reducing what all workers can earn? And does this process of "self-exploitation"—working for wages that are lower than the cost of the labor itself (Guthman 2004)—make it hard for workers to feel good about their jobs, their coworkers, or their existence? That is, does it actually *increase* what Marx (1964) identified as the social condition of "alienation" in capitalist societies? And then, if successful, do worker cooperative members come to view themselves less as socially stigmatized workers and more as socially elevated owners, and act in ways that perpetuate the social and economic relations they formed worker cooperatives to escape (Kasmir 1996)? Or is cooperative workers' self-exploitation actually a useful way to collectively coordinate savings, and support and sustain economically marginal communities (Sobering 2016), as has been seen in less democratic forms of worker ownership like employee stock ownership plans, where the company is wholly or partially owned by a trust that allocates shares in the company to employees based on their hours, pay rate, and/or seniority (Kruse, Freeman, and

Blasi 2010)? Does it offer workers the practical experience of management and autonomy that inspires further action for broader worker control and develops necessary skills when those actions prove successful?

These important concerns raised in Marxist debates have been productively joined with questions regarding the significance of race/ethnicity and gender in the workplace and within relations of production, and the degree to which the allotment of power and resources can be made broadly egalitarian. How do these debates sidestep the gendered nature of the division of public waged labor as work and the private, unwaged "reproductive" labor of feeding, cleaning, and clothing as nonwork (Dalla Costa and James 1973; Federici 2004)? How do they address the exclusions and marginalization white workers enact towards workers of color (Bonilla-Silva 2014; Roediger 1999; Taylor 2016), and cisgender men workers towards women, transgender, and nonbinary workers (Hartman 1981; Schilt 2010; Ward 2008)? To what extent does the overt elimination or reduction of class inequalities within economic organizations address or ignore their ethnoracial and gender inequalities, or more subtle *cultural* class inequalities? For instance, is a worker cooperative in fact pure *self*-exploitation, or do some (white, men, educated) workers within an organization exploit others more than themselves? Despite questions that point out the inherently intersectional quality of work and workers (Crenshaw 1991), the primacy of class has come to define the Marxist tradition over time (Wright 2006).

As this chapter shows, the history of American worker cooperation has consistently, if not always overtly, grappled with these issues—often as it grappled with the American labor movement's increasingly exclusive commitment to the labor union as the organizational vehicle for the empowerment of economically oppressed and devalued workers. As I will discuss, the proximity to and distance from the labor movement affected conceptions of which problems could be addressed, and even who or what a worker was. In turn, these imagined workers mobilized and also restricted cooperators' ideas about how worker control could be realized, and particularly what organizational form it could—and should—take, from partnerships with capital-controlled workplaces to autonomous spaces questioning the public/private division.

The way cooperative members have attempted to address these issues offer important lessons about what is possible and desirable within economic and social limitations. Yet these struggles and their lessons have remained relatively obscure, with few people even understanding what a worker cooperative is or how its financial structure can benefit workers. Therefore, I first explain how cooperatively owned businesses may benefit workers, and then offer an overview of the past 150 years of worker cooperatives in the United States. Identifying three distinct eras, I explore the extent and breadth of worker empowerment within them: the origins of the mass creation of worker cooperatives, the way these organizations were structured, the imagined worker they aimed to promote, their connection to labor and other social movements, and the reasons their era ended. To understand how these elements create the whole, I end each section with a case of a cooperative or cooperative region. This chapter sketches a history and terrain of American worker cooperation in aid of mapping the choices made by the contemporary cooperatives that are the focus of subsequent chapters.

How Worker Cooperatives Work

As I noted in the first chapter, worker cooperatives are businesses entirely owned and controlled by their working members. This means that there are no external investors and that the membership as a whole has democratic authority over any elected board (unlike a corporation), and that all workers have a path to ownership (unlike a limited partnership). Unlike other kinds of cooperatives—housing cooperatives, consumer grocery cooperatives, utility cooperatives, or agricultural cooperatives—the basis of membership is employment. Yet, similar to many other kinds of cooperatives, a central organizational goal is member financial empowerment.

Like other cooperatives, worker cooperatives face hard decisions about how the wealth they produce is distributed (see, e.g., Ferguson 1991). In a typical capitalist firm, some portion is distributed to workers as *wages* and some gets retained as *working capital*, or the money needed to make purchases, maintain or upgrade facilities, pay insurance premiums and other professional fees to keep the business going. Everything else goes to owners and investors as *profit*. Consumer, agricultural, and financial cooperatives face similar struggles over what should go to the (hired) workers as wages and the user-owners as profits. Worker cooperatives, on the other hand, do not have to make that decision: a cooperative's owners and workers are one and the same. Instead they must decide how the cooperative should address and reward (or penalize) members as owners and as workers within the context of a capitalist economy.

As *owners*, worker cooperative members are entitled to a share of annual profits—or losses—proportionate to their share of the whole workforce's annual hours. That is, if a worker's annual hours total 1 percent of all the labor hours that go into the business, that worker is entitled to 1 percent of the profits. For instance, someone who puts in a typical full-time workweek of forty hours with two weeks of annual vacation will have contributed two thousand annual labor hours (forty hours per week times fifty weeks). Someone who only works an average of thirty hours per week would contribute fifteen hundred annual hours, while someone who works an average of fifty hours would contribute twenty-five hundred. In a cooperative of a hundred people, where 70 percent of the people worked full-time, 20 percent worked part-time, and 10 percent regularly worked overtime, the total labor hours of the entire cooperative workforce would be 195,000. A full-time worker's share of those labor hours would be 1.03 percent, a part-time worker's share .77 percent, and a chronic overtimer 1.28 percent. If—after deducting what the company has paid for its materials, machinery, facilities, wages, taxes, and so on—the company's profits were $2 million, a full-timer would be entitled to shares of the profits in the amount of $20,513 (1.03 percent), a part-timer $15,385 (.77 percent), and an overtimer $25,641 (1.28 percent).[1]

But worker cooperatives also operate within the state regulation of an economy that is not accustomed to workers collectively owning their firms. Because tax codes in the United States currently benefit owners far more than workers (Piketty 2014), individuals pay higher taxes on earnings from wages than from profits. Firms are liable for payroll taxes at the national, state, and local levels, but do not pay taxes on distribution of dividends (the cash portion of profits given to a firm's shareholders on a regular basis). It is therefore a huge savings for the cooperative and individual members to take as much of their share of the cooperative's wealth as they can in annual profits, reducing both their own tax liability and the organization's share of payroll taxes. But there are two barriers to this: the Internal Revenue Service (IRS), and workers' own need for cash flow.

The IRS is the biggest *external* constraint on sharing most wealth through dividends. To prevent companies from evading payroll taxes, the IRS imposes steep fraud penalties if it finds that a company is substituting profit sharing (for instance, as commission earnings) for wages. What seems to satisfy the IRS is the deferral of profit sharing for a significant period of time, and worker cooperatives have therefore usually only distributed between 20 and 50 percent of each worker's annual shares in cash. The remainder of the profits earned is retained by the cooperative as working capital for the expansion, improvements, maintenance, and repair vital to the survival of smaller businesses. For this reason, cooperatives often only pay out shares in full when a worker separates from the cooperative (either by quitting, being fired, becoming permanently disabled, or dying).

With wages kept low to minimize taxes for the firm and for workers, and with firm needs and the IRS constraining the amount of cash distributed annually, workers can wind up with very little actual cash compensation—particularly cooperatives in industries, like groceries or food production, that operate close to the margin. Workers may want higher regularly paid wages to provide more day-to-day control over their finances. As workers' shares build over many years but continue to be held by the cooperative, workers may quit in order to access the full cash value of their shares—perhaps to buy a home or start their own side business. Such member flight is costly in terms of lost institutional knowledge and retraining, and can undermine members' trust in the cooperative's future. Workers' lack of cash liquidity between dividend pay-out periods therefore creates an *internal* incentive to increase wages.

A further problem arises, however, when trying to determine how much those wages should be. While it seems easy to come to collective agreement on the distribution of profits as an outcome of hours worked, it is more difficult to decide what, if any, differences there should be among the wages of cooperative members. Although some cooperatives pay all their workers the same hourly rate, most differentiate to some degree. Cooperatives have historically kept the ratio between the highest and the lowest earners fairly low—from 3:1 through the 1980s to more like 6:1 in the present day. In comparison, the average earnings of CEOs of S&P-indexed firms are 287 times that of their median earner (AFL-CIO 2019). But in worker cooperatives, the criteria used for even the smallest differences in wages is often a highly loaded topic that typically invokes different logics: those of the social good or issues particular to the organization versus "market" logics that squarely focus on productivity and profitability (Cobb 2016; Taylor 1994). Should worker cooperatives act as a model of egalitarian regard for different skills and abilities, aiming at ensuring all members can provision for themselves and any dependents, or should those whose training and abilities could command higher return in the mainstream labor market be enticed and retained through higher wages?

A comparison with non-worker-owned firms can help clarify when and why worker cooperatives use social and market logics. The classical free market theory of wages contends that the upper limit on wages is the market value of what workers produce, and the lower limit is what they need to stay alive and productive as workers (Smith 1994). The value created by workers—their productivity—is seen to derive from their human capital, or the physical and mental skills and abilities they have developed before and during their employment that are necessary for such productivity. Employers will try to pay as little as possible for labor because their profit is the difference between what they pay workers to create whatever product, information, or service and how much they can sell it for on the market. Workers will try to demand as much for their labor as possible, but their bargaining position depends on the available resources (state policies, unions, or social movement activism) that can be deployed to raise the lower limit, as well as how many people are available and willing to do their jobs for lower wages.

Contemporary sociological studies of workplaces reveal additional social factors shaping wage ranges. Across national economies, state policies can legitimize or criminalize unequal wages by race/ethnicity and gender (Kelly and Dobbin 1998; Wilson 1996). At the organizational level, employers place greater value on—that is, pay more for—skills typically exercised by men than those typically exercised by women (Steinberg 1995); knowledge generated among professional and managerial workers than that generated among service and manual workers (Bourdieu 1986); and interactional styles typical of whites than those typical of people of color (Moss and Tilly 1996). And, individually, managers still make decisions about workers based on their own beliefs regarding gender, class, ethnicity, and race (Castilla 2008; Ray 2019; Ridgeway 2011). This does not mean that such disadvantages "add up." For instance, racial gaps are closing between low-wage women, but mostly because the overall picture is so grim for all low-wage workers (Branch and Hanley 2014); and white men are suffering more from the "precarization" of work than are other groups, but only because they historically had less precarious employment (Kalleberg and Vallas 2017). Yet it does reinforce the ubiquitous embedding of gender, class, and race in the concepts of human capital and skill that are supposed to drive any wage differences.

This creates what Joan Acker has called "inequality regimes" (2006a, 2006b). She argues that our acceptance of workplace hierarchy and the practice of paying the CEO more than the personnel manager or the janitor tends to make us view CEOs as more valuable *people* than personnel managers, who are in turn more valuable *people* than janitors. That these jobs are also unequally apportioned by race/ethnicity and gender has a spillover effect in terms of making us feel that white men possess more valuable qualities than others, in part because this is similar to hierarchies we see outside the workplace—in politics, families, and schooling (Collins 1990). But Acker says that we not only accept ethnoracial and gender hierarchies because they seem so socially "natural" but also reimport these implicit beliefs about leadership, strength, or compassion into the workplace, mutually reinforcing cognitive and practical links between power and social characteristics that become difficult to interrupt.

The factors that shape wage differentiation thus also affect the demographic composition of worker cooperatives. Cooperatives have historically been undercapitalized, and those founded by men and women of color and white women even more so given institutional racism and sexism in lending and other wealth-building practices (Alkon 2012; Chang 2006; Gordon Nembhard 2018; Oliver and Shapiro 1997; Stevenson 1986). Due to this undercapitalization, cooperatives often pay below-market wages to build necessary capital for continued survival and growth to a secure foothold from which to generate shareable profits and raise wages. While there are many reasons workers choose to join cooperatives, being structurally positioned by race/ethnicity and gender to have few or only low-wage options in the regional or national labor market can certainly increase the attraction of even low-wage cooperative employment. In the same vein, having higher-earning options can make it less so. Indeed, the lower wages cooperatives typically pay for expertise that has high value in the labor market— a practice intended to equalize unequal labor market practices—can create disincentives for joining a cooperative. Only those people who have had the luxury to develop skills without needing to return the investment as support of their families, or who may have other sources of income (spouses, parents, trust funds, etc.), may be able to afford such wage egalitarianism (Jackall and Crain 1984; Scott 2005). Yet if cooperatives pay higher rates for expertise and training to attract more skilled workers, they also attract workers who can push to the front of what Barbara Reskin and Patricia Roos (1990) call "job queues": those whose combination of class status, race/ethnicity, and/or gender is more socially valued in an unequal society. Using "skill" to sort them into organizational positions then replicates the inequalities scholars have found in the broader labor market (Cohen 2013; Kmec 2003, 2005; Rivera 2012), even in cooperative organizations intended as forms of resistance (Kasmir 1996; Kleinman 1996; Ostrander 1999; Ward 2008).

The struggle between the economic commitments of cooperatives and their value-based commitments to narrower or broader versions of social egalitarianism has been waged across generations of worker cooperatives. As Rosa Luxemburg noted in the second epigraph to this chapter, worker cooperatives need to generate profits to keep from "dissolving" within a capitalist economy, but in doing so they risk becoming "pure capitalist enterprises" that pursue profit for its own sake rather than in support of its workers. Yet despite the persistence of this struggle, its results have varied across history—indeed, the "great social experiment" that Karl Marx called them.

Worker Cooperation in America: Three Periods

Although there were a small number of mostly spontaneous, short-lived instances of industrial worker cooperation prior to the mid-1800s, most American worker cooperatives were created during three distinct periods. The best known of these are the labor republican era (from the post–Civil War period to the late 1880s) and the countercultural collectivist era (from the early 1970s through the early 1980s), but cooperatives also flourished during the self-help era of the Great Depression in the 1930s. Each had its own flavor: the labor republican era was the only historical moment in which worker cooperatives were a clear part of the (nascent) labor movement; self-help cooperatives were deeply (though not originally) dependent on state support; countercultural collectivist organizations were markedly comprised of the children of economically privileged rather than economically marginalized families and communities. But in all periods, intensive worker cooperative formation occurred as an attempt to deal with broad and lasting economic crises: the Long Depression of 1873–96, the Great Depression of 1929–39, and the 1970s period of global economic restructuring that persisted through the early 1980s.[2] That is, the history of American worker cooperatives is a history of workers' responses to crisis through direct means. And although there was little to no crossover of membership between eras, each generation drew lessons from preceding ones and thus left its mark on contemporary worker cooperatives' efforts to improve economic conditions, deliver control over working conditions, and address workplace inequalities.

The Labor Republican Era, 1860s–1890s

Origins. Between the moment of Marx's hopeful praise of worker cooperatives in 1864 and Luxemburg's bleak assessment of their failures in 1899, North America saw its first mass organization of worker cooperatives, a site of labor organizing (Leikin 1999) amid a larger foment of American voluntary associations (Crowley and Skocpol 2001).[3] When most American workers were struggling to make a living in the Long Depression following the Panic of 1873, tens of thousands came together under the umbrella of a labor republican ideal of an autonomous citizenry in control of their economic destiny and day-to-day labor conditions (Gourevitch 2013); they were the only legitimate owners of the value they produced, free from the precarity of wage fluctuations and the tyranny of supervising bosses (Leikin 2004). Coordinated by the Knights of Labor, the first American mass labor organization (Voss 1993), and the National Grange of the Order of Patrons of Husbandry, an association of Northern white people hoping to stitch together the divided post–Civil War nation with a shared agriculturalist identity, up to five hundred producer cooperatives were linked to consumers, political reformers, and social theorists (Cerny 1963; Curl 2009; Leikin 2004; Parsons et al. 1983; Saloutos 1953; Schneiberg, King, and Smith 2008). At the same time, and often without affiliations, formerly enslaved African Americans pooled their resources to create mostly communal farming and mercantile associations, but also a few jointly held worker cooperatives (Du Bois 1907). Located throughout the nation, both urban and rural cooperatives were credited not only as a forum to challenge the inevitability of the rule of capital over labor (Leikin 2004) but also as a site for neighbor interaction (Buck 1913; Leikin 1999; Osterud 1993), a path for integration of European immigrants in the national project (Fink 1983; McMath et al. 2008), a form of self-sufficiency for the recently enslaved (Gordon Nembhard 2014), and a staging ground for political activism (Baum and Calvert 1989; Lurie 1974). In regions with a high concentration of cooperatives and a high degree of intercooperative coordination, membership benefits might include not only shares in profits but also the ability to shop at a consumer store or get a discount on cooperatively produced goods, although in less dense or loosely coordinated areas these benefits were limited to cash. Yet this thriving countereconomy evaporated well before the end the century—going bankrupt or transforming into limited partnerships hiring labor—due to tensions between collective solidarity and individual profit, economic barriers sponsored by the state, and electoral defeats.[4]

Organizational structures. A key tension in the labor republican cooperatives emerged between the egalitarian ideals of the Knights and the Grange and the organization of typical cooperative enterprises—whether in shipbuilding, printing, glassblowing, shoe and cigar making, plumbing, mining, garment manufacture, cooperage, or the other industries in which these cooperatives were developed. Despite the labor republican rhetoric of the autonomous worker, neither authority nor return on labor were entirely democratic in their distribution. There is little record of day-to-day interactions in labor republican cooperatives, but what history exists reveals minimal variation from other firms' bureaucratic hierarchies and formal rules and processes despite recurrent resistance to top-down management (Goodwyn 1976; Leikin 2004). Two characteristics tended to aid the "degeneration" (Webb and Webb 1897) process of cooperatives into corporate associations of founding members hiring labor. First, a number of labor republican cooperatives were formed as joint-stock companies, with legal ownership—although not necessarily the ownership claims that are typically recognized in a corporate firm—assigned not per person but per dollar of investment (Cerny 1963), and some cooperatives were unable to prevent the development of unequal power. Second, in keeping with the birth of the "scientific management" practices of the day, managers were often appointed by the firm's board of directors rather than elected or even approved by members (Jones 1984), undermining workers' sense of control. This uneven use of cooperative principles weakened organizational traction for labor republican ideals; in their place a rhetoric of efficiency and profitability made social rhetorics more difficult to maintain (Taylor 1994; Weber 1978).

The cooperative subject. The labor republican ideal cast cooperative members as the cornerstone of a new and inclusive society: they were workers capable of transforming the world by applying republican principles to the act of engaging in labor (Leikin 1999). Women drew strength and empowerment from valorization both as workers organizing industrial collectives from garment factories, such as the New York collar-manufacturing Troy Laundry Women's Cooperative (Curl 2009), and as housewives engaged in provisioning labor, like the Joan of Arc Assembly's bread baking cooperative in Toledo, Ohio (Levine 1983). Despite ongoing struggles with white-owned competitors and landlords, Black cooperatives such as Maryland's Chesapeake Marine Railway and Dry Dock Company developed skills among their workers that, even where cooperatives failed, gave them access to union membership in the trades (Du Bois 1907). For workers excluded from or marginalized in the labor market, the labor republican cooperatives could provide more stable and enjoyable employment.

Yet the labor republican actor primarily emerged as a white man. First, while at the national level the Grange actively developed white women's leadership and fostered a culture widely perceived as feminist (Marti 1984, 247; Tontz 1964) that opened space for women to organize their own cooperative firms and, eventually, gain a place in the labor movement (Curl 2009; Leikin 1999), the Knights' conception of workers was located in the public space of work, a site only then becoming distinct from the simultaneous feminization and privatization of the home (Kerber 1988; Kessler-Harris 2003). Materially, the industrialization of work (Gourevitch 2013) was embraced in all its "appropriateness to a masculine readiness and hardness" (Willis 1990, 193). Thus, it was men who, both in the abstract and in practice, were called into cooperative engagement (Leikin 2004).

Second, although both the Grange and the Knights were (unlike the overtly whites-only American Federation of Labor) outwardly integrationist (Kantrowitz 2000; Voss 1993), and the estimates of Black cooperator participation were only a slightly smaller fraction than their proportion of the national population at the 1886–87 height of labor republican cooperatives (Gordon Nembhard 2014, 50), the organizations' operational practices were not consistently integrationist, and their commitment to integration decreased over time. The Knights, for example, refused to directly confront white working class repression of Black American communities (Leikin 2004; Roediger 1999), supported anti-Chinese immigration restrictions (Curl 2009), and refused cooperative membership to those of Chinese descent (Gerteis 2002). Similarly, the Grange policy of local rule was criticized as a "convenient device to permit Southerners to exclude Negroes from the locals and still enable the national organization to boast hypocritically that it did not exclude anyone on racial grounds" (Saloutos 1953, 477). Critically, as Cedric de Leon (2016) has argued, the labor republican "successor discourse" positing capitalism as the great equalizer of all "wage slaves" both insulted the experience of recently enslaved people and evacuated discussion of racial inequality.

Together these practices narrowed how the cooperative labor republican worker was ethnoracially defined.

Labor and social movement relations. The connection of labor republican cooperatives to the labor movement was stronger than in any other era because they were planned as part of the Knights' alternative economy. As Steve Leikin (2004) notes, Terence Powderly, the highest-ranking Knight from 1879 to 1893, strongly supported the development of cooperatives and insisted on a dedicated member "tax" to create a cooperative loan fund. Yet with mixed leadership support and even less from the rank and file, the tax wobbled back and forth between compulsory and voluntary, and the link between cooperative worker-owner identity and increasingly industrial workers was less than firm. In contrast, the Grange offered strong financial support for cooperative development but was more focused on consumer and agricultural cooperation (Parsons et al. 1983) than the industrialization that could not as easily be joined to their narratives about the agrarian essence of America (Lurie 1974). Thus, while worker cooperatives were connected to these movements, they remained at the periphery rather than at their imaginative—or financial—centers.

The cooperative barrel makers of Minneapolis. The case of the formation of a relatively egalitarian cluster of cooperatives in Minnesota exemplifies the external and internal challenges faced by cooperatives in this period. In Minneapolis a small group of mostly European immigrant barrel maker men—some of whom had connections to the Knights of Labor, and all of whom were tired of seasonal unemployment after farmers' harvests were shipped—formed a cooperative in 1870. This was not a joint-stock company but instead gave all members an equal stake (payable out of wages over an extended period), with profit distributed based on the share of hours contributed to the whole (Virtue 1905). Even the shop floor of the cooperage was democratically run, including equal distribution of opportunity, mutual moral and social expectations, and limited disciplinary power by the foreman (Leikin 2001). In the busy season, members invested in an off-season fund so that they could pay themselves when demand went slack. Their model was successful, and they were able to both enlist the support of the Knights and support striking journeymen coopers, which helped to generate many more cooperative cooperages (Engberg 1941). By 1886 it was claimed that two-thirds of all Minneapolis coopers worked in cooperative shops (Curl 2009), and they inspired cooperative house painting, housing, loan and insurance, publishing, library, and laundry businesses, and grocery and dry goods stores that raised the total number of Minneapolis cooperatives to at least thirty-two (Leikin 2001). While most members were men, the labor republican ideals of autonomy and egalitarianism not only attracted women but also undermined men's gendered claims to women's unpaid labor in the home. Thus, the cooperative retail stores began to employ women as well as men, and an entirely women-run laundry cooperative was founded. It was even noted that women's cooperative labor participation created more democratic allocations of household chores (Curl 2009).

Yet this cooperative economy was all but gone by the turn of the twentieth century. Not only did mechanization reduce the number of coopers needed to produce Minneapolis's grain barrels, but barrels were being abandoned in favor of boxes and bags to transport agricultural products (Virtue 1932). Further, "poor management and internal strife" were noted as widespread problems (Virtue 1905): one cooperage dissolved in lawsuits over how and whether a manager could fire a worker despite the worker being largely loathed by his coworkers (Leikin 2001). On both the local and national scenes, the Knights' focus and strength began to dissipate in the last decade of the nineteenth century. Battles over territory with Samuel Gompers's American Federation of Labor (AFL), which rejected the geographic and social orientation of the Knights for more trade-specific and wage-oriented strategies, left the Knights with few financial or personnel resources to devote to preserving Minneapolis cooperatives or the culture they shared with union members. As the remaining cooperative cooperages first consolidated and then ceased extending membership to new employees, a 1905 study by a University of Nebraska economist found that up to half of those employed were simple wage-earners drawing no share of profits (Virtue 1905); twenty-five years later, the same economist noted that the last of these former cooperatives had closed (Virtue 1932).

The end of the era. The Minneapolis case paralleled the national experience of the era: despite their many successes, the integrated cooperative economy collapsed permanently in the late 1880s. The Knights were neither able to reconcile the contradiction between individual autonomy and collective responsibility nor to fight off coordinated legal and sometimes physical attacks by the state and private businesses. Black cooperatives faced not only similar harassment but also massacres similar to those visited by white supremacist mobs on other Black-owned businesses in the post-Reconstruction era (Du Bois 1935; Gordon Nembhard 2018). The Sherman Antitrust Act of 1890, heavily lobbied for by labor and farmers, was used far more often to break up nonagricultural cooperatives— and unions—than capitalist trusts (Curl 2009; Voss 1993; Zinn 2003). Many Grangers poured their energies into the People's Party (commonly known as the Populists) but, unable to elect a president in the 1896 election (Goodwyn 1981), they withdrew from the political promotion of cooperatives. Although most cooperative firms survived as long or longer than similar enterprises in their industries

(Jones 1979), the legacy of this era was more popularly the "death or degeneration" cautionary tale told by the socialist labor critics Beatrice Potter Webb and
Sidney Webb (1897, 1920).

Perhaps more insidiously, the connection of worker cooperatives with the
Knights and feminist and socialist strands of political thought linked them to a
radicalism that was increasingly dangerous in America in the wake of the death
sentences and executions of the labor activists arrested at Chicago's Haymarket
rally in May 1886.[5] Although union leaders such as Gompers supported *consumer*
cooperatives (Parker 1956), *worker* cooperatives seemed to threaten workers' class
consciousness by blurring the line between workers and owners (Foner 1977) and
also potentially driving down wages by dividing earnings between wages and
profits (Virtue 1905). As the Knights weakened, unions in cooperative strongholds
such as Minneapolis shifted allegiance to the growing AFL powerhouse (Engberg
1941), severing the earlier connection of worker cooperatives to the labor movement and helping to stabilize unions as the sole legitimate voice of the working
class.[6] Many of the more activist cooperatives went bankrupt when they were cut
off from a consumer base that now regarded them as suspiciously left-wing rather
than laudably supportive of working communities (Curl 2009).

In the following years consumer, agricultural, housing, utility, and insurance
cooperatives continued to grow, particularly in the 1920s (Frank 1994; Sazama
2000; Schneiberg, King, and Smith 2008). Worker cooperatives, on the other
hand, largely disappeared from mainstream America in the early decades of the
twentieth century as unions took over as the agent of change for the growing
population of industrial workers (Greene 1998). This division between workers in
unions and consumers in cooperatives shaped narratives of class, race, and gender in meaningful and often problematic ways, framing and separating these dimensions of people's lives as distinct identities. While the vision of organizational
solutions to the problem of worker exploitation was kept alive to some extent in
African American community self-reliance enterprises—particularly among fol-
lowers of Marcus Garvey's Black nationalist movement (Gordon Nembhard
2014)—and a few northwestern associations of consumer cooperatives (Frank
1994), for the most part the labor republican moment was over.

The Self-Help Era, 1929–1939

Origins. Mostly overlooked in histories of the Great Depression, and shorter in
duration than the labor republican era, the era of "self-help" cooperatives—the
name this generation gave itself—were motivated by the persistent and paradox-
ical national crises of hunger and food surplus (Nestle and Guttmacher 1992).
They produced a vibrant patchwork of farms, dairies, workshops, canneries,

mines, mills, foundries, garages, and factories, as well as domestic and groom-
ing services, consumer cooperative stores, and housing (Curl 2009; Rose 1988,
58n6) involving up to a half million Americans in cooperative ventures (Kerr
and Taylor 1935) and swelling the ranks of active worker cooperative members
to nearly seventy-six thousand in 1932 alone (Pasha 2014, 6). Although the self-
help era was more ideologically ambiguous than the earlier labor republican or
later countercultural collectivist eras—both of which were critical of the way
capital maintained an impoverished reserve pool of labor, but also advocated
shelter for workers until capitalist enterprise could absorb them again—the sheer
numbers of participants and cooperative enterprises suggests important lessons
about how and why cooperatives form in times of economic crisis.

Initially, self-help cooperatives emerged spontaneously to coordinate informal labor exchanges between unemployed workers and farmers, with successive waves mainly composed of neighbors or former coworkers (Curl 2009).
Later these cooperatives were developed as part of planned and geographically
broader campaigns by community organizations such as the urban Unemployed Exchange Association in Oakland, California, and the rural Southern Tenant Farmers' Union that rapidly expanded from its local Arkansas base. Given
the residential rather than occupational basis of formation, most reflected the
ethnoracial segregation of American life. In the white and white-dominated cooperatives, men and women were apt to perform distinctly different labor too
(Kerr 1939). Although this generation of cooperatives eventually received funding from New Deal programs aimed at addressing poverty, such support proved
to be their undoing both in terms of the conditions imposed by the state and then
by the evaporation of working capital as the New Deal ceded territory to private
ownership (Rose 1988).

Organizational structures. A community self-help logic did not easily lend
itself to organization at the national level. Derek Jones and Donald Schneider
find that most self-help cooperatives began as decentralized democratic organizations: "Participation was direct, and most issues were voted upon" (1984, 65).
As they grew and developed coordination, cooperatives sent representatives to
their local cooperative association. This group not only coordinated the labor
exchanges of the cooperatives but also applied for support from local businesses
and local state agencies and might organize "mass demonstrations, direct action,
and appropriation"—often described as "chiseling"—of food, housing, water, and
heating for community members (Pasha 2014, 101–3) or raw materials and production facilities necessary to the cooperative endeavors (Curl 2009). These items
were needed, because although most cooperatives began on the basis of barter,
they often found themselves needing cash for items they were unable to produce
or trade for (Leab 1966). Yet despite these powerful actions, the cooperative

associations did not dictate policy or action to the cooperatives beyond the principles of equal democratic vote. There was therefore a great deal of variation in how value was distributed (ranging from pure need-based to hours-based to differential skill-value allocations; Curl 2009; Rose 1988; Tselos 1977), whether work was self-directed or hierarchically managed, and who could become a cooperative member.

The cooperative subject. The ambivalence of the self-help era towards both socialism and capitalism played out in the strongly masculine but ambiguously classed and ethnoracialized self-conception of its members. Few self-help cooperatives were ideologically rooted in labor concepts of *worker* power. Instead, as a form of local community "self-help" (Kerr and Taylor 1935), they made claims on local businesses or the state as heads of households, neighbors, or even consumers as often as they did as unemployed workers (Pasha 2014). Although the self-help era of cooperation was far from a racially egalitarian paradise (Barrow 2007), these other logics could advance markedly less exclusionary practices than the earlier, more rhetorically inclusive labor republican era (Pasha 2014). In some places self-help cooperatives were founded or became interracially integrated (Pasha 2014, 53). For instance, the Southern Tenant Farmers' Union grew out of an Arkansas meeting of displaced sharecroppers, "seven blacks and ten whites" (Mitchell 1973, 343), who agreed to a platform of nonviolent action to protect the more vulnerable Black members. In Northern California, the Oakland-based Unemployed Exchange Association was formed in a white community but soon coordinated labor and goods exchange among white, Black, Chinese, and Pilipino neighborhoods (Pasha 2014). In other places, however, a logic based on residential status could be used to restrict members by race/ethnicity and religion (Leab 1966).

The meaning of gender for cooperative participation was similarly complicated. On one hand, there were women in the cooperative units, including several all-women "auxiliary" cooperatives that coordinated consumer purchasing; manufactured clothing; or distributed, prepared, and preserved surplus produce (Rose 1988). The contemporaneous observer Clark Kerr notes that "Negro" garment salvage and quilting cooperatives in Los Angeles were managed and almost entirely staffed by Black women and were, when compared to more contentious mixed-gender cooperatives, "comparatively harmonious" (1939, 198). On the other hand, the manual labor origins and the narrative about the unemployed worker—and, in the rare unionized cooperative regions like Seattle, an overt discourse about women undermining the masculine work prerogative (Frank 1994)—invoked a masculine worker, a "natural" head of the family that could legitimately later claim a share of state relief funding as his entitlement (Rose 1990; Storrs 2006).

Lack of resolution regarding the class, ethnoracial, and gender characteristics of the imagined cooperative worker enabled more community empowerment projects than previously possible (particularly for men and women of color and white women) but also limited egalitarian achievements. Self-help cooperatives offered a nonmarket vision of how life could be provisioned but, in failing to specify who was welcome into this identity, did little to make the role of cooperative worker truly inclusive.

Labor and social movement relations. This ambiguity was in no way clarified by organizational-level connections to social movements; indeed, such connections were markedly absent compared to those of both earlier and later cooperative generations, and there was far more variation between the cooperatives than there were common threads. The deeply repressive Red Scare in the post–World War I period (Murray 1955) and its focus on deportations of radicals (Goldman 2011) had stigmatized and reconfigured both the Left and labor movements. The anarchist and socialist groups that had experimented with cooperatives in previous years were weakened compared to the Communist Party and had little institutional effect on cooperative development. And despite the central role Communists gave to the industrial worker (Naison 1968), worker cooperation's ownership aspect remained at odds with the Communist dogma regarding the opposition of labor and capital's interests. Labor alliances, although not entirely absent (Frank 1994), were infrequent: the labor movement continued to deride cooperatives as ineffective at best, and at worst a force driving down wages with their use of an informal scrip for brokering labor-exchange credits (Elvins 2012; Leab 1966). There was strong support for cooperatives within African American communities in this period, but they were almost always consumer rather than producer co-ops (Gordon Nembhard 2014).

While robust oppositional organization and activism helped to generate transformational goals in some locations (Leab 1966), this was not the predominant cooperative model. Instead many worker cooperatives positioned themselves as friendly to local businesses: distributing unsalable produce, making unfashionable clothes for charity donations instead of sales floors, and helping to preserve a generation of consumers (Pasha 2014). In return, as Lauren Martin notes, the business community "offered rewards for loyalty and threatened punishment when the movement seemed prepared to engage in more confrontational collective political action" (2013, 37). These alliances protected cooperatives in ways the labor republican cooperatives had not been protected, but they also articulated cooperatives as reformist but pro-capitalist, a movement of plucky and entrepreneurial citizens (Tselos 1977; Valocchi 1990).

Similar connections to the emerging welfare state, made out of need, addressed problems of undercapitalization and the difficulty retaining young and skilled workers (Curl 2009; Jones and Schneider 1984; Martin 2013; Tselos 1977). Following the passage of the Federal Emergency Relief Act in 1933, most cooperatives sought a share of the federal grants being made available through local state agencies to supplement their production. But engagement with the New Deal agencies profoundly affected cooperatives' day-to-day operations. The act's rules prohibited cooperative use of cash compensation or competition with traditionally owned firms, limiting the attraction and long-term futures of cooperatives as market enterprises (Jones and Schneider 1984; Rose 1988). These rules also prompted a transfer of responsibility and power to managers through what were initially voluntary guidelines but later became funding requirements. Thus, on one hand, federal New Deal funding provided enough support for a generation to experience worker cooperation. On the other, despite the highly participatory roots of the self-help cooperatives and the economic innovations they were beginning to discover (Jones and Schneider 1984), this funding crippled the cooperatives both democratically and economically by transforming them into managerialist firms unable to compete for workers or markets due to regulations imposed by the state.

The Unemployed Cooperative Relief Association (UCRA) of Los Angeles. The history of this organization is a case of tensions among the self-help cooperatives' relationship to capitalism, the undetermined parameters of membership, and the potential of a relationship with the new welfare state. The UCRA emerged from cooperative wildfire: after a single unemployed, white veteran offered to exchange his labor for food with Japanese farmers in the truck farms at the edges of the city in 1931, a cooperative developed in early 1932 and proliferated within months into more than a dozen involving an ethnoracial mix of perhaps twenty-five hundred men. By the end of 1932 the UCRA had been created to coordinate labor, capitalization, and transportation support among the cooperatives, the business community, and the state (Martin 2013; Pasha 2014). Within the next two years, over 125,000 people (Pasha 2014)—roughly 10 percent of the Los Angeles population—would benefit from 130 UCRA cooperatives, including twenty-five thousand actively working members (Kerr 1939, 103).[7]

The UCRA cooperatives combined a relatively conservative individualist rhetoric and faith in capital with a fiercely local democratic practice and a needs-based system of compensation: members received a share of food based not on hours worked or skill but on family size (Kerr 1939, 188–89). The spontaneous emergence of the cooperatives that would form the UCRA occurred in the context of notoriously anti-labor and "open shop" Los Angeles, where individual union membership could not be compelled in a unionized establishment, and labor was portrayed as Communist-affiliated and thus an enemy of the pre–Great

Depression economy on which workers depended (Davis 1997; Nicolaides 2002). But it was also noted as the second biggest center of socialist and Communist community in the nation (Bernstein 2011), and thus the echo of labor and the Left's overt disdain for what they termed cooperative "self-starvation" (Martin 2013, 46) or "collective panhandling" (Leab 1966) had wide resonance. Perhaps for this reason, the UCRA cooperatives found support first from the business community, which preferred the work orientation of the cooperatives to the socialist city councilors' calls for the end of private enterprise, and who lobbied city hall to funnel relief funds and supplies through the cooperatives (Martin 2013). Stabilized, cooperatives then successfully sought New Deal funding. Although the central UCRA included the involvement and partial leadership of outspoken white supremacists (Pasha 2014), several of its cooperatives were either interracial or entirely "nonwhite" for 1930s Los Angeles, identified as "Mexican," "Negro," "Jew," and "Italian" (Pasha 2014, 54). And although the UCRA sprang from men's labor exchanges, women eventually made up a quarter of working members in some of the longest-lasting and best-performing cooperatives (Jones and Schneider 1984), which made lunch for farm laborers, canned excess produce exchanged for labor, sewed clothing and household goods from salvaged and donated fabric, and performed clerical work (Martin 2013).

Four factors eventually brought the UCRA and the self-help movement down: infighting over unsettled ideological tensions; market and state collaboration to limit cooperatives' ability to compete; uncompensated expenditure of resources on a failed electoral campaign; and withdrawal of state support.

First, in statewide conferences intended to build a broader cooperative economy (Kerr 1939), power scrambling between white men leaders over the role of cooperatives in a capitalist crisis led to expulsions and defections from the UCRA. Former members joined alternative cooperative organizations or found cash-based jobs in the mainstream market or those that, in 1933, began to be offered through a variety of New Deal agencies (Kerr and Taylor 1935). Second, these jobs drew workers away not merely because they were exciting or stable but because they were in firms that had no constraints on how they did business—unlike the UCRA cooperatives, whose business and state (local and federal) support came with stipulations both forbidding cooperative products from being sold in the open market and mandating cooperative scrip in place of cash wages. A representative-democratic organizational model was disseminated by the primary New Deal funder, the Federal Emergency Relief Agency, and although most UCRA cooperatives used a participatory-democratic process, they reformed their structure, viewing adoption of agency guidelines as key to securing funding. Third, these conditions combined to undermined cooperative operations and stability (Jones and Schneider 1984, 65) to the extent that, when Upton Sinclair made a Socialist Party run at the 1934 California gubernatorial race (Blake and Newman 1984), his failure proved disastrous to the UCRA by absorbing the few resources it had left.

But it was the fourth factor that definitively ended the era: success. Although UCRA membership dropped from its high of 30,335 in 1932 to 5,715 in 1935, with numbers continuing to fall until 1937 (Pasha 2014, 7), the trend then reversed and cooperative membership almost doubled in 1938 as the cooperatives stabilized and began to reach full productive capacity (Kerr 1939), competing with noncooperative firms. In 1940, the federal government abruptly defunded cooperatives through legislative decree and repossessed all state-funded machinery and production space. This effectively closed the book on the UCRA (Pasha 2014).

The end of the era. Although self-help era cooperatives were more varied in membership demographics or industrial niche than the previous labor republican or future countercultural collectivist generations, their dependency on the state limited employment and sales, remade organizational practices, and undermined long-term success. Self-help cooperatives proved vulnerable when state priorities and policies changed and when capital began to win back the ear of federal leadership. By the end of the decade, only the African American cooperatives—few of which had received federal support, and even fewer of which were primarily worker cooperatives (Gordon Nembhard 2014)—and the Pacific Northwest plywood cooperatives—equally independent of both New Deal funding and the labor movement, and almost entirely composed of white men (Pencavel 2012)—remained.

The other cooperatives that survived were almost entirely consumer or agricultural (Schneiberg 2011; Storrs 2006), and the increasing industrialization of agriculture in this period shifted the focus of most white-dominated agricultural cooperatives from socioeconomic goals to marketing ones (Hogeland 2006).[8] Most consumer cooperatives were grocery stores set up primarily in reaction to rising food prices and, secondarily, to food safety rather than as democratic or workplace projects (Herrmann 1970). Although many consumer cooperatives—well-known examples such as the Washington, DC, Greenbelt Co-op and the Consumers Cooperative of Berkeley (Sommer and Fjeld 1983)—had roots in radical social thought and working-class communities (Chambers 1962), most became vehicles for the urban middle class (Gordon Nembhard 2014; Herrmann 1970). Just as the agricultural cooperatives were shifting to incorporate external managerial expertise (Hogeland 2006), so too were the consumer cooperatives functioning much like noncooperative firms, with workers hired and supervised by managers (Evan 1957). These transformations produced a fairly strong distinction between worker cooperatives and other kinds in the following decades.

The Countercultural Collectivist Era, 1970s–1980s

Origins. The third wave of worker cooperatives in the United States differed significantly from the eras that preceded it in terms of its class composition and its focus on workplace organizational practices. Its members were primarily (but certainly not only) the children of postwar white affluence arising from the 1950s and 1960s near-full employment and historic lows in wealth disparities (Piketty 2014). But this gave way in the 1970s to a worldwide contraction in the labor market. Between domestic unemployment and a sharp rise in global inequality (Block 1990; Harvey 1989), this expectant generation struggled to find work and initiated a national pendulum swing from optimism to pessimism about capitalism. As they were no longer content to follow in their parents' footsteps—nor able to step into their shoes with the ease that had been promised—a counterculture, or alternative movement, ethos, and set of social norms and practices, emerged (Roszak 1995; Yinger 1960) and turned its attention to the organization of work.

The focus on work brought together the insights of "politicos" in the so-called new social movements—active members of the anti-war, racial justice, and gender liberation movements of the day (Cohen 1983; Echols 1989; Offe 1985)—and lifestyle-focused "hippies" more interested in expanded consciousness, often through sexual, chemical, and spiritual human connections (McMillian and Buhle 2003). Although they were in many ways distinct, politicos and hippies found common ground in the potential of radically democratic and intentionally egalitarian *collectives*—small friendship-based groups of people sharing values and using participatory democracy towards shared goals. Using collectives as sites of community good and self-actualization, these spaces knitted together a shared subculture. Unlike earlier cooperative generations, a sizable portion of the counterculture's members had access to their affluent families' wealth, which combined with depressed urban real estate to make communal housing, entertainment, and alternative businesses possible (Miller 1999).

The collectives provided goods and services necessary to the counterculture, including legal advice for conscientious objectors to the draft, medical care for illegal drug users and reproductive health seekers, and news provision for unreported countercultural activities (Rothschild and Whitt 1986). A distinct subset of worker cooperatives engaged in food production and distribution (Alkon 2012), where their provision of pesticide-free produce and multigrain baked goods combined with their small size to create an unexpected mixture: a throwback to the old-time general store that had been replaced by national chains in the 1950s and 1960s (Levinson 2011; Spellman 2016), and a step forward towards the "foodie" emporium, with its specialized and even "artisanal" wares (Johnston and Baumann 2014). With the relatively greater access to capital that came with their class demographics, roughly a thousand worker-owned cooperatives in a wide range of industries were in business by the late 1970s (Jackall and Levin 1984).[9]

That is not to say that all cooperatives of this period were dominated by white, educated, middle-class youth. Retail, production, transit, and employment cooperatives served working-class Black communities in the US Southeast and Midwest (Gordon Nembhard 2014), and working-class Black and white women organized print shop and publishing collectives on both coasts (Davis 2017). In the United Kingdom, working-class women took collective ownership of their factories after their employers shut them down, setting up shifts to accommodate their children's school schedules (Mellor, Hannah, and Stirling 1988). While these were the exception among this generation of cooperatives, their members similarly reported pride and accomplishment in learning new skills, providing important goods and services, and stabilizing their employment.

Countercultural collectivist cooperatives were uniquely concerned with the *cultural* effects of bureaucracies (Mellor, Hannah, and Stirling 1988), and the materialism, industrialization, and emotional disconnection of mainstream culture. The collective goal of *empowerment* was elevated above profits even among those cooperative enterprises that produced or sold goods or services, even as the meaning of the term was not clearly specified. Countercultural collectivist cooperative founders united the hippie value of human connections with the politico value of reducing inequality in an attempt to change the meaning and experience of work. Yet despite their access to capital and their almost uncontested command of countercultural niches, the legacy of this era has been primarily the rejection of participatory democratic control as "inefficient" and responsible for the evaporation of worker cooperation.

Organizational structures. The antibureaucratic collectives were "collectivist-democratic" organizations (Rothschild-Whitt 1979): officially leaderless authority structures characterized by "participatory democracy," a consensus-based and decentralized system of allocating and exercising power (Polletta 2002). Countercultural collectivist cooperatives were notable for their awareness of how race and gender—and, to a lesser extent, class—served as criteria for sorting or rewarding workers (Mansbridge 1980; Mellor, Hannah, and Stirling 1988). Prefiguring a more egalitarian world to come (Breines 1989), they identified earnings and power differentials as key practices of inequality and instead used flat wage structures and democratic control of the firm. Rejecting the uneven development of expertise and exercise of managerial hierarchy as central mechanisms of inequality, countercultural collectivist cooperatives insisted that most people could do most things; thus, task specialization was replaced by cross-training and intentional job rotation (Davis 1991).

Yet the commitment typically generated by a bureaucratic career and the workflow typically organized by managers were still needed, so, in their stead, these cooperatives utilized friendship and shared values. *No Bosses Here! A Manual on Working Collectively and Cooperatively*, a 1981 publication written by members of various cooperatives, advocates that it is "important to find people who have similar goals, since starting a collective is hard enough. People can become frustrated if political views are so diverse that very little work actually takes place" (Brandow, McDonnell, and Vocations for Social Change 1981, 15). The camaraderie of friendship and shared values also compensated for lower pay; the integration of social and emotional goals with the more standard financial and creative ones was perceived as a rare good within the antibureaucratic collectives (Jackall 1984).

The cooperative subject. In popular memory, countercultural collectivist cooperative members are white hippies, children of affluence (Hoover 2008), and exclusive despite the generation's overt aspirations for inclusion (Mansbridge 1980; Swidler 1979). Yet these cooperatives were at least fairly gender balanced, and many women worked in what were then nontraditional positions, such as printers, lawyers, or factory workers (Davis 2017; Jackall and Crain 1984; Mellor, Hannah, and Stirling 1988; Santa Barbara Legal Collective 1982). To be a cooperative member typically involved a challenge to normative gender roles and the gender hierarchy: the masculinity of the traditional worker was minimized if not absent in cooperatives of this era. This is not to say that there was no gender inequality in the countercultural collectivist cooperatives. In some places gender remained an unspoken but significant mediator of power and resources (Kleinman 1996); in others, women members found sexism so intolerable that they expelled men and created an explicitly feminist collective, like the printshop that became the seminal lesbian publishing house Diana Press (Davis 2017). The feminist and lesbian collectives that developed to provide goods and services—including those that provided women's health care—endowed their members with new skills, new competencies, and new confidence in themselves and each other (Bart and Bart Schlesinger 1982; Oerton 1994; Rothschild and Whitt 1986), as well as new arenas for personal and principled disappointment and betrayal (Davis 2017). But what was most important was that, unlike previous generations of cooperatives, gender was no longer a legitimate criterion for determining the kind of work, the level of power, or the earnings a member might try to claim.

Another significant difference from earlier generations was the low level of cooperative involvement by those who self-identified as working class or came from less economically and educationally privileged communities. This was an unintended but direct effect of antibureaucratic ideology and organization. First, the countercultural claim of "dropping out" of capitalism (Miller 1991) extended more broadly into a disdain for money itself: profit was suspect among this generation. While this allowed members of the counterculture more freedom to pursue value-oriented goals (Rothschild and Whitt 1986), it also led to business decisions that reduced earnings—often to poverty or near-poverty levels (Jackall and Crain 1984). Anti-materialism was not a novel enticement to people who grew up with material deprivation. Low wages acted as a barrier for those without independent sources of wealth that could be used to supplement cooperative earnings (Gamson and Levin 1984). This was a significant factor in creating a generation of cooperatives composed primarily of members raised in affluence.

But it was also the use of friendship—as both a recruitment and retention practice—that led to the predominance of elites. Because nearly all aspects of American social and emotional life in the 1970s (and certainly no less so thereafter) tended towards class segregation (Halle 1984; Lamont 1992, 2000; Sennett and Cobb 1972; Wilson 1987), the more "human" use of social bonds in hiring and organizational assimilation acted as a class-screening mechanism. Friendship worked as a large-grain screen in the hiring process, and then as a finer-grain screen in the incorporation of new members, whose assimilation required knowledge that was more specifically *cultural* than *technical*.[10] It was also a *race*-screening mechanism due to similar and overlapping forms of ethnoracial segregation in America (Massey and Denton 1993; Stainback and Tomaskovic-Devey 2012), bolstered by a seldom explicit belief in homophily (McPherson, Smith-Lovin, and Cook 2001) that "similarity" increased collective stability (Gamson and Levin 1984; Rothschild and Whitt 1986).

Even beyond low wages and the sort of homophily just described, antibureaucratic organizational structure also limited countercultural collectivist participation by class. Although few empirical studies of the collectives of the time focus on members' class background or identification, those that do find that members were far more middle-class (and whiter) than the general population (Jackall and Crain 1984; Rothschild and Whitt 1986). Even more important, working-class people across ethnoracial groups were rarely able to wield power within middle class-dominated cooperatives (Mansbridge 1980). This may very well be for the same reasons that Jo Freeman (1984) noticed in political collectives of the time: organizational "structurelessness"—a refusal to implement formal policies and procedures for transparently distributing and facilitating organizational power—allowed those with organizational and interpersonal skills and abilities developed over a lifetime of middle-class social training (what Pierre Bourdieu [1984] would call their "habitus") to prevail over those of working-class members, whose habitus meshed far less easily with a business world. Thus, despite the overt egalitarian claims and intentions of the collectives, countercultural collectivist worker identity was gender-inclusive but class- (and, typically, race/ethnicity-) exclusive.

Labor and social movement relations. Countercultural collectivists were not strongly tied to labor movements, as labor republican cooperatives had been, but neither did they reject self-conceptions as workers in the way many of the self-help cooperators did. Indeed, it was as workers that they articulated their critiques of capitalism, bureaucracy, and ethnoracial and gender inequality. Yet although *No Bosses Here!* (Brandow, McDonnell, and Vocations for Social Change 1981) lists over fifty organizational resources for current and potential cooperative members, not a single one is part of the organized labor movement. The overlap of goals between the labor movement and the counterculture makes it worth asking why this youth counterculture chose to develop worker cooperatives instead of unionizing existing workplaces.

A popular narrative holds that countercultural collectivist separation from the labor movement resulted from unions' tendency to be bureaucratic, right-wing, sexist, and racist organizations (see, e.g., Faue 2017; Gouldner 1954; Wilensky 1961). Yet in the 1970s union leadership faced an internal democratic reform movement (Cowie 2012; Lucas 1997), some unions joined the Vietnam War protest movement (Lewis 2013), and many rank-and-file workers openly challenged fellow members' racism, sexism, and homophobia (Brenner, Brenner, and Winslow 2010; Hunt and Bielski Boris 2007; Nussbaum 2007). That is, labor and cooperatives had many similar concerns.

What primarily kept unions and worker cooperatives apart was simply that most union members emerged from the working class. What debates they had over the meaning and potential of workplace-based action were often confined by the discourse of the American Federation of Labor and Congress of Industrial Organizations (AFL-CIO) and its goal of a greater share of the value within capitalism (Piore 1986). Labor movement discussions of gender and ethnoracial inequality could only make sense in terms of how sexism or racism undermined workers' attempts to achieve realization of the value they produced. In contrast, most members of worker cooperatives were raised among the middle class, and their debates took place within the discursive new social movement vision of an egalitarian, creative, noncapitalist society (Jackall and Levin 1984).[11] Discussions of workers' power, a staple of the labor movement, were therefore only meaningful to the extent that such power was seen to make society more egalitarian. AFL-CIO themes such as the family wage (with its seemingly patriarchal family) or even the eight-hour workday (which presumed a distinction between alienated and joyless paid labor and authentically fulfilling nonlabor hours) did not articulate this vision of an egalitarian and thoroughly creative life. The values based in differing class cultures that had come to attach to each movement's reaction to the capitalist organization of work thus largely separated labor and new social movement actors.

The Cheese Board Collective. Like most cooperatives of this era, the Cheese Board Collective in Berkeley—initially a cheese shop, but eventually also a bakery and pizzeria—emerged from the San Francisco Bay Area counterculture.[12] Although created in 1967 as a private enterprise by a married couple, in 1971 it transformed into the kind of democratically run "food for people, not for profit" small collective that was beginning to pop up all over the Bay Area (Ferguson 1991, 109). Its popularity in the so-called Gourmet Ghetto developing in Berkeley—a nonconformist but increasingly affluent food-centered shopping district north of the University of California flagship campus (Alkon 2008)—gave it breathing room to experiment with combining fulfilling workplace relations and customer satisfaction and to question the focus on growth assumed in the mainstream business community. By 1975 the fourteen regular members and eight substitutes serving at least three hundred customers per day vetoed significant expansion of their collective or business, later describing their decision as "a philosophical distaste for society's dependence on and glorification of growth and expansion" and a "natural inclination to take it easy and keep things on a smaller scale" (Cheese Board Collective 2003, 13). Instead of its own expansion, the Cheese Board supported the local cooperative community with low- and no-interest loans and training.[13]

On its face, Cheese Board membership was inclusive: buy-in was nominal (one dollar), and upon payment new members had all the rights of longer-term ones. But there were barriers to full inclusion. As cooperative ethnographer Robert Jackall noted in the Cheese Board's first decade, conventional help-wanted advertisements were not used to attract new members: "No one is even considered for the collective unless he or she is known, and known fairly well, by an established member" (1984, 112). Such friendship-based screening practices may have contributed to the Cheese Board's ethnoracial and class uniformity: all members were white, almost all were from professional families, and most had either college degrees or some years of college. This uniformity may also have resulted from their low earnings, which Jackall attributed to being "satisfied with a generally modest, low-consumption life-style" (1984, 128). Such satisfaction also allowed the implementation of a "completely egalitarian pay structure" (Cheese Board Collective 2003, 4), and whether because pay equity was more attractive to potential women members or more *unattractive* to potential men members, women were the majority.

Cheese Board decisions were made by consensus, requiring the agreement of all workers on major decisions, or at least their agreement not to actively dissent. Members rotated through tasks that appealed to them and that needed doing: interacting with customers on the floor, receiving and cutting cheese in the back areas, or performing clerical or janitorial duties. Jackall found, however, that "some tasks . . . are considered choice ones, and . . . workers must fight for them" (1984, 116), and the more hours a member worked, the better chance they stood to win the fight—perhaps resulting in subtle gender inequalities to which Jackall was not sensitized but other scholarship has found in worker cooperatives (Hacker 1989; Miller 2011).

This "fight" was an ongoing issue in the collective. Jackall meant that Cheese Board members encouraged each other to be blunt in their disagreements—"Meetings in the first years were frequently loud, argumentative, and unstructured," noted the Cheese Board Collective itself (2003, 5)—with the aim not only of prompt and direct address of problems, but also as an "an integrating factor" that "creates a bond of deeply felt experience and heightens feelings of familial intimacy" (Jackall 1984, 111). Thus, disagreements were transformed into emotional commitments that, along with preexisting social ties, helped to facilitate the use of consensus decision-making. Yet they also created what Jackall called the "central paradox" of such collectives: that such openness also produced "an ongoing state of open conflict" (1984, 110). In the San Francisco Bay Area such conflict was often political and sectarian, and often split local collectives apart (Drew 1998). Perhaps for this reason, and perhaps because several members of the Cheese Board Collective were also deeply engaged in more hippie than politico pursuits, the collective refused to commit the business to any particular political or social cause even though many individual members were deeply involved with such causes. Thus the "contentious but connected" culture remained almost entirely internal and was only weakly affected by outside currents; this is arguably the reason it remained one of the few surviving countercultural collective cooperatives.

The end of the era. Popular wisdom has it that the participatory democracy of countercultural collectivist cooperatives reduced their ability to be nimble or innovative—an argument made both by scholars (Okun 1975; Viggiani 1997) and participants (Thompson 1992; Yasukochi 1992) to account for the financial battles that most of the generation of cooperatives fought and lost. But longitudinal studies have shown that these cooperatives were at least as likely to survive as other small businesses (Ben-Ner 1988; Olsen 2013). More significant in the sharp drop-off of this generation was the countercultural collectivist combination of member homogeneity with embrace of a "small is beautiful" (Schumacher 1973) ethos—a practice of intentionally limiting organizational size to one that allowed members to meet face to face, not only to preserve friendship relations internally but also to approximate the neighborly feel of a small business of the past.

In the face of growing corporate entry into what were previously entirely countercultural niches like "natural foods," which set itself against the chemical processing that had come to dominate food production (Belasco 1989; Johnston, Biro, and MacKendrick 2009; Thompson 1992), small worker cooperatives found themselves unable to compete with national companies' strong commodity chains and ability to sustain below-cost sales to eliminate competition (Aschemann et al. 2007). Like other small businesses of the era, countercultural collectivist cooperatives suffered during a period of national and transnational chain growth, particularly as customers continued to move to the suburbs, transforming frequent pedestrian shopping trips into weekly ones in their cars (Levinson 2011; Lichtenstein 2009).

But this small business problem was compounded by its member demographics. First, the labor market had not only contracted but more sharply bifurcated, creating what sociologist Arne Kalleberg calls "good" and "bad" jobs (2011), and hollowing out the middle, in which the low pay but good conditions of cooperative jobs were located. The whiteness and class culture of cooperative members (who were aging out of the youth culture and acquiring family responsibilities of their own) offered a privileged path back into the noncooperative labor market. A less privileged workforce might have stuck around to make its cooperatives work for longer; a more evenly distributed economy might have allowed an economically privileged workforce to withstand ongoing marginal earnings created by the pressure of Home Depot and Whole Foods entering previously protected market niches. Instead, the demographic that founded the cooperatives largely moved on. Although there may have been thousands of democratic worker cooperatives in the mid-1970s, they declined precipitously in the 1980s (Curl 2009); by the beginning of the twenty-first century, there were only about two hundred in existence (Deller et al. 2009).

Lessons from American Worker Cooperative History

Although it is not necessarily the case in other parts of the world, in the United States the history of worker cooperation is intimately bound to the rise and fall of the country's economy, with each period of mass cooperative formation mapping onto a particularly lengthy and deep crisis of capitalism. In all periods, loss of economic opportunity and faith in capitalism's ability to sustain communities presented worker cooperators with three challenges that remain central to contemporary and future cooperation: creating *economic empowerment* by generating and returning value to workers; *democratic empowerment* via a transformed distribution of organizational authority; and *egalitarian allotment* of resources and power among their members.

The labor republican era demonstrated that, as Marx insisted (1864), workers could self-manage production on a large scale, reduce if not eliminate inequalities, and model an alternative to the capitalist organization of production. That it was delegitimized by the institutionalization of the labor movement in organizations such as the AFL and the CIO, and crippled by the coordinated efforts of capital and the state, does nothing to undermine this achievement but does suggest that market efficiency is not the only influence on how particular organizational forms come to predominate.[14] Union disparagement of worker cooperation was at least as much about solidifying unions as the sole vehicle of workers' interests as it was about Luxemburg's (2006) concerns over cooperative members themselves becoming capitalists. Without the support of the labor movement, it is not that surprising that the next generation of worker cooperatives would instead seek the support of other powerful forces: the business community and the state.

The critical lesson of the self-help era is how quickly and successfully working people could organize collectively to "chisel," or demand resources, that enabled first distribution and then production networks. Some of the poorest and least socially connected members of society, unemployed and "unskilled" laborers, were able to identify and satisfy the needs of their communities almost entirely autonomously. Yet this independence combined with their impoverishment to make them vulnerable to, and then dependent on, corporate and state aid. They were driven by a fundamental ambivalence: Should cooperatives simply sustain displaced workers until the market could reabsorb them, or should they offer an alternative vision of provisioning for communities? As businesses, they benefited from inclusion across race and gender in terms of increased labor and skills but also suffered from submerged raced and gendered expectations regarding how work was performed and by whom; as social justice organizations, race and gender inclusion tested the investment in cooperation between workers who ran the gamut from self-declared anti-racists and anti-sexists to outright white supremacists and defenders of work as a masculine prerogative. Although the self-help cooperatives proved safe from Luxemburg's (2006) fears of self-exploitation, in the end the institutionalization of spontaneous collective economic action provoked by the Great Depression was unable to sustain a mix of ideologies or independence from a state that was not committed to long-term worker ownership.

At multiple generations' remove from mainstream labor, countercultural collectivists reinserted middle-class habitus into a new definition of work and workers, and returned issues of creativity and autonomy to discussions of what a social movement for labor could do. They rejected the dichotomy suggested by Marx (1864) and Luxemburg (2006) by rejecting bosses entirely, and proposed the blunt and contentious but democratic workplace in their stead. Yet they faced a paradox not fully addressed in cooperative studies of the time: that the noted similarity of countercultural collectivist members that facilitated contention without conflagration and allowed their cooperatives to become deeply democratic and egalitarian workplaces *also* effectively excluded most of those who did not share their white and middle-class *habitus*. That is, countercultural collectivist cooperatives created a more egalitarian space *internally* while *externally* (and opaquely) denying access to those without the shared culture knowledge necessary for entrée and integration into countercultural spaces.

Thus, as *economic* projects, periods of worker cooperation respond not only to the availability of labor or capital but also to the social and labor movements of which they were part. The autonomous labor republican model—the most economically successful of the worker cooperative models—demanded shop floor control in a way that the more family- and neighborhood-oriented self-help subject did not. This paved the way for government influence over self-help ability to compete in the open market and organizational structure (and eventually control over cooperative assets), particularly given the labor movement's refusal to engage with worker cooperatives as allies. Indeed, union demands on the state that resulted in the National Labor Relations Act of 1935 (which protected the rights of workers to form unions without fear of reprisal) and the corresponding corporate pushback in the form of the Taft-Hartley Act of 1947 (which limited union actions and gave greater legal powers to the state to act against unions and union members) focused the labor movement on unionization issues. Worker cooperatives could not find a home in a labor movement entirely dedicated to protecting unions. Yet it was this abject state that made the worker cooperative available to countercultural collectivists in the 1970s as a relatively unregulated and even undefined form of enterprise that could be retailored to suit the needs of those raised to be members of a professional and managerial class.

Struggles within the labor movement have also affected worker cooperatives as *democratic* projects. Democratic control has emerged repeatedly in the history of the American labor movement, but as often as not as a site of contention between rank-and-file union members and their leadership (Milkman and Voss 2004; Polletta 2002). Worker cooperatives have experimented with workplace control, moving from theoretical to practical beliefs about workplace democracy, and from representative to participatory ways of understanding democracy. Labor republican enterprises were sometimes brought down by conflict between the autonomy enshrined in the origins of the era and the top-down managerial structures that were almost unthinkingly put in place. Self-help cooperatives' democratic voting represented a significant departure from the norms of capitalist firms and showed the potential of aligning day-to-day operations with ideals. Such alignment was central to the countercultural collectivist cooperatives and attempts to prefigure a future society, and they offered models of worker control that have made their way into "high performance" and other employee-participation approaches to even mainstream workplaces—despite the regular finger-pointing at the high degree of participative control as the cause of countercultural collectivist era failure.

As *egalitarian* projects, the labor republican and countercultural collectivist eras proposed conceptions of workers that were increasingly at odds with both capital and union conceptions. Like unions, labor republican cooperatives articulated worker subjectivity as something that comes into being through its relation with capital and that is endowed with rights to the value it creates. But they offered an alternative to union insistence that this subjectivity is concrete and maintained through an antagonistic relationship to owners of capital: because the cooperative worker is always also becoming an owner, cooperatives defeat capital by stealing away its labor rather than through union confrontations. Yet by delimiting the birthplace of the worker to its relation with capital, labor republicanism had no easy or convincing way to make a case against the casual, thoroughgoing, and institutionalized sexism and racism that kept men and women of color and white women from accessing this "citizen-producer" self in any consistent manner. Sidestepping this problem, self-help cooperatives largely rejected the worker role: *workers* received cash wages and produced goods for sale on the open market; *cooperators* bartered and chiseled for their families' needs as heads of households. It was, perhaps, the distance from the white and masculine worker role that allowed self-help cooperators to be most broadly inclusive of all the eras. Yet this ambivalence about *workers*—by the 1930s a firmly union-centered concept—made it difficult to attract and keep members who saw labor as work, with all its attendant responsibilities and (financial) rewards. Perhaps for this reason as much as the fact that their members were rarely facing significant economic privation, countercultural collectivist cooperatives firmly declared themselves workers but also announced their intention to redefine workers and the workplace: not merely what people do in order to provision for life but also to connect with others and explore their human potential. Their recognition of workplace inequality as encompassing gender and ethnoracial barriers was a significant transformation in terms of being able to identify and thus address workplace inequalities, but their inability to recognize the class and ethnoracial inequality effects of their friendship-based relations kept the egalitarian project from being fully realized.

Thus, it seems as if the labor movement and worker cooperatives have been at odds since the institutionalization of collective bargaining. Union leaders derided worker cooperatives as too extreme in the labor republican era, as a form of "self-starvation" in the self-help era, and as hopelessly bourgeois in the countercultural collectivist era. In doing so they attached meaning not only to the economics of worker cooperatives but also to their egalitarian democratic control—as ineffective, frivolous, and anti-American. And by the 1970s it seemed that worker cooperatives had accepted, at least, that while cooperatives could be a model for broader adoption at some later date, they were not for economically marginalized folk who were not members of the counterculture. But buried in this history is the shared foundations of unions and cooperatives as vehicles for working people to take control of their productive lives, and the idea that workplace control and participatory democracy have a long—albeit disowned—history across all sectors of the labor movement (Polletta 2002).

What does this suggest for contemporary and future worker cooperatives? First, that worker cooperatives offer important potential avenues of resistance to the control of capital over workers' lives, which—regardless of their connection to the labor movement—were not acknowledged by mainstream labor for decades (although this began to change in the twenty-first century; Hoyer 2015; Schlachter 2017; Witherell 2013). For one thing, worker cooperatives can offer practical *organizational* alternatives for workers' livelihoods when unions are under attack from big business and the state. For another, in an era of such diverse processes as graduate student unionizing and the rise of the gig economy (Milkman and Ott 2014), they offer *conceptual* alternatives to think about what it means to be a worker and perhaps to think about class itself.

The meanings of *work* and *worker* have become historically coupled with the union organizational form promoted by the labor movement and with the labor movement's ability (but often failure) to examine workers through lenses of race/ethnicity, nationality, gender, sexuality, religion, and other social forces that shape work experiences. Thus, an important lesson this history of worker cooperation reveals is not only the power of the *worker* construction but also its limits. Worker cooperatives experimented with inhabiting the labor movement's worker conception in the labor republican era (and thus largely excluding men and women of color and white women), trading it in for another identity in the self-help era (increasing inclusion but only weakly making claims to creating and maintaining workplaces), and attempting to transform its parameters in the countercultural collectivist era (increasing gender inclusion and rights as workers, but reproducing ethnoracial and class exclusions). These different struggles suggest that contemporary and future worker cooperatives need to consider not only the material structures of their economic and democratic projects but also the cultural meanings embedded in the conceptualization—and then recruitment and retention activities—of the cooperative worker.

Summary: Alternative Versions of Labor

As collectivities, worker cooperatives have attempted to advance workers' economic and democratic interests over time and within the parameters of what is possible for the organizational form. This has been accomplished while addressing internal differences of class, race/ethnicity, and gender to greater and lesser degrees. Although cooperatives operate within limits regarding how they can distribute economic and social benefits (see the "Worker Ownership" section of chapter 1), when they occur en masse, as they did in each of the historical eras discussed in this chapter, they are capable of changing rules and practices. Examples of this include the labor republican era's support for union wage increases among noncooperative shops; the self-help era's insistence on interracial cooperation in a time of deep racial segregation; and the countercultural collectivist era's demonstration of the value of direct worker control over working conditions. Yet the cooperatives and their members that helped to win these rewards have largely been forgotten.

Each cooperative era ended decisively—a radical break that severed connections between generations of cooperators, requiring each generation to start from scratch. There are some advantages to this: the unknown quality of the cooperative enterprise allowed each generation's participants to imaginatively fill in blank spaces, creating new forms of economic and democratic empowerment and new configurations of people within them. Yet the gaps between cooperative eras also have their drawbacks: the self-help generation failed to consider how the noncompetition requirements set by the state could potentially be used to cripple an alternative economy like that of the labor republicans; the countercultural collectivists failed to consider how their minimization of the economic benefits of worker cooperation shaped their recruitment of members; and the current generation's pursuit of state sponsorship (for instance, the Worker Cooperative Business Development Initiative funded by New York City's Department of Small Business Services) fails to consider how dependence on state funding and the shared control of assets with the state makes cooperatives especially vulnerable to shifts in the political winds. Without this understanding of how cooperative era advances are *connected to* their limits, contemporary and future worker cooperatives are less equipped to make the kinds of decisions that could transform cooperative development from an era—whether "experiment" or "contradiction"—to a permanent transformation of labor.

METAMORPHOSES
Worker Cooperatives in the Golden Valley

> **We were a cult of personality. And our Jim Jones left and we didn't have enough Kool-Aid to go around, so we had to try to make it work for us all.**
>
> —Herbert Gubbins, People's Daily Bread Bakery

> **One World was working fine. That wasn't the issue. . . . We just knew we needed something more formal than our meetings.**
>
> —Bob Imperiale, One World Natural Grocery

Why do some alternative organizations persist when others of their generation dissolve? Why do some worker cooperatives abandon egalitarian foundations? And what explains those organizations that defy this "law of oligarchy" (Michels 1959) and the demands of market and state to conform to capitalist business norms? This chapter traces the origins and development of People's Daily Bread Bakery and One World Natural Grocery and explores their mutual journey beyond the collectivist model of their era as well as their divergence. In so doing it makes an argument that worker cooperatives are indeed viable businesses but that their ability to address inequalities changes as the organization evolves.

While chapter 2 identified markedly different ways workers have organized cooperative enterprises over time—from the managerial firm of the labor republican era, to the decentralized but integrated "chiseling" operations of the self-help era, to the friendship-based collectives of the countercultural collectivist era—it did not address variation *within* each of these eras. This chapter focuses on what differences among contemporaneous cooperatives says about the limits of egalitarian commitments in capitalist economies. Both People's Daily Bread Bakery and One World Natural Grocery developed a critique of the "small is beautiful" and friendship network dogma of the period, and these adaptations seem critical to their survival. But they differed in their embrace or critique of the decentralized and distributed authority so widely used by their peer organizations, and in their sense of what it meant to be a member of a cooperative. As

I will show, neither the managerial or member identification practices each developed were inevitable choices, but each choice was deeply consequential for workplace democracy and egalitarianism.

Theories of Survival and Divergence

The rise and fall of worker cooperatives present a challenge to organizational theorists, who try to explain the growth, institutionalization, and transformation of social movements, offices of the state, religious institutions, community groups, and, of course, work organizations. Structuralist approaches call attention to foundational actors and practices (e.g., Stinchcombe 1965), looking inside organizations for clues to the structures and practices—including ones that generate or remediate inequality—that they preserve, adopt, and discard. This focus on organizational histories and actors helps to explain how and why workers might choose cooperatives instead of unions as a vehicle for social change, and it also directs inquiry regarding the survival of certain cooperatives: the particular people, values, or organizational practices adopted either initially or at an early critical juncture (Baron et al. 2007; Hannan, Burton, and Baron 1996). This approach preserves agency, or the potential of workers to collectively change their circumstances, for both organizations and their inhabitants; the key is to be found in setting up the right conditions early on. But the structuralist approach sets aside the larger social conditions and environments in which organizations operate, and thus cannot account for the difference described in chapter 2 between the direct attacks faced by the nineteenth-century labor republican cooperatives and the subtle withdrawal of resources faced by the self-help cooperatives of the Great Depression.

In contrast, neoinstitutionalist approaches offer usefully macrosocial frameworks, such as the "institutional environment" (Rowan 1982) and the more sociocultural "field" (Ray 1999) to explain the periods of worker cooperative flourishing within the norms and regulatory pressures exerted by the field of social movement organizations and weakened legitimacy of traditional capitalist businesses. But while both institutional environment and movement field help explain why very similar types of worker cooperatives emerge (and fail) in waves, it makes it difficult to explain differences between cooperatives. Why don't *all* worker cooperatives in a given period either transform the field, cease operation, or "degenerate" into more traditional, investor-owned firms (Webb and Webb 1897)? What explains the organizations that seem unaffected by "institutional isomorphism" (DiMaggio and Powell 1983), or the various pressures to conform to existing and legitimated institutional forms and actions, persisting as outlier or resistant organizations that often inspire or train a successive cohort? Indeed, like the structuralist path dependence approach, neoinstitutionalist attention to an organization's environment obscures the effects of ongoing human interactions within organizations.

To account for both actor agency and their surrounding socioeconomic environments, the "microinstitutional" (Kellogg 2009) or "inhabited institutions" (Hallett and Ventresca 2006) approach directs attention to what Tim Hallett and Marc Ventresca term organizations' "embeddedness." This is a relational or processual focus on the interplay among organizational actors and between them and their institutional environments, and on how these actors make meaning through the imperfect and dialectical process of organizational "collective combat," or the "face-to-face" struggles between individual actors within organizations that are nested in larger environments (Kellogg 2011, 14). In the case of the bakery and the grocery in this study, this would mean considering the external (or what Kellogg calls "extra-local") conditions that might have affected decisions by cooperative members, the local relations within each cooperative that increased or decreased the sense-making power of relevant institutional logics, and the meanings created through interchanges between these extra-local and local relations and conditions that affect how organizational members act. I will argue that understanding the *accretion* of these embedded local meanings better explains how these cooperatives became organizations that were not only different from their generational peers but eventually also considerably different from each other.

In this chapter, I first provide a brief political economy of the Golden Valley, outlining the regional conditions that shaped the proliferation of worker cooperatives instead of traditional labor movement involvement or consumer cooperative formation. I then present the early histories of the two worker cooperatives in this study, using excerpts from meeting minutes and other documents that each cooperative allowed me to examine in their on-site archives between 2003 and 2005, as well as interviews with longtime and former members conducted between 2001 and 2005. Following that history, I offer explanations for how the bakery and the grocery survived the end of the countercultural collectivist era, how they transitioned away from the collectivist-democratic organizational structure common at the time, and why their transformations took different shapes from each other despite their proximity and interconnection. In this part of the chapter, I propose a microinstitutionalist theory of organizational accretion as better suited than structuralist or neoinstitutionalist theory to explaining such organizational transformation. The chapter concludes by linking the insights of this historical analysis to the exploration of the relationships between organizational structure and culture and workplace inequality in the subsequent chapters.

Worker Cooperatives and the Political Economy of the Golden Valley in the 1970s

The Golden Valley is a physically and economically lush region of Northern California. Although, like most of the country, its cities were shrinking in the 1950s and 1960s and leaving pockets of poverty and joblessness, the region's new suburbs increased the overall population. The 1970s global financial restructuring (Block 1990) diminished the Golden Valley's prosperity: all over California, unionized jobs disappeared as steel, auto, and rubber tire factories packed up and moved overseas. Youth raised on the American dream of financial reward for hard work expected to step into stable jobs,[1] but instead faced an unstable, contracting economy. While some of the lost employment opportunities were replaced by ones in new information technology industries (Rhode 2001), these were more like the service jobs that were also replacing manufacturing: they were less likely to be white-collar jobs, and more likely to be routinized and technologically or managerially controlled (Saxenian 1983).

These economic changes transformed not only the Golden Valley labor market but also the way young people thought of and interacted with the labor movement. Even though California was one of the most densely unionized states and had one of the highest populations of union members in the country, this was primarily in the public sector. Young workers, on the other hand, were going into the private sector, which had some of the lowest national rates of unionization (Hirsch and Macpherson 2004). Yet this disconnect between unions and most young Californians did not necessarily create a rupture with the labor movement as whole. In the Golden Valley, the earlier blacklisting of labor and left-wing organizers in the 1950s had created an alternative network of employment, housing, and cultural institutions even before the counterculture became a national phenomenon. This parallel social world expanded its participants' ideas about what counted as "labor activism" as it came to encompass countercultural communal living and educational experiments in the 1960s and 1970s, and it nurtured some of the key activists in social movements for ethnoracial, gender, and sexuality justice. These overlapping social and cultural projects provided a rich base of both rhetorical support and material resources for the development of a wide range of labor challenges to capitalism and bureaucratic relations.

One focus of this social justice subculture was the experience of work, and particularly the psychic pain of job routinization and worker dehumanization across the class spectrum. While such insights fueled union-oriented labor movement action on the national scene (Brenner, Brenner, and Winslow 2010), in the Golden Valley they found ideological congruence with the participatory democracy of the time and material support from professional and managerial family financial reserves. That is, unlike the majority of those who put their energy into organizing existing workplaces, members of the Golden Valley counterculture had just enough capital to combine with others to start small businesses (Jackall and Crain 1984). And unlike other youth from similar backgrounds, they were exposed to a critique of work and a vision of alternatives that made cooperative enterprises both alluring and imaginable. Cooperatives, rather than unions, became the vehicle for transforming the experience of work.

Golden Valley worker cooperatives were influenced by two other types of organizations that were also located at the edges of the economy: the established institution of consumer cooperatives and a new institution of "free stores." First, leadership from an established and nationally-emulated chain of Golden Valley consumer cooperatives provided training and advice to would-be worker cooperators. Their documents suggest that some of their left-leaning leadership helped guide the early food-oriented Golden Valley youth away from the managerial model favored by the anti-communist Cooperative League (Parker 1956) and instead towards a highly participative organizational form that could operate independent of this Cold War artifact.

Second, the intersecting "hippie" lifestyle- and "politico" social change-oriented mentality (Echols 1989) of the San Francisco-based Diggers had created the "free store" space, stocked with donations and scavenged or stolen items, in which the youth counterculture could both get minimal provisions like food, clothes, or household items and also connect with each other to plan and carry out new projects (Curl 2009). One such project was the worker cooperative, which visitors to free stores carried back to their own communities with the flush and bloom of religious converts (Roth 2011). The worker cooperative project was sustained by a Diggers-founded distribution network connecting their free stores to alternative producers (Alkon 2012), and that eventually solidified into a more formal and rule-bound organization than the Diggers seemed comfortable with (Howard 1969).

It seems that the Golden Valley hit the sweet spot of opportunity, lowered entry costs, the ideological satisfaction of anti-materialist and antibureaucratic desires, and the personal satisfaction of social needs. By some estimates the Golden Valley was home to nearly 20 percent of *all* countercultural collectivist worker cooperatives in the United States. The contracting economy made it more difficult for young people to work entirely without pay, but it also reduced operating costs to the point where family capital was good enough to keep such enterprises afloat. The abundance and then evaporation of material resources and expectations, the disappearance of ready employment and the availability of union benefits, a locally broadened notion of "progressive" culture encompassing labor and new social movements, and the direction and inspiration of established and innovative forms of cooperation provided both concrete and symbolic resources to create innovative workplaces. Two of these were People's Daily Bread Bakery in Colina, a smaller city at the southern end of the Golden Valley, and—only fifty miles away—One World Natural Grocery in Edgefield, the region's urban center.

People's Daily Bread Bakery: Making Community, Making Money

> It started with a buying club. . . . And then they got a warehouse to store the food, and then they had a store to sell the food, and they got a trucking company, and then they wanted to start a bakery. . . . And then the bakery people didn't feel like they could get everything that they needed in the vote, because they were always outvoted . . . so they decided they wanted to buy out and go it on our own.
>
> —Adam Delaney, People's Daily Bread Bakery

Foundations: Collectivist "Openness and Unity"

Adam Delaney's description of the founding of People's Daily Bread Bakery in 1979 identifies the shift from a weakly defined collection of individuals within the Redwoods Workers Circle Community Store in the suburban college town of Colina to a fully purposeful and self-supporting worker cooperative. As one of the original bakery collective members, Adam, a white man with a high-school education raised without access to family wealth, explains that they chose to follow their interests in baking rather than making what might be a more prudent financial choice of staying in a larger, diversified company. Luckily, they were quickly integrated into a regional cooperative network, the Food for People Consortium, which modeled its connection of producers and retailers of natural foods after that of the Diggers (Alkon 2012). The earliest photos depict almost stereotypical hippie "dropouts": three young white women and two white men with long hair floating over Indian-print clothing, grinning with the even, white teeth of a lifetime of middle-class dental and orthodontic care. The bakery's founding mission statement commits the organization to economic support for its members and healthful food for the community, adding that members will "treat each other lovingly using communication techniques to share feelings in order to maintain a sense of openness and unity with each other." In short, the bakery exhibited the kind of typical countercultural collectivist ideals and material conditions described in chapter 2, "The Countercultural Collectivist Era, 1970s-1980s."

The bakery's founding and survival in the early days relied heavily on its members' ability to draw from the financial and cultural resources of their families and communities. Greybo Sofer, a white woman hired in 1988 who had become the bakery's safety coordinator after years of production work, heard that "all of [the founders] were able to go to their parents and borrow this *obscene* amount of money. I think it was five thousand dollars or ten thousand dollars [each]." Although buy-ins for subsequent members were closer to $1,000 in the next decade, Herbert Gubbins, a white man who dropped out of an Ivy League college, the first company CEO and the second-longest worker at the time of my study, still remembers that "the average college education when I started here was bachelor's or master's." Yet this amount of capital and education did not translate into immediate success: financial weakness and instability meant there was little profit to be shared, with starting wages just barely more than the national minimum, and only meager raises—some of which were wiped out during the bakery's financial crises in the mid- and late 1980s.

Yet from such small and undercapitalized beginnings, a business emerged. Through its use of the Food for People Consortium's warehouse and West Coast "countercuisine" distribution network and its fulfillment of the booming new "natural foods" consumer niche (Belasco 1989), the bakery was able to increase its reach and sales. By retaining most of its profits as working capital, the bakery was able to lease a commercial plant in 1982 that allowed it to double its capacity. (For a discussion of how cooperatives generally allocate their resources, see the "How Worker Cooperatives Work" section of chapter 2.) The eager markets for its bread helped to convince the membership that expansion was viable. The bakery increased its small fleet of local sales and delivery trucks, and within five years the founding population of five had multiplied to over forty full- and part-time workers—still more women than men, still almost all white and college-educated.

The division of labor varied in the beginning. On one hand, for some it was relatively weak and egalitarian, and bakery photo albums from the early and mid-1980s reveal both men and women—again, almost all white—in production, shipping, maintenance, and administrative roles. There was a board of directors for incorporation purposes, but it was composed of the entire membership and its meetings were folded into the general membership meetings, where decisions were made. Adam described to me the lack of specialization in either maintenance, distribution, or production that his first schedule entailed: "I had one janitorial shift, I had three delivery shifts, I had a breadcrumbs shift, and on Saturday I would drive transport." Yet meeting minutes and other bakery records from the time indicate that other workers' shifts were more focused in a single area and that power began to concentrate. First, responsibility for scheduling and supervising worker absence and lateness was given to bread mixers—positions that involved the skills of maintaining product consistency and setting a viable pace for other production workers, and appear to have been entirely filled by men. Then a production coordinator position was created, with both men and women being elected or self-selecting into the role.

As was the case in many noncooperative enterprises, this increased responsibility did not increase pay, however: at the bakery at this time, only seniority produced differences in earnings, not merit or skill. Akin to what Sherryl Kleinman (1996) has found in a similar organization, recollections and meeting minutes reveal a mix of desire for *and* hostility towards higher pay for specialized skills and knowledge. Still, in the early years the countercultural collectivist practice of uncoupling earnings from role or responsibility held.

Crisis: "Management by Committee" and Conflict

Despite the countercultural collectivist insistence on the broad sharing of responsibility, the bakery membership chafed at the long meetings its completely flat organizational structure generated. By 1983, members were ready to try a little more delegation, and voted in "management by committee," or the election of members to task groups to organize work schedules, production cycles, and product sales. Adam ruefully recalled, however, that "people love to be on the committees because they get to vote for raises or vote for whatever, but they really don't want to do any *work*. They just want to be on a *committee* because they didn't want anybody else to mess with anything, mess with their job or whatever." That is, rather than increasing efficiency or effectiveness, Adam felt that committees were less organizational management and more personal territorial control. Meeting minutes and recollection reveal member struggles during the seven years of "management by committee."

This was at least in part because of the numerous interpersonal conflicts, which Adam saw as an outcome of what had and had not changed since the bakery's founding:

> ADAM: Collectives seem to work when they're small, and you have a few people that are like-minded individuals. You're all a bunch of hippies and you're in this business together to save the world and make organic bread, and it kind of works, although you certainly have the arguments and knockdown drag-outs, and all the rest of that. But it's a little easier to make it work. As it grows, it becomes an impossible task to try and get everyone to agree, especially if you're trying to be unanimous. What do they call it? Making decisions by . . . [*voice trails off*]

JOAN: Consensus?

ADAM: Consensus. Ooh! That's the word. No way! It's just about impossible when you have strong-willed people who really have strong opinions and are really attached to them.

Although Adam initially seemed to claim that the difficulty of consensus is size ("a few people"), it became clear that the "like-minded" criterion was at least as important: the "strong opinions" at the bakery increasingly centered around race and gender. Conflicts began to be addressed in meeting minutes first as "employment harassment" (September 1984), and then as "unorderly conduct" (August 1985) and "unacceptable conduct" (September 1986). By 1986, comments and behaviors in a conflict between two "strong-willed" white women and an African American man were specifically labeled "sexist" and "racist," and by early 1989 workers articulated a policy to address "sexual harassment." At times the bakery's organizational solutions were as unusual as its organizational structure: bakery members approved, but did not seem to ever use, an absurdist 1986 proposal requiring parties in unresolvable conflict to use noisemakers, don Groucho Marx glasses, and conduct a duel with rubber chickens. However, just as often they were legalistic and standardized, documenting specific actions as worthy of termination in just the way a noncooperative firm might do.

These interpersonal conflicts combined with the weak committee accountability to produce dangerous—and expensive—working conditions. Herbert, a mixer and member of various committees, felt that workplace conflicts were primarily managed by keeping people apart, but in practice this meant that "good workers were in bread, not-so-good workers [were] doing bagels, and shitty workers went to the pizza place." While "good" workers helped enforce norms and practices that kept workers safe on the job, others did not. The monthly board meeting minutes from November 18, 1985, include a safety report, which reads in its entirety, "Sherry tripped over floor dolly and fell. Vernea slipped on wet floor and twisted her ankle. David had a back injury while delivering." The bakery's higher-than-average rate of injury—attributed to poor bodily mechanics, sloppy workspaces, and overwork—hurt workers and diverted profits to cover rising insurance premiums. As Herbert saw it, this was because the committees were unable to compel safe practices: they had no power to sanction workers whose actions were unsafe for themselves or their coworkers, nor did they have access to resources that could remediate physical issues like an uneven floor. With fewer than ninety bakery members, he recalled that "we had forty-four injuries, and twenty-two of them were voc[ational] rehab[ilitation]s" involving a lengthy period of physical therapy and/or career transition services paid for by the bakery. In 1989, membership minutes show that he warned the membership that their inability to demonstrate procedures to address unsafe conditions would cost the bakery up to $1 million per year in excess insurance payments, as well as hurting workers and depriving the bakery of those workers' skills and knowledge. Indeed, in the following year, falling profits forced the bakery to cut wages across the board.

As the bakery teetered at this edge of strife and financial turmoil, it also experienced a crisis of leadership. The lack of organizational processes or practices to rein in potentially dangerous individual member behaviors had also permitted charismatic power and informal leadership to develop. White, middle-class James Heinz, one of the founding members, was repeatedly referenced in interviews with senior workers as a "visionary," "genius," or, self-mockingly, "our guru." A well-liked mixer, James was known to circumvent the bakery's democratic practice. For instance, he once used his own money to purchase labor-saving and production-enhancing devices deemed too expensive by the membership, and then convinced members to reimburse his outlay once the devices were incorporated into the work processes. Despite this subversion, his actions were not only protected from criticism but enhanced his personal credibility for several years. Eventually, however, a financial audit revealed significant losses from a side project he had claimed was profitable and the collective voted to shut the project down. James resigned shortly thereafter, reportedly angered by having his authority challenged. Herbert likened the bakery to the San Francisco–based Peoples Temple, the countercultural religious organization whose infamous 1978 mass suicide and murders in Guyana were still fresh in the minds of Californians: "We were a cult of personality. And our Jim Jones left and we didn't have enough Kool-Aid to go around, so we had to try to make it work for us all."

After James left, the bakery struggled to develop its leadership. As Adam saw it, James's departure created suspicion of informal authority but no commitment to delegating formalized authority. "There would always be one or two people on a committee who would end up taking on all the work, and they'd have to develop skills to be able to do that work, and once they developed the skills they realized they could go almost anywhere else and make twice the money. . . . You always had people who had that desire—that drive—to make things work and to get involved, and to learn the skills . . . the people who naturally float toward these management positions." Adam felt that only a minority of people have leadership skills, and that they tended to leave for (financially) greener pastures to be managers. When I asked if he meant that the bakery's structure encouraged the exit of skills and knowledge, and that the membership felt that a solution to this problem was key to the bakery's survival, he replied, "Exactly. 'Why can't we just have managers and get paid?'"

Other members disagreed about the loss of expertise.[2] But after James's departure and a further round of increased insurance premiums, the bakery saw its customer base begin to respond to a late 1980s recession by purchasing cheaper, mainstream baked goods. Productivity and profits were not rising to support the bakery's workforce. Herbert felt that the exacting chemical reactions and timing of sourdough starter and yeast were incompatible with the diffuse accountability of democratic management, that "bakeries are harsh mistresses when it comes to things like being on time." At this point the membership was in broad agreement that the crises—struggles regarding worker diversity, a poorly functioning democratic management system, and financial instability— threatened the bakery's survival and that, without significant changes, it would go out of business.

Adaptation: The "New Model"

As Adam saw it, change really began when Lisa Paris, a white, middle-class founding member, demanded increased compensation for her accountancy skills:

> ADAM: Our financial person at the time said . . . at a meeting, big membership meeting, and everybody's there . . . "In order for me to stay here, I'm going to have to make *this* much money." And that was like *blasphemy* at the time . . .
>
> JOAN: To talk about money?
>
> ADAM: To talk about "*I* need more money, or I'm going to have to leave."

Why was this request "blasphemy"? Because, as bakery members understood, rewarding some more than others is rarely based purely on merit but rather on skills that class, gender, and race/ethnicity combine to produce. Thus, paying one person more than another risked reproducing an "inequality regime" (Acker 2006b), a system of increasing the financial worth of members of socially dominant groups in ways that allow them to reproduce those skills in the next generation—a self-reproducing system that the countercultural collectives of the 1970s and 1980s had consciously sought to end. Paying more for particular skills would reintroduce the mainstream logic of human capital: valuing college educations over manual labor experience, middle-class paths over working-class paths. Yet *not* participating in this system could mean losing this human capital; the company's consultants described members as feeling "blackmailed" by Lisa.[3] Her "blasphemous" demand went to the heart of the bakery's conception of itself as a worker cooperative, and debate raged for many months.

The turning point came when Lisa reported to the membership that the National Cooperative Bank (NCB)—one of the few financing institutions available to cooperatives, and the bakery's most likely lender for an equipment upgrade—was "looking for . . . democratic control, not necessarily a co-op corporate structure" (board minutes, August 23, 1988). Indeed, the NCB, whose mission was historically more connected to consumer and agricultural cooperatives, has funded numerous noncooperative organizations since its founding in 1975 (National Cooperative Bank, n.d.). "Democratic control" could be as simple as having *stakeholders* vote on alternatives presented by an organization's leadership, while a cooperative involves far more areas and degrees of *shareholder* control. This framework helped relieve the membership of the burden of its collectivism and allow it to freely pursue alternatives. In late 1988, seeking to create more impersonal fairness, greater accountability, and a competitive footing in the stratified world of capitalist firms, the bakery membership voted to hire consultants to help it transition. As Adam summarized, "We wanted to develop a hierarchical management system. We call it *the new model* . . . with different wages for different work groups, and different skill sets, and things like that." When the first consultants tried to preserve the bakery's participative management, they were quickly replaced by a second group that was more responsive to the membership's vision. This consultancy helped the bakery transition from "management by committee" to a more hierarchical system of managers still called—as late as 2014—the new model. This shift became a turning point for the bakery not only in terms of its organizational roots in the collectivist-democratic worker cooperatives of the 1970s but also in terms of its class, race/ethnicity, and gender diversity.

The new model, as depicted in figure 3.1, formally separated most democratic governance from positional management. Long-range and big-picture planning was delegated to a nine-member board of directors elected from the membership with some degree of proportional representation of work group (e.g., production or maintenance), authority (at least two managers and two nonmanagers), and gender (at least two men and two women). Day-to-day and weekly organization of jobs was shifted entirely to managers of the specific work groups, who reported to the "general coordinator" (later, "general coordinator/CEO"). This was Herbert, who was responsible for the creation of annual business plans and budgets and who reported to the board of directors. Mediating between them was the membership meeting, which held the power to affirm or veto Herbert's proposals, and an elected grievance committee. The new model also created greater variation in earnings. First, wage ranges were more highly differentiated based on the position's autonomy and skill, and managers were given the power to set wages within ranges voted on by the membership. Second, sales and delivery drivers began to derive a significant portion of their earnings from sales commissions. Third, management was converted from waged to salaried positions.

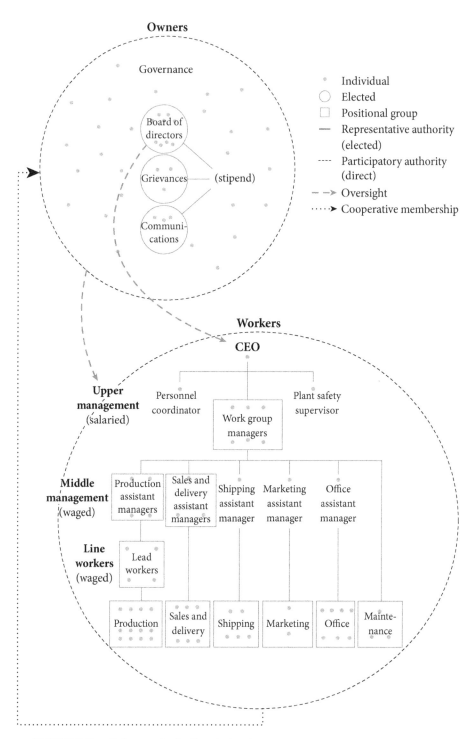

FIGURE 3.1. Bakery organizational structure

There were two other important phenomena that were not connected to or formally part of the new model. First, concurrent with the new model adoption was a period of national economic growth as the recession faded. It is possible that if the recession had continued for another year or two, the introduction of the new model would not have been able to counter these larger economic effects and might not have been associated with greater prosperity by bakery workers (if, indeed, the bakery had survived at all). Second, the bakery's growth following this period led to diversification by class and race/ethnicity, although primarily among its men. Increased production demanded workforce expansion, and by the end of 1991 there were a hundred workers, many more of them Chicanx and African American due to the efforts of a Chicana manager and an African American man's direct recruitment efforts. At the same time, many of the early white, middle class-raised members left, and managers filled their positions with workers who had relevant job experience rather than a cooperative or counterculture background. This may account for the greater proportion of new hires who were working-class and men, as both groups were more likely to have prior manufacturing experience.

Workers' increasing class and ethnoracial differences created new kinds of conflict among the workforce, particularly over religion and sexuality. In an extreme case, a new straight, white, self-proclaimed "Christian" production hire discovered that two of his white women coworkers were romantic partners and grew threatening. Almost ten years later, one of the two women recalled,

> He wanted to get our addresses . . . and *kill* us! So Herbert talked to him and said, "Well, people are that way. If you can't handle it, you need to leave." So the guy left. . . . But then he started hanging out on the corner of our house, kind of watching us. And then we found out he killed somebody at a party and was in jail. So from that point on, one of the questions [managers] are *supposed* to ask when hiring is, "There are gays and lesbians here, people different from you. There are African Americans, all this stuff. Do you have a *problem* with any of that?" I don't know if they always ask it . . .

According to workers who witnessed these changes, the first generation of managers struggled to address these new kinds of conflicts. Managerial interventions short of terminations were often ignored or overtly resisted: in meeting minutes from the period, Herbert described the bakery as having "a basic anti-management culture" (board minutes addendum, August 5, 1992), with workers complaining openly about managers' decisions and attitudes, and managers complaining of more subtle sniping and distrust. Herbert even refused to appear at what he deemed "hostile" membership meetings. Indeed, other than him, the first set of appointed managers had all resigned by 1992, and the second round of managerial hires was similarly brief.

Eventually, though, the cooperative came to accept management. By 1994 many of the former countercultural collectivist era members had resigned, and later managers got far less flak from their newer workers, most of whom had always worked under managers and brought with them the more common institutional logic of managed employees. Almost all of those I interviewed identified 1994 as the time the bakery began to stabilize, and most of them attributed this to the effect of managerial hierarchy fulfilling its promise of greater accountability and impersonal fairness (Kanter 1977; Weber 1946). In practice, this was described as better enforcement of rules governing interpersonal conduct and safety rules, which resulted in fewer costly injuries, more efficient production, and better use of planning skills.

The year 1994 also marked a significant change in financial practices for cooperative members: the implementation of "rolling payouts": a three-to-five-year deferral of payment of the cash value of workers' shares of cooperative profits rather than deferral until employment ended.[4] This reduced incentives for members to "cash out" by quitting, and thus killed two birds with one stone: working capital was protected as fewer members cashed out, and workforce turnover (and its financial and social costs) were reduced. At the same time, the bakery also reserved a portion of profits to share with *all* workers—members or not—to help induce loyalty and guarantee a source of funds that could be used by member applicants to pay buy-in costs. Both practices were extremely popular. Productivity increased, earnings began to rise well above state minimum wages, and the proportion of workers seeking membership began to rise again.

The bakery's success in finding a consumer market opened the way to growth, but the introduction of management was perceived as at least as important in the bakery's generation of meaningful levels of profit. By addressing its accountability problems, the bakery seemed able to create more jobs and a more stable workforce. Yet it was also a workforce whose ideological aims and cultural interests were becoming less similar, and this dissimilarity was also less directly addressed among members in board or membership meetings. What began as a fairly homogenous collective that prioritized its shared cultural values had transformed into a relatively traditional organization of increasingly diverse members whose shared material interests now formed their common ground.

The bakery's managerial turn from the participatory democratic practices of the countercultural collectivist generation of worker cooperatives challenges structuralist accounts of firms' foundations as explanatory of later outcomes (Baron, Hannan, and Burton 1999; Hannan, Burton, and Baron 1996). The bakery was originally just as committed to egalitarianism and democratic control, just as white and middle-class and young, and just as inexperienced in either business management or its industry as were peer cooperatives. That is, in its founding the bakery had no meaningful differences from the many similar cooperatives that either went out of business or trudged along for a while longer in their (fairly impoverished and ethnoracially homogeneous) collectivist-democratic mode (Jackall and Levin 1984; Mellor, Hannah, and Stirling 1988).

The neoinstitutionalist approach, on the other hand, seems to offer a better way to understand why the bakery diverged from the path of other cooperatives by considering the isomorphic pressures of the larger market: as the cooperative institutional environment evaporated, the bakery legitimated itself by mirroring or adopting many of the organizational practices, structures, and identity narratives typical of the noncooperative business world (DiMaggio and Powell 1983). Indeed, such adoption was believed to produce a level of stability in the bakery highly desired by the (eventual) workforce. But this approach suggests the futility of a social change strategy based on creating alternative organizations under existing conditions, that the institutional environment will irresistibly exert too much pressure for workers to change their lives "by deed instead of by argument" (Marx 1864). Further, this approach also contains an implied binary division of organizations as conforming to the institutional environment or resisting it. Such a division leaves it poorly positioned to explain the very similar changes but very different outcomes of a worker cooperative with a similarly alternative organizational founding form, One World Natural Grocery.

One World Natural Grocery: From Dogma to Democracy

> A lot of us didn't want to work for a living. We didn't want to make money. We just wanted to live and serve, and so One World was a place where you could go and do that. . . . We were a collective . . . we weren't a group doing business, we were a group running a grocery store.
> —Bob Imperiale, One World Natural Grocery

Foundations: "The Service Orientation"

Like Adam Delaney at the bakery, the grocery's Bob Imperiale was a white, working-class man—albeit one who had completed college and joined the cooperative while in graduate school. Like Adam, he was drawn to cooperatives by his belief in people over profits. When Bob distinguished "doing business" from "running a grocery store," he elevated the "value-rational" aspect of provisioning food for a community over the "instrumental" aspect of making money (Weber 1978). Yet it was not only the grocery's focus on values over money that made it exemplary of the countercultural collectivist era. If bakery workers like Herbert Gubbins liked to joke about having had a "guru," grocery workers were completely serious when they used the term. The grocery emerged in a working-class Latinx neighborhood in Edgefield when members of a spiritual commune of self-described "devotees" of a teenage Indian spiritual leader with a worldwide "New Age" following (Roof 1999) formed a buying club to secure the "natural" diet he recommended. Demographically, it was similar to the counterculture in which it was situated; an early member recalled, "We had one Black guy, one Asian woman, a few gay people. We had some diversity in the beginning, but it was, as you said, a little more white, and most of us were college educated."

The buying club, a holdover practice from cooperatives in the 1930s self-help period in which consumers pooled shopping lists to make weekly volume purchases directly from a wholesaler, was increasing beyond a manageable size due to neighbors' interest. In 1975 the commune's members decided to open a small produce market around the corner from their residence to fulfill their spiritual commitment to community service. Because one devotee was a member of the regional Food for People Consortium distribution network, the grocery became the third of an eventual network of ten Edgefield stores. Bob felt, however, that the Consortium "always looked at us with some level of disdain because we lacked this sort of, 'We're going to go out and change the world!' kind of core value. We were doing service. They were doing something else." This "service" captured the provisioning that retail stores offered but also subtly implied that, unlike the more revolutionary Consortium, the grocery was attuned to what people unlike themselves might want and prioritized those desires above their own. In addition to a shared morning meditation in front of the store, Bob claimed that

> the service orientation of a lot of the people made the store incredibly sensitive to the needs of customers. And maybe unlike a lot of the other collectives—especially the ones that were really white—we were in a very mixed neighborhood and we very quickly had a very mixed clientele because we sold rice and beans cheaper than anybody and all the Mexican ladies came. We had such an outrageously high percentage of purchases on food stamps—without any fraud going on! . . . Half to two-thirds of our deposits were on food stamps, but it was because all of the poorest people in this poorest part of Edgefield . . . they just found us. And they'd ask us for stuff and we would buy it.

The grocery was, in Bob's view, different from other countercultural collectivist cooperatives in two ways: its spiritually motivated service orientation predisposed it to bridging a gap between its members and its community; and its community was perceived more geographically (as its Latinx, working-class and immigrant neighborhood) than ideologically (as coreligionists or even the greater, and whiter, counterculture). For both of these reasons, the grocery quickly became far more welcoming across class and ethnoracial difference than it had been at its founding.

This community service orientation also led to greater overall growth. Customer (and member) desires for nonfood items like preservative-free toothpaste or phosphate-free laundry soap led to the opening of a second storefront next door for nonperishable items, then to a warehouse in an industrial park a few miles away to handle the volume of goods being sold, and finally to a fourth collective to coordinate clerical and administrative functions among the other three. As Bob recalled, "I don't remember us ever having slowing down growth as an issue. Nobody ever said, 'We don't want to do this.' It was, 'How can we do this?'" Like the bakery, the grocery had found its footing, and it became solidly established in the Edgefield counterculture.

Crisis: "Areas of Authority"

Like the bakery, the grocery also faced challenges regarding the differences between workers, accountability and interface problems with its collectivist-democratic organizational structure, and financial instability. The way Diana Flores, a white, middle-class mother of two who was living a downwardly mobile countercultural life in 1979, describes how she came to work at One World Natural Grocery is illustrative of how the first differences emerged among grocery workers. Diana had patronized the grocery as a customer supportive of countercultural spaces, but economic considerations changed her relationship:

> I moved to a little, tiny house and that made my rent go up. *Way* up! So I needed to work, so I went into the store and said [*in a plaintive voice*], "I need a job!" And some of them said, "Work here!" . . . It was about fifteen people. Very small. . . . [Some]thing I liked about the store was when I went shopping there, I got to recognize the people that worked there and they seemed friendly and interesting, they seemed to know each other and enjoy each other's company. . . . And so I joined!

On one hand, the way Diana "joined" the grocery collective through social connections rather than being hired through a newspaper ad or placement agency was typical of the countercultural collectivist era, and this reinforced ethnoracial and class homogeneity similar to that of other cooperatives of the period (Jackall and Crain 1984, Rothschild-Whitt and Whitt 1986). But on the other, Diana did not describe joining a spiritual community, and her story highlights the changes underway at the grocery: the transition from a spiritual community to a worker cooperative. Between the guru's ambivalence about his own leadership, a charge of international luxury goods smuggling, and the collective's discovery that a devotee had been stealing from the till, the guru's influence was significantly weakened within two years of the grocery's founding. Bob, who began as a devotee, explained that by the time the embezzlement was discovered, a hiring question they used—"Is this a *good* person?"—now meant, "Is this someone who shares our anti-materialist, pro-community, pro-spiritual-reflection values?" It became a more *generally countercultural* than *specifically spiritual* term. New workers—including Diana and the poor, young hippies described in the "Worker Control" section of chapter 1 by Burgundy Levine, a white man who was himself one of the early post-devotee hires—were increasingly drawn from outside the spiritual community. Their presence interrupted the foundational basis of member unity based on service as devotion but proposed a new set of unifying values. Although new members brought to the grocery a distinct institutional logic of withdrawal from capitalism, it recombined with that of founding members into a third anti-materialist logic that was neither explicitly spiritual nor political.

Having managed to diversify spiritually, the grocery then began to diversify ethnoracially. Photos and films of parties in the store from the early 1980s show that the organizational culture remained overwhelmingly white (only rock music is heard, and only typically European-American foods are displayed), but a number of Latinx immigrants became members in short succession when positions opened due to the illness and death of gay men during the 1980s AIDS crisis. Although this produced a natural form of "cluster hiring" (Guinier and Minow 2007) that may have provided solidarity for these new workers and protected them from being singled out as highly visible and closely monitored representatives of their demographic group (see Kanter 1977), several of these new Latinx members were partisans and even combatants from both sides of the Nicaraguan Revolution and El Salvadoran civil war in the 1980s (Funkhouser 1995; Wood 2003). In interviews, members recalled bitter feuds and sabotage between these new members, and factions that drew other members into the fray. As at the bakery, growth at the grocery was producing an organization of people with less in common than before.

It was also producing an organization with fewer shared informal channels to share information. Previously the devotees' daily meditation practice—sitting cross-legged on the sidewalk in front of the store each morning—had easily been followed by informal discussions of the business. That was now impossible not only because devotees were a minority of the members but also because the workers were spread across the different locations. In membership meetings, workers complained that inefficient practices at one site were impoverishing members at another, and that the lengthy collective deliberation of decision-making was hurting the business. A widely discussed example of the latter was the failure to make a timely offer on a lease for the bigger building they had wanted to unite the three collectives. And there were grumblings that individual accountability practices were fuzzy at best.

In fact, informal leadership had become the norm. In interviews, three people were consistently identified as "leaders" despite the lack of any title: Bob, a member of the warehouse collective; Burgundy, in the general store; and Greta Straka, a white office worker. While Greta's financial acumen was credited as key to the cooperative's expansion, Bob and Burgundy were the "entrepreneurs," as Burgundy put it. Articulating what other observers of alternative organizations have found (see, e.g., Kleinman 1996), Bob claimed that, "If you're entrepreneurial but you're not taking any benefits for yourself, then you have a moral authority." Because Bob had abandoned his free ride to a scientific PhD for the spiritual and communitarian reward of the collective, he achieved this moral authority. And Burgundy confirmed Bob's degree of influence, describing it in terms of merit: "Bob had smarts. If you had an idea and convinced [other members] it was a good one, you were given the ball and you ran with it. Of course, there wasn't tons of money so you couldn't run too far. . . . [But] people who showed aptitude were ceded areas of authority." For Bob, this area was the warehouse, into which he directed grocery funds to bring it up to code and to operate as a Golden Valley regional distributor, and over which he was regarded as the de facto general manager. But when he began to explore expanding it into a massive West Coast distribution center, the cooperative membership balked at his demand for higher wages and commissions for the warehouse staff, which they felt would have introduced earnings inequalities. Frustrated, Bob and a few others in the warehouse quit the cooperative to set up their own distribution company. The grocery shut down the warehouse and absorbed what Bob had put into the building as a loss. The departure was bitter on both sides.

Part of the bitterness resulted from increasing financial strain. Members who had formed the cooperative in their twenties were entering their thirties, forming families, and discovering health issues that required more than aspirin or shiatsu massage. While the recessions of the early 1980s helped to preserve the low cost of housing, and the rental vacancy rate trended upward throughout the decade, they also affected customers' spending and therefore the cooperative's earnings. Although, unlike the bakery, the grocery never reduced wages or laid anyone off, it had to impose hiring freezes from time to time and—in one year that would later be painfully recalled—suspend members' health and vacation benefits.

In short, the grocery experienced what the bakery did; like the bakery, it had crises of internal diversity and distrust, struggles with participative democratic workplace control in terms of both fitting into existing capitalist institutions and creating internal accountability, and conflict over scarce financial resources. But although many worried about the future of the grocery, there were key differences that kept grocery workers from choosing the path that the bakery workers did.

Adaptation: "Something More Formal"

At this point one might expect that the grocery's members would act like their counterparts at the bakery, taking stock of their troubles and reconsidering the benefits of traditional structures. That they did not was likely because they had already initiated a restructuring process. This project was coordinated by the Shire,[5] a local countercultural association of small business owners, academic researchers, community activists, and early high-tech innovators focused on alternative organizational structure and culture. As Bob recalled, "They didn't come in to help us run our store. They came in for that specific purpose of creating a corporate structure. . . . One World was working fine; that wasn't the issue. . . . We just knew we needed something more formal than our meetings." Articles in the Shire's newsletters suggest that its members saw the grocery as a test case to experiment with engineering a balance between the demands of profit and community, and so the association lent its support—for free—for roughly two and a half years. Shire members came to work group and membership meetings to observe and assist the grocery's development of overlapping authority among a representative board of directors elected from the workers, the membership as a whole, and the various subcollectives (see figure 3.2). By 1980 a basic set of bylaws was created, and by 1983—when the cooperative had moved into a building large enough to house all three remaining collectives under the same roof—it had thoroughly documented its unusual overlapping democratic organizational structure between direct democratic authority (the membership meeting) and representative democratic authority (the board of directors), along with numerous policies and procedures regarding work groups' labor practices.

The organizational structure continued to evolve over the next ten years, with a series of significant changes being put in place in the early 1990s following the cooperative's purchase of a nearby building large enough to unite the food, nonfood, and administrative subunits. The cooperative's sales increased by 50 percent in the first year in its new location and by lesser but positive increments for more than ten years after that. Hiring resumed and, within two years of the move, the membership had doubled to more than 150 workers. Wages

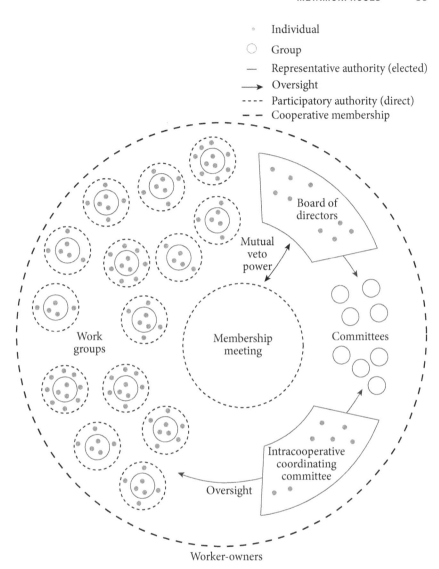

FIGURE 3.2. Grocery organizational structure

and profit sharing also rose to the point at which working-class members approvingly compared their earnings with those of their parents.

The speed of this growth tested the Shire-initiated accountability processes. Many new workers had only a weak understanding of what a worker cooperative was, and in the mid-1990s a rumor spread among the newer hires that the grocery was secretly owned by an inner circle profiting from their labor. After the rumors were silenced by a special membership meeting, "An Evening of Fine

Food and Finance"—where the store's financial structure was explained over a candlelit dinner—senior workers identified the problem as the rapid inclusion of a large number of new workers. A white man known as the Doctor, who had joined the general store side of the cooperative in the mid-1980s, explained, "All you had to do [to be eligible for membership] was nine months or a thousand hours, and boom, buy a ten-dollar share and you were a member! But part of the growth was, 'Okay, we need to teach people what it is to be a co-op. We need to teach people what the history of the collective is, we need to teach people about finances, we need to make sure everybody understands all these things.' They can't just come in and be a member and not know what's going on anymore. So these orientations got created." From this point on, the membership required first financial and then various other information sessions for all new workers, and new workers were given the option to have seasoned workers as "buddies" to accompany them to meetings and answer their questions. In short, the grocery had strategized and formalized its hybrid democratic system well before it faced major crises and thus had more democratic processes in place to address its problems than the bakery did.

Grocery workers were probably also less likely to seek managerial solutions because their financial injuries were less severe. Although they had to contend with hiring and even benefit freezes, their wages were never cut in the way bakery members' were. Indeed, although the 1980s recessions reduced the size and spending of its customer base, that reduction also left One World Natural Grocery as one of only three remaining cooperative groceries in Edgefield by the end of the decade, solidifying its market position. As the Doctor explained, "It was a spirit, like, 'Round *down* on your time card, don't round *up*.' . . . When it comes down to it, I think that that kind of spirit runs *deep* here. That we need our jobs." Certainly, the increasing loss of alternative employment opportunities— well before the introduction of chain competitors like Whole Foods—created incentives for workers to protect their business. Yet, even if that spirit was not inherently stronger for grocery than for bakery workers, the experience of first urging each other to sacrifice a few cents here and there and then seeing it pay off in stabilized earnings may have produced a stronger faith in the possibilities of this alternative organization.

And this faith in alternatives may also have been strengthened at the grass-roots level by seeing how it worked to protect and support ethnoracially marginalized grocery members. Although the white majority membership had initially taken a "business" approach to diversity (Herring 2009), articulating the value of hiring Latinx workers who could better communicate with local consumers in their densely Latinx neighborhood, the new members shifted the grocery's expressed beliefs about diversity. The new Latinx workers and the white allies they helped to develop critiqued the store's practice of conducting its internal and customer-facing business in English only. They drew on the hybrid participatory/representative democratic organizational structure to demand bilingual signage, simultaneous interpretation for membership meetings, and Spanish translations of meeting minutes and employee manuals to ensure a multidirectional flow of members' knowledge. Although most work group meetings continued to be conducted in English,[6] the primarily Latinx janitorial work group drew on the formalized right of work groups to autonomous practice, and began to hold its meetings in Spanish instead. Perhaps only in the wake of this shift to valuing diversity in itself rather than instrumentally to service consumers, grocery hiring became more broadly ethnoracially diverse, including more people of African American, Asian American, Indigenous, and Pacific Island descent.

Over its first two decades, the grocery changed from being a path towards spiritual enlightenment into a vehicle of democratic and economic integration in an urban community. Although the grocery's class and ethnoracial makeup transformed along very similar lines as those of the bakery, its unifying practices were focused more on social and civic membership in an organization and community than on shared economic interests. The implications of this key difference will be explored in chapters 4–7. But the reasons for this difference still merit further exploration.

Instead of entirely discarding its original informality and spirituality, the grocery *enriched* these aspects with additional formalized and rationalized structures, policies, and processes. This allowed it to preserve a degree of participatory democracy rarely seen in firms that have grown past their ability to have all workers sit down and make decisions together on a regular basis (Jackall and Crain 1984; Kasmir 1996). Much of the internal justification for this preservation was based on a positive assessment of the organizational origins: that it was "working fine" and that all it needed was adjustments to accommodate its growth. Such an explanation sounds very structuralist—that the grocery's founding principles of democracy and service shaped later actions in an almost path-dependent manner (Mahoney 2000). Yet this path was not followed by the countercultural collectivist generation in general, which largely resisted such formalization and rationalization (Jackall and Levin 1984; Mellor, Hannah, and Stirling 1988). And this explanation does not account for why the white, middle class-raised bakery members felt their participatory democracy was leading to financial and political crises while the white, middle class-raised grocery members did not. The structuralist approach has a hard time explaining the role of external forces in shaping organizational actors' perceptions and narratives.

While neoinstitutionalist logic is much better at linking these organizational perceptions and narratives, a comparison with the bakery weakens this analysis: in the wake of the evaporation of the dense network of alternative and worker cooperative food producers and retailers, the grocery faced similar struggles as the bakery in finding legitimacy (and therefore financial support). The disintegration of the countercultural collectivist institutional environment and community affected members of both cooperatives similarly. The nearly exclusive neoinstitutionalist focus on processes and forces outside organizations makes it hard to understand how such similar external conditions could produce such different outcomes.

Surviving the End of an Era

Looking at this history, two key processes emerge in explaining the continuation of the bakery and the grocery, and how they differed from the countercultural collectivist era that spawned them. The cooperatives' openness to growth and the formalization of their practices and policies seem critical to their survival. Yet their growth and formalization were accomplished in different ways, and this difference affected both how the organizations were structured and how their memberships perceived organizational goals.

The openness to growth was different from that of most countercultural collectivist cooperatives, where the strong degree of personal connection deemed necessary to compel responsibility to group outcomes seemed to require restricting growth to a size capable of face-to-face communication among all members. Instead the bakery and the grocery used a logic of community service to justify expansion, whether the bakery's production or the grocery's supply of goods that were otherwise hard to obtain in the period before "Big Organic" (Pollan 2006). In both cases, as the demand for organic food began to emerge, growth permitted critical cost-saving economies of scale, allowed the bakery to survive local economic fluctuation with a bigger national market (Haedicke 2016), and gave grocery customers the more familiar experience of "superstore" shopping (Fullerton 1992).[7] They also made room for more workforce diversification without the individually burdensome effects of tokenization; being one of thirty people of color among ninety coworkers gives you many more possible allies than being one of three in a collective of nine.

Formalization of rules, policies, and procedures also seemed to violate the autonomy-seeking norms of the era's cooperatives, but many bakery members viewed its originally informal collective decision-making—which requires a fairly strong degree of shared values and goals—as inefficient and even undemocratic as they pondered James's charismatic power. At the grocery, collaboration with the Shire's consultants had similar effects in terms of persuading members that documenting and disseminating formal guidelines for action was to their benefit—a belief that was tested and affirmed when Bob tried to convince the grocery to differentiate wages by job.

Yet although both the bakery and the grocery welcomed growth and formalization, they did so in markedly different ways. The bakery linked formalization to a managerial hierarchy in an effort to be accountable, effective, and efficient. In meeting minutes and recollections, bakery members cited awareness of an increasingly working-class membership, and a belief that better management would increase the bakery's ability to compete in the national market and thus create more financial stability for its workers. In contrast, the grocery repeatedly rejected centralizing management in either jobs or elected bodies but put equal emphasis on the ways that informality undermined both its financial and democratic process, such as in the narrative about how rumors substituted for standardized information sharing and created a divide between newer and more long-standing workers. As at the bakery, this transition away from the collectivist model produced stability. The grocery discovered that such stability and growth supported working-class members, and these members in turn supported the unusual but functional organizational structure.

Unlike many countercultural collectivist cooperatives[8]—whose members were either so committed to participatory and hyper-egalitarian ideals that they could not run a functioning business or conversely were not committed *enough* to such ideals and left the cooperatives for more traditional forms of employment—the bakery and the grocery survived by rejecting face-to-face size limits and informal, friendship-based normative control. But in leaving behind their collectivist-democratic caterpillar selves, they metamorphosed into very different butterflies: a managerial hierarchy at the bakery and a hybrid democracy at the grocery. Grocery workers expressed bafflement at the bakery's choice to "go back" to managers, as one put it, and bakery workers repeatedly asked me to explain how a business could run without managers unless it completely burned out its members with "all those meetings." What explains the different choices members of each cooperative made when faced with similar economic and social challenges? What accounts for why they transformed when others of their generation did not? And why did their transformations bring them to such different destinations? In the next section, I will argue that the microinstitutionalist insight regarding repeated encounters between organizational actors and external forces explains why the grocery continued to develop its participatory democratic control while most other countercultural collectivist cooperatives either ceased to exist or transformed into managerial hierarchies.

Explaining Survival and Divergence

In the Golden Valley and across the nation, almost all countercultural collectivist worker cooperatives were out of business by the end of the 1980s. The bakery and the grocery, however, stabilized during the 1990s and are still operating at the time of this book's publication, but are now different—both from their origins and from each other. While conclusive claims cannot be drawn from a study of only two organizations—and particularly a study based on the kinds of recollective interview data that always already include a narration of the present within a narration of the past—comparison of these two histories is nevertheless suggestive. Although they are helpful, neither structuralist nor neoinstitutionalist explanations satisfyingly explain the bakery and the grocery's ability to survive their cohort's demise in a way that can also account for their divergence. I therefore follow this analysis by advancing an argument that an accretion of micro-institutional processes linked local individual actors with local and extra-local conditions to produce two consequentially different organizations.

A structuralist explanation for the different developments of the two worker cooperatives might focus on key ways in which the bakery and the grocery both differed from *other* countercultural collectivist organizations, and certainly their willingness to grow past face-to-face limits was a critical difference. Yet although Bob asserted that the grocery's growth was a direct result of its founding service orientation, many other cooperatives with a similarly spiritual orientation chose to limit their growth, and the bakery pursued growth quite apart from a spiritual path. Indeed, despite Bob's emphasis on the distinction between the provisioning and the profit-generating aspects of the grocery, the foundational elevation of customer over worker desires within the retail realm could easily support a logic of managerial control of workers in aid of customer satisfaction—and seems far more likely to be coupled in this way than the bakery's foundational revolutionary socialist mission of worker empowerment.

Thus, the neoinstitutionalist demand to look outside the organizations to understand their growth seems, on the face of it, quite sensible: the willingness to grow can be seen as a bit of zigzagging between what Paul DiMaggio and Walter Powell (1983) describe as the "coercive isomorphism" of banks seeking growth-oriented business plans and the "mimetic isomorphism" of alternative organizations seeking legitimacy—particularly in the context of a fading counterculture. Here, though, the presumed isomorphism of the post-countercultural collectivist era fails to match its reality: variation among survivors ranges from, at one end, the Cheese Board Collective, a gourmet cheese shop and bakery in Berkeley (described in chapter 2, "The Countercultural Collectivist Era, 1970s–1980s" section), which stayed small and informal long beyond the end of its era

(Cheese Board Collective 2003) and, at the other end, the growth and elected managerialism of Burley Design Collective, popularizers of the bike trailer (Schoening 2006). At the bakery and the grocery, internal logics for growth were far from meaningless, and indeed undergirded further organizational movement away from the countercultural collectivist model that, rather than making them more similar to each other, made them even more different than they had originally been. If the institutional environment exerts external pressure, it is diffuse and varied. There are, therefore, significant problems with explanations from both approaches to explain the cooperatives' survival and their divergent strategies for doing so.

What can better explain these trajectories is a microinstitutionalist approach focused on organizational *accretion*: the persistent and idiosyncratic interplay of actions and meaning making within each organization, and between each organization and its institutional environment. Both cooperatives developed meanings that informed and were informed by actions at the local (intraorganizational) and extra-local (institutional, social, and economic) level: the timing of their origins and their internal social and financial crises affected how they responded to "collective combat" (Kellogg 2011) among their members, which in turn affected how they responded to internal and external pressures, and which then affected how each cooperative experienced their crises.

In both cases, the cooperatives were somewhat late arrivals to the countercultural collectivist era, being founded at the end rather than the beginning of the decade, and quickly had to contend with the dissolution of the Golden Valley cooperative networks—an extra-local event fraught with the impermanence of alternative organizational strategy and participatory democracy. For the bakery, this was followed locally by the debunking of a charismatic leader at the same time that a financial shortfall was discovered: the informal relations that allowed the development of charismatic leadership took on an association with financial failure and the perception of a leadership vacuum. These two things became crises in an extra-local landscape where alternative organizational employment was disappearing. Soon afterwards, local demands for more wage differentiation were linked to an extra-local logic of less explicit democratic control (in place of participatory democratic control), which allowed the National Cooperative Bank's definition of democracy to infuse the bakery's definition. The local development of the bakery's new model—where members explicitly chose pro-managerial hierarchy consultants over those urging more functional reform of existing participatory management—dovetailed with the ethnoracial and class diversification of the workforce, creating a visible moment of transformation in the early 1990s. This also coincided with the extra-local improvement in the economy (which may also have siphoned off middle-class bakery members) and the expansion of an organic market that benefited the bakery. Thus the bakery's improved financial state became narratively linked to its local managerial hierarchy but not to its workforce diversity due to ongoing local ethnoracial and gender conflict. In the end, bakery members accepted reduced democratic control and reduced egalitarianism in favor of greater financial reward. In this way they tied a local logic of worker cooperation to an extra-local, wage-focused logic of unionized (and masculine) "breadwinning" (Willis 1990).

While the grocery struggled to make sense of its place in an environment with fewer and fewer cooperatives, and also faced a failure of charismatic leadership, its response was subtly different. Although, like the bakery, grocery members introduced a much greater level of formalization to block the concentration of informal power, they did not swing entirely over to a traditional bureaucratic hierarchy. This was not only due to the grocery's relationship with the Shire, but perhaps also because, as urban dwellers, members were brought into regular contact with other cooperative and alternative businesses—and potential employers—in a way the suburban and rural residents at the bakery did not. Such contact offered even more extra-local democratic logics to support the grocery's local participatory democracy. This mixing of local reorganization with extra-local values may have made financial constraints easier to bear. The local logic of rounding down time card hours may have indeed been perceived as a badge of anti-materialist honor and collective heroism, but it became part of the lore primarily because the uptick in the extra-local economy meant stabilization of local earnings. While the Shire-guided hybrid democracy did not prevent some grocery members from translating an extra-local logic of investor capitalism into believable rumors about the "real" grocery owners, it did squash the growth of those rumors by providing a local space for the sharing of facts and, by extension, for the development of local trust in this novel organizational form. Although grocery members never enjoyed as much in real wages as bakery workers, they developed a compensatory narrative about how valuable ethnoracial, gender, and class egalitarianism had been produced through a deeply democratic practice.

Neither outcome was predestined by the cooperatives' (highly similar) founding, nor by the state of their (nearly identical) institutional environments at the (almost simultaneous) moments of their organizational crises. Nevertheless at each step of their parallel development the accreted logics made some options possible and undermined others. A microinstitutionalist approach argues that any social setting contains multiple options for meaning making (Friedland and Alford 1991). Some of the meanings available to the worker cooperative members included primarily viewing their enterprises as a way to contend with capitalist exploitation, as a form of economic citizenship, as a family-like group of people who care and look out for each other, or as some combination of the three.

Determining what the cooperative meant was, in both cases, a site of collective combat: historical minutes document proposals to consider managerial control at the grocery and to reject its implementation at the bakery. What becomes clear in comparing these two cooperatives is the importance of workplace democracy at each cooperative in generating their divergence from each other: that the worker-owners of both the bakery and the grocery had the authority to determine their own goals and methods with which to reach them. While there are other ways to shake loose a logic from its institutional setting—for instance, when the labor bargains made by unions are attacked and dismantled by globalizing capital—democratic control provided each cooperative's workers with powerful and uncommon tools to unsettle meanings that have cohered in particular places: a capitalist logic in a workplace, a political logic in a social movement, and a social logic in a group of friends or a family (Haedicke 2016).

At both the bakery and the grocery, members drew on local and extra-local meanings in conflicts and contests, accreting reasonably coherent rationales for the organizational structures and practices that came to shape what was seen as both practical and possible. There was no single moment at which organizational alternatives were foreclosed: foundations and institutional environments were influential but not determining, as new battles over meanings could redirect organizational practices entirely. Thus, explaining organizational development—both survival and divergence—requires careful attention to the interplay of power in organizations, organizational actors, and their environments.

Summary: The Institutional Accretion of Difference

People's Daily Bread Bakery and One World Natural Grocery were shaped by the 1970s and 1980s countercultural collectivist responses to and calls for significant changes in social structures described in chapter 2: economic contraction and uncertainty, generational hope and commitment to social justice, dissatisfaction with the results of an efficiency-focused bureaucratic structuring of work (and life), and the availability of a young, largely white and middle-class, labor force. The bakery and the grocery exemplified many aspects of this generation but developed more complicated relationships to social justice and bureaucratic organization as they also became more ethnoracially diverse and working-class.

As I have argued in this chapter, this is not because they contained some hidden seed of difference from their peer organizations, nor because they were privileged by their institutional environment—or at least no more so than were the hundreds of other Golden Valley cooperative enterprises. Nor could their divergence from each other be predicted by structuralist or neoinstitutionalist theories, particularly given the similarities in their trajectories beyond the countercultural collectivist era. Instead a microinstitutionalist approach better teases out the practices and processes through which these organizations became financially viable firms and through which their democratic actors transformed their collectivist-democratic cooperatives into new and distinct organizations with diverging forms of workplace authority.

This microinstitutionalist approach also allows for the identification and evaluation of the ways in which these different organizational structures produce, reinforce, interrupt, or undo practices, processes, and regimes of inequality in the moment. While collective combat appears as the most common practice of organizational fortification and change in this chapter, that may be an artifact of a historical approach: noncombative processes are less well remembered and less likely to become part of organizational archives. The next two chapters do not shy away from describing combat, but they also examine the less dramatic ways in which organizational meanings, practices, and power accrete in the day-to-day lives and actions of cooperative workers. In chapter 4, the perceived benefits of the bakery's hierarchical management are described in more detail; in chapter 5, the potential and limits of undoing inequality through the grocery's organizational processes are more closely mapped out. Together the two chapters provide a clearer view of both how democratic workplaces can function economically and how they produce different social and economic outcomes for their workers.

PEOPLE'S DAILY BREAD BAKERY
Worker Ownership, Working-Class Empowerment

We are not a collective. We were once a collective; we are no longer a collective.

—Herbert Gubbins, chief executive officer/general coordinator

It's a capitalist widget factory, but you get a piece of the action for coming in and doing your part.

—Dutch Henry, sales and delivery work group member

You can smell the bakery before you see it, that delicious scent of wheat fermenting from the sourdough starter that goes into People's Daily Bread Bakery's organic buns, mini baguettes, and sliced bread. With the freeway and a sprawl of big box stores to the east, suburban lawns and roses side by side with goats and horse enclosures to the west, a state college due north, and a high-tech campus a mile south, the area is an almost perfect cross section of the five-county Golden Valley region. The bakery itself is located in a nondescript industrial park, and nothing on the sign out front gives away the fact that this business is owned by its workers. Still, there are some clues. Most workers drive, but only those who arrive during the late-night or early-morning "unsocial" bakers' hours are likely to find a space in the parking lot. Mercedes Delgado, the morning receptionist, tells me that there's no reserved parking for anyone, including managers, "because we're a co-op! I'm sure there'd be issues if we did that."

I have not arrived early on this particular day, so I have to park about twenty yards up the road. The bakery is, in fact, a complex of three leased neighboring buildings in an industrial park at the edge of the county's metropolis, Colina. One houses the production and national shipping work groups downstairs with administrative offices upstairs, a second is used for staging deliveries to the local routes and remote depots, and a third contains an additional production line with marketing offices upstairs and maintenance offices in back. Each work group has a separate break room in its own building, and this spatial division minimizes interaction among members of different work groups. But today is Friday, and almost everyone streams through reception to pick up paychecks from Mercedes, who calls to them all by name, sometimes in Spanish and sometimes in English, asking after their families and health, and filling me in on their lives. "It's good me being Hispanic because there are a lot of Hispanics here," she says.[1] I also notice that, other than the office workers, they are all men.

Linda Kemp, who takes over (although only in English) when Mercedes leaves at 2:00 p.m., points out a few other divisions besides buildings or work groups: management "makes me nervous, looking over my shoulder"; if you are politically conservative, "it can grate on your nerves . . . like, if your religious beliefs mean you're against homosexuality" (she is a member of a local conservative evangelical church, and several drivers, arriving back at the bakery in the late afternoon, are out lesbians); some of the men from production are using the women's bathroom located between reception and the production floor and not cleaning up after themselves if they miss the toilet, and their manager seems unwilling to try to make it better. Linda complains that, now that "we've gotten so big," company management just "want us to be plug-and-play." Sherry Ferrar, the shipping manager, would not let a woman transfer from the office to shipping due to a lack of forklift experience. Yet Linda says that the bakery's egalitarian gender relations were more of a draw to her than its cooperative status when she was looking to leave her old job at another national natural food company, where the boss "owned his wife like you own a dog." Nevertheless, she became a member of the cooperative as soon as she could once she understood what it was. Some people here, she says, are passionate about making sure it stays democratic, and names an out lesbian couple as a positive example. "I'm passionate too," she tells me, which is why she cares about big things like transfer policies and little things like pee on the floor.

A Working-Class Cooperative

The very existence of the bakery acts as rebuttal to those who have claimed that investor capital and expert management are necessary to provide jobs for working people. At the same time, it raises questions about the limits of functional workplace democracy, particularly across differences of race/ethnicity and gender. On one hand, almost twenty-five years into its existence, the bakery's broadly diverse workforce—not only in terms of race/ethnicity and gender but also religion and nationality—indicates that cooperatives can address the needs of the contemporary labor market and offer support to the increasingly imperiled working class. But its particular way of organizing labor and of distributing workplace political rights seemed to fall short of some of the promises of earlier generations of worker cooperation, such as those described in chapter 2.

The bakery of 2003, when I did my most intensive fieldwork (see appendix A), could hardly be more different from its original incarnation. Its business park location corresponded to its profoundly industrial scale, and the size of its work-force: 115 permanent and three to five temporary workers at most times. Managers now made most decisions[2]—from work group transfers to rates of pay to scheduled hours—and while the bakery was still democratically controlled by its workers, that control was, as I will show, much more representative than participatory. Its members were no longer a like-minded group of (white and middle-class) friends but instead ranged across ethnoracial and cultural differences, and most were—like Linda and Mercedes—from working-class backgrounds. What was not different was that the bakery was deeply valued by its members, although this value ranged from the provision of good, stable jobs to fairness and opportunity.

And this was important in the Golden Valley, a rapidly prospering part of the country in the early years of the twenty-first century. Colina, where the bakery was located, was transforming in response to this growing wealth. Despite its rural identity, local fruit orchards and processing plants around the bakery had given way to boutique vineyards and shopping malls; in 2003, county revenue came almost equally from retail and manufacturing (including food and beverage processing), with health care and service work following closely, and agriculture trailing well behind. Information technology was the county's fastest growing sector, but it mainly employed the non-Latinx whites who comprised roughly three-quarters of the county's population. Most of the rest of the population was Latinx, with small numbers of African Americans, Asian Americans and Pacific Islanders, and Indigenous people. More than 80 percent of the county's residents were primary English speakers, and almost one-third had a bachelor's or postgraduate degree, although its median household income was just below the national average.[3] It was a relatively ethnoracially homogeneous area whose residents had a fairly average level of household income.

Theorizing Worker Spaces within Capitalism

The stability and success of the bakery more than twenty-five years into its existence flies in the face of commonsense "death or degeneration" beliefs about worker cooperatives (Webb and Webb 1920): that working-class people cannot run their own businesses and will either go bankrupt or devolve their broad ownership into a smaller set of hands. That worker ownership is impossible is the logic of business schools, which claim sole right to the creation of necessary technical expertise for firm management through MBA programs (which, like other forms of higher education, have been typically populated by people from middle- and upper-middle-class backgrounds). But it is also the logic of the once-dominant strand of the labor movement, which ceded responsibility for business planning and even most day-to-day operations to capitalist ownership, aiming at best for regulation of pay, safety, and dignity (Clawson and Clawson 1999; Fantasia and Voss 2004; Milkman and Voss 2004). The question worker cooperatives like the bakery pose, then, is if workers can truly "go it alone." Can they banish capital and the logic of profit extraction, and instead operate their own functional, economically productive organizations that offer fair and equitable divisions of wealth and of power? And how can this be accomplished under capitalist conditions, where extraction of wealth not only animates business schools and unions but is written into state laws regarding corporate profit maximization?

This chapter therefore explores the *how* and *what* of this puzzle: the ability of a worker cooperative to function as a democratic organization benefiting workers within the structure and national culture of managerial capitalism. The first section reviews bakery members' *economic rewards* in relation to the local community, and how these rewards differed by member role. The second section explores the bakery's workplace *political rights*—the ability of workers to legitimately participate in the direction and day-to-day operations of the organization and themselves—and reveals some of the outcomes of dividing workplace control into governance and management functions. The third section explores the degree to which these rewards and rights were *egalitarian*: accessible and enjoyed across class, race/ethnicity, and gender. The chapter concludes with a summary of how the bakery challenges commonsense assumptions about the limits of democratic workplaces, as well as questions about how the bakery's managerial bureaucracy limited integration with a broad workers' movement.

Economic Rewards: "The Closest to a Utopian Workplace"

Once a small and struggling collective, the bakery's growth now generated much greater wealth for its membership. With 2003 net revenues of $17.5 million from its dozen different organic, whole grain sourdough products, and with a workforce of a size that put it in the top 15 percent of bakeries nationally (US Census Bureau 2004), People's Daily Bread Bakery was no "artisanal" bakery. Its various baked goods were sold in supermarkets nationwide under its own label as well as a national grocery chain's private label, leading to net profits of $1.5 million over and above operating expenses (including wages and benefits given to workers). Some was reinvested in the business, but more than $1 million was redistributed to the workers in the form of higher earnings. Starting wages were only 10 percent lower than median wages for bakers in the county (and almost twice the minimum wage), and they were quickly supplemented with hourly raises, work group bonuses, and profit sharing for members. Because almost all bakery employees worked forty hours per week, with four weeks of paid vacation, this added up: even nonmanagerial bakery workers averaged over $57,000 in earnings per year,[4] or almost twice the county's median income.

These financial rewards were widely appreciated. Even one of the most cynical bakery workers, Dutch Henry, a driver in his thirties, was blunt in his assessment: "It's a capitalist widget factory, but you get a piece of the action for coming in and doing your part. Which is great, especially today. Look at these cats that have stolen the people's money. *Stolen the people's money!* Out from underneath them! If [profits] are constantly being disbursed amongst the actual members of the widget factory, as a product of the bylaws, that's the cooperative there!" As he saw it, corporations had been skimming profit off workers' labor for years and were now fleeing to overseas labor markets with less regulation; a cooperative was a vehicle for workers to recuperate the value of their labor, regardless of what it was they actually produced.

Nonmanagerial workers also appreciated the narrow difference between their earnings and those of managers. Brushing a loose strand of blond hair off her khaki work shirt and behind her ear, shipping work group member Anne Bush explained that she liked not feeling like she had to try to climb the management ladder because "we almost all make the same amount of money!" Indeed, compared to the average 334:1 ratio between CEOs and median employee earnings in the United States (Anderson et al. 2007), the bakery CEO's $125,000 per year was only four times the earnings of the lowest paid permanent worker ($32,000). This tight ratio was a direct result of the cooperative ownership structure. While many forms of corporate profit sharing are typically only given to those in upper management (Carberry 2010), the bakery distributed profits far more broadly: about 60 percent of worker-owners' annual incomes were delivered through lump-sum work group bonuses and hours-based cooperative profit sharing (tracked by time clock for nonmanagers and weekly self-reporting by managers).

Eligibility for the ownership share of the profits required membership in the cooperative. Cooperative membership eligibility required: nine months of full-time employment; nine hours of orientations in the bakery's history and that of worker cooperatives globally, fiscal statement interpretation, and worker-owner personal tax preparation; an open-book exam based on the orientations; and observation of a quarterly membership meeting. Eligibility was also contingent on the ability to buy a cooperative share (refundable upon departure from the bakery) that, in 2003, cost just under $1,600. Recognizing the difficulty this posed to people with little savings or access to family wealth, the bakery set up a long-term payroll deduction plan. Greybo Sofer, a former production worker who was now the bakery safety coordinator, described how this practice eliminated a class barrier that had shaped the bakery's founding:

> Twenty-five years ago, that's real America, to be able to say, "Hey, Mom, I want to try this business. Can you and Dad give me, like, five thousand dollars please?" And, "Sure, hon, here's some money." To me, it's, "Mom, I need two hundred dollars. I have to pay my car insurance. I'll pay it back next week because I know you have rent due." It might have started out that way, but it didn't keep growing that way because of how it became structured where anyone could buy in in small amounts. I think I bought my share at six dollars a week over three years.

The middle-class "real America" she refers to no longer supplied most of the bakery's members: in 2003, ten-dollar weekly membership payroll deductions were barely felt by most members, and many told me they used their first member profit-sharing check to pay off the balance. The restructuring of members' share purchase opportunity represented a significant break with the bakery's more elite past and reaffirmed the cooperative's commitment to ownership by working-class people.

While bakery managers' earnings in 2003 were higher than those of nonmanagers—an average of slightly more than $94,000—they were lower than earnings for comparable positions in the county, where the average pay for operational managers was over $100,000. Several managers, indeed, said they had taken a small pay cut to come to the bakery. The expected limit of forty-hour workweeks for managers, however, provided some compensation. Pam Jorgeson had finished an advanced degree and left a higher-paying job to become the bakery's fiscal controller and manager of the office work group. She explained, "If I went to get some other job that paid more of a base salary, maybe, I'm sure I'd be working . . . fifty, fifty-five hours a week for the first year or two. And a lot of the places, if you report to the CEO, they just want you there all the time anyway, face time. And we don't really have that here." If nonmanagerial workers appreciated the increased pay, managerial workers appreciated reduced time commitments. The lack of market rate salaries for managers did not seem to be detrimental to the bakery's ability to attract talent and created more class similarity between managers and nonmanagers than typical of American workplaces.

Differences in bakery worker earnings differences did not simply result from the managerial hierarchy: some types of jobs paid more than others. As CEO Herbert Gubbins claimed, "[Wages are] based, again, on market value and relative worth. In other words, we say, 'How much money would we need if that person leaves to hire somebody who could do a good job?' And retain them. We look at wages as just something for recruitment and retention." This, he asserted, explained why office jobs started at a higher rate than production jobs, the physically grueling "hot and dirty" labor of baking and packaging. Although there was some cross-training for redundancy in the office, some rotation for ergonomic reasons in production, and some sales and delivery drivers rotating between other drivers' permanent shifts on their days off, the wage differential restricted real job rotation. As Adam Delaney, the worker with the most seniority, pointed out, his 1980s experience of responsibility for tasks ranging from bookkeeping to janitorial "would be pretty im—it wouldn't be *impossible*, it would just be really confusing. You would be getting different wages for different areas."

Almost twenty-five years after its founding, the bakery had become a thriving business that not only provided strong financial compensation for its working-class employees to do working-class jobs but also allowed those doing more middle-class work to balance a decent living with time to pursue commitments outside the workplace. One of the keys to this success was the introduction of a managerial hierarchy. The specialization of jobs and corresponding market wages (although not necessarily salaries for managers) had introduced more differentiation, but Pam saw it as pretty much the ideal, saying, "There's never going to be this utopian workplace. So for the most part, this is probably the closest to a utopian workplace as one could get." Economically, the bakery was delivering on its promises.

Political Rights: "We Are No Longer a Collective"

By the time of my study, the bakery had fully separated its democratic governance from its positional management. The separation of long-term from day-to-day decision-making created more efficiency but absolved managers of democratic responsibility to their work groups or the cooperative more generally.

Governance structure. Members of the bakery widely attributed its financial success to the 1989 change in organizational structure described in the "Adaptation" section of chapter 3, replacing collectivist-democratic control with hierarchical management and representative democratic governance. Looking across his desk from me, Herbert baldly stated, "We are not a collective. We were once a collective; we are no longer a collective." Where collectivist-democratic organizations merge three kinds of workplace political rights—organizational governance through long-range and big-picture planning, labor management at the day-to-day and small-group level, and individual autonomy over tasks and time—the more bureaucratic "new model" separated these out into distinct areas of action (see figure 3.1 in chapter 3).

By 2003 democratic participation was now limited to the quarterly meetings, where workers voted annually on the business plan, budget, and election of members to the board of directors (who held hiring and firing power over the CEO) and to three less powerful committees. On an as-needed basis they would also vote on bylaw amendment proposals and on whether to extend membership to self-nominated candidates. These quarterly membership meetings, held in a nearby community hall, were mandatory. Despite a free hot dinner (meetings were always in the evening, requiring a brief shutdown of production) and door prizes of up to fifty dollars for a randomly selected attendee, attendance was primarily compelled through the threat of loss of benefit: missing more than one meeting per year could result in the suspension of membership and loss of quarterly profit sharing.

Governance accountability. Meetings were streamlined to deliver information and elicit approval or rejection. Board meeting minutes were disseminated, but in summary form: meeting attendance, agenda items, and decisions were all that was published. A similar efficiency was at play at the quarterly three-hour membership meetings. Members sat in rows facing a podium where managers would describe the bakery's financial progress to date, the proposed annual business plan or budget for the coming year, and any changes to health care or other benefits. Sometimes other proposals that had already been vetted by the board—that is, brought to a board meeting and refined until approved—were read and briefly described.

Sometimes workers would question what was being presented to them. Pam felt that pushback largely came from only the sales and delivery work group, which she said tried to "incite" people against management in a manner she compared to union organizers in a corporate factory:

> JOAN: When you say people don't trust management as much as they should, I'm wondering where you see that and where that comes from.
> PAM: It's probably the vocal minority of people that stand up and say things at the membership meeting which, yeah, maybe they just incite things. . . . It's almost like they have to be like that even though—even when things are good, they have to find something to complain about. You're never going to make those people happy. And I think they are a minority, it's just that they're vocal about it. They think

that they're protecting other people's rights, people who didn't really
ask them, you know? What was that Sally Fields movie [*voice trails
off*]?

JOAN: *Norma Rae?*

PAM: *Norma Rae.* Yeah. People like that.

Yet, unlike the 1979 film about a textile mill worker who dramatically provokes
her coworkers to shut down the production floor mid-shift while organizing a
union, what was more typical at the bakery was a short question and answer period followed by a secret ballot vote. Theoretically, members could make proposals from the floor, but this never happened during my year of observation,
nor could anyone recall a proposal from the floor that had passed in the last ten
years. As Pam, who had been a board member, explained, "The members would
say, 'Do we want to waste our time? Is this lady off the wall? She didn't even go
to the board.'" That is, despite some heckling from the crowd, the bakery's democracy was very strongly *representative* in form.

Yet democratic control was part of everyday discourse at the bakery, often
using "the co-op" to mean a commitment to democratic principles of equality,
as Mercedes did when she dismissed the possibility of preferred parking for managers. This extended to performances for outsiders like me. During my very
first visit to the bakery, Keith Assis, the personnel director, briefly interrupted
my interview with Herbert, who usually bicycled to and from work, to tell him
that it was raining and that Stuart White—the marketing manager and long-
term president of the board of directors—had a message for him: "Being in the
cooperative, your boss, who is as well your subordinate, who is the same person, is offering you a ride home." Smiling, Herbert kept the joke going: "Could
you tell my boss-as-well-as-my-subordinate to not leave without me?" In this way
bakery members both reminded managers that they served at the discretion of
the workers—the board of directors could, at any time, replace Herbert as CEO—
and reminded elected representatives where their places were in the hierarchy
of managerial power.

Workers could take part in this democratic process by becoming members
of the cooperative, which was an option open to all directly hired workers after
meeting the membership requirements.[5] At that point a worker could make a
formal request to the membership for ratification by filling out a form to be distributed prior to the quarterly meeting with a short essay making their case for
their value as a worker and a cooperative member, and standing up in the membership meeting and making a short speech summarizing his request. One night
I witnessed two new production workers stand for membership, speaking Spanish and using the on-site interpreter. The first, Gregorio Nava, declared in a

flowery way, "Like the workers in the field, I want to be a worker in this field." The second, Efrain Gutiérrez, was more of a wisecracker, saying, "I think I'm going to be here until you throw me out." They were peppered with questions in English and Spanish: "What are your ideas that could benefit the bakery?" ("Well, they're not that concrete, but I'll let you know.") "Are you interested in running for a committee?" ("Not at the moment.") "How's your health?" ("I'm fine. I intend to be at all the meetings.") Pam felt this process could be "intimidating," but more than 85 percent of the bakery workers with more than nine months of full-time work under their belts had found their way past any such dread.

After this verbal application, the prospective member would leave the room, and it was then typical for the worker's manager to offer words of support (and, indeed, I was told that workers would usually check in with their managers to vouchsafe support before standing for membership) before the floor was open for general comments. At this meeting it was almost only Gregorio and Efrain's production coworkers who spoke, describing both of them as hardworking, committed, and capable of helping to train others (entirely in English, although some were primary Spanish speakers). The election committee then distributed a yes-or-no ballot regarding accepting their membership, tallied the results, and welcomed back the new members with cheers and pats on the back—and often nominations for committees. I was told that it was extremely rare for anyone to be turned down for membership, but it had happened within the memory of several sitting around me: a driver pointed out a production worker who had refused to apply for membership for years as a protest of the rejection of a former worker's application.

Upon attaining membership, workers could vote for board and committee members, and could run themselves—which was why Efrain had been asked about his readiness. The three task committees were, respectively, in charge of running the series of elections in each quarterly meeting, producing a twice-yearly newsletter, and arbitrating grievances. The nine-member board of directors was also entirely elected from the membership, and, in addition to its supervision of the CEO, met monthly to review policy, adjudicate sensitive personnel matters, and advise the CEO on long-range planning. Board terms were for three years, with one-third of the seats coming up for election each year. Bylaws created in the 1989 organizational overhaul required the board to have members from each of the five work groups that existed at that time, as well as at least two managers, two nonmanagers, two men, and two women. These stipulations were disparaged by Herbert as "vestigial," and more reservedly but also publicly criticized in Keith's orientation sessions as "unnecessary," but they remained in place as it seemed few had the appetite to organize a membership vote to change the bylaws.

Management structure. While these bodies facilitated the governance of the bakery, the day-to-day and long-range operations of the specific work groups were now in the hands of managers—sometimes multiple levels of managers. In production, the largest work group, the salaried manager who answered directly to the CEO oversaw four waged assistant managers, each in charge of one of the shift crews that had its own waged "lead man" responsible for setting the pace of production (see figure 3.1 in chapter 3). Although assistant managers and lead workers had the most day-to-day contact with nonmanagerial workers and often made wage and firing recommendations, managers were the only ones who could officially hire or fire workers or set their wages.

Given the four layers of management, it was not surprising that most of the forty-two nonmanagerial production workers described feeling quite distant from the CEO. But some of the smaller work groups had a closer relationship to him. The six-member office work group, with only two layers of management and located next door to Herbert's office, knew quite a lot about his likes and dislikes and were able to joke with him—even to the extent of teasingly accusing him of creating a "coopHERBERTive" when they felt he was overstepping his power, while similar joking was made out of Herbert's earshot by other work groups. The number of managerial layers varied among the work groups and were not entirely a function of size: the shipping work group, for instance, had only five members in total, including both a manager and an assistant manager, while the four-member maintenance work group only had a manager.

Managers generally determined their work group's goals with the CEO, not with their workers. They set penalties for those who undermined goals or otherwise disobeyed, but their assistant managers usually carried them out. For instance, when Charlie Navarro, the production manager, arrived for work at 6:00 a.m., he noted to Mark Costa, his graveyard shift assistant manager, that a new worker had called out sick too many times. While he and Mark shared a theatrical laugh, Mark took over the process of telling the new worker that he had one more chance: new workers who called out sick too many times could be fired. Later, when another worker with a longer tenure called out sick, Mark was charged with disciplining him, too, as this worker's shift started within an hour and workers could be—and regularly were—suspended for a week for failing to give enough warning before the start of their shift.

Many managers tried to balance penalties and coercion with a more hegemonic, or consent-based, form of control. For instance, the production manager described his "second-grade teacher trick" for enforcing safety: a marble in a jar for each potential or actual safety problem documented by a member of a shift crew, and a shift crew party when the jar was full. Workers seemed to appreciate not only the party but also getting to call attention to unsafe practices.

Management accountability. Greybo, who visited the different work groups regularly to conduct safety trainings, compared the early days of the introduction of management to the present: "When I go to those meetings now, some of them are just the manager talking and people listening, and then [the work group members] leave. Not all of [the meetings], but I'd say half. And it used to be the *people* would talk and the *manager* would listen, and then they'd dialogue." In my own observation, this was indeed the norm. There was very little discussion *among* work group members. Instead, managers made decisions based on their observations, discussions with other managers, and/or discussions with their assistant managers, and then checked to confirm that those decisions were carried out.

Although Keith and Pam claimed that at times workers would complain about managerial power, mistaking the elicitation of their opinion as delegated decision-making power, I only witnessed one direct challenge when Herbert included a line item in a business plan that changed payroll from weekly to biweekly. He did not explain this as cost cutting (and, when pressed, said that it would only save $5,000 per year) but as a "mental health" measure in terms of requiring workers to learn longer-range control of their personal finances. At the contentious membership meeting reviewing the business plan, workers, assistant managers, and managers alike abandoned the Roberts Rules of Order they typically observed to have loud side conversations and angrily yell at Herbert without being recognized by the meeting chair. Mark, the graveyard shift assistant manager, stood and denounced Herbert's proposal as undermining workers' mental health by making it harder to cover weekly costs of living and as taking a patronizing approach to workers' lives and checkbooks. His angry comments met with loud approval from the assembled bakery workers. Herbert glowered at the assembled members from the podium until he finally declared the change to be within his managerial jurisdiction, and curtly asserted that it would only remain weekly if the membership voted down the entire business plan. Indeed, the membership only had the right to approve or reject business plans; they had no line-item power. The membership voted to approve the plan. That night and in the days afterwards, some members told me they'd voted for the plan to avoid the risk of a disgruntled Herbert quitting the cooperative and taking his valuable leadership and vision with him. Other members grumbled to me and any nonmanagers who would listen about how this was not right, was not part of "the cooperative," that it was a "coopHERBERTive." But no one proposed to make a bylaw change mandating weekly pay, to revoke the business plan, or to fire Herbert.

Indeed, it seemed that most bakery workers were willing to leave the responsibility for day-to-day organizational processes to their managers. While there was an elected grievance committee, it had been several years since a grievance had been brought to its members. When I asked Herbert about this, he said, "I always say that the grievances—or the lack thereof—is because managers are fair within the policies and protocols. Other people could say, 'Well, it's just because the system sucks,' or whatever. I mean, I don't believe you keep *all* the people happy *all* the time. I think what you need to look at in an organization is whether or not people leave or if they stay. 'Cause it's not a gilded c—well, it *could* be a gilded cage. But if it's a gilded cage, it's still *gilded*!" To Herbert, any degree of unfairness due to managerial control was more than compensated for by the economic rewards of managerial efficiency.

The "management by committee" days described in chapter 3 did not seem to have become part of institutional memory, or at least not in any positive way. At one point, while I was shadowing Linda in the office, her coworker Peggy Printz, who had expressed interested in my comparative study, leaned over to ask me how the grocery's participatory democratic control worked. As I explained the intricate system of self-managed work groups, elected committees, and monthly membership meetings I describe in the "Political Rights" section of chapter 5, the two office workers rejected the idea of such a thing at the bakery. Peggy said, "You'd have to *really* participate!" and then rolled her eyes as if imagining having to add such an enormous burden of managerial tasks to those for which she was already held responsible by her supervisors. Linda seemed to be trying to be polite as she said delicately, "It's like everyone becoming your boss," which I agreed seemed to be a view held by grocery workers. Like many others at the bakery, Linda and Peggy preferred to let their managers make decisions instead of having to hash it out with their coworkers.

Individual autonomy. Although suspicious of the work required for distributed management, bakery workers still craved some control over how and when they did their jobs, over their personal job autonomy. As was the case with authority, the bakery's allocation of individual autonomy followed neither the broad distribution of collectivist-democratic organizations nor the narrow band of a typical corporation, but instead distributed autonomy unevenly across work groups, and sometimes even combined high regulation with high autonomy.

One example of this odd mix of regulation and autonomy was in the production work group. Like many low-wage workers in non-worker-owned firms (Schneider et al. 2019), production workers' schedules were managerially regulated at the granular level. Production workers were disciplined by managers for being more than fifteen minutes late; had to be on call on at least one of their days off each week; had no say over which days or hours they would work within the twelve-hour shift period each week (only learning their schedule as little as a week beforehand); could only switch shifts with managerial approval; and could be disciplined for switching shifts with coworkers too often.

Yet the production process itself was structured to provide real autonomy. Instead of a single continuous production line, such as those made famous in Charlie Chaplin's *Modern Times* (1936) or the *I Love Lucy* chocolate factory episode (1952), where each worker's efforts affected those farther down the line and was affected by those before them, production in this bakery took place in three noncontinuous areas: mixing, ovens, and packaging. Mixing, in bowls taller and wider than workers, was accomplished by one person who roughly set the pace of production by how much dough they mixed for automatic shaping, loading into pans, and sending through an automatic proofing machine to rise. But while it was best to get the risen loaves baking in the next production area, the ovens, panned loaves could wait on racks until workers could get to them. Ovens was the hottest and most physically challenging work area. It involved first loading the risen loaves onto the shelves of the stall-like ovens, then unloading the ovens and depanning the hot bread onto the ten-shelf wheeled cooling racks, and then pushing the hot racks into an open space to cool and await the attentions of workers in the third and last area, packaging. Packaging was where cooled loaves were fed onto a conveyor belt to the slicer and bagger, then caught by workers and quickly stacked in boxes destined either for local delivery truck runs or for the massive freezer room, from where they would eventually be shipped to distributors beyond the bakery's local routes.

Graveyard shift assistant manager Mark took one look at me, considered the safety and time issues involved in having me at either the loading or depanning points, and put me on packaging under the supervision of "lead man" Valentín Rios. Although Valentín explained that he was setting a slower pace than usual as he trained me and helped me so I would not get too backed up, and although he and others encouraged me with smiles and nods over the noise of the machinery, like Lucy and Ethel in the chocolate room I could not keep up. The work required physical strength, excellent hand-eye coordination, and a constant mental calculation. As I fell behind, cooling racks lined up or bagged loaves dropped on the floor. Unlike the *I Love Lucy* episode, eventually someone would press the button to stop whatever part of the machine I was working. I apologized, but Valentín and the others would tell me, no, this is how it is when you train new workers. The noncontinuous manufacturing process used at the bakery allowed each shift crew to adjust the work flow, take breaks, and rotate positions. The speed of each part of the packaging machine—the feeder belt, the slicing arm, the bag tie, the output conveyor—could be separately adjusted, just as the three-stage production line could be staggered. While they could not decide how much bread to bake, how to make the dough or bake it, or in what it should be bagged, production workers were able to tailor each step to their pace rather than having to meet the machine's.

But beyond these mixtures of autonomy and regulation in one job, there were disparities between workers within work groups and between work groups as a whole. Within work groups, disparities were primarily related to where a worker was in the hierarchy. For instance, the assistant managers in production had as much latitude in their scheduling as their work group manager, as I discovered one night while I waited for a half hour to meet Mark. Production workers coming and going in their regulation steel-toed boots, hairnets, and earplugs joked with me, "Oh, Mark? ¡Surete! Good luck!" One of them, Alejandro Barrera, disapprovingly asserted that both Mark and his brother John Costa, the morning assistant manager, were always late but he, Alejandro, had never been late in his life. But most of his coworkers seemed to accept as a natural fact that managers would have certain freedoms they did not. On the other hand, neither lead workers nor assistant managers were able to give up their positions once they had taken them. John complained openly that he would prefer to step down into the nonmanagerial position he had once held, but had been told for the past two years that he had to either keep his position or "step away" from the bakery entirely. Similarly, Valentín complained about being stuck as the lead worker during the unsocial hours of the graveyard shift, but that Mark valued him too highly to let him transfer to another shift. In both cases, their places in the hierarchy were determined by those higher up the ladder; there was no individual autonomy when it came to position.

At the other end of the spectrum from the most managerially regulated production work group was the sales and delivery driver work group. Adam Delaney, now a medium-distance transit driver, had started on the production line and recalled what he disliked about it: "When you're working in a factory setting you have people in front of you who have jobs to do, and then it gets to you, and then there are people behind you who have jobs to do, and you're always relying on both parts to keep up their end of the thing and, you know, sometimes people don't. So . . . sometimes you feel like you have to do your job *and* their jobs in order to make everything flow correctly." Now he was one of the two men who drove eighteen-wheelers full of bakery product to the remote depots just beyond the edges of the Golden Valley. When I went on a run with Adam one night, a homemade CD bouncing his eclectic blend of music off the walls of the truck's cab, he told me he liked to be out in a truck alone at night. "You're kind of your own boss. You're out there just dealing with insane traffic, but you're kind of on your own." While drivers had route time estimates they were expected to meet, there was no other direct supervision—and there were few penalties imposed for exceeding estimates.

Somewhere in the middle of the autonomy spectrum, office workers were given some freedom over scheduling, some latitude to complete tasks in their own way, and even some say in hiring. Pam described a recent hire of a new accountant, saying that she "just let the work group have that interview" because she felt that they were capable of selecting a good candidate. But Pam also felt that managers should determine when that power should be shared, agreeing with Keith that the ambiguity in this area should be resolved in managers' favor: "People think that giving input or having input into the process means taking [their] suggestion. And so we try to say, 'Thank you for your suggestion, thank you for that input, we did look at it, we decided not to do this, the reason why is because—.'" In this way, managerial hierarchy motivated the flow of authority as much in the office as on the production floor.

"If it's a gilded cage, it's still gilded": Balancing participation and profits. Political rights at the bakery were neither entirely reserved for management nor widely distributed among the workers, but instead were parceled out to each body within specified limits: management created forward-looking plans for the company, but required a majority of workers' approval to enact them; managers controlled most but not all daily operations, but were overseen by a board of directors elected from the whole of the workforce. The contradictory feelings about management and autonomy largely stemmed from the two sets of workplace expectations the bakery straddled: that a traditionally hierarchical bureaucracy was best for financial matters, and that democracy could level problematic inequalities like pay or preferential parking. Absent regular interaction with a larger community of democratic workplaces, the collectivist vision of democratic control had shifted to one that was more representative than participatory, more formalized than informal, and increasingly articulated as distinct from daily business operations. As most workers saw it, the bakery had struck a balance between democratic participation and managerial efficiency practices that worked for most workers most of the time.

Yet despite generating significant economic rewards without entirely sacrificing democratic control, the bakery struggled to do this in an egalitarian manner. Getting and keeping a bakery job, earnings, organizational power, and day-to-day control over one's actions on the job differed by systems of class, race/ethnicity, and gender.

Inequality and Inclusion: Class, Race/Ethnicity, and Gender

In some ways the bakery was a remarkable advance against inequality, leveling earnings—particularly across class and gender—and becoming a far more ethnoracially inclusive organization than it had been originally, or than most of its countercultural collectivist generation of cooperatives had ever been. But it also had developed subtle forms of gender exclusion and ethnoracial earnings inequalities, few of which it acknowledged.

Class

Where the bakery truly excelled as a form of remedy to social injustice was in its attempts to level inequalities based solely on class.[6] As was noted earlier in this chapter, the earnings of workers in manual jobs were excellent—more than twice what other bakery workers in the local area earned, and nearly twice the median county income. To some extent this was at the expense of bakery managers' earnings, which were in no case more than four times the rate of the lowest-paid permanent bakery worker. But this compression—the relatively small difference between average nonmanagerial and managerial earnings—was not the only aspect of management that helped to level inequalities. Of the eleven salaried managers and three other professionals at the bakery, only three had business-related advanced degrees. Some—including the managers of production, transit, the local delivery depot, and the CEO—had not even completed an undergraduate college degree. Because a large body of research has demonstrated that higher education whitewashes class advantage as merit (Bathmaker, Ingram, and Waller 2013; Lareau 2003; Mullen 2010; Stuber 2011), the promotion of working-class people to managerial positions based on work experience rather than advanced educational credentials leveled purely class-based inequalities. This was not only true in terms of economic rewards but also in terms of the workplace political rights of management and, by extension, individual autonomy and firm governance: working-class managers were identical to middle-class managers in having almost total autonomy in scheduling their on-site time and arranging and carrying out their duties, and were just as likely as middle-class managers to be elected to the manager-heavy board of directors.

Yet there were few workplace political rights for the almost entirely working-class nonmanagerial bakery workforce. Managers determined schedules, instituted "best practices" for completion of work, offered the carrot of parties and prizes for meeting certain goals, and used the stick of reduced hours for those who failed to adhere to the rules, policies, and procedures they set. In the same way that workers who had wanted to keep being paid weekly had been forced to choose between accepting (white, upper-middle-class) Herbert's biweekly pay scheme or rejecting the business plan entirely—and maybe Herbert with it—workers who wanted more control could only "vote with their feet" by quitting. That is, although the bakery created viable pathways for working-class people to move into management, the positions of most working-class people gave them little day-to-day or long-range power. In this way, it could be argued that the cooperative was no more able to secure working-class workplace political rights than noncooperative firms.

Race/Ethnicity

On one hand, the bakery had become far more ethnoracially diverse not only when compared to its founding but also when compared to the surrounding county, having twice the proportion of Latinx bakery workers as Latinx county residents.[7] Compared to median earnings of just over $30,000 for Latinx men full-time workers in the county, the median wages of Latinx bakery men were about $54,700, and the mean only slightly lower (Bureau of Labor Statistics 2003).[8] In this way the bakery was not only welcoming but economically advantageous for Latinx workers.

But such welcome did not preclude a degree of internal ethnoracial segregation and inequality: no bakery work groups approached an ethnoracial balance, and more than half were at least 85 percent white, a "skewed" condition that has been argued to generate disadvantage in itself (Kanter 1977). While the production work group was not ethnoracially skewed (see table 4.1), 85 percent of the bakery workers of color were concentrated there. Despite the widespread and admiring talk of the hard work done by production, this work group had the lowest average total earnings (wages, work group gainsharing bonuses regardless of cooperative membership, and member profit sharing): an average of $9,000 less per year than what was made by all other nonmanagerial bakery workers. This was partly due to seniority: turnover was far higher here. Nonmanagerial workers in other work groups had an average of roughly three more years' tenure, and pay rose by seniority. But there was also another explanation: lower membership rates among those eligible for membership.

Less than three-fourths of eligible production workers had joined the cooperative, while in other work groups almost all other eligible workers had done so. No one in production described buy-in cost as a barrier, but the requirement to literally stand and address the entire membership did seem to be one. At the end of my study, two primary Spanish speakers got cold feet the night they were scheduled to stand for membership. Although one applied and was approved the following quarter, and another the quarter after that, the delay cost the first worker almost $7,000 and the second about $13,500 in gross profit sharing for the year. Pam, the white, middle-class office manager who called the process "intimidating," recalled a few other workers "chickening out," and all the examples she recounted were of Latinx production workers. The conflation of production employment with Latinx heritage and Spanish-language primacy may explain

TABLE 4.1 Bakery work group by race/ethnicity and gender in 2003

	WORK GROUP SIZE	WHITE MEN	WHITE WOMEN	MEN OF COLOR	WOMEN OF COLOR	WORK GROUP % MEN	WORK GROUP % WHITE
Administrative (exempt)	3	1	1	1		66	66
Sales and delivery	20	13	5	2		75	90
Exempt		1					
Non-exempt		12	5	2			
Maintentance	5	4		1		100	80
Exempt		1		1			
Non-exempt		3					
Marketing (exempt)	2	2				100	100
Office	7		5		2	0	71
Exempt			1		1		
Non-exempt			4		1		
Production	45	8		37		100	19
Exempt				1			
Non-exempt		8		36			
Remote delivery depot #1	6	4		2		100	66
Exempt		1					
Non-exempt		3		2			
Remote delivery depot #2	7	7				100	100
Exempt		1					
Non-exempt		6					
Shipping	4	2	2			67	100
Exempt			1				
Non-exempt		2	1				

Note: During my observation in 2003, two Latinx men had been hired into shipping on a temporary basis, but had not become permanent workers eligible for membership yet; both became permanent workers/ members in 2004.

why Latinx bakery workers had a shorter tenure than non-Latinx white workers, earned lower wages, and were less likely to become members: inclusion was not ethnoracially neutral.

Politically, Latinx bakery workers were underrepresented in both governance and management compared to non-Latinx whites. During my four-year observation period, only four Latinx members sat on the nine-member board of directors, and not all at the same time. All had jobs that gave them a fair degree of time autonomy: three were the only three exempt workers of color (the production manager, office manager, and personnel director), while the fourth was a waged assistant manager in production. Of the eleven bakery managers, only two were not white, making up less than half the proportion of Black or Brown bakery employees. At the more individual level of job autonomy, the story was similar: white bakery workers held a disproportionately greater share of jobs that provided more control and creativity. The highly autonomous local and long-distance drivers in the three depots were almost all white, while production workers were more than three-fourths Black and Brown (see table 4.1).

Thus, while the bakery was a more inclusive and egalitarian employer than most others in the area, ethnoracial inequality permeated its economic and political arrangements. White workers made more money, held more managerial power, had more of the desirable nonmanagerial positions, and had more positions with greater job autonomy than workers of color—almost all of whom were Latinx. In terms of a workers' movement, this cooperative made only partial progress towards ethnoracial equity.

Gender

Compared to the earnings and political access inequalities between whites and people of color, at first glance the differences between bakery men and women seemed to tell an entirely different story.[9] Unlike the direction of national trends in gender inequality (Cotter, Hermsen, and Vanneman 2004), bakery men averaged only 89 percent of women's annual earnings, while women workers were 50 percent more likely to be members and twice as likely to be managers as men workers, and consistently held at least twice as many board seats as their proportion of the workforce. And, like Latinx members' advantages over local Latinx full-time workers, with average annual earnings of $68,100, bakery women far outpaced local county full-time working women, whose median incomes were just over $40,000. For those women who had achieved bakery employment, both economic and political rewards were real and substantial.

But in that last sentence lies the rub. Although women were a majority of founding members and maintained this majority until after managers were fully installed in the early 1990s, by 2003 they made up only 15 percent of the permanent workforce. More than a third were concentrated in the all-women office work group, while there were none in six of the work groups. Some of this had to do with scheduling. Mercedes, the Hispanic middle-class morning receptionist, was one of only two part-time workers. Mercedes had proved herself a highly competent worker early: she been called into Herbert's office after her first two weeks and commended as the best receptionist in twenty years. "I was so relieved!" she said, laughing, and used that to her advantage when she pressed for a twenty-four-hour workweek. "I wouldn't be here if I wasn't on this shift," she said as she described driving her children to various after-school activities around the Golden Valley. With her husband's income, she was able to balance what she characterized as an interesting, good-paying job with the kind of care she wanted to provide to her family.

Such shifts, however, were not available in production, where most bakery job openings were. For this reason, perhaps, it had been several years since a woman had been hired. When asked, managers and workers across work groups told me that women did not like "hot and dirty" work. That the office, the cleanest kind of work in the most spatially distinct area of the bakery on the upper floor, was composed only of women seemed to add weight to this assertion. Some shrugged: What could you do if no women wanted production jobs? Yet, at other moments, managers' stories suggested other reasons, ones that were not about choices based on internalized norms. Mark recalled some "girls" he had met at a family party who asked about production jobs, and how he had told them that they would hate it because they would get sweaty. Production manager Charlie, a Latinx, working-class man who had skipped college to provide for his younger siblings' education, described some recent women applicants he had disqualified based on lack of experience, and laughed sheepishly when I pointed out how this contradicted the claim he had just made about women not liking "hot and dirty" work. Whether perceived as gender socialization or some essential characteristic of women, more important seemed to be organizational barriers: the fact that production jobs were full-time, and that schedules could change by hours every two weeks—all of which posed a major challenge to anyone who was the primary caretaker for young or elderly family members. Moreover, whether internal or external, barriers affected everyone: the high turnover in production led to a steady stream of temporary labor, suggesting that *men* disliked "hot and dirty" work just as much as women did. Yet this went unnoticed by Charlie and other workers who instead naturalized gender segregation as gendered preference.

That women were such a small proportion of the workforce had implications for their managerial power as well. In general, being a man seemed to amplify managers' authority, status, and respect, while being a woman seemed to reduce it.

Men managers' roles as members of the board of directors were described by work group members as proof of their value; women managers were patronized as "mothering." Similarly, at a membership meeting I attended toward the end of my time at the bakery, I sat flanked by Matt Schroeder and Tommy Lowden, two white, working-class men from the sales and delivery work group. Describing the typical meeting structure where Pam presented the annual report and was followed by Herbert presenting the annual business plan, Matt whispered, "First Pam'll tell us how good we're doing . . ." and Tommy picked up the line as if part of a practiced routine: ". . . and then Herb'll tell us how terrible everything is!" But while Herbert's unwanted criticism was generally described as financial vision, Pam's positive assessment was brushed off as more emotional than professional.

Although women held twice the share of management positions as their 15 percent of the total workforce, in real numbers this meant only three women managers: Pam and also Latinx, middle-class Alicia Bermúdez in the office, and Sherry, a white, working-class woman in shipping. Alicia and Pam seemed to have no more than the normal modest friction common between workers and managers, and turnover in the office was very low. Sherry, however, was widely pointed out as the most difficult manager and it seemed significant that she was the only woman supervising men. Although both Herbert and Pam spoke glowingly of Sherry's work, several shipping and production workers who interacted most regularly with her complained that she was a micromanager, and that this led to high turnover in the shipping work group. They described her assistant manager, Toby Sparks, a white, working-class man in his thirties, as having been hired more to compensate for Sherry's lack of people skills than to fulfill any other administrative needs in their small work group. Although Sherry was an out lesbian (like several other bakery workers in the office and the sales and delivery work groups), I heard nothing that seemed tinged with homophobia. Indeed, even the other lesbian in Sherry's work group focused on her managerial skills. Anne, also a middle-aged white woman, told me that the problem was that, since Toby had been hired, Sherry was primarily doing logistics but still tried to make shippers coordinate labor her way: "Toby can just tell us what to do and we'll do it. We don't need more instruction. Sherry's more of an office person. She probably wouldn't even know what I do if she came out here now." Anne claimed that several young men had quit in frustration.

Yet, in contrast, Charlie, who had risen from floor labor to manager like Sherry and whose scheduling was often overtly punitive, did not seem to face the kind or degree of criticism leveled at Sherry. He had a social awkwardness that drew teasing but he was generally well regarded—even though he also spent more time in the office than on the floor and also relied on his assistant managers to implement direct supervision. He was well aware of this and, as he stood for hours grilling carnitas and sausages in the hot sun during the annual Labor Day barbecue, cannily joked that "the guys" needed to see him sweat once a year. Indeed, I had never seen him work on the line and rarely saw him on the production floor. A week earlier, when I had been telling the white, working-class assistant manager for the morning shift, John, about Charlie's assessment of my "tryout" on the production line, John had opened his eyes wide and mugged, "So he went down on the floor because you were there?" in a half-joking critique of Charlie's usual place in his upstairs office. But no one ever suggested this was anything more than Charlie's proper role as a manager, whose concerns should be more global and less local. That is, his similar managerial actions were not criticized in the way Sherry's were.

The organizational reproduction of managers as the "strong, technically competent, authoritative leader[s]" (Acker 1990, 153) worked to women's disadvantage. The general bakery disparagement of Sherry's managerial skills showed the precarity of women managers of men in and out of their work groups. Regardless of their perceived femininity or masculinity, women managers were affected by what Rosabeth Moss Kanter (1977) describes as tokenism: their persons, rather than achievements, were highlighted and the scrutiny was more intense. Sherry was "more of an office person," while Charlie's absence was unremarked; Sherry had problems with "young guys," while office workers' lack of intimacy with Pam was considered normal. While Ellen Scott (2005) has found that organizational minorities can successfully wield a disproportionately greater share of power when organizational discourses legitimate it, the lack of such discourses at the bakery meant that the number of women's managerial positions did not improve their status or increase levels of inclusion for women generally.

Indeed, what best explained bakery women's economic and political advantages was their overwhelming whiteness: while whites were only a bare majority of bakery men, thirteen of the fifteen bakery women were white. As I have noted, whiteness accounted both for a sizable increase in earnings and for the likelihood of being a manager—and being a manager then increased earnings and also the likelihood of being on the board of directors. But because women were such a small proportion of the workforce, their actions were critiqued in a way that attributed their actions to their gender, while men's were not, thus limiting these benefits to the small group of white women able to access bakery employment.

Summary: Ownership and Inequality

By the bakery's third decade, it had found a way to make a worker cooperative a thriving business capable of supporting a primarily working-class membership.

In a region dominated by whites, it had opened its doors to a Latinx workforce proportionally double that of the county. It had narrowed the earnings gap between workers doing the dirtiest and most physically demanding labor and those doing the highest-status mental labor; developed effective management; and preserved ultimate political control with the membership as a whole. If individual levels of autonomy were far lower than in the collectivist-democratic days, the trade-off involved in creating this "gilded cage" seemed to satisfy its inhabitants.

"By deed, instead of by argument" (Marx 1864, 11), the bakery demonstrated how working people could manage their enterprises: by tempering bureaucracy with an egalitarian commitment to working people. First, as described in chapter 3 and fleshed out in this chapter, the bakery created specialized positions such as driver, shipper, packager, or manager; staffed those positions based on experience- or certificate-based expertise; delegated responsibility and power to impersonal positions, such as "manager," rather than to persons, such as "James"; and formalized every practice and expectation in documents containing rules and regulations. But, second, the bakery aligned the interests of the managerial strata with nonmanagerial workers in two ways: by reducing the gap in pay between managers and nonmanagers, and by including managers as members of the cooperative rather than separating them—as is common, for instance, among union bargaining units.

Yet although these two kinds of actions provided significant benefits for its working-class members, Pam's designation of the bakery as "closest to utopian" is questionable. By the early years of the twenty-first century, many of the bakery's pay, power, and autonomy practices were more similar to traditional workplaces than 1970s and 1980s collectives—with troublingly traditional outcomes. Jobs were more likely to be apportioned along mainstream lines, with a small group of (mostly white) women doing "clean" office work while most of the Black and Brown (men) workers did the "hot and dirty" production jobs. As in the larger labor market, this produced few opportunities for women of color. Latinas were largely blocked from bakery jobs accessible to Latinos and were unable to achieve the pay and power of white women. Power and autonomy were largely delegated to managers, and managerial positions reflected white labor market privilege. While white women had more managerial power than might be expected for their proportion of the workforce, management was still overwhelmingly composed of men. The bakery challenged the mainstream labor market's class-stratifying processes, but was less proactive when it came to gender and ethnoracial inequalities. Even the bakery's distribution of wealth was, while far less extreme than elsewhere, increasingly linked more to the unequal labor market and its valuation of jobs than to an internal sense of worth in the value of labor. The relatively high earnings of manual workers and relatively low ones of managers seemed to justify the internal stratification of not only earnings but organizational power and job autonomy.

In short, People's Daily Bread Bakery offered some important answers to questions about how a worker-oriented workplace could model a transformation of class relationships but seemed to have far less to say about ethnoracial and gendered workplace inequalities. It also proposed problematic answers to questions about workplace democracy, suggesting that economic success and direct worker control were antithetical and that only a highly representative form of worker democracy that ceded large areas of authority to a managerial stratum could be used to run a business within a capitalist economy.

But the bakery was not the only model of worker cooperation in the Golden Valley at the beginning of the twenty-first century. Chapter 5 explores a different cooperative approach to the democratic management of a workers' enterprise under capitalism, and a different approach to the intersecting roles of class, race/ethnicity, and gender in the struggles and successes of the new century's workers.

ONE WORLD NATURAL GROCERY

Managing without Managers

No one understands how we work.

—Sara High, cashiers work group member

It's so free here. Most Americans have no idea what it could be like.

—Juanita Cole, produce work group member

On the large gray building tucked under the freeway between big box stores, warehouses, and small single- and multifamily homes, the words "a WORKER-OWNED COOPERATIVE" stake a claim in three-foot high capital letters below One World Natural Grocery's name. While workers trickle in on bike or by foot from nearby neighborhoods or the public transportation system, an idling line of customer cars wait for one of the thirty or so spaces in the small garage to avoid the risk of smashed windows on side streets. Dozens of homeless men and women push their possessions or camp between the beams holding up the freeway overhead, and there is frequently human waste on the sidewalks. In the early years of the twenty-first century, this is one of the more run-down parts of the city of Edgefield. Like many similar social enterprises situated at a "border zone" between wealth and poverty (Borowiak et al. 2017), it is unclear whether its future is a few blocks east, where scores of new loft condominiums are going up every year and being bought by high-tech and professional workers, or a few blocks west, where those displaced by the lofts are squeezed into single-room occupancy hotels and tenement buildings.

I have the time to notice all of this while I wait outside the store for Shane Romero, who has agreed to let me shadow him today. Shane, a young Chicano[1] in his twenties who has recently become an owning member of the cooperative after his first year of employment, is more than fifteen minutes late for his cashier shift, but no one seems to notice as Shane exchanges English and Spanish greetings with the cashiers and floor workers: men and women of a range of ethnoracial groups and ages. We walk across the store, a former automobile showroom, with its soaring ceilings, daylight harvesting panels providing the illusion of constant sunlight, its twenty-five bilingually labeled aisles of natural food, personal, and household products. It's really beautiful. Then we step through an open doorway labeled Workers Only, up the stairs, and into another, more chaotic world: the inexpertly-framed Sheetrock cash room that Shane disappears into (after consulting with an older coworker about the advisability of bringing me in), a cramped set of offices, a surprisingly light kitchen, a break room overlooking the retail floor below, some multipurpose rooms full of mismatched folding furniture, and a hallway lined with more than a dozen boards covered with notices, agendas, meeting minutes, policies, and schedules. One bulletin board has Polaroid headshots of members of committees and non-sales-floor work groups like the office and maintenance that help me (and any newer worker) sort out who to ask about what. After a few days, there's also a sign with a clear headshot of me, my contact info, and a brief description of my research plan.

Shane sets up at a register next to Sara High, the mixed-race daughter of a current and a former worker. Although Sara's "home" work group is cashiers, she still has shifts in the personal care work group that hired her and in herbs, and occasionally picks up shifts in vitamins, her father's work group. Sara is a member of the cashiers coordinating committee, an elected body that meets weekly to oversee scheduling and ensure that time cards are correctly filled out. She starts talking to me about a cashier who was scolded for wearing a button with a political slogan for a highly contentious current issue by a customer who complained, "I thought your management told you that you can't wear that!" Sara sighs, "No one understands how we work." Even if customers accept that, unlike nearby supermarkets, uniforms are not required here, they cannot imagine this level of worker autonomy. But she can understand the customers' confusion; even through her parents had worked at the grocery for years, Sara did not really understand that there were no managers until she began working here herself. Next to her, eighteen-year-old Chicano Theo Vallin turns and exclaims, "Wow, I thought I was the only one!" He grew up in the neighborhood, and his mother, Luisa, has been a cashier at the grocery for more than ten years. But he says he used to tease his mother for talking about "our" store, and says that during his first week he kept asking the "buddy" assigned to orient him, "Who's the guy or lady in charge? Who really owns it?" Now, though, he understands. He tells me with no small degree of pride, "I don't bag [customers' groceries] because I'm an owner. Customers have to respect us because we're owners."

An Experiment in Democracy

Like People's Daily Bread Bakery, the grocery's worker ownership provided a set of living answers to questions about worker self-management. After more than twenty-five years of operations, it had its own highly developed set of practices and procedures to produce economic stability and distribute workplace political rights. But where the bakery had replaced collectivist-democratic workplace control with managerial bureaucracy in an explicit attempt to best protect its working-class membership, the grocery's similarly working-class workforce instead expanded and formalized its democratic, distributed management. Where the bakery had reintroduced the kinds of gender exclusions and ethnoracial inequalities typical of the mainstream labor market, the grocery had reduced them.

Yet, like the bakery, the grocery was nothing like its original incarnation as a provision service to a New Age, white-majority spiritual community: there were over two hundred ethnoracially and spiritually diverse members in 2003, working anywhere from three to sixty hours per week, sorted into fourteen self-managing work groups. The structure outlined in figure 3.2 in chapter 3 had been augmented with additional elected bodies, creating an even denser—although, as I will show, not total—form of democratic control. And this densely clustered democracy did not require worker homogeneity but instead drew on its gender and ethnoracial diversity.

While the bakery was located in a semirural and mostly white metro area, the grocery was in the center of the densely urban Edgefield, a much more ethnoracially diverse and wealthy city. By the time of my study, the process of "exurbanization" (Nelson and Dueker 1990) was already displacing Edgefield's working class (and significant portions of its middle class) to rural and suburban areas just within a commutable range. Education, health, social services, and professional and business services dominated Edgefield's labor market and were closely followed by tourism. Relatively affluent (median incomes above the national average), it was also a "minority majority" city: non-Latinx whites made up less than half the population in 2003, followed in descending order of population share by Asian Americans and Pacific Islanders, Latinx people, and African Americans, as well as much smaller numbers of Indigenous and mixed-race people. It was also an intensely cosmopolitan city, with almost half its residents speaking a language other than English at home, almost half having a bachelor's degree or higher, and a median income just above the national average.[2]

Theorizing Workplace Democracy within Difference

Like the bakery, the grocery offered an alternative to the supposed truism that worker cooperatives either failed economically or ceased to be operated cooperatively (Webb and Webb 1920). With more than a quarter century under their belts at the time of my study (and still in business when this book went to press), both demonstrated the potential of worker cooperatives to provide good, stable jobs. As I have described in chapters 3 and 4, the bakery's solution to the demands of a surrounding capitalist economy was for labor to hire a form of management that would be accountable as much to its workforce as to the demands of the market. Yet this process had also been accompanied by a significant reduction in the numbers of women (including the near exclusion of women of color) and an ethnoracial segregation of jobs and power. While the bakery's managerial regime helped to overcome many of the *exclusions* common to the white, middle class-dominated 1970s countercultural collectivist generation (see chapter 2, "The Countercultural Collectivist Era, 1970s-1980s" section), it did not produce either ethnoracial or gender *egalitarianism*.

Historically, broad and egalitarian distribution of power has only seemed possible within highly homogeneous groups, where shared values—for instance, the overthrow of capitalism, being "woman identified," or "godly duties" (Lindenfeld and Rothschild-Whitt 1982; Radicalesbians 1970; Taylor 1983)—sustain commitment in the face of social challenges. Yet, as the countercultural collectivist cooperatives showed, such *value*-based homogeneity seemed to code or conceal shared *cultural* backgrounds and helped to produce and maintain ethnoracial and class homogeneity. This suggests a dilemma for the grocery and similar organizations: How does an egalitarian-oriented organization maintain its participatory and highly deliberative democracy within a diverse, heterogeneous membership? Is it possible to coordinate organizational action while respecting and protecting the variety of values that arises from a variety of social locations? Thus, where the bakery asked if workers could free themselves of investor ownership without going bankrupt or profiting off the labor of others, the grocery asked if they could do so in a directly democratic fashion without either devolving into chaos or internally reproducing social inequalities of class, race/ethnicity, and gender.

To see if and how the grocery was able to balance its egalitarian and democratic goals–while also providing stable, good jobs—this chapter first explores the allocation of earnings within the grocery, and contextualizes them at its locale. The second section describes the grocery's political organization, detailing the workings of a complex and decentralized form of organizational power where governance and management overlap in unusual ways. The third section addresses the grocery's successes and failures in distributing economic and political rewards and rights across differences of class, race/ethnicity, and gender. Finally, the chapter summarizes the potential and limits of such a densely clustered democratic structure for an alternative market organization, and what lessons the grocery might offer to workers more generally.

Economic Rewards: "Customers Have to Respect Us Because We're Owners"

Like the bakery, the grocery was by many measures a successful business. By the time I was conducting ethnographic study in 2003, it had expanded into a far larger physical space and generated almost $25 million in annual sales. Its workforce of 214 put its size, like the bakery, in the top 15 percent size-wise of its industry nationally (US Census Bureau 2004).[3] While its offerings now included expensive European cheeses and "artisanal" organic breads, and the grocery's neighbors would critically compare its prices to those of the many ethnic markets a few blocks away, it still did a brisk business in bulk commercial rice and beans and was acknowledged to have the cheapest organic produce in the city. Its distribution of over $2 million in profits to its members meant that 2003 hourly average earnings were almost twice that of those working in large California supermarkets and similarly greater than that of other retail workers in Edgefield (Dube and Lantsberg 2004; US Department of Labor 2003),[4] and the grocery's benefits packages were rich even in comparison with unionized stores. Nevertheless, grocery workers' median annual income—just under $40,000—was almost $2,000 *less* than the local median income. This was largely due to grocery workers' shorter full-time work hours—thirty per week on average—and the fact that more than one-fourth did not even average the twenty-four hours needed to be eligible for medical and dental coverage, including extensive complimentary care coverage and up to fifty-two mental health visits per year. All workers, however, were eligible for other benefits: pretax income shelters; 401k subsidies; public transit subsidies; store discounts; annual gym memberships; unpaid leaves of absence that allowed full-time workers to keep their health insurance if life events required them to stop working for weeks or months at a time; child care subsidies of one dollar per hour per child (with an upper limit of five dollars per hour); at least two (and up to eight) weeks of paid personal time off; and—last but not least—piles of free nonsalable food.

Grocery workers seemed to struggle to balance their desire to make a living with their desire to have time away from work to enjoy it. They often spoke with pride about their *hourly* earnings—which averaged over twenty-eight dollars, with a median hourly rate about ninety cents less—but were less vocal about their *annual* earnings. Juanita Cole, a member of the produce work group, seemed shocked when I responded to her query about pay ranges at the bakery: "I bet they own houses!" she exclaimed.[5] Homeownership was out of reach for many grocery workers in the inflated Edgefield housing market. She had been critical of the bakery's decision to install managers but smiled wistfully as she said, "I'd like to own a house, a bit of land." Nevertheless, later at her work group's weekly meeting, she requested and was granted a two-week leave to tour with her band; there was nothing at the grocery compelling the forty-hour workweeks mandated by bakery managers that generated bakery workers' higher annual take-home pay. Despite often identifying pay as one of the chief attractions of their jobs, most grocery workers chose to work less rather than earn more.

Grocery earnings did not just mean wages. Like the bakery, profit sharing based on annual hours worked as a member and dividends paid on the shares retained by the cooperative were a significant part of earnings—more than one-third of workers' average incomes at the grocery. Yet the grocery's distribution of earnings differed in two important ways from that of the bakery. First, the grocery did not allocate any part of its profits to nonmembers as gainsharing, as the bakery did; only members were eligible for profit sharing. This was largely because there were hardly any nonmembers: new workers who did not satisfy membership requirements and were not approved as members within a year were fired on the anniversary of their hire date. These requirements were very similar to the bakery's, and including working at least one thousand hours (about seven and a half months of thirty-two hour workweeks); completing a written, open-book membership exam after a series of orientation sessions in cooperative structure, meeting process, customer service, safety, and financial literacy; observing a membership meeting and a meeting of a key elected committee with an assigned volunteer "buddy"; and receiving a vote of confidence from their work group. The last step was buy-in, but at a price that was just under an hour's starting wage, this was no real barrier.

And this comparison was true for all new workers because the biggest difference from the bakery was, second, that everyone—regardless of position, expertise, or years to attain an educational certification—began at exactly the same starting wage. Every grocery worker was hired into a "home" work group with disciplinary and firing power. The division of labor that began in the 1980s had proliferated into work groups representing ten sales categories (vitamins, household goods, personal care goods, refrigerated food, cheese, produce, packaged food, bulk, baked goods, herbs) and four nonsales categories (cashiers, maintenance, the office, and customer service). But neither the work groups nor the jobs within them affected earnings; in 2003, everyone started at $11.35 per hour. The decoupling of wages from job or task allowed workers to specialize or cross-train as they liked: cashiers could take shifts in packaged food that did not tax their injury-prone hands and wrists, office workers could pick up cashier shifts in the busy consumer season between Thanksgiving and New Year's Eve, and workers having conflicts with members of their work group could transition to another one without harm to their income.

Similarly, neither work group nor task affected the amount of profits each worker was entitled to share in. Profits were not simply distributed by annual hours but also slightly multiplied by wage (this to compensate older workers whose contributions had laid the foundations for the grocery's current financial success but who had gone years without significant profit sharing or 401k subsidy). Unlike the bakery, the grocery tended to distribute workers' shares in cash as much as possible without triggering an Internal Revenue Service audit—that is, closer to 50 percent than 20 percent cash payments. The grocery did not distribute the rest in the three- to five-year "rolling" payouts as the bakery did, but instead paid a 5 percent annual dividend on retained profits and allowed members to withdraw any amounts over $30,000 in their retained-profit accounts.

Thus, the earnings differences that existed among grocery worker wages were mostly due to seniority: increased dividends and the accrual of biannual wage increases. Twice a year, the grocery's board of directors allocated each work group a lump sum equal to a per-person hourly raise (typically between twenty-five cents and a dollar), and the work group then apportioned it among its members. Some work groups simply divided the amount equally, while others with many longer-tenure workers voted more money to newer workers to better equalize wages, often in recognition of new workers' longer hours or more physically challenging tasks. Other work groups used these wage allocations to reward new or recently developed expertise (e.g., a packaged food work group member who took a training course in forklift operation) or to punish poor performance. Yet despite the variety of rationales and processes for dividing wage increases, no work group described using education or credentialed expertise and wages to implement differentials.

For this reason, while workweek variation drove profound differences in annual earnings—the highest paid member earned almost $128,000, while the lowest earned only $2,300—the highest hourly earnings ($43.74) were less than two and a half times that of the lowest hourly earnings ($18.96). This was not only within the ideal 3:1 cooperative ratio of the International Cooperative Alliance (n.d.), but it was a closer ratio than most real-world cooperatives (Tonnesen 2012) and a tiny fraction of that of the average Fortune 500 company (see chapter 4, "Economic Rewards").

The grocery enjoyed a measure of success financially, providing stable and decently compensated jobs, and socially, giving workers more control over both their work/life balance and their workplace task allocation. This degree of autonomy was very much appreciated by grocery members, but the tug between money and time became particularly pressing as the Golden Valley's real estate market heated up, and grocery workers felt less secure in their housing. Juanita's lament regarding opportunities for homeownership served as a sober reminder of the limits on organizational autonomy regarding grocery members' well-being. Yet most workers continued to limit their hours, and—as I will describe in the following sections—to use their political will to protect rather than reduce the grocery's egalitarian distributions of power and resources.

Political Rights: "We're Not Just Here to Tell People What to Do"

Grocery governance was not entirely identical with its management—the board of directors was no longer composed of the whole membership as it had been in its early days—but the two were still deeply entwined. Yet rather than a completely inefficient and ineffective organizational form, the grocery had produced a hybrid democratic governance structure that supported a highly democratic and largely distributed form of management.

Governance structure. In its third decade of existence, the grocery still had no positional management: it was no one's sole job to coordinate labor, processes, or people. But neither was the grocery like the countercultural collectivist generation of small, direct democratic collectives, where most decisions were made together and could get bogged down in endless discussion, or where interpersonal struggles over power could only be tamed by rotating everyone through all tasks (see "The Countercultural Collectivist Era" in chapter 2). Since the grocery's restructuring in the early 1980s (see figure 3.1 in chapter 3), governance and management functions were often rolled in together and dispersed through its expanded hybrid of representative and participatory democratic control, with nearly a dozen temporary and permanent committees allocated responsibility for specialized tasks, many of which combined governance and management functions.

Governance operated through both direct and representative democracy. Direct democratic governance primarily occurred at the monthly membership meeting and by secret balloting. Membership meetings were places to enact changes to bylaws, propose new actions, or veto actions by either the most powerful representative governance body, the seven-member board of directors, or the most powerful representative management body, the Intracooperative Coordinating Committee (ICC). Individual monthly membership meeting attendance was paid at regular hourly wages but was voluntary rather than mandatory. And despite simultaneous Spanish interpretation, on-site meetings, and alternation between mornings before the store opened and nights after it shut, membership meeting attendance was often low. Sometimes it even fell below the quorum of 20 percent of membership required for binding decisions. Even when there was quorum, low attendance was seen as a problem. A sign advertising a summer meeting, "Don't Let 21 People Decide the Fate of One World!," warned the membership that, with two hundred members at the time, a simple majority of a meeting barely at quorum could reject a change to health care coverage or veto the annual board-determined per-person wage increase. For changes to bylaws, however, a two-thirds majority vote was required at membership meetings. Further, when an action proposed was deemed by the board to have a strong financial impact—such as a boycott of the then-popular Odwalla line of juices when they were acquired by Coca-Cola Inc., or a proposed boycott of all French goods in response to the country's ongoing nuclear testing in the Pacific—the board would provide secret ballots to all members to cast over a two-week period.

Representative democratic governance was primarily accomplished through the elected seven-member board of directors, whose jurisdiction was the grocery's legal and financial (largely budgeting) decisions. The board determined wage increases and shares of profits paid out as cash and as dividends. To the extent that it believed work group practices might affect the store's financial health as a whole, the board could override their decisions. For instance, when two work groups chose to participate in a different and more contentious boycott, the board intervened and insisted on secret ballot polling of the membership to determine boycott policy for the store as a whole. Elected annually from the membership, board members committed to a two-year term, and some had served for three or more terms. The board met weekly for three hours and made decisions by majority vote. Any other worker could sit in on most meetings, but only board members and those who requested or were invited to make a presentation were paid to be there—like all other work, board participation was paid at each worker's regular hourly wages and counted towards their share of the cooperative's annual hours.

Governance accountability. Given the diffusion of governance power, it is perhaps unsurprising that accountability mechanisms were also dispersed among work groups, the membership meetings, and elections of representatives. Unlike the bakery, meetings were far from streamlined or even uniform in their process. Some work groups seemed to make decisions by majority vote, while others used a partial consensus process: usually talking until everyone could nod their heads in agreement, but switching to a two-thirds vote if not. Consensus is commonly understood as a process of deliberation until all members of a group can agree. Even a sole dissenter can block consensus and refuse to allow the group to take a particular action. Its use has been found to create stronger decisions and more member investment (Epstein 1991; Polletta 2002), but also a loss of speed and nimbleness (Viggiani 2011) and the erasure of internal dissent (Mansbridge 1980). As a decision-making process, it is usually contrasted with voting, where action can be taken even in the presence of a few or many dissenters. I was initially confused by claims that workers made about valuing consensus, because most decisions—in work groups, elected committees, and the membership meeting—seemed to be made by voting. For instance, the membership meeting facilitator—a representative of the four-member elected Successful Participation Committee (SPC)—would call for a straw poll of approval for my presence rather than call for consensus, and although sometimes someone voted against me being there, I would be allowed to stay.[6]

But grocery members expected and encouraged both the intensive process of deliberation and the decisiveness of voting. Deliberation was built into governance processes. For instance, any proposal at membership meetings had to be submitted a week in advance to the SPC (which, in addition to facilitating membership and other meetings, also reviewed proposals for "completeness, accessibility, and accuracy"). The SPC had no power to block any proposal from going to the membership meeting for a vote, but could include a statement outlining any objections or noting a failure to respond to review—and in practice, I never saw a proposal go to the members without SPC approval. Proposals made from the floor could not be put to a binding vote, but had to wait a month until the next meeting. Membership meeting agendas and proposals were distributed a week before each meeting, and I heard informal discussions of items in the lunchrooms, meeting rooms, hallways, and outdoor smoking areas throughout the week leading up to each meeting. For particularly controversial proposals, a "wall poll" in the form of a large sheet of butcher paper would be posted in the upstairs hallway a week before a meeting to allow members time to gather and express their thoughts on a subject on sticky notes affixed to the butcher paper; wall polls then commonly generated greater meeting attendance. Any member could also propose a "CoCo"—a Cooperative Concerns forum—to discuss contentious or complex issues that were likely to be the subject of a membership meeting proposal and, if at least four people signed up for a proposed topic, the ICC would schedule and convene the focused discussion. CoCos had been initiated as a way to control the length of monthly membership meetings by separating what was seen as necessary deliberation from efficient decision-making. During my observation period, CoCos varied in size from twelve to more than fifty participants. Regardless of size, CoCos were recorded and transcribed verbatim within forty-eight hours, with transcripts placed in a binder in the worker lounge for all to read.

With such a level of pre-meeting governance debate, it was typical for most membership meeting discussion to be relatively brief and for voting to be more of a formalization of established support than the discovery of it. Jan Bridges, a member of the small baked goods work group, asserted that the presence or absence of voting did not define the use of the consensus process: "At One World, we use almost all of the other aspects of consensus. And then, toward the end, we vote."

This level of deliberation seemed to also produce investment in accountability from representatives at the grocery. One example was the case of a well-liked man in his forties, Brian Cleary. Brian's experience in and knowledge of the construction industry and local permitting process was often described to me as crucial to the store's successful mid-1990s move to its current location. After that, Brian had enjoyed easy and repeated reelections to the board of directors and had consistently been the store's liaison with the city of Edgefield when it came to legal and financial matters. Yet it emerged that, despite grocery policy requiring board consent for major financial decisions, Brian had signed significant financial contracts with the city on his own. Even though almost no one found fault with the contracts' contents—most workers I asked viewed them as beneficial to the store—Brian's failure to follow democratic protocol ended his time as a board member after he failed to win a seat in the next election. Being liked and effectively managing city contracts did not, it seemed, trump democratic accountability at the grocery.

Management structure. Another way to view the membership's rejection of Brian was as a managerial action, albeit in this case an action of distributed management. Much of what a small group of managers would do in a traditional business was accomplished by the entire workforce through direct democratic practices in the fourteen work groups, through eleven representative democratic committees, and through individual workers acting in accordance with the expectations of grocery policies and practices.

"Power is in the work groups," I was told when I asked what made people come to their weekly meetings. During these meetings, both member and probationary workers allocated raises, articulated requirements for extended leaves, coordinated coverage when workers were unable to find their own shift substitutes, and activated penalties up to and including firing members. Within each work group a rotating three-member committee was also elected to—at a minimum— hire, coordinate annual worker evaluations, check time cards for accuracy, and deliver disciplinary decisions as needed. Other tasks could be delegated to this committee, leading to a continuum of configurations among the work groups. At one end, the eighteen-member produce work group delegated only the required minimum, while at the other, the thirty-one-member cashiers work group tacked on scheduling, vacation coordination, tracking lateness and absences, and terminating work group members to its committee's responsibilities. Cashiers tended to see their work as harder than that of other work groups (explored in the "Many Flavors and Many Facets" section of chapter 7), particularly in terms of customer interactions. But they were different in other ways too. Most cashiers favored the centralization of their work group policies, while members of other work groups disparaged the cashier committee structure as "becoming managers." Work groups offered both rationalized reasons for devolving duties to their internal committees (that time card checks should be coordinated with schedules, for instance) and affective ones for refusing to do so (that it was "fun" to talk about people's vacation plans during weekly work group meeting scheduling sessions). Yet no matter where they were on the continuum, that these committees were both elected and expected to rotate meant that responsibilities typically given to managers were distributed across most of the workforce.

In addition to internal work group management, grocery members carried out managerial functions in a range of committees such as the Successful Participation Committee (SPC). Other elected committees assessed and addressed security risks; evaluated and responded to community applications for donations of cash and goods; mediated interpersonal conflicts; or monitored and adjusted material resource waste (trash, recycling, and energy consumption). The most powerful managerial committee was the seven-member Intracooperative Coordinating Committee (ICC), which had been created in the mid-1990s when the board felt it was making too many day-to-day managerial decisions. Like the board, ICC members were elected annually but could be reelected for several continuous terms; unlike the board, few ICC members stood for reelection more than once or twice in a row. This was mainly because the ICC had to make difficult and often unpopular decisions, and its members found both the process of making those decisions and the reactions of the coworkers stressful. The ICC was assigned responsibility for mediating conflicts between work groups that the grocery's mediation committee could not resolve, and for maintaining the physical structure and infrastructure of the store. While the ICC had no financial authority, its decisions could have indirect financial effects on workers individually (investigating and firing a worker accused of theft who was neither suspended nor terminated by their work group) and on work groups as a whole (recommending to the board the withholding of wage allotments when the household goods work group repeatedly failed to meet cleanliness standards, which the board did).

Historically, participants in organizations with direct democratic control have struggled with what Francesca Polletta (2002) has astutely identified as the complaint of the "endless meeting": the way "leaderless" organizations are seen as demanding unpaid labor, and often in increasing amounts. Such unpaid labor taxes organizational members unequally in terms of (often gendered) domestic responsibilities or (often classed) abilities to rely on unearned wealth to compensate for labor time. It can also taint donations of labor as literally stripping members' efforts of value (Kleinman 1996). The grocery, however, sidestepped these problems by recharacterizing meeting labor as work and paying workers at their hourly rates. In thus revaluing meeting participation, the grocery redistributed what another business might pay a small managerial tier across its whole workforce.

In addition to meetings, this redistribution of responsibility and reward was woven into other forms of communication. Grocery members were expected—and paid—to spend fifteen minutes per shift reading various work-related documents: their own work group's communication log, weekly meeting minutes of the board and the ICC, and ad hoc minutes of any other committee that might affect their work. These minutes were not mere summaries, but were usually verbatim accounts of the deliberations of each meeting, and thus allowed workers to review not only the decisions but also how they were made and who had made them. While not every worker seemed to fulfill these expectations, I regularly saw people eating meals in the workers' lounge with an open binder of meeting minutes in front of them.

Management accountability. Because management was both participatory in work groups and representative in committees, managerial accountability was necessary in both ways. Within and between work groups, accountability was expected to be both deliberative and informal. I noted this deliberative norm in the verbatim meeting minutes of the ICC, where workers attempted to address a rash of personal and store thefts from a "backstage" area shared by the spatially-adjacent cooler, produce, and cheese work groups. The thefts were attributed to outsiders sneaking in through a street door that, complained a cooler worker, the produce work group kept unlocked for the ease of their numerous, staggered vendor deliveries. The ICC responded to the complaint with a policy requiring all vendors to use the gated loading dock, and thus for workers to unlock and relock the gate for each delivery. The produce work group reacted angrily to being asked to do extra work. Colleen Norris, a cheese work group member of the ICC, reported at the next ICC meeting that Sarah Drum, a produce worker, had belligerently told her, "It's not gonna happen." When Colleen attempted to explain the thinking behind the policy, she said another produce worker, Michael Goetz, erupted, "'Who do you think you are, the fucking police? What do you

know about anything in produce or receiving? No, it's not going to fucking happen. You should mind your own business and maybe you should join produce if
you want to do whatever you want to do.' He said that I was an idiot and I told
him that he was a mean jerk. It was a really ugly situation."

Further ICC minutes revealed that some of her fellow committee members
reacted with anger. Gabriela Guinn, a personal goods worker who had been at
the grocery for over fifteen years, grumbled, "Fuck it, we tried, fine. Let One
World get ripped off because produce doesn't care." But her coworker Alana
Banks suggested discussions with produce and cooler members in a meeting two
weeks later, where she explained, "[The ICC] need[s] to have open communication with people about whatever our ideas are—so we can come up with ideas
together. Because we're not just here to tell people what to do." This meeting resulted in a compromise acceptable to all three work groups. Eduardo Secar,
a longtime member who was at the time in a romantic relationship with Gabriela,
emphasized the expectation of deliberation and collaboration between work
groups instead of direction and punishment from an overseeing body when he
thanked the ICC for addressing the problem but reproached them, "It would have
been great if you'd come to the work group right from the start."

This collaborative interaction could also be informal. Work groups, for instance, did their own hiring and set their own scheduling; there was no other body
within the organization that could require more or less staffing. But each year the
office would compile and publish a labor-to-sales ratio list, which was a break-
down of how much each work group spent on labor compared to how much it
generated in sales. Of course, non-sales-category work groups like the office or
cashiers could not be assessed this way, and it was generally understood that some
work groups, like produce, had thinner profit margins and required more hours of
prep work than one like packaged goods. But there was a lot of ribbing—and only
some of it was good-natured. Members of the household goods work group, which
sold pricy items with high markups, reported feeling under attack. This feeling of
being scrutinized by the entire membership tended to compel work groups to
scrutinize their hiring and scheduling practices, anxious as they were to keep their
labor-to-sales numbers looking healthy. Normative processes employed—but far
exceeded—formalized processes to put a check on wastefulness.

In contrast, where representative committees were being held accountable,
formalized processes were primary. This was evident in a case where a decision
regarding a work group's termination of two of its members was overturned by
the ICC and then challenged by the membership meeting. Jennifer Ruud, who
had been on the ICC at the time, exasperatedly recalled both the emotionally
taxing investigation and the subsequent frustrating and expensive accountability process afterwards:

This weird thing—this never happened before in the history of One World—the membership said, you know, "We don't trust these people making that ICC decision, especially one that big, where people get fired." And they overthrew us. [The membership] wanted to know what happened, what the [ICC] investigation was about. And they wanted to make up their minds, basically, on what happened. Which, first of all, was a *nightmare* the first time around. On the second time around, for me, I was just looking at this huge pile of money that was blowing out the window. "Here's the hair dryer, here's a stack of money. [*Laughter.*] Here you go! Here, you guys read all those minutes, have a great time!"

Jennifer complained about the cost of the process the grocery used to balance between its culture of decentralized information sharing and participatory management on one hand, and state privacy laws mandating limited access to personnel files on the other. Under advice from its lawyers, the grocery provided each person who attended that month's membership meeting with copies of the two appellant workers' personnel files—including work group and ICC meeting minutes—but only to be read on-site and during the meeting itself. At the meeting's end, all copies were collected and shredded. Because everyone was paid for the time it took the slowest reader to finish the documents, it was expensive: almost a hundred workers were paid for more than four hours of meeting time. Jennifer found it particularly frustrating "to pay people to be in a meeting and to discuss what had already been discussed *for three months* by the ICC. You know, the people they *elected* so that we don't have to have a hundred people sitting here reading the minutes!"[7]

Yet while the process struck Jennifer as costly and grossly *inefficient*, it was nonetheless highly *effective*. Not only did the membership reverse itself after this meeting to uphold the ICC's decision on the terminations, but ICC and board minutes suggest that the process increased the workers' trust in their representative bodies' decisions: for at least a few years thereafter, few workers questioned committee decisions. The ability of the membership to review the decisions of any one of its representative bodies was mainly held in reserve, but these committees were always on notice that their decisions could be scrutinized. Through the use of both informal and formalized deliberation, the grocery integrated managerial accountability at both the participative and representative levels.

Individual autonomy. Worker autonomy—or the ability to determine how and what one's work consisted of and when it was performed—was produced by both external and internal forces at the grocery. Workers tended to speak proudly and often of their autonomy as a benefit of the grocery membership, and limits to it as entirely due to direct or indirect actions by customers. Indeed, I found markedly different levels of autonomy among the workers based on how much customer contact their jobs entailed. Yet this was not an automatic outcome: work group practices also affected workers' autonomy.

The store as a whole struggled to balance workers' claims to respect and autonomy with the broader cultural ethos of "the customer is always right." Grocery workers' most common theme of self-reproach was "rude service," but that ongoing discourse did not seem to change behavior. For instance, one night as Shane, the young man I had shadowed earlier in the week, and Deb Scharf, a woman in her twenties, chatted animatedly about weekend plans across the aisle separating their registers, a customer asked Deb, "Are you open?" in what sounded to me like a friendly voice. Deb, however, shifted gears abruptly, her face suddenly blank, and flatly replied, "Yes. I'm open." To me, this was a prime example of "rude service." Later, though, Deb explained that she felt like the customer was telling her to get back to work and not talk to her coworkers—that she was trying to "manage" Deb. Raised by a single mother who worked as a housekeeper in the most affluent part of the Golden Valley, Deb was acutely sensitive to the ways in which the wealthy tried to compel desired behaviors from those who served them. At the time I thought it was a misunderstanding; when I had shopped at the grocery, I often could not tell if a cashier was working or not, and easily imagined myself posing the same tentative question. But what I saw as Deb's rudeness was, to her, a necessary protection of her autonomy. Elena Guzmán, another cashier, proffered a narrative to push back on what she saw as the main challenge to grocery worker autonomy: the customer service norms of non-worker-owned supermarket chains. She grew animated as she insisted, "I'm real friendly all the time, but customers are used to Safeway. They're spoiled! We have the right not to be acting. Here workers can express and be themselves. If they don't like it how we are, I'm sorry! We're humans! And it's something they need to learn." From the viewpoint of Elena and Deb, the ongoing "us versus them" struggle of service workers and customers required both sides to reframe and review customer actions as potentially oppressive and thus practice a different form of interaction.

Perhaps surprisingly, this kind of perceived direct customer pressure seemed easier for grocery workers to resist than the indirect kind. For example, workers bowed to the pressure to increase staffing in the "food season" that started in the week before Thanksgiving and only ended after New Year's Eve, even though this was a hardship for those whose family's schedules required or made attractive more time at home in these weeks. More insidious was the adoption of the rude service discourse as a form of *co-monitoring*, or the kind of surveillance among workers that could feel, as Elena put it, "like you have two hundred bosses." Elena complained about pressure from other cashiers to take fewer bathroom breaks despite what she described as medical need. Unlike "a regular job with one boss, where you can do things behind his back," Elena said, "here everyone is your boss." In this way imaginary customers were deployed to limit worker autonomy.

Having no expectation of customer contact, office members were widely regarded as the most autonomous workers, especially regarding their schedules. Once, when laughter broke out at the May Day party karaoke jam over two office workers' duet of Dolly Parton's "Nine to Five," I thought the joke was that the grocery had no "boss man" who would not let them "move ahead," per the lyrics. But I was corrected: the point was that the grocery's office workers never came in by 9:00 a.m., regardless of scheduled hours or the need to connect with East Coast vendors. I had experienced this myself on my very first morning of grocery observation when I waited over half an hour for the office worker I had arranged to shadow, who shrugged off her lateness when she eventually arrived at 10:30 a.m. And, when the surprise arrival of an out-of-town relative compelled me to cut short my last day of office observation by more than an hour, office workers teased that I had "gone native" by leaving early, that I was a "fast learner" to figure out how to "skip out" before the end of the day. There was no disagreement that office workers—housed upstairs and literally above the fray of the shop floor—were free from the demands that customers directly or indirectly put on almost all other grocery workers.

Yet there were still differences among work groups with customer contact. Work groups' official practices and informal norms, or their work group culture, also affected workers' ability to exercise discretion and creativity over their work. Both the produce and household goods work groups were based on sales categories that required both a high degree of customer interaction, and a fair amount of backstage labor (washing, prepping, and stocking of heavy and dirty fruits and vegetables in produce; constant inventory of expensive and delicate items in household goods). But I found that only the household goods work group limited worker autonomy with numerous formal rules and policies that often substituted for direct informal communication between work group members.

One afternoon during my week of shadowing household goods, recently hired Douglas Whyte was approached by Philip McGowan, who had been at the grocery for more than fifteen years. Philip gave a nervous laugh as he asked, "No apron?" Unlike most large stores (grocery or otherwise), workers were not required to wear any kind of uniform: in public meetings, most members of other work groups rejected this practice as overly conformist, and in private conversations as making them too available to customers. Household goods was one of only two work groups whose members regularly wore a store-logo apron or T-shirt to identify themselves. But Douglas calmly replied, "No apron. I don't usually wear one." Philip grimaced, "Uh, well, you're really supposed to wear one," and walked away. Douglas shrugged; he told me he thought that customers could identify him without grocery-branded clothing because, unlike others in his work group, he was always stocking or cleaning instead of talking to friends and coworkers. At the next work group meeting, Philip had an agenda item: "We all need to wear our [store-logo] aprons or T-shirts," bewildering the majority of his work group, who almost always wore one of the two items. But this, I discovered, was a common practice in household goods: a conflict between two workers was rarely direct but instead was turned into policy and rule proposals that seemed more sniping than problem solving, or in complaints to each other (or me) about issues that were never raised at meetings. The specter of customer complaint was deferred from direct communication between workers to regulating policy.

In contrast, no members of the produce work group discussed feeling watched by their coworkers, even when they were aware of failing to perform as expected. At the end of one night, Juanita, the woman who envied what she imagined as bakery workers' ability to become homeowners, and Sarah, who claimed that she had simply used produce's motto when she responded to the ICC street door edict with "It's not gonna happen," realized that they had not cleaned the produce area to work group standard. Juanita wrote, "Oops, no sweep or mop!" in the produce log book. She explained to me that her work group members would understand because two people had been absent from that shift, and "as long as you're sincere, people can't get mad at you." Indeed, produce was known for its direct—at times even blunt and contentious—communication. Direct communication was used as the rationale for hiring English/Spanish simultaneous interpretation for weekly meetings of the work group, about a third of whom were primary Spanish speakers. As a value, direct communication seemed to transform "two hundred bosses" into a more equal form of participatory management, and to push back against customers, as a laminated sign on one of the produce bins demonstrated:

> Dear customers: Please, please do not spit or leave cherry pits on our tables. It's disgusting. Thank you, -One World Produce Workers

Verging on the "rude service" other workers worried about, produce workers' direct communication enhanced their individual and group autonomy. Juanita grinned as she told me, "It's so free here. Most Americans have no idea what it could be like."

"Two hundred bosses": Benefits and drawbacks of worker control. Grocery political rights were both widely distributed—in direct and representative democratic forms of governance and management—and densely clustered, with the jurisdictions and responsibilities of organizational bodies often overlapping with each other. This intentional design did not devolve into ongoing and retaliatory battles because there was a culture of intensive deliberation and participation, because democratic election allowed grocery workers to take on more leadership when they felt the ability or duty but then lay it down without financial penalty as needed, and because so many important decisions had been delegated to the decentralized work groups. And, perhaps because so many were regularly exercising some kind of workplace political right, grocery workers tended to identify external factors, primarily embodied in customers, as the cause of perceived limits to their autonomy—despite often also being constrained by decisions made among their direct and representative organizational bodies. Although formally distinct, workers perceived little separation between themselves and their leadership bodies similar to the lower boundaries noted in more participatory organizations (Polletta 2002) but also retained the kind of concentrated decision-making ability seemingly necessary for "efficiency" under capitalism (Kasmir 1996; Taylor 1994).

The struggles between workers described above make it clear that the grocery was no utopia. Yet its innovations offered real advances in the long struggle to balance autonomy and democracy with survival in capitalist markets. But were these advances evenly enjoyed within the cooperative? In the next section, I take up the question of how economic and political rewards were shaped by class, race/ethnicity, and gender and how the grocery addressed inequalities and exclusions.

Inequality and Inclusion: Class, Race/Ethnicity, and Gender

Unlike the bakery, the grocery had not been founded specifically to address class or any other kind of inequalities, and, as stories from its early days (see the "Crisis" subsection of the "One World Natural Grocery" section in chapter 3) make clear, it was unexceptional in preventing power from collecting around charismatic white men. Yet few of these patterns or processes remained by the turn of the twenty-first century.

Class

Like the bakery, the grocery had minimal class-based workplace inequalities.[8] Also like the bakery, experience was the most important factor in grocery hiring and this tended to privilege people from working-class backgrounds who had done working-class jobs. Although people spoke admiringly of workers who brought ideas from other cooperatives—a work history more common to middle-class people at the time—almost all members I spoke with recalled ranking previous job experience over cooperative experience when they had been on a hiring committee. Chris Badger, a white, middle-class man in packaged food, first said that he liked candidates who could "be pretty much self-managing, you know, or work in a nonhierarchical situation." But he immediately followed this by claiming, "If a person's got that, great, that saves you a couple of steps. But it wasn't something that would make or break an application." I found that, with the exception of teenagers, those hired within the past five years had done similar work in non-cooperative businesses before coming to the grocery. Because most grocery jobs were primarily working-class occupations—cashier, retail sales, maintenance—"previous experience" increased the likelihood of hiring working-class people.[9]

Valuing experience offered cooperative job access to working-class people at both the grocery and the bakery, but it was the grocery's wage policies that preserved class equality after the initial hire. When the state minimum wage was $6.75 per hour, grocery workers were all started at $11.35 and accrued similar proportions of the hourly wage allotments each year. This meant that there were even smaller differences between high and low earners at the grocery than at the bakery: the office's personnel coordinator (a white law school graduate in her thirties from an upper-middle-class Midwestern neighborhood) and the cashier hired the same week (a Latinx teenager from the grocery's working-class Edgefield neighborhood with a newly minted high school diploma) earned within a dollar per hour of each other two years later. The most common way in which class is reproduced within workplaces—by allocating greater value and reward to the skills and certifications associated with middle-class life paths than to those associated with working-class paths (Acker 2006a)—was largely absent.

Political power had a somewhat more classed aspect: grocery members with middle-class backgrounds—and associated skills and certifications—were more likely to be elected to the board or the ICC. To some extent this was because the office hired more of the small proportion of grocery members with college degrees (roughly 10 percent of the membership total) than other work groups.[10] But as a white, middle-class office worker known as the Doctor claimed, "You know, you're in the office, money goes by you, so you're aware of it and so you want to participate in that kind of stuff." He felt that the day-to-day tasks of office workers, rather than class background, made them more likely to choose to run for leadership offices. The office, he said, was "seen not so much *as* the boss but *wanting to be* the boss. The people that work in produce would never want to push paper. It's like, 'Ugh, these paper pushers, these number crunchers! Why would you want to do that?'" The Doctor contended that spatial arrangement combined with ideas about—rather than material relations of—class to separate office workers from other parts of the grocery, the "societal constructs that get imposed, that we bring, each of us individually, to this work environment because of our upbringing, our surroundings, because we grow up in Western capitalism. We've had ingrained in us these societal constructs of top-down management. So somebody working on the floor looks up at the office and says, 'Those motherfuckers.'"

Yet this resentment did not stop the membership from repeatedly electing office members to the board. In part, this might be because grocery power was still largely in working-class hands: most decision-making power was distributed to the work groups, and most of the members of those work groups were working class. Culturally, too, there were organizational aspects that returned control to workers. Grocery members valued passion in their elected leadership regardless of experience. Jennifer, the white, working-class woman who had complained about the instance of membership-meeting oversight of the ICC as akin to blowing money out a window with a hair dryer, had never held decision-making power in her previous natural food store jobs. Nevertheless, she ran for the ICC as a member of the refrigerated food work group because "I do have really good ideas, I believe. I really feel like a lot of things at One World could go better. And I talk to people about it. And they're like, 'Yeah, yeah! You should do something about it!'" In fact, Jennifer's experience with the two contested terminations on the ICC led to a successful run for the board, where she helped enact bylaw changes regarding how work groups fired their members. "Yeah, I like to play boss, I guess!" she laughed. "I'm bossy! Well, I mean, I'm just—I just care a lot about how our business is run." Although the association of leadership with being "bossy" could be problematic, it did not prevent political power from being accessible. For working-class grocery members, participatory governance combined with distributed management to ensure a high degree of equity in earnings and decision-making.

Race/Ethnicity

Like the bakery, the grocery was more ethnoracially diverse than its founding membership had been and had become demographically very similar to other large California supermarkets (Dube and Lantsberg 2004). Yet unlike the bakery, whites were not only the majority of cooperative workers, at 62 percent, but were a disproportionate majority, one that did not reflect the neighborhood or county. This disparity was not simply because whites from the old days stayed longer: Black workers had a similar average tenure of eight years, and Latinx workers were only two years behind, at six. Rather, there was a

TABLE 5.1   Grocery work group by race/ethnicity and gender in 2003

	WORK GROUP SIZE	WHITE MEN	WHITE WOMEN	MEN OF COLOR	WOMEN OF COLOR	WORK GROUP, % MEN	WORK GROUP, % WHITE
Bakery	4	2	2	0	0	50	100
Bulk	14	6	3	0	5	43	64
Cashiers	31	10	8	3	10	42	58
Cheese	12	5	5	0	2	42	83
Customer service	9	0	2	4	3	44	22
Herbs	4	1	1	1	1	50	50
Household goods	10	1	6	1	2	20	70
Maintenance	7	4	1	2	0	86	71
Office	18	7	6	2	3	50	72
Packaged food	20	6	5	5	4	55	55
Personal care goods	15	1	4	3	7	27	33
Produce	18	4	6	3	5	39	56
Refrigerated food	8	1	5	2	0	38	75
Vitamins	14	10	1	1	2	79	79
Totals	*184*	*58*	*55*	*27*	*44*	*46*	*61*

lingering hiring privilege enjoyed by whites, at least partially facilitated through personal networks. While people of color were benefited more by the intercession of family members (of fourteen such connections between workers, only five were between whites), whites benefited more from having "a good word" put in by a nonrelative worker. As Chris put it, "When there's a one-foot stack of [job] applications, that helps." In this way, the white majority reproduced itself.

Yet although the grocery did not reflect local demographics, it was, like the bakery, a relatively ethnoracially balanced organization. Indeed, only two work groups had such a large proportion of whites that a "tokenized" situation of unfavorable attention and stereotyping in day-to-day interactions might be expected (Kanter 1977). As table 5.1 shows, more than half the grocery workers were in ethnoracially balanced work groups (no more than 60 percent of any one ethnoracial group), and there was little mapping of race and ethnicity onto the good/bad job dichotomy (primarily regarding customer contact and physical arduousness). For instance, janitorial labor—an occupational category dominated by Black and Latinx workers in California and typically performed in isolation from all other workers—was distributed to each work group. Furthermore, there was very little difference in earnings between ethnoracial groups: while the *hourly* earnings of people of color were fractionally less than those of whites, the *annual* earnings of whites were fractionally less than those of other ethnoracial groups due to working about two fewer hours per week on average than all other ethnoracial groups.

In terms of governance, there were similarities between ethnoracial and classed access to grocery power: like middle-class people, whites were overrepresented on the board of directors. In the summer of 2003 only one woman of color held a seat alongside two white women and four white men, and this was criticized as typical by several workers of color and white workers. Yet because the membership meeting had (and sometimes used) veto power over board decisions, this state of affairs did not mean white domination in the same way it might elsewhere. Further, authority usually accorded to managers was far more ethnoracially diversified at the grocery: the 2003 ICC composition consisted of one white man, two white women, three women of color, and a man of color— a composition typical of the ICC and in striking contrast to most US firms, where it has been estimated that 60 percent of managers are white men, 19 percent are white women, 14 percent are men of color, and 7 percent are women of color (Elliot and Smith 2004).[11]

These mixed effects were also found in terms of grocery workers' autonomy. On one hand, the highly autonomous office work group had a higher proportion of whites (72 percent) than did either the workforce as a whole or the cashiers, the least autonomous work group (58 percent). On the other hand, five sales work groups had higher proportions of white members than the office, including, at 83 percent white, the cheese work group, which was one of the least autonomous due to an extremely constrained workspace and to the degree and nature of customer interaction. Three work groups—including fiercely autonomous produce—had higher proportions of people of color than cashiers.

Overall it appeared that while ethnoracial privilege had not been eliminated from the grocery, it had been significantly reduced: whites had some advantages in access to power and resources, but these were neither deep nor pervasive. Whites did not make more money, did not have more day-to-day control, and did not have significantly more job autonomy—a notable difference from the ethnoracial state of affairs in the American workplace (Stainback and Tomaskovic-Devey 2012).

Gender

Like class and ethnoracial inequalities at the grocery, gender inequalities were minimized but not absent.[12] On one hand, occupational segregation was hard to find. Women made up a slight majority of the grocery's workforce and contributed 53 percent of the cooperative's annual hours (large Californian supermarkets at the time had roughly the opposite gender ratios; Dube and Lantsberg 2004).[13] Women were integrated throughout the work groups (see table 5.1), and only four work groups would not be considered gender balanced. Even the four-person maintenance work group, the in-house construction crew, had a woman member. More broadly, the grocery was widely known for flaunting gender norms: women workers' hairy legs and armpits were the basis of a regular and mostly good-humored repertoire of outsiders' jokes, and although my fieldwork did not focus on customers, when I was on the floor I could not help but over-hear customer comments about how many women were doing gender-transgressive work like lifting heavy boxes or driving the forklift. Within work groups, tasks were far less stereotyped than might be expected in a grocery (Skaggs 2008). For instance, the small proportion of men in the household goods work group did more of the emotionally intensive labor of floor sales while women's labor was more physical (receiving) or analytical (buying).

On the other hand, despite the significant reduction in gendered work at the grocery, women's annual earnings were about 10 percent lower than men's, al-though this varied by race/ethnicity, from more than double the average gap be-tween African American men and women, to only slightly greater earning by white men than white women, to almost no difference between Latinx workers, to an almost exact reversal in the average gap between Asian American and Pacific Islander, Indigenous, and other ethnoracially marked men and women.[14] As at the bakery, length of tenure was part of the story, with white and Black men aver-aging an extra year's membership over similarly ethnoracialized women. But the opposite was true of the relationship between Latinas and Latinos, and average tenure was almost indistinguishable among other ethnoracial groups. Indeed, in terms of hourly earnings, the gender gap for the workforce as a whole was tiny, ranging from just over $1.50 per hour between African Americans to less than ten cents per hour between Latinx workers. Rather than resulting from tenure disparities, the gendered gap in annual earnings was largely due to a women's choices to schedule fewer working hours: with only one exception, all the women (and men) I spoke with claimed that their schedules corresponded pretty con-sistently to the number of hours they wanted to work. Although it would be a mistake to attribute this gap to individual free will—the differently gendered so-cial expectations of family and domestic responsibilities are well documented (Jacobs and Gerson 2004; Sirianni and Negrey 2000)—it was also not the case that grocery women were blocked by managers' gendered allocations of time or the kinds of external conflicts with rigid work schedules that have been amply demonstrated to limit women's employment or promotion (Acker 1990; Blum 1991; Clawson and Gerstel 2014; Correll and Bernard 2010; Hossfeld 1990; Kelly et al. 2010; Lee 1998; Salzinger 2003). This was made clear as I shadowed office work group member Betty Penrose, a white, working-class woman in her forties with three school-age children and a civil servant husband. I discovered that Betty had easily scheduled her graphic design tasks around her children: arriving after bringing the youngest to school, leaving before 3:00 p.m. to pick him up, and then coming back to the grocery after spending the afternoon and dinnertime with her family, often working past 10:00 p.m. And this was not just the notable flexibility of the office. I noted how an Asian American woman in the cheese work group took regular nighttime cleaning shifts to give her daytime hours with a disabled family member, and a Latina cashier worked six-hour shifts to allow her to trade off childcare with their father. That is, whatever barriers existed for grocery women were not organizational.

There also seemed to be few other barriers in terms of political rights. While the board often had slightly more men than the general grocery population, the ICC regularly had more women (significantly, women of color) than would be proportional for the workforce. While one of the most autonomous work groups, maintenance, was three-fourths men, the office was evenly divided by gender, and the two work groups with the least autonomy, cashiers and cheese, were almost identical in gender composition to the store population as a whole (see table 5.1). Politically, there was very little correspondence between the greater labor market opportunities conferred by masculinity (and particularly white masculinity) and power at the grocery.

Summary: Growth and Egalitarianism

As the grocery entered its third decade, it had, like the bakery, included those largely left out of the countercultural collectivist cooperatives—particularly people of color across class and gender, and working-class whites across gender. These were jobs that provided both economic empowerment and an unusual degree of control over their long-term and day-to-day fates. With average job tenure nearly twice as long as that of the average American worker, it seemed to work for its members.

Like the bakery, the grocery offered a living model of working-class and ethnoracially diverse worker ownership. But where the bakery demonstrated how labor could *hire* management for its benefit, the grocery exemplified management *by* labor, showing how a business could be both effectively and democratically run by the kind of people written off in business schools as in need of the expert financial and labor supervision (ideally of the type developed by those business schools). Where the bakery set up practices and processes that allowed men of color and (mostly white) women to access their benefits, the grocery reduced the salience of race/ethnicity and gender to jobs and allowed for broader inclusion.

These achievements on the part of the grocery were accomplished through its densely clustered and highly formalized democracy. That is, its mixture of inclusive participative governance and management in work groups and membership meetings allowed all workers to have a voice in matters in which they had a stake; and its representative governance and management via the board and the ICC was able to act more nimbly and decisively without compromising its participative side. The success of this hybrid democratic self-management was made possible by the grocery's formalization of organizational policies and structures to preserve and protect this balance of democratic processes. Enmeshed and codified in organizational practice, the grocery was able to function within the demands of the market but also remain accountable to its diverse worker needs and desires.

Like the bakery, though, the grocery was not utopia. Grocery workers struggled financially more than bakery workers, earning less but living in a part of the Golden Valley with a higher cost of living. Although I was sympathetic to the creation of nonstandard shifts that allowed workers to have an inspiring work/life balance, I found myself frustrated with what felt like the shortsighted choices of grocery workers to undermine their chances of financial stability (including homeownership) with short workweeks or extended leaves to pursue artistic or personal projects. The grocery also employed a lower proportion of workers of color than did the bakery despite the grocery's location in more multiracial Edgefield, and whites held a disproportionate share of governance power within the grocery. Despite regular self-castigation by the white membership, there was little headway made to institute practices like ranked voting, which has been found to benefit white women and people of color (Barber 2000; John, Smith, and Zack 2018). And while all workers had more scheduling autonomy than their counterparts elsewhere, such autonomy was far more pronounced for workers with more elite class and educational backgrounds. Despite significant advances in generating empowerment and egalitarian relations, the grocery had not solved all the economic and social problems of twenty-first-century life under capitalism.

Nevertheless, the grocery demonstrated that broad-based and highly participative democratic control is not incompatible with either effective organization or a diverse and even unharmonious workforce. Like the earlier generation of cooperatives, it aimed at equalizing reward regardless of background or certification, maximizing autonomy as feasible, and balancing paid labor with all the other things a worker does to make life worth living. But, unlike that earlier generation, its relatively flat structure did not subtly concentrate power in the hands of dominant social groups. The preservation of egalitarianism resulted from a degree of formalization entirely foreign to the countercultural collectivist era. That is, while far from perfect, the grocery resolved many long-standing and seemingly immutable inequalities at the intersection of class, race/ethnicity, and gender through its specific combination of organizational processes.

Viewed together, the bakery and the grocery provided strong evidence that working-class people have no need of "a class of masters employing a class of hands" (Marx 1864, 11). Both cooperatives harnessed the tacit knowledge of on-the-job experience and learning to organizational formalization, with distinct expertise-based jobs and jurisdictions and a multitude of policies and procedures enshrined in volumes of written documents, to become successful, where "success" meant both a viable business and the delivery of rewards to workers. In short, both organizations had *bureaucratized*. The main difference in how they did this was the organization of power: hierarchically at the bakery and in densely clustered democratic form at the grocery. As I will argue in chapter 6, although hierarchy is generally seen as inherent to bureaucracy, nonhierarchical organizations can be proactively examined as bureaucratic variations. And, can be proactively examined as that chapter will argue, such variation is deeply consequential for organizational inequality and its remedy.

MANAGERIAL AND PARTICIPATORY BUREAUCRACIES

Varieties of Inequality Regimes

Sometimes in a membership meeting you'll hear, "Oh, I think that management has too much power." Okay, well, define that. In what way? And it always comes back, "Well, I made a suggestion at a work group meeting, and they didn't implement it." [*Chuckles.*] And it's like, "Well, wait a minute here. There's a difference between input and participating in the decision-making, rather than making that decision." And when you decide that you're going to have pay differentiation built into your system, and you're rewarding responsibility—i.e., making decisions—[the manager] knows they're going to be accountable for their decisions. The input that you gave doesn't necessarily mean that you're going to be held accountable!

—Keith Assis, People's Daily Bread Bakery

There's a difference between a leader and a ruler. Leaders take initiative to get things done. A ruler's someone whose permission you need to get something done. So I don't have a problem with leadership. . . . To me, that just means people have faith in themselves. They participate. And that to me is the greatest thing about One World, is that people don't step on you when they disagree with you. You know? We work it out. And then when you see that your ideas are heard, and sometimes they get implemented, I, personally, I feel like a capable person. I feel like I can get more done, I have more confidence in myself, because I have to take this responsibility.

—Jan Bridges, One World Natural Grocery

In chapters 4 and 5, I described how People's Daily Bread Bakery and One World Natural Grocery created economic rewards, distributed day-to-day and long-term authority over work processes, and remedied and/or reproduced social inequality within their respective organizations. Both cooperative firms created stable jobs for their ethnoracially diverse and primarily working-class memberships. But there were also important differences: gender and ethnoracial inequalities were greater at the bakery than at the grocery, and—despite having a workforce twice the size of the bakery's—the grocery's management was distributed and exercised by the entire workforce while the bakery concentrated it in a fairly small group of management positions. In this chapter and in chapter 7, I examine how these organizational differences contributed to the different kinds and degrees of inequality found in the cooperatives: the strong address of class inequality at the bakery that primarily benefited white men, and the weak direct address of class at the grocery that nevertheless produced surprising class egalitarianism across race/ethnicity and gender. The discussion in chapter 7 is more cultural, focusing how each cooperative produced a legitimating "worker identity," while this chapter explores the effects of organizational structure.

Together the two chapters take up different strands of what Joan Acker calls "inequality regimes," or the "loosely interrelated practices, processes, actions, and meanings that result in and maintain class, gender, and racial inequalities within particular organizations" (2006b, 443). While chapter 7 focuses on *meanings*, this chapter will analyze the *practices*, *processes*, and *actions* of inequality regimes. Research has been divided as to whether bureaucracy generates or limits inequality (Britton 2000), but it has hewed towards a "hierarchy plus formalization equals bureaucracy" model, ignoring not only the possibility of formalized but nonhierarchical bureaucracy, but also how such a bureaucracy might affect inequality outcomes. In this chapter, I contend that the combination of organizational formalization with distributed management—what I describe as *participatory bureaucracy*—provided tools and resources for the minimization of inequality within the grocery. In this way I describe it as *protective* of members of marginalized groups. In contrast, the organizational formalization of managerial hierarchy into a *managerial bureaucracy* permitted and fostered the proliferation of inequality, *subordinating* members of (most) marginalized groups.[1] This difference of organizational structure, I argue, goes a long way towards explaining why two historically similar and neighboring worker-owned cooperatives would develop such different inequality regimes.

To say that the difference in level and type of workplace inequality is largely a result of the cooperatives' bureaucracies is to make two associated claims. The first is that deeply bureaucratic effects may be overlooked in organizations that do not exhibit a specific subset of bureaucratic characteristics outlined some hundred years ago by Max Weber (1978): hierarchy, impersonal rules and documentation, and expert specialization. Organizations that lack one of these characteristics but are otherwise highly rationalized are too quickly labeled antibureaucratic and thus assigned the qualities of informal relations, personal allegiances, and a lack of expertise. These antibureaucratic qualities were, indeed, claimed as a positive value by scholars of the countercultural collectivist era of collectives and worker cooperatives (see, e.g., Ferguson 1991; Iannello 1992; Jackall and Levin 1984; Rothschild and Whitt 1986) from which the bakery and grocery in this study emerged. But such a bureaucratic/ antibureaucratic bifurcation obscures a growing population of organizations that do not fit neatly in either box. Hierarchy is certainly not unique to bureaucracy, and what distinguishes bureaucratic control more than the direction of power—vertically distributed through a managerial hierarchy or horizontally across permanent and temporary democratic bodies—is organizational *rationalization*, the privileging of instrumental goals like production and profit over value-oriented or affective ones. Although the grocery did not overtly seem to exhibit bureaucratic characteristics, this chapter illuminates its highly rationalized and instrumental organizational life and thus suggests closer examination of what has been considered anti- or nonbureaucratic organization.

The second (and related) claim concerns how these different bureaucratic configurations reduce or reproduce inequality. This chapter explores bureaucratic *formalization*—the specification of rules, policies, and procedures in organizational documents—as a characteristic that operates differently when authority is organized vertically in a managerial hierarchy than when organized horizontally as distributed management, as shown in table 6.1. The different combinations of formalization and authority, I argue, reproduce and remediate inequality through different kinds of processes: the informal and flat collectivist-democratic organizations of the countercultural collectivist 1970s and 1980s were just as likely to reproduce inequality as bureaucracies. However, participatory bureaucracy—with formalized but distributed management—offers alternatives to both the inequalities of collectivist-democratic organizations and the more typical managerial variety of bureaucracy. That is, I do not contrast a bureaucratic bakery with a nonbureaucratic grocery. Instead, this chapter compares

TABLE 6.1 Authority and formalization

	FORMALIZED	INFORMAL
Vertical authority	Managerial bureaucracy	Cult
Horizontal authority	Participatory bureaucracy	Collectivist cooperative

managerial with participatory bureaucracy and explores the ways in which formalized managerialism reproduces inequalities that formalized participatory control disrupts.

The chapter begins by unpacking the meanings of bureaucracy and the variations discovered in the years since it was first proposed as an organizational type. This context helps to situate both resistance to and rationales for viewing the grocery's organizational structure as a variety of bureaucracy. I review the bureaucratic characteristics of the bakery and the grocery—described, respectively, in chapters 4 and 5—and build a more robust definition of bureaucracy by distinguishing the managerial from participatory variety. In the second section, I explore how managerial and participatory bureaucracy reproduced or reduced workplace inequality in hiring and firing, earnings, autonomy, and power and influence. The third section addresses the question of whether these inequality differences were organizational or about the people in each cooperative by looking at exceptions: the formalization of participatory management on one production shift at the bakery and its effect on ethnoracial inequality, and the de-formalization of participatory management—"structurelessness" (Freeman 1984)—in the selection of grocery buyers and its effect on gender inequality. At the end I summarize my argument about how organizational structure affects inequalities.

Varieties of Bureaucracy

What is *bureaucracy*? This originally pejorative term, meaning "government by desks," was first introduced in 1751 by Jacques-Claude Marie Vincent de Gournay, an economist and court consultant from the nascent bourgeoisie, as a specific complaint about the constraints imposed on the emerging merchant class (Harrington, Marshall, and Müller. 2006; Parker 2008). Bureaucracy's enduring signification is a more generalized sense of overregulation: getting sunk in the concrete of narrowing formal rules, the routinization of daily life, the papering over of joy with a thousand needlessly repeated tasks.

Max Weber's early twentieth-century use of the term to capture established but undertheorized post-feudal administrations was similarly a critique of the subordination of action to goals (Weber 1978). It was also descriptive of the new kinds of economic and political organizations Weber observed in turn-of-the-century northern Europe. Distinct features of modern workplaces across Europe and elsewhere came into view through Weber's paradigm: organizations composed of *specialized positions* based on *expertise and ability* instead of birth or monarchal favor; organized in a *hierarchy of authority* neatly ordering not only persons but *offices* and thus preserving official autonomy not only from below but, to some degree, from above; administered on the basis of *universally applied rules and policies* encoded in a multiplicity of *documents* instead of the whim of a monarch; and threaded along the string of a *career* where experience, rather than monarchal permission, led to promotion into more powerful and responsible positions.

Although the specific bureaucratic organization was distinct in its composition, the flow of authority downward through a hierarchy of diminishing power and jurisdiction continued the pattern of feudal life. For Weber, what was novel about bureaucracy was the logic animating this hierarchy of official power. In his bureaucratic "ideal type"—an interpretative abstraction of common and central characteristics of a class of social objects into a seemingly concrete standard of measurement (Weber 1978)—each function and practice illustrated what he saw as bureaucracy's true distinguishing feature: its "legal-rational" core, or what Ann Swidler calls "the regulation of relationships between leaders and led on the basis of principles and rules" (1973, 41). Thus, officials have power over their office and those who work within it because the rules stipulate those conditions, not because the rules were given by a monarch or spiritual leader. It is the rules that rule.

Despite Weber's assertion that ideal types were never meant to represent any one real organization (Courpasson and Clegg 2006), and despite bureaucracy's primary popular usage as "red tape" in the form of numerous procedures sparked and funneled by numerous rules and regulations, it is the hierarchical ordering of power that is most perniciously attached to the concept of bureaucracy in organizational scholarship (Iannello 1992). Other Weberian characteristics have been entirely dispensed with: no one thinks, for instance, that the American corporation has become nonbureaucratic despite the disappearance of the lifelong career within one firm (Davis 2016; Tilly 1997). But once the vertical direction of authority is shifted to a more horizontal distribution, the existence of bureaucracy is called into question.

For some scholars, the renegotiation of authority suggests entirely different kinds of organizations—for instance, the "post-bureaucratic organization," where "everyone takes responsibility for the whole" (Heckscher and Donnellon 1994, 24); the "heterarchy," where accountability maps horizontally rather than vertically onto the "patterns of knowledge and communication" and the evaluation criteria for actions shift in relation to shifts in the networks in which organizations and individual actors within them are embedded (Stark 2009, 23–24); or the "networked organization," where "constellations of social networks that are dynamic over time . . . [tie] in with the degree to which innovative knowledge can flow within the organization . . . [and] previously separated knowledge is joined" (Aalbers and Dolfsma 2015, 6–7). Such conceptualizations may beg the empirical question of whether such alternative organizational configurations manage to fully or permanently displace rationalization and hierarchy (Ames 1995; Diefenbach and Sillince 2011). Yet in all cases they infer a recognizable organizational form, bureaucracy, that, conforming to the Weberian ideal type, is regular in its features and consistent in its operation. But is that true? Similar to conceptions of capitalism as far more varied than monolithic (Block 2012), better understood as practices than a singular system (Gibson-Graham 2006), bureaucracy can be viewed as a set of variations. Indeed, the known organizational universe contains many such variations of how much power is legitimately or nominally shared with workers (Adler 2012; Ashcraft 2001; Gouldner 1954; Hales 2002). Given that, like all theory, Weber's ideal type concept was bound to its time and place (Kallinikos 2004), it is useful to reexamine nonhierarchical organizations as sites of potential—and potentially egalitarian—bureaucracy.

Rather than demanding compliance with a laundry list of bygone organizational features or attempting to generate names for each new wrinkle in organizational formation, bureaucracy itself can be better understood as the logics and discourses that organize power through a mesh of *largely explicit rules* that *govern and rationalize actors' behavior* to *create accountability and predictability* for their actions. Bureaucracies are, as Peter Blau has noted, organizations "designed to accomplish large-scale administrative tasks by systematically coordinating the work of many individuals" (1956, 14). An organization may be deficient in certain Weberian characteristics but no less bureaucratic if, on the whole, its organizational structure embodies and advances these bureaucratic logics and discourses (Baron et al. 2007; Kallinikos 2004). Indeed, Alvin Gouldner's (1954) point that these logics can shift and take new forms even in the same location is as revealing today as it was nearly seventy years ago. By viewing the grocery as a *participatory* bureaucracy—one that adopts a systematic and instrumental approach to labor coordination but also to egalitarian and empowering relations between workers—its work process rationalization is easier to see and understand.[2] Formalization can transform decentralized and democratic worker control into rationalized and productive organizational processes that preserve worker ownership.

Managerial and Participatory Bureaucracy

PEOPLE'S DAILY BREAD BAKERY: MANAGERIAL BUREAUCRACY

I initially saw my study as a contrast between a bureaucratic and an antibureaucratic worker cooperative. Indeed, the contrast of the bakery's highly rationalized organizational structure with most worker cooperatives of the time made it stand out strongly to me. In chapter 4, I described its efficient, effective, and very *familiar* delegation of authority to managers; the firmly drawn boundaries

around job and work group tasks and responsibilities; the centrality of expertise in hiring and promotion decisions; and the promotion of rules, policies, and
procedures to ensure an impersonal standard of reward or punishment. But key
to its bureaucratic status was its instrumentality, its pursuit of profit in aid of
the material empowerment of workers. As I explained in chapter 3, its worker
ownership was conceived and increasingly developed as a means towards an end:
security and stability for an endangered working class. Yet in this economically
focused instrumental goal, the bakery tended to internalize the capitalist valuation of money above all else, generating a logic of profit that legitimated its actions. Bureaucratizing was positive, in this logic, because its efficiency generated
profit that gave bakery workers what they wanted—or, at least, what they needed.

Bakery management seemed genuinely concerned about protecting the primary asset working-class people possess—their bodies—and the bakery's commitment to safety was enshrined in formal (and informal) documents everywhere.
Signs in every work area prominently displayed the number of days that had
passed without a work group accident or injury; ergonomic and health posters
were placed in all break rooms and bathrooms; handmade safety illustrations
from a children's competition were scattered throughout the company; workers
sported bakery logo T-shirts with slogans such as "People's Daily Bread Bakery:
Our Success Is No Accident!"

Safety was also policy: workers received encouragement and reward for completing "near miss" reports any time they spotted a safety concern. This could be a
piece of equipment left out of place, a wet floor, a worker not following safety protocols, a potential repetitive strain risk or anything else that was out of compliance
with the safety rules in which workers were regularly drilled. The reports that
workers filled out would be reviewed and rectified by the assistant manager or, if
beyond their scope of authority, passed on to the work group manager for remedia-
tion. After the manager reviewed the problem and its remedy, they would write a
brief report for Greybo Sofer, the white, working-class woman who had become the
safety director. She would often follow up with observation of the effectiveness of
the remedy, and then pass her report on to the white, upper-middle-class CEO,
Herbert Gubbins, at the top of the managerial hierarchy. This level of formalization
was *effective*: accidents were well below average for a bakery of its size, saving up to
$200,000 annually in insurance payments. Production workers themselves com-
pared their conditions to those of other bakeries, noting that unlike Hostess workers they knew, everyone at People's Daily Bread Bakery had all of their fingers.

But it was not only safety that was bureaucratized. As Herbert explained, "We
became more formalized in our management . . . we document *everything*. We feel
highly confident that if something is being done wrong here, we will change it and
fix it. We don't want anybody to be treated capriciously." Although it had, like the

grocery, started out in the late 1970s as an organization suspicious of bureaucracy—strongly committed to decentralized democratic control and the power of friendship to compel good organizational citizenship—by the time of my study the bakery functioned as a largely conventional managerial bureaucracy. Indeed, its managerialism was grounded in rules, policies, and procedures that did not stem from a need to see itself as a "legitimate alternative" (Kleinman 1996) or even a legitimate traditional business (DiMaggio and Powell 1983), but to address the problems of its past: the unequal access to power and resources enjoyed by the more charismatic or easygoing described in chapter 3. The bakery was attempting to be meritocratic, to allocate rewards and risk through impersonal criteria of ability and performance. Yet, as the next section shows, the formalization of managerial hierarchy was unable to function in a truly meritocratic way.

ONE WORLD NATURAL GROCERY: PARTICIPATORY BUREAUCRACY

In contrast to the bakery, the grocery could be hard to recognize as bureaucratic. As I explained in the "Political Rights" section of chapter 5, the grocery had an unusually wide delegation of authority to the membership, a variety of democratic processes in each of the work groups, and impermanent elected committees rather than permanent managerial positions. There were far more permeable boundaries between positions than is typical of a bureaucratic organization chart. For instance, Burgundy Levine, a white, working-class man who was the nominal president of the board of directors and who indeed took on projects that made good use of the expertise he had developed in finance and city regulations, could be found just as often consulting with shoppers regarding the best nutritional supplements for their bowel impairments as with the grocery's bankers. Office workers often took cashier shifts during the busy early winter holidays. There was no upward trajectory of power: after the emotionally taxing three years on the personnel-oriented Intracooperative Coordinating Committee (ICC) reported by Jennifer Ruud (see chapter 5), she happily chose not to run again but was instead exploring running for the financially oriented board of directors.[3] When a proposal to introduce some degree of permanent positional management came up at a membership meeting I observed, shouts of "Go work somewhere else!" proceeded its overwhelming defeat in a vote. That is, the grocery's organizational status did not fully conform to Weber's ideal type model in terms of hierarchy, specialization, or career.

Yet at its core the grocery was all about the rationalization of organizational economic life—the creation of *effective* (if not strictly efficient) processes for running a successful business that aimed to empower workers and minimize inequality. Capitalist logics make profit seem like the primary—if not sole—

legitimate activity of business, but worker ownership reframes profit as a source of worker empowerment. That the grocery was not always entirely profit oriented was due to its instrumental pursuit of worker empowerment more broadly conceived: material, but *also* nonmaterial. Numerous empirical studies have demonstrated that workers want far more than increased pay; they want respect, creativity, autonomy, authentic connection to others, safety, security, and a sense of the intrinsic value of their labor (Berry and Schneider 2011; Blauner 1966; Freeman and Rogers 2006; Gouldner 1954; Hacker 1989; Hodson 2001; Kalleberg 2011; Lamont 2000; Nishii 2013; Padavic 1992; Sallaz 2002; Schilt 2010; Smith 2001; Stacey 2011; Turco 2016; Vallas 2003). As a worker cooperative, the grocery's organizational structure was constructed to pursue this wider set of worker wants and needs. And, in aid of such goals, the grocery incorporated what are arguably the most rationalized characteristics of bureaucracy: the use of specified technical expertise as impersonal criteria for filling positions; the creation and use of rules, policies, and procedures to direct workers' actions; and the use of written documents to instantiate these other characteristics.

For instance, it was not the case that there was no specialization or division of labor. Although roughly one-third of grocery workers had at least one regular shift in another work group and another third occasionally picked up a shift in a work group when needed, work group jurisdiction was generally clear—and if it were not, the ICC would step in to help work groups clarify, as the case of the loading dock door and the conflict between the produce, refrigerated food, and cheese work groups illustrated in the "Political Rights" section of chapter 5. The grocery delegated hiring to three-person elected (and typically rotating) committees of workers who were required to learn a basic level of local and national employment law, and these committees then used job descriptions developed in work group meetings to choose between applicants (see figure 3.1 in chapter 3). While I was unable to observe an actual hiring meeting, former hiring committee members reported looking for related job experience or training, and indeed the only grocery workers I spoke to without such experience or training had been at the store since its days as a small collective or were teenagers. That is, while countercultural collectivist worker cooperatives were staffed on a moral and social basis, grocery staffing decisions were far more likely to rest on an applicant's skills and abilities as a worker.

Bureaucratic policy making, developed in representative bodies like the board or the ICC, or in decentralized ones like work groups, was also a key feature of the grocery. From the grocery's orientations and the buddy program that walked new workers through the grocery's idiosyncratic organizational structure and culture, to policies that encouraged workers to purchase protective clothes or gear for reimbursement, to procedures that existed for individuals or groups in conflict to find mediation and resolution, rules and policies mobilized and disciplined workers' actions. Indeed, as chapter 5 described, the sheer volume of grocery policies had been determined to be more than any worker could be expected to grasp on their own, and instead required five separate orientation sessions. This also applied to terminations: policies required work groups' three-member committees to first offer verbal and written warnings before a vote could be held at a weekly membership meeting to terminate employment and cooperative membership.

Finally, all rules, policies, and procedures were thoroughly documented in handbooks, handouts, and examinations. What did not appear there was literally in the face of workers as they made their way to the kitchen or the lounge: numerous eye-level bulletin boards presented everything from meeting minutes and agendas (some with notes from workers who were not members of that work group asking for time to speak or consideration of an issue), to advertisements for workers' side projects (some more artistic, others more commercial), competition-generating work group labor-to-sales ratios, to local and national labor and safety regulations. There were also binders full of verbatim meeting minutes, including (as instances in chapter 5 show) informal teasing or cursing between meeting participants. Work group minutes were primarily in English only, but those of the board, the ICC, and the membership meeting were translated into Spanish and collected in an additional binder. And while binders certainly had the potential to be ignored and forgotten, I consistently observed work group members reading and writing in their work group's logs, and also often saw members of other work groups using them for information or discussion. Interaction with documents was a regular and routinized part of grocery life.

Together these three characteristics produce organizational *formalization*, or the explicit and accessible system of rules, processes, and procedures governing action within and operations of an organization (Blau 1956; Walsh and Dewar 1987). This formalization cannot be overlooked when considering the grocery as a bureaucracy, or assessing its ability to avoid the inequalities of earlier "structureless" cooperatives. For instance, produce worker Sarah Drum, a white, working-class woman, and Juanita Cole, an African American, working-class woman, described policy formalization as key to distributed management in their work group when they explained how they had come to the decision to fire a coworker. Sarah teased Juanita about having an overly developed work ethic when she referred to Juanita's military job history ("The soldier! The drill sergeant!"), but came around to Juanita's view that a recent internal hire, a man whose size they had mistaken for strength and willingness to do physical labor, needed more than the verbal appeal they had made to him to "pull his weight." When a written warning they collaborated on for their three-person committee failed to effect changes, they called for a practice that had recently been developed and written into work group policy: a vote for continued support in the work group meeting. This vote of confidence replaced a previous practice of a vote of no confidence, which had required the emotionally difficult task of publicly announcing one's perception of a coworker's incompetence. With abstentions now counted as negative votes, terminations were reported as easier to make. It was policy, not individual personality, that allowed this change to happen. In the documentation and dissemination of rules, policies, and procedures, formalization acted as an important agent in the grocery's coordination of labor.

While the grocery was not easily recognizable as a bureaucracy due to its distributed management—the relatively flat and decentralized distribution of authority described in chapter 5—its near total embrace of formalization rationalized almost all corners of the organization. Although far more participatory than typical bureaucracies, this was an organization that, indeed, systematically coordinated the labor of many.

A Tale of Two Bureaucracies

Both cooperatives introduced organizational formalization as part of their commitment to worker ownership and their desires to overcome countercultural collectivist-era problems. The bakery's rationalization in pursuit of material empowerment for its workers justified its managerial bureaucratic structure, while the grocery's inclusion of nonmaterial empowerment justified both bureaucratization and distributed management. But the different ways formalization operated within distributed and hierarchical management systems were not only felt in day-to-day job experience but also in how—and by whom—power could be accessed. The next section explores both similarities and divergences, and particularly divergences in terms of gender and ethnoracial inequalities among the working-class members of both cooperatives. These, as I will show, are issues that emerge from the subordinating effects of formalized hierarchical control and the protective effects of formalized participatory control.

Varieties of Inequality

Theories of bureaucracy's inequality effects have been contradictory. On one hand are claims that bureaucracy requires and promotes inequality. Kathy Ferguson (1984), for instance, theorizes bureaucracy's inherent masculinity in a power binary, requiring domination and submission and thus "feminizing" all those who are subordinated by the power hierarchy; Catherine Alter posits a clear distinction between the "diverging organizational objectives—social equality or technical efficiency" of democracy and bureaucracy (1998, 262). This gender analysis is broadened into a more general one of domination supported by empirical findings of gendered, classed, and ethnoracialized inequalities of autonomy, power, and resources (e.g., Blauner 1966; Collins 1997; England et al. 1988; Kennelly 1999). But on the other hand, as Weber himself notes, "Bureaucratic organization has usually come into power on the basis of a leveling of economic and social differences" (1946, 224), and indeed other empirical studies have found that that bureaucratic organizations are more likely than nonbureaucratic organizations to level such inequalities (e.g., Eisenstein 1995; Martin 2003; Reinelt 1995; Reskin 2000; Sirianni 1993; Wickham et al. 2008). As Dana Britton notes, "under some circumstances, more bureaucratized settings may be less oppressively gendered than those that also exhibit informal and/or collegial structural characteristics" (2000, 423). We might ask if they might also be less oppressively ethnoracialized and classed.

Further, just as the theorization of bureaucracy itself has either glossed over its significant variations, or reified them (and itself) as distinctly different organizational forms, so too has analysis of bureaucracy's inequality effects presumed a stable and consistent set of characteristics. This is most commonly found in studies that conflate formalization with hierarchy, focusing on the minimization of informal networks used by historically dominant actors and the increased utilization of formal processes for inclusion and advancement (e.g., DeHart-Davis 2009; Roth and Sonnert 2011; Wickham et al. 2008). Yet, as Alexandra Kalev and Vincent Roscigno point out, "in the real world there is some level of disconnect between how organizations officially operate, what actors do, how they interpret rules, and whether the rules are actually applied equally" (2016, 115). Bias, they note, can be built into the very procedures formalized in organizations. But bias on whose part, and how does it get there? The difference between formalization and hierarchy, then, is how these policies get put into place, whose viewpoint gets represented in the process, and who gets a say in how the policies and processes are used. These issues require us to ask specific questions about the bakery: How did the their bureaucratic variation affect workers' empowerment materially (i.e., access to jobs and earnings) and nonmaterially (i.e., autonomy, authority, and influence)?

Managerial Bureaucracy and Inequality at People's Daily Bread Bakery

As I described in chapter 4, the bakery's introduction of a managerial structure helped it attract capital, stabilize pay and turnover, and extend membership beyond its almost exclusively white and middle-class founders. Yet, hiring, job type, and pay coalesced in gendered and ethnoracialized patterns. Because women were primarily absent from manual labor, the most common kind of bakery work, they had a very small share of bakery jobs; although Latinx men were over-represented in bakery employment, they were clustered in the most physically strenuous jobs. In contrast, whites were overrepresented in the best-paid and most autonomous jobs. In this section, I explore how the formalization of managerial hierarchy contributed to these conditions and functioned to subordinate certain populations of the bakery workforce.

BAKERY HIRING

Research (e.g., Ridgeway 2011) has revealed the difficulty of overcoming or removing implicit biases, and at the bakery these biases were obscured by its formalization of hierarchical authority. Bakery managers' individual biases—just as likely implicit as explicit—about who could or should be performing certain duties were buried in the formalization of the hierarchical hiring process itself. In the same way as Charlie Navarro, the Latinx, working-class production manager, had instantly offered a worker-side gendered preference explanation for his work group's gender homogeneity (see the "Gender" section of chapter 4), white, middle-class office manager Pam Jorgeson also saw her work group's gender uniformity as an issue of workers' individual choices. "Most men don't like to work in an office where it's all women," she claimed, ignoring the presence of Hispanic,[4] middle-class personnel director Keith Assis less than three yards away, whose desk and duties were squarely situated in the office despite reporting directly to the CEO instead of to Pam. A day later she ignored her part in the construction of this uniformity as she described her subtle pressures to resign on the last man who worked under her.

Pam and Charlie's beliefs in tight links between worker-side gender preferences (and abilities) and the type of work performed were unaffected by experiences that contradicted these beliefs—even to the extent that they could each report conflicting information to me without questioning themselves. Even cruder versions of gendered work preference/ability theory were advanced by assistant managers in both work groups: that men did not like to sit still all day, or that women did not like to get dirty. These submerged, stable beliefs permeated the hiring process in often unobserved ways, acting invisibly to segregate labor by gender.

The transformation of individual bias into job segregation was a result not only of workplace hierarchy but also of its formalization. For instance, white, working-class office worker Linda Kemp's complaint in the first pages of chapter 4 about a coworker's inability to transfer to shipping was not directed at white, working-class shipping manager Sherry Ferrar's personal bias but at the "plug-and-play" policies that resulted from being "so big now." But this combination—Sherry's seemingly gender-neutral requirement of certified forklift skills in the job description and the externally gendered labor market—all but ensured her of a workforce of men, many of whom would resist supervision by someone who was most likely the first woman to manage them.

Charlie's formalization of "related work experience" in production job descriptions was not identical to Sherry's requirement of a certificate, but it similarly gendered the hiring process. Many Latinx production workers had previous landscaping, rather than food processing, experience. Charlie explained that these experiences showed an ability to do "hot and dirty" work, apparently unlike local Latinas' housecleaning work histories. Charlie's formalization of job experience requirements to include "manual" but not "domestic" labor ignored the dirty work, heavy lifting, and acute time constraints that characterize housecleaning (Hondagneu-Sotelo 2007), and invisibly—and thus unassailably—further gendered his hiring process.

Charlie was also concerned about injury when it came to hiring women. He described an unnamed former worker who "almost got chopped in half" when she failed to properly disconnect the power from the mixing bowl before climbing inside to clean it. Greybo also offered injury as explanation for women's absence from production in our initial interview, but two years later she created a spreadsheet going back more than a decade that revealed that not only were women—white and Latina—injured less often, but their injuries resulted in less medical treatment and lost work time. Indeed, in the interests of safety and savings, Charlie should have avoided hiring white men, the most frequently and seriously injured.

The formalization of managerial hierarchy had mixed effects on bakery inclusiveness. To its credit, the bakery's documented job criteria replaced hiring processes that have been shown to reproduce homogeneity, like recruitment through friendship networks or demands for shared values (Bonilla-Silva 2014; Kleinman 1996). But those job criteria were created by individual managers. When managers created and then used formalized job criteria in hiring, any cultural beliefs about how gender (as well as class or race/ethnicity) affected job performance were transformed from individual bias into seemingly impersonal organizational standards. Using managerially created job criteria, therefore, hid from view any processes that might account for the shrinking involvement of women in the bakery and made it almost impossible to address such gendering of bakery jobs.

BAKERY EARNINGS AND WORK VALUATION

Perhaps an even more potent aspect of the formalized managerial hierarchy was the way it made unequal pay seem normal and natural. Despite the widespread claims of admiration for "hardworking" production labor, such praise did not transform into pay. Between Herbert's market-oriented justification of "wages as just something for recruitment and retention," and Keith's expertise-focused claim in the first epigraph to this chapter that accountability means "rewarding responsibility—i.e., making decisions," managerial hierarchy within a stratified labor market meant pay inequality. Thus, the heavily Latinx production jobs were, as described in the "Race/Ethnicity" section of chapter 4, the lowest-paid work at the bakery. Then, because these ranges were, like job descriptions, seemingly neutral and even democratic documents (the membership voted to pass or reject the wage ranges proposed by management), the ethnoracial dimensions were rendered invisible, making direct address of inequality almost impossible. That is, even if the bakery's growth and stability (and thus its ability to recruit and retain a working-class membership that required good and stable earnings) resulted from the managerially bureaucratic administration of its labor process, the same administration also stratified these earnings based on race and ethnicity.

The formalization of managerial hierarchy directly and indirectly shaped earnings stratification through ethnoracial and gender meaning-making processes. There were small direct effects of formally attaching wage differentials to management: because management was largely white and men, managerial hierarchy directly funneled greater wealth to managers. Yet the difference in earnings between managers and nonmanagers was much smaller at the bakery than at most corporations. In fact, the bakery's lower managerial pay than at other places might partially account for the higher concentration of women in management than in the larger workforce: white men's options elsewhere might have reduced the bakery's attraction.

BAKERY FORMALIZATION AND SUBORDINATION

At the bakery, managerial use of formalized safety and efficiency policies and procedures was justified through a logic of worker benefit: a classed understanding of the healthy, functioning body as a worker's primary asset, and a commitment to worker empowerment through the distribution of profits. Any reduction in autonomy, therefore, was a necessary concession to these collective goals. Herbert claimed that before its reorganization, the bakery used to have "more than our fair share" of workers who "would come into these places and want anarchy, which is like, 'You're not the boss of me now! I'm just gonna do what I wanna do.'" Managers had dispensed with that illusion, he felt. Indeed, cooperatives have historically struggled to match the safety protections of noncooperative firms (Greenberg 1986), partly due to workers' refusal to surrender bodily autonomy to managers (Hoffmann 2001). But managerial control over the formalized safety and efficiency policies and practices at the bakery meant that benefits and concessions were not evenly allocated.

Bakery safety was organized with an expectation of managerial discretion. The bakery's safety regime relied on its near miss report cycle: workers documenting potentially hazardous conditions to be investigated and resolved up the managerial ladder. For instance, if Latinx, working-class production worker Alejandro Barrera nearly slipped on a wet patch of concrete, he would fill out a near miss report and pass it on to his assistant manager, white, working-class John Costa. John might observe the area and discover that sales and delivery drivers were tracking moisture in from their trucks, and pass the report across to Pete McCraig, the white, working-class sales and delivery manager, to address it in his work group. Or he might notice that mixers in the production work group were spilling liquid from the mixing bowls. John could then ask Charlie, the production manager, to implement a new policy for mixers to check and wipe each bowl and themselves after pouring in dough ingredients. Charlie could make this policy, and then pass Alejandro's original report, John's suggestion, and the work group's new policy up the ladder to Greybo, who would include all of these documents in her regular report to the CEO. She would also report back to Alejandro on the determination of his original report.

The formalization that protected physical bodies, however, was not as equally available to workers as it was to managers. While workers sometimes discussed using near miss reports to try to convince managers to change working conditions—to let them use a particular piece of equipment in a particular way or pace a process differently—they often said they felt that they really had little to no effect on how managers coordinated their working conditions. Nor could they use formalized safety practices to change managers' behavior. Production workers could not, for instance, have compelled white, working-class graveyard assistant manager Mark Costa to wear earplugs by filing near miss reports unless Mark's supervisor decided to discipline him; in contrast, Mark could send production workers home for the day if they refused to wear theirs. Although the bakery's safety practices were overtly aimed at protecting working people's bodies and thus a long-term form of empowerment, the attachment of health and safety to the managerial system transformed safety, at best, into a paternalistic gift, with the wisdom of managerial givers elevated above workers' understandings of their own bodies. At worst, it became one more tool for managerial discipline. It was at once a site of working-class empowerment and working-class subordination.

Similarly, efficiency practices were ostensibly aimed at increasing workers' financial stability, but enacted through managerial discipline in a way that curtailed autonomy and reproduced inequality. Work group managers and their assistants could threaten and dock pay, threaten or enforce unpaid time off, and threaten or enact termination for worker actions that jeopardized productive efficiency. That is not to say that such actions were arbitrary. Indeed, numerous employment manuals, orientations, and posted signs, all of which were reviewed with workers repeatedly in work group and membership meetings, made rules and policies clear not only regarding infractions but also their discipline by managers. But in this way they became part of the bakery's inequality regime. Indeed, it was formalization in the hands of management that created such different conditions by race and ethnicity.

The centrality of formalization to ethnoracial inequality was both most pronounced in the ethnoracial autonomy division between production workers and sales and delivery drivers, and also most obscured. To some extent the fact that 85 percent of the bakery's Latinx workers were concentrated in production reflected the privilege that white job seekers brought with them: a greater ability to access more autonomous jobs (Stainback and Tomaskovic-Devey 2012). That is, white workers had more autonomous and/or prestigious options in the Golden Valley and the broader labor market. But in order for workers to be sorted into more and less autonomous jobs, businesses like the bakery must organize jobs more and less autonomously. This organization also reflected the bakery's engagement—or lack of engagement—with the ethnoracial division of autonomy in the company.

The intense supervision and surveillance of the disproportionately Latinx production work group was described as essential to profitability. Herbert insisted that the product dictated the process: the fickle nature of yeast and sourdough required a diligence incompatible with the pre-managerial informal coordination, excessive absences, and practice of self-selection into shift crews of varying quality (see the "Crisis" section in chapter 3). To ensure consistent quality, each assistant manager in production had to ensure a minimum number of salable baked goods. This was why the assistant manager of the graveyard shift did not want Valentín Rios, his lead worker, to transfer to a daytime shift, why workers were not allowed to informally switch shifts, and why formal shift switching was only possible if the assistant manager unlocked the glass cabinet where the schedule was posted and changed it himself. Even too many formally switched shifts would result in negative annual evaluations. Suspending workers who compromised production by calling in sick with too little notice to reliably replace their labor seemed reasonable given the stakes: loss of profitability, loss of company earnings, and loss of individual wealth. Rules were made for a reason and, it seemed, management simply enforced them.

Yet the intensity of rules and policies was not applied to the mostly white sales and delivery drivers, who had a remarkable degree of control over how they completed their tasks. The job of a sales and delivery driver was not *inherently* more autonomous than that of a production worker. The handheld electronic inventory tracking devices used by drivers could have included time oversight features for managers to review and then use to discipline drivers in terms of pay or route allocation. The rudimentary GPS available at the time could have allowed managers to surveil drivers' compliance with route times and breaks. Grocery store receivers at delivery sites could have been surveyed to assess bakery drivers' safety procedure compliance, with time or money penalties attached to low scores. Implementation of such formalized accountability processes would have reduced drivers' autonomy to a level similar to that of most other bakery work groups, and that of most noncooperative sales and delivery drivers in the region. But sales and delivery managers did not implement such rules and processes; instead, they gave their drivers a degree of valuable autonomy. The bakery's goal of creating better lives for all its workers through the formalization of work processes was warped by managerial hierarchy, with individual managers having latitude about the creation and enforcement of policies and procedures. The different decisions made by work group managers undermined the egalitarian intentions of bureaucracy by weakening the potentially protective effects of formalization.

MANAGERIAL WORKER DEMOCRACY

When the bakery reorganized in the late 1980s, democratic worker governance was distinguished from the managerial supervision of workers. By the time of my study, these two systems stood largely apart. Only the fact that the membership was composed entirely of bakery workers and that the all-member board of directors had oversight of the CEO connected governance to management. Like similar cooperative businesses (e.g., Comisso 1979; Hoffmann 2005), the intent of separating these systems was to preserve workers' organizational power. Yet over time, managerial power had become ascendant due to both the predominance of managers on the governing board, and manager-directors' ambiguous governance power over the CEO.

Although bylaws required at least two nonmanagerial workers on the board, it had become dominated by managers and assistant managers. At times it was difficult to find nonmanagers to run for board positions. When asked, some bakery workers opined that leadership interest in democratic control mirrored job interest in labor control: managers just cared more, and board participation could be put down to an individual's particular interests. Herbert claimed that it was precisely the lack of required collective decision-making that had made the bakery a welcoming place for working-class people. Almost echoing Jo Freeman's (1984) claims that participatory democracy advantages those with the training typical of the middle classes, Herbert insisted that the countercultural collectivist cooperatives in fact ignored the interests of working-class members despite the stated equality of voice among all members. As he saw it, middle-class members got their way by using the kinds of skillful oration and persuasive strategies sociologists have found to be more commonly developed in middle-class educational and familial settings (Lareau 2003). And while this seems likely to have been the case (see chapter 3, "People's Daily Bread Bakery" section), the bakery's changes had created new organizational reasons for the dominance of managers as board members.

One part of this managerial imbalance on the board had to do with who had the time to serve for three years on a committee that paid less than a hundred dollars per month but required a monthly multi-hour meeting and additional subcommittee work. While this had not stopped driver Laura Marks, a white, working-class woman in her forties who was looking for ways to get more non-managers to join her on the board, she pointed out that "there's no guarantee that hourly workers will get their hours made up another way if they attend board meetings, while salaried [managers] can find the time somewhere." She also felt it was an obstacle for workers with childcare responsibilities. Indeed, the two nonmanagerial workers on the board during my observation were childless men. One of them, a college-educated white man in his twenties named Tom Rowe, agreed that it required extra time but shrewdly described his service as a way to move up, to demonstrate his commitment and managerial potential. Tom had recently returned from a monthlong Spanish immersion course in Costa Rica. He viewed this language skill development not only as beneficial in his current position on the afternoon production crew, but an asset to his long-range goals: first, promotion to assistant manager, and eventually becoming a salaried manager in the expanded network of cooperative bakeries he hoped to develop during his tenure on the board.

It was difficult to show this kind of long-range planning skill if you were not a manager at the bakery. Managers and assistant managers were generally seen as smarter and more capable that those they supervised, which made them more qualified candidates for the board. This perception was heightened by the bakery's hierarchy because they were the only ones who were *visibly* out there making and implementing decisions. The bakery's managerial system fostered an illusion in which the hierarchical structure seemed a natural outcome of the unequal distribution of talent in society at large, with managers seeming to inhabit their positions purely by virtue of similarly natural talents. Yet, as in other hierarchical organizations, the opposite was just as likely the case: their talents were visible only because the positions they held spotlighted their actions and obscured those of others. Disruption of this recursive illusion was difficult because decision-making was the prerogative of managers. Even in the case of proposals from the floor of the quarterly membership meetings, one of the few instances where more participatory demonstrations of leadership were authorized, a lack of managerial vetting could be stigmatizing. As Pam explained in the "Political Rights" section of chapter 4, proposals from the floor were liable to get the membership wondering, "Is this lady off the wall? She didn't even go to the board." With this participatory option discredited, only managers could legitimately demonstrate leadership.

The board's managerial overrepresentation also created problematic dissonance in the intended control of management by the bakery's democratic governance structure: the majority of board members were directly supervised by the person they were charged with "governing." Some board members took this conflict as part of the job. For instance, Stuart White, the marketing manager, persisted as long-term president of the board despite regular, open, and often strident arguments with the CEO throughout the time of my study. Other board members, like Sherry and Keith, would express trepidation about confronting Herbert but would do so nevertheless, although with gentleness and appeasing tones. But most other bakery workers told me they tried to avoid arguments with Herbert whenever possible; while workers' "coopHERBERTive" comment was generally intended as a joke, it was also a way of citing the CEO's fierce protection of his prerogative. Both Keith and Pam raised the difficulty of trying to exert control over the person who was their direct supervisor when describing their decision to step down from the board. Although archival meeting minutes show that Herbert himself had predicted the potential dilemma posed by these conflicting relationships when managerialism was being introduced in the late 1980s, he did not seem to notice its manifestation in practice, or at least recognize the manifestation as a problem. Using aggressive phrases, vocal tones, and body language, he forcefully advanced his desires when facing resistance from board members he directly supervised.

Thus, democratic worker control was less muscular in practice than it appeared on paper: formalized policies gave long-term control of the bakery to the board; managerial hierarchy allowed only managers to demonstrate the kind of leadership necessary for board members; and because manager-directors were directly supervised by the CEO they were supposed to oversee, there was little functional worker control. Indeed, the very formalization of the separation of governance and management was what subordinated the former to the latter.

SUBORDINATION VIA MANAGERIAL BUREAUCRACY

The leadership and the workers at the bakery were in no way bad people. Much of the leadership had openly expressed organizational and personal desires for a welcoming and inclusive workplace. But this did not stop them from creating policies and practices that, in different ways, systematically disadvantaged people of color and white women, and extracted the value of their labor to fund the greater employment and enrichment of white men. It was not only that the turn to managerialism streamlined authority into the hands of a few, provided no mechanisms to check the implicit and maybe unconscious bias of individual managers, and protected managerial prerogative with seemingly neutral formalized policy and practice. If it were only the case that managerial power had become outsize, the egalitarian desires of managers like Sherry or Herbert should have been able to create more egalitarian outcomes. Instead, even highly social-justice-minded managers were trapped within the bakery's formalized policies and practices and a traditionally classed logic of material empowerment through worker ownership. Because "organizational policies and practices are not gender neutral in their influence on employment outcomes" (Kmec 2005, 345), here they were not ethnoracially neutral either. While the bakery's classed logic was able to minimize earnings inequalities (for instance, the relatively small 3:1 ratio between the highest-earning manager and the lowest-earning worker), it provided no resources for worker control. Even overtly democratic governance had morphed into another form of control by management due to pay and scheduling policies. The bakery thus seemed to echo Robert Michels's (1959) infamous "iron law of oligarchy," the contention that the need for efficiency erodes even the deepest democracy as power becomes concentrated into the hands of a small group.

Participatory Bureaucracy and Inequality at One World Natural Grocery

As chapters 3 and 5 describe, the grocery had taken a very different route from its days of financial crisis and domination by its white, middle-class founders to the profitable and accountable organization I observed. While it had rejected positional management and a rigid division of labor, it also rejected the inequality-generating informal structure of earlier collectivist-democratic cooperatives. Instead it had adopted the other aspects of bureaucracy and rationalization in aid not only of material support but of more broadly defined empowerment. This section explores how, as at the bakery, the grocery's formalization of policies and procedures was intended to create worker empowerment. Yet unlike the inequality generated by the bakery's formalized hierarchy, only minimal differences in hiring and earnings existed at the grocery. In terms of power, while the long-range planning of the grocery's board of directors was still disproportionately in the hands of middle-class whites, day-to-day oversight and management was proportionately representational in the ICC and directly exercised by the gender- and ethnoracially-mixed democratic work groups. The grocery's formalization combined with its distributed management to provide egalitarian protection of its workers in what this section outlines: a participatory bureaucracy.

GROCERY HIRING

While managerial bias is a common barrier to gender and ethnoracial equality in hiring (Chatman 2010; Greenwald and Krieger 2006), the grocery's formalization of distributed management weakened these effects in two ways: its use of committee hiring first required grocery workers to externalize any biases, and it then subjected them to deliberation. A description of hiring by Chris Badger, the white, middle-class packaged food worker who saw cooperative experience as a useful but not necessary job applicant quality (see chapter 5, "Class" section), provides clues to the key components of the grocery's hiring system:

> CHRIS: The first hiring committee I was on, it was the first time for all three of us to do hiring. And so we were looking through applications and just going, "I don't know, none of these look all that great but, you know, what do we know?" And so we went to the files and pulled our own applications out that we got hired with, to think, "What was it about these applications that made us look interesting?" . . . And we kind of saw, wow, you know, okay, these are solid applications, and you could see why the people who saw them said, "Okay, well, let's talk to this person."
>
> JOAN: What sort of things do you remember?
>
> CHRIS: Well, I think it was experience. In my case it was collective experience, that I had some small working knowledge of herbs, that I was a vegan for several years. I remember claiming that with herbs I could cure the common cold. [*Laughter.*]

Besides immodest medical claims, Chris's account reveals a rationalized approach to hiring: the reliance on predictive power in job applications, and the use of job experience and product knowledge as certification of expertise. In using these measures, the committee also rejected an earlier era's reliance on friendship networks and emotion-based criteria (see chapter 2, "The Countercultural Collectivist Era, 1970s-1980s" section). But Chris's account also reveals the participatory character: the discussions and collective process of determining an applicant's value rather than a decision made individually or even through voting. Chris's recollection of turning to historical applicant files reflects my observation of floor workers easily and regularly accessing office files that would typically only be seen by personnel workers. Such use of records weakens the possibility of arbitrary and biased hiring decisions, particularly because these records were being jointly viewed. That these processes were routine was important to later hiring, as I found when I asked, "Are there affirmative action sort of policies in place in hiring, or is that ad hoc?"

Chris replied,

> We don't have any sort of quotas or anything like that. I can't really say how it works in other work groups. I know, when I've been on hiring in package[d foods], that we're always psyched not to get some regular schmo, someone who's culturally or genetically not one of the average folks. You know, whether that's, you know, "Oh good, we're hiring a woman," or "Good, we're hiring someone who speaks another language," or "Good, we're hiring someone who's not straight," or "Good, we're hiring—" You know, whatever. I mean, occasionally we've had so many *women* in the work group that it's like, "Oh good, we're hiring a man."

Although Chris's own implicit bias is revealed in his characterization of the "average" applicant as an English-speaking straight man, his comment also shows that it was not an accepted practice at the grocery to privilege men, English speakers (and language was often used to draw a distinction between Latinx or Asian Americans and Pacific Islanders and white people), or heterosexuals in the hiring process. Indeed, the discussion-based process of hiring undermined the potential for stereotyping and implicit bias in the consideration of job applicants, making it difficult for even an overtly prejudiced hiring committee member to argue for or against a candidate using such criteria.

The significance of the grocery's reliance on highly formalized practices was most clearly illustrated to me when I attended my first Cooperative Concerns forum, or CoCo, convened by African American, working-class ICC and personal goods work group member Gabriela Guinn. As described in the "Political Rights" section of chapter 5, these ad hoc meetings were intentionally designed as fairly unstructured assemblies for members to discuss issues in advance of a vote. This time the topic was the grocery's underrepresentation of African Americans. Perhaps reflecting the grocery's ethnoracial demographics, more whites than people of color attended. Yvonne Miller, a white, working-class member of the cheese work group, grew animated as she described the grocery's need for more African American members. At one point she implied that a long-term Black member of personal care goods had been left to fend for himself by describing him as a "unicorn." While there were at that time four other Black men in the store, and three Black women in that man's work group, the CoCo's participants were accurate in their self-criticism of the store's failure to at least mirror the city's 8 percent African American population. As members discussed the issue, white, working-class office work group secretary Elaine Kimble outlined and recorded what would later be distributed as verbatim minutes. At the end of the allotted hour, Elaine abruptly ended the session, the assembled workers thanked each other for coming, and everyone left without proposing further action: the abrupt and completely routine conclusion of a CoCo.

To me this process seemed chaotic and ineffective. Could discussion without further steps—the drafting of a formal plan of organizational analysis and centralized hiring policies at the very least—possibly translate into a change in practices? For grocery members, though, the CoCo was just one part of a larger set of interlocking practices. CoCos formalized the informal talk typical of any institutional setting, and the distribution of documented minutes (also translated into Spanish) spread the discussion throughout the store. Discussions about the minutes occurred in the lounge, in hallways near agendas, and on the shop floor—and all counted as the same kind of paid time as reading a work group log or any other sets of minutes. By turning member complaint into documents that all were expected and paid to read, a shared discourse emerged: underrepresentation was real, was a legitimate organizational concern, and that internal work group policies contributed positively and negatively to this underrepresentation. Indeed, in the year following this CoCo, a larger proportion of African Americans were hired than in the three previous years, and most of them survived their first year to become cooperative members where roughly a quarter of all new hires were fired or quit in their first year. And all of this happened without the top-down policies or managerially mandated diversity trainings that are most commonly—and unsuccessfully—used to increase workplace diversity, equity, and inclusion goals (Kalev, Dobbin, and Kelly 2006).

GROCERY EARNINGS AND WORK VALUATION

That there were almost imperceptible earnings differences among workers by race/ethnicity and gender (see chapter 5, "Gender" and "Race/Ethnicity" sections) was certainly due in part to the grocery's policy of requiring membership—and thus shares in profits—for all workers. But more important, "managerial" work and pay were distributed across the workforce through formalized policies and practices. Tasks that would most often be managers' work at corporate firms—hiring, scheduling, discipline, and goal setting—were meted out to the participatory work groups and representative committees. As members of these bodies, workers' weekly hours included expectations of—and pay for—review of the documents produced by them. Such democratic participation was seen as work, and formally valued as such by the grocery. Workers were paid the same for all their working hours, whether washing and prepping vegetables, reviewing personnel files, attending work group or committee meetings, reading log books or meeting minutes, conducting orientations or acting as guides for new workers, or performing any other tasks designated in the bylaws. By paying workers to perform the planning and coordination traditionally done by managers, and by building compliance through formalized policies, the grocery spread managerial responsibility *and* reward across the workforce.

GROCERY FORMALIZATION AND PROTECTION

Calling the grocery's formalization "protective" may seem counterintuitive given its worker injury rates. Once, nearly slipping on a lettuce leaf near a produce bin and seeing customers also just barely avoiding a spill onto the hard concrete floor, I found myself wishing I could fill out one of the bakery's near miss reports to trigger a cycle of inquiry and remedy. But the grocery had no such practice. Indeed, despite the fact that California bakery and grocery workers at the time had very similar injury rates (USDLBLS 2003), One World Natural Grocery's "X-mods" (the actuarial number representing the history of actual injury compared to expected for firm size and industry; WCIRB 2019) were higher than those of People's Daily Bread Bakery. This was not because grocery workers or board and committee members were insensitive towards grocery worker suffering. Rather, the grocery's refusal to intertwine safety with discipline led to more worker injuries at the same time as it minimized the reproduction of societal inequalities within the cooperative.

The case of the cashiers work group illustrates this issue well. Cashiers suffered the most injuries at One World Natural Grocery, and while the work group had voted to shorten shifts from eight to six hours, no policies had been put in place to forbid double shifts or in other ways limit strain on workers. Thus, when Luisa Portillo, a Latina, working-class cashier, left a shift in pain and then signed up for extra shifts the following week, Latina, working-class Mari Rivas complained that the remaining cashers were "the ones who get stuck with it when she gets hurt": they had to work more quickly to check out more customers in ways that forced them to choose between safe work practices and rapid ones that potentially contributed to more injury. Even in this work group that was internally considered to be the most managerial in the store, there was no one to tell workers to take steps to protect their bodies—and protect the grocery's profits from rising insurance rates.

Why did the grocery allow such conditions to persist? It was not that no one cared about workers' suffering. Joe Peterson had petitioned the board to fund him in a safety coordinator position a year before I began observations. A young white and proudly working-class man, his zeal for safety had previously been expressed in a semicomical song he performed with coworkers that included the lyrics,

> We gotta be careful: our bodies, our tools
> We gotta be careful till these injuries cool
> Injury! Injury! I need a rest
> Injury! Injury! God, I wish I had stretched

But other than keeping first aid kits stocked and putting up safety posters, Joe described himself as unable to effect change. Sometimes he said that he might be the wrong person for the job, that someone more "results-driven" and less concerned about "process" might be better. For instance, similar to the way the cheese and refrigerated foods work groups had asked the ICC to address the thefts from a "backstage" area they shared with the produce work group (see chapter 5, "Political Rights" section), Joe could have asked the ICC to ban cashiers' double shifts. I privately wondered if he was right, that someone else should do the job. But as I spent more time at the grocery and read ICC meeting minutes recounting the resistance the ICC had faced in their attempt to impose a gate-locking policy, I understood his dilemma. Coercively "acting like a cop," as he put it, was unlikely to be as effective in the long run as the generation of consensus. He planned a longer campaign of convincing work groups to develop their own safety policies. For instance, cashiers would need other work groups to offer partial shifts to help them make up for the lost hours, but that could also be a good solution for the coverage gaps faced by some of the smaller work groups. Joe helped me understand that formal policy was neither reliant on the presence of management nor even more efficiently implemented from above. Both safety and discipline could be effected without hierarchy.

Because discipline was certainly not absent from the grocery. Despite the sense that work was "free," as Juanita put it in chapter 5, and that autonomy was described by many workers as a central benefit of cooperative employment, formalization put limits on workers' autonomy at the grocery, too. Storewide policies allocated many responsibilities to each work group's internal three-person committee (see figure 3.2 in chapter 3): tracking the accuracy of time cards, offering "coaching" when they or other work group members had complaints, and initiating firing processes when oral and written warnings failed to produce desired changes in behavior. But formalization was also used to distribute disciplinary power more broadly across work groups. For instance, the cashiers had a policy that if someone wanted to leave their shift early, they had to elicit unanimous agreement from all the other cashiers who were working. Mari recalled a time when she had had to stay on her shift because one cashier had refused to allow her to leave. Theo Vallin, the second-generation member who in the first pages of chapter 5 recalled how little his mother's grocery membership had helped him understand cooperative ownership, suggested a policy change from unanimous to majority approval. "Yeah," said Mari, "because sometimes it's a personal thing," a power struggle between coworkers. "It's not like you have a boss. You have to convince *everyone*." This was, in Mari's telling, frustrating— an example of bureaucratic red tape. But it was also about the way formalization blocked the kinds of individual as well as gender and ethnoracial biases retail workers are typically subject to in managerial settings (Williams 2006). Theo's response then highlighted the dynamic potential of this formalized policy to become even more fair and impersonal.

What behavior was subject to discipline and how quickly behavioral change was expected varied across the work groups. This was to some extent related to jobs and tasks but also to a work group's culture of democratic authority. Thus, on one end of the spectrum was the largely working-class and ethnoracially diverse cashiers work group, whose members had the most customer contact built into their jobs and were widely perceived to have the most "managerial" culture in terms of numbers of rules and centralization of scheduling and discipline. On the other end was the largely middle-class and mostly white office work group, whose members rarely had contact with customers and were seen as overly lax in their adherence to schedules (as self-reflectively acknowledged in their teasing comments about my having "gone native" and become a "fast learner" when, as described in "Political Rights" section of chapter 5, I cut one day of observation short for personal reasons). It was not that office members worked fewer hours (in fact, members of that work group tended to have longer workweeks than the average), but that their jobs did not have customer-driven pressure to be physically present during store hours.

If only cashiers and the office were compared, it would seem that the sorting of workers into work groups replicated social inequalities, translating social marginalization and privilege into greater and lesser organizational scrutiny and discipline. But this pattern did not prevail across the store. Housewares, for instance, a white- and middle-class-dominated work group, was also known for its ever-increasing number of rules and disciplinary policies (including the wearing of grocery logo clothing, unlike most floor workers); produce, the work group known for its "anarchist" resistance to centralization and top-down authority, was even more evenly balanced across race and ethnicity (as well as gender) than were the cashiers (see table 5.1 in chapter 5). That is, the different degrees of autonomy between work groups—with the cashiers at one end and the office at the other—were dictated neither by task nor by ethnoracial privilege. There was no greater push by white men to the front of "job queues"

(Reskin and Roos 1990) for the most autonomous positions at the grocery. Instead work groups' different autonomy levels resulted from a decentralized process of negotiation and interrupted the reproduction of social privilege that typically happens at work.

The grocery also used formalization to protect workers from customers' attempts—or perceived attempts—to control workers. It was not simply about allowing workers to adorn themselves with political slogans that angered many shoppers, as in chapter 5, when a customer told a cashier with a contentious statement pinned to her chest, "I thought your management told you that you can't wear that!" It was also about protecting workers' ability to control the way they organized their labor or balanced their personal and productive time. As highlighted by cashier Elena Guzmán's insightful comment in the "Political Rights" section of chapter 5 about "spoiled" customers demanding inauthentic friendliness, retail work typically includes a high degree of emotional labor—what Arlie Hochschild (1983) describes as the transformation of workers' emotions from private feelings into commodities intended to improve company profits. Indeed it was, for instance, this perceived customer demand for Deb Scharf's attention and emotional labor that accounted for Deb's resistant surliness to what I initially viewed as innocent confusion over Deb's availability (see chapter 5, "Political Rights" section). Formal policies allowing workers to control their time and interactions—and a pronounced lack of policies typical of supermarket chains like mandatory name tags or compelled smiles—reduced the amount of emotional labor Deb and her coworkers had to perform. Framing customer demands as akin to managerial ones at a deeply democratic cooperative workplace allowed the grocery to reject common supermarket practices, and undermine the gender- and ethnoracially unequal demand for emotional labor in retail work (Guy and Newman 2004; Leidner 1999).

Thus it was not only formalization but also the *democratization* of formalization—its detachment from hierarchical authority—that offered important protections for workers' autonomy. Autonomy inequalities are one of the common ways inequality is reproduced at work (Hodson 2001). The grocery's participatory bureaucracy instead offered those protections across class, race/ethnicity, and gender.

PARTICIPATORY WORKER DEMOCRACY

Grocery workers were a lot like bakery workers. One similarity was a belief in a naturally occurring distribution of abilities. Workers at both cooperatives generally ignored the ways in which racism and classism shape the development, expression, and recognition of so-called personality traits like confidence or intelligence (Tilly 1998; Wingfield 2009). Many grocery workers also expressed a belief in the value of what R. W. Connell has termed "hegemonic masculinity," or the "'currently accepted' strategy" of masculine embodiment (1995, 77), defined against both a white-collar middle class and femininity. That is, cooperative membership neither screened out nor transformed internalized class, ethnoracial, or gender biases. Yet grocery members' internalized beliefs were not harnessed to a hierarchical pyramid of authority, as they were at the bakery, nor were they amplified through informal friendship relations as so often happened during the antibureaucratic 1970s countercultural collectivist era. The grocery's decentralization and formalization of authority created very different expressions of power than individual beliefs might suggest would occur.

The overrepresentation of white men (and proportionate but still substantial representation of white women) on the board of directors was acknowledged as a fact—and concern—of grocery life. Board members seemed to be elected on the basis of their long-range vision, ability to interact with the corporate world, and financial savvy to guide the cooperative. The grocery seemed to reproduce typical workplace rewards for hegemonic masculinity in the aggressive and mental work of managerial leadership when conducted by white men but not men or women of color or white women (Collins 1990; Collinson and Hearn 1994; Pierce 1995). Grocery workers struggled over possible solutions in CoCos and membership meetings. The membership generally elected all the people of color who ran for the board but, perhaps due to those noted social penalties of seeming dangerous or offensive, very few did so.

The disproportionate share of board seats held by whites and by men did not, however, mean disproportionate *organizational* power. The decentralization of grocery authority and the formal policies and practices that minimized individual social advantage instead spread authority much more widely across class, race/ethnicity, and gender. When the board and the ICC tried to institute new storewide or multi-work group policies, they were usually faced with resistance from work groups (as the case of the pushback against the ICC's locked-gate rule in chapter 5) and the membership as a whole. Bylaws allowed the membership meeting to veto board decisions (a power it seemed to exercise roughly every two years) or recall the board entirely (which had never been done). Through these formal policies, the reach of the grocery's board and ICC were made more narrow than a comparable board and managerial structure at a typical corporation. As suggested by the cautionary tale in the "Political Rights" section of chapter 5 of Brian Cleary's fall from grace after obtaining a city contract without first getting membership approval, and in the one in the "Crisis" section of chapter 3 recounting Bob Imperiale's inability to get the cooperative to approve a differentiated pay structure, hegemonic white masculinity offered little protection to those who tried to skirt or bend the rules.

Some grocery policies were designed to compensate for the class advantages via the advanced formal education typical of the middle class. Several workers used the terms *university* and *college* as metaphors for their time working at the grocery—perhaps in part to make it sensible to me, a researcher from a university, but also to capture their experience of learning new skills. For instance, the formal jurisdiction of the Successful Participation Committee (SPC) included running membership meetings and helping work groups develop communication practices as requested, but also providing research and writing assistance to members trying to craft thorough and well-written proposals and agenda items. This allowed the many grocery workers who had ended their formal education at high school to draft documents as strong as those who had honed those skills on college papers. Organizationally, this practice helped to level the playing field among grocery workers by universalizing this subtle asset.

Such practices seemed to increase participation across class and race/ethnicity in the many non-board committees. The incoming elected Public Relations Committee, which managed both advertisement and community outreach, was comprised almost entirely of Black and Brown grocery members. The self-reproducing (new members selected by current ones) Front End Committee that addressed problems among or between customers, cashiers, and the customer service work group had actively shifted from a white to a nonwhite majority. Similar to the (unintended) egalitarian effects of corporate cross-functional teams and training (Kalev 2009), grocery members' experience of seeing their coworkers innovate new solutions and demonstrate leadership across class, race/ethnicity, and gender weakened the ability of individual biases to become organizational barriers.

Why did workers take on committee work, and particularly the less glamorous tasks like front end coordination or keeping the indoor and outdoor plants alive on the Ecology Committee? While a key enticement was monetary—all committee work was paid at the exact same rate as regular hours and credited towards profit sharing by the hour—workers almost always offered one of four other reasons they took on this extra work. The first was variety: to temporarily spice up a routine workweek or to ergonomically compensate for repetitive stress. The second was about status creation or enhancement. Mari, for instance, recalled feeling distrusted by coworkers when she first joined the grocery, and was delighted to be recognized as capable and hardworking in her nomination to the Front End Committee. The third reason was control over working conditions, as Jennifer, the refrigerated food work group member who described liking "to play boss" in the "Political Rights" section of chapter 5, noted when she ran for the board. Finally, the fourth reason was a sense of collective obligation. Jan, who, in the second epigraph to this chapter, described leadership as the broad participation that creates a feeling of capability, stated this most clearly: "If I can do it, and it needs to be done, then I should try." While pay surely played a part in grocery workers' decisions to take on committee work, the relatively modest compensation—at least compared to the extreme degrees of managerial pay in corporate settings—allowed workers to discover and articulate important personal and collective motivations for performing managerial labor.

It was also notable to me that Jan's description of a moral obligation to the cooperative did not seem to undermine the standing of workers who did not serve. In the early days of my research, I heard some criticism of a perceived mercenary attitude to grocery membership among "paycheck people" compared to "co-op people" who took on leadership roles. But when I asked my interviewees about this distinction, only one agreed. Most of the rest expressed appreciation for the grocery's openness to different levels of engagement, pointing to the kind of "complex equality" democracy theorist Francesca Polletta describes when "different skills, talents, and interests are seen as equally valuable" (2002, vii). For instance, Chris, who had laughed at his former claim of mastery over the common cold, said, "There are people who, even now, I've got a really high respect for them as workers, but don't expect to really see them at meetings." In his opinion, the grocery needed a variety of efforts by its members, not only leadership participation. He went on to explain, "Yeah, it's great when more people step up, but things are basically getting done. You know, if everyone in the store, if all two hundred plus of us were [*uses a chipper voice*] totally stepping up to the plate to make this co-op work because we're owners and we're down with the whole thing [*returns to normal voice*], then, you know, things would get divided out so thin that we'd basically *all* be paycheck people with just one or two little chores." For Chris the grocery was a place where participation could mean the kind of work typically less valued in corporate settings—the work not done typically by professionals or certified experts—and could still be respected as vital contributions to the cooperative.

Indeed, I saw this respect when I asked workers who they saw as "indispensable" at the store (see appendix B). While a small handful of white men—mostly board regulars—were repeatedly cited, their names were almost always followed by those of less visible workers who were not on the board. For example, Jennifer first named Burgundy, who had been on the board almost without a break for over a decade, and Ed Storey, the white primary cheese buyer who had been on the board twice. But she then added Mariana Contreras, a Latina member of the cashiers work group who had never been on the board but had successfully lobbied it to fund hours to coordinate workers' meal preparation and the cleaning of the single shared kitchen. Jennifer was enthusiastic as she described Mariana's contributions: "She's probably a staple too. Just on a completely different level. . . . She's involved, I mean, she's not committee-wise involved, but . . . if she didn't work in the kitchen, the kitchen would be a mess. She really just has this insight that no one else has of how to make things work well. Especially in that situation where two hundred people share one kitchen." While companies often delegate in-house domestic tasks to women, and especially women of color, recognizing (and compensating) these human reproduction tasks *as work* is more rare. Rather than describing Mariana's kitchen committee involvement as shirking her "real" job as a cashier or overlooking these tasks as natural to her (ethnoracialized) gender (Hondagneu-Sotelo, 2007), Jennifer described Mariana's effort as a "staple" of organizational function. Formalization of both decentralized authority and such human capital development appeared to create noticeable appreciation for capabilities across class, race/ethnicity, and gender and a resulting "complex equality."

Grocery workers were not noticeably different from their bakery peers in terms of implicit class, ethnoracial, and gender biases, and they valued the social pleasures of informal friendly relations with coworkers just as the previous generation of worker cooperators had. But the grocery had developed egalitarian distributions of power and resources: unlike the bakery's repayment of its Latinx production workers' labor with lesser pay and profit sharing, someone managing the kitchen at the grocery made no less than someone managing the financial accounting or the marketing. Through the formalization of egalitarian reward and decentralization of democratic worker control, the grocery thus avoided developing the kinds of organizational inequalities seen at the bakery and at most countercultural collectivist cooperatives. Formalized policies and processes reined in the organizational manifestation of implicit bias, and decentralization not only limited the impact of biased decisions to a particular work group but also provided numerous visible examples of people from socially subordinated groups displaying "insight that no one else has" or otherwise demonstrating valuable leadership. Together, this undermined a logic linking leadership ability to socially privileged groups.

PROTECTION VIA PARTICIPATORY BUREAUCRACY

Bakery members were not villains: many were fierce and active proponents of class, ethnoracial, and gender justice. Similarly, grocery members were not saints: many seemed only to want to come to work, do what was formally required, and leave, and they were just as likely to express the kinds of implicit (and sometimes explicit) biases researchers have found to be a pernicious source of organizational inequality (Castilla 2008; Reskin 2000; Ridgeway 2011). But the grocery, unlike the bakery, had developed an organizational form that protected rather than subordinated its socially marginalized members. By combining formal policy and procedure with a hybrid of participatory and representative democratic authority, the grocery had become more inclusive in its hiring and more egalitarian in its apportioning of earnings, autonomy, and authority than either a typical supermarket or the managerial cooperative bakery fifty miles to the south. Formalization limited the spread of implicit bias among workers, while decentralization limited the effect of decisions made from such bias.

Exceptions: Where Subordination and Protection Faltered

By contrasting managerial and participatory bureaucracies, I have called attention to the importance of organizational structure in the inequality differences between the bakery and the grocery. Alternative explanations—such as differences between founding memberships or a different local or occupational institutional environments (Rowan 1982) or social movement fields (Ray 1999), or different degrees of individual commitment to social justice—have been reviewed in chapters 3, 4, and 5 and rejected as unsupported by what I found at the bakery and the grocery. While the nature of the work itself—industrial production versus service—might seem to evoke a gendered binary of masculinized factories and feminized retail, this logic accounts for neither the extent of gender inequality in *other* cooperative bakeries and groceries nor the *ethnoracial* inequality differences between People's Daily Bread Bakery and One World Natural Grocery. Indeed, a closer look at spaces where the bakery and the grocery did *not* exhibit their respective managerial and participatory bureaucracies reveals exactly how meaningful organizational structure was in the reproduction or reduction of inequality. This section first explores an unusual instance of participatory democratic control at the bakery, and then a case of the absence of grocery formalization that allowed members of socially privileged groups to seize and hold power.

Bakery Participatory Bureaucracy: The Egalitarian Afternoon Shift

Francisco Soto, the afternoon assistant manager, supervised the production shift crew with the most normal, daytime working hours. It was unlike the nighttime sanitation crew, which conducted its Spanish-language meetings among its native Spanish-speaking workers and assistant manager, or the predominantly Spanish-speaking graveyard and morning crews that conducted their meetings in English per their monolingual English-speaking assistant managers. With the highest proportion of English-speaking white workers, Francisco's shift crew was the most ethnoracially and linguistically diverse. Francisco was a bilingual native Spanish speaker who had developed an innovative meeting format in which information was presented in English or Spanish and then translated into the other language by either himself or another worker. The translation could be imprecise, and other men would jump in to clarify phrasing or a point. This practice allowed both information and decision-making to be shared much more widely than was common at the bakery, and did so in the part of the bakery that was most representative of the baking industry.

For instance, at one meeting Francisco announced that production workers were no longer supposed to use the pallet jack to move stacked crates of bread. Safety supervisor Greybo had deemed it an unsafe practice; large hooks had been ordered so that much smaller stacks could be hauled manually from production to shipping. Tom, the ambitious young white man recently returned from studying Spanish in Costa Rica, exploded in English that this would be worse not better, that there were *more* accidents with hooks. When he somewhat haltingly expressed the same in Spanish, his words were gently corrected by Ricki Nieves, a Latinx, working-class man in his thirties, who added in Spanish that he agreed, which a Spanish-speaking man to his left echoed. Francisco looked concerned and said, in English, "Let's document this with near miss reports so that we can prove it." Ricki replied, in Spanish, that they would be writing too many reports to get the bread on the truck. Tom translated Ricki's remark into English, and Dave Jackson, one of the few African American workers, let out a snort and said in English, "Let Greybo and [production manager] Charlie try to do it!" Other workers first translated and then threw out quick remarks in Spanish, and the meeting momentarily broke down into chaos. Then Francisco whistled and said, first in Spanish and then in English, "I'll talk to Charlie, and if any of you guys want to show him, you should." Dave frowned as he countered, "He already made his decision." There was some nodding from both English- and Spanish-speaking workers, but Francisco insisted in English, "Yeah, but if we can prove it to him," and waved a sheaf of papers as Ricki's neighbor called out in Spanish to urge the work group to prove the hooks were bad by filling out a lot of the formal paperwork: "*¡Escribamos muchas* near miss reports!"

Sometimes information was very complex and difficult to communicate correctly, but this communal responsibility seemed to free others up to speak. On almost all points—including some company-wide bulletins that had dropped like lead balloons at other work groups' meetings—there were lively discussions among the shift crew members that switched rapidly back and forth between English and Spanish and left any visiting guest (e.g., the personnel or safety coordinator, the CEO, another crew's assistant manager) sitting patiently on the sidelines. Francisco was a skillful facilitator, closely tracking his shift crew during the discussion to see when comprehension was clear on enough faces, and then summarizing the points workers had made in both Spanish and English. Each meeting of the afternoon shift I attended generated new ideas about improving safety, making production more efficient, or balancing individual needs with those of the work group. I heard no such innovations at any other work group meetings. This pocket of formalized participatory management allowed a greater range of creativity to flourish and seemed to deeply engage the shift crew.

Yet this model of creativity and innovation did not spread to other shift crews or work groups, despite regular formal discussions among work group managers in formal biweekly meetings or informal hallway and email exchanges. As an informal practice that originated among workers, there was no obvious way for the practice to move upward or outward without its adoption by the work group's manager, Charlie (see figure 3.1 in chapter 3). Even if he had done so, the resistance to learning Spanish by two of the bakery's assistant managers (described in the "Diversity Regimes" section of chapter 7) might have spilled over to a resistance to bilingualism among their shift crews. There were no forms comparable to the manager-originated system of near miss reports that could share organizational innovations. Without a formal system of "management from below" (Ward, Wilbert, and White 2011), participatory practices were stuck where they started.

Grocery Structurelessness: Men's Privilege as Buyers

It was in the rare non-formalized part of the grocery that it was most clear how formalization combined with participatory democracy to produce more egalitarianism. One of these was the appointment of buyers. Buying was a coveted position for many at the grocery. While buyers were in the hot seat in terms of profitability, these positions—conducted upstairs at a desk, mostly on the telephone—offered many hours away from customer interaction and physically demanding floor work. A buyer position often came with little perks: free samples, invitations to tasting parties, restaurant meals. The cheese buyer even got a free trip to the cheese cellars of Europe. Neither elected nor appointed, buyers for the more profitable work groups had more informally assumed control of particular areas or accounts. Rather than being seen as having lucked out into a high-markup area, they were bathed in an almost heroic light: workers whose financial prowess supported those in less profitable work groups. Many of these hero-buyers were regularly elected to the board. And year after year, their profitable actions—as well as their arcane and complicated knowledge accrued over years of buying—kept their work groups from challenging their continued unelected hold on the position.

While the gender composition of the official buyers list tended to map onto the workforce gender composition (twenty-one men and twenty-eight women), and while there were some men and women of color with buying responsibilities, I was cautioned that "the list doesn't make any difference between people who buy one or two things and people who buy pages and pages." It was the buyers of "pages and pages" who spent a significant portion of their workweek doing paperwork or phone coordination off the sales floor, and who were most likely to be offered gifts by vendors. Minor buyers of "one or two things" continued to spend most of their working hours engaged with customers on the floor, and were unlikely to get any meaningful vendor gifts. With an office worker's guidance, I discovered that all eight of the major buyers were white, and all but one were men.

Some workers expressed their concern about this pattern to me and each other. Jan, whose baked goods work group had intentionally chosen to equally divide buying and shelving among its three members, pointed out, "Buyers, the guys pass accounts off to each other. They do! There's definitely an old-boy buyer thing going on. You know, like Burgundy [buyer for vitamins, the most profitable work group], he's finding the young man of his choice to train up to his position. And the women just aren't even in the same realm, you know. I don't think he considered it, and I don't think he knows he's not considering it." Indeed, Douglas Whyte, the household goods worker who refused to wear an apron on the floor (see chapter 5, "Political Rights" section), described Burgundy's mentorship in vitamins to me, but cast it as validation for how focused he had stayed on his tasks rather than unequal treatment based on his race or gender. Jan was agitating to formalize the process of selecting buyers during the period of my study. "There's not a storewide policy," she explained. "I mean, there really should be. It should be clear to everybody how a buyer gets hired and, in my opinion, information should be available to everybody." As she saw it, inequality flourished due to a lack of written and disseminated policy, and creating policy would necessarily make the selection of buyers fairer. Burgundy, for instance, would not only have to justify Douglas's superior qualities to his work group but would have to open the position up for application throughout the store.

That there were no formal buyer selection policies allowed inequality to creep into the grocery, but its overall bureaucratization provided an accessible set of tools for workers to begin to address those issues. Jan called my attention to the recent termination of a packaged food work group buyer, Paul Butler, a white man and long-term member who had many of the biggest and most lucrative accounts. During his reign as buyer, Paul had refused to cross-train anyone in his work group and had ignored work group member requests to comply with several work group policies. When threatened with termination, he would claim that the work group would fall apart without his specialized and tacit knowledge. Jan recalled, "He maintained an image of being indispensable, but someone [in his work group] complained to me once that he was working a lot of overtime. And *he* would say, 'Yeah! I worked a hundred hours a day!' So I just went into personnel and said, 'You know, I just don't think it's true [that he's working a lot of overtime]. Can you look that up for me so at least we won't have to deal with this complaint?' . . . And it turned out he worked an average of forty-one hours a week for the last three years. So he was lying in order to be perceived as indispensable." Eventually Paul's behavior and claims had annoyed so many of his work group that they called for a vote of confidence and, when he failed to get enough positive votes, he was fired. Jan chuckled and then spoke seriously, "It turned out that person was *not* indispensable. Not even close. One of the other buyers walked up, picked up his notebook, and started doing the job in fifteen minutes." That is, these positions were not protected from formalization due to the expertise that developed in one position. Indeed, the formalization that permeated the rest of grocery workers' day-to-day practices transformed "expertise" into a transferable routine. Although the absence of formalized criteria to become or remain a buyer allowed white masculine power to proliferate, other aspects of bureaucratic formalization were available to curtail its spread.

A lack of formal procedures for selecting and retaining buyers was not unusual in cooperatives: Robert Jackall (1984, 16), for instance, found the same informal accretion of knowledge and therefore power at the Berkeley countercultural collectivist firm he studied. Yet the grocery's bureaucratization had two important effects that differed from that era of cooperatives. First, Paul's informal buying authority contrasted jarringly with the formalized democratic distribution of authority across the rest of the grocery, highlighting the gendered and ethnoracialized social inequality at play, and spurring Paul's coworkers and Jan to challenge his claim to the position. Second, because this informal authority was entirely surrounded by formalized processes and practices—from personnel files to votes of confidence to buyer record keeping—Paul's coworkers and Jan had easily available remedies to address what they saw as the problem with him. It was not because its members were a serendipitous collection of magically bias-free people that the grocery was strikingly egalitarian in its opportunities and rewards. It was instead the grocery's distributed but formalized democratic management that translated egalitarian ideals into egalitarian practices.

Neither Industry nor People, but Bureaucratic Structure

The places where the bakery and the grocery's normal bureaucratic patterns either had not developed or had broken down demonstrated how each cooperative was shaped by its bureaucracy variation. At the bakery, Francisco's afternoon crew developed an egalitarian and productive form of distributed management that was bureaucratic but not hierarchical. At the grocery, informal practices regarding the staffing of the vitamins and packaged food buyer position had transformed implicit bias into active exclusion, and a participatory bureaucracy into structurelessness. Two lessons can be found in these counterexamples. The first is that in neither the case of the bakery nor the grocery could either the labor process of baking or retail sales nor the collection of individual characters account for the difference in organizational structure: alternative organizational arrangements popped up within the same group of people despite the similarity of their working conditions to others around them. The second is that the impact of these exceptional cases on the immediate degree of inequality at each site—more ethnoracial equality in the bakery's afternoon crew, and more gender inequality in vitamins and packaged food—indicates how powerful even the most local organizational structures can be. Bureaucracies are more varied than has been allowed, and their variations are more relevant to organizational inequality than has been considered.

Summary: Bureaucratic Solutions to Bureaucratic Problems?

Both the bakery and the grocery managed to overcome historical worker cooperative problems: lack of accountability, inefficient and ineffective communication, subordination of financial stability and profitability to social justice values, and/or monopolization by members of socially privileged groups. Drawing on their observations as factory and retail workers, and as cooperative owners within a universe of primarily corporate but also cooperative enterprise (see chapter 3), both bakery and grocery workers formalized and standardized policies and practices organizing their labor, management, and governance. At the bakery, managerial bureaucracy was seen as a necessary concession to the greater good of improved material gain and bodily protection; at the grocery, somewhat reduced earnings and safety were viewed as a worthwhile trade-off for the broader distribution of autonomy and authority inherent to participatory bureaucracy.

Yet the different bureaucracies they developed led to different organizational inequalities. Although bakery members made a strong case that their managerial bureaucracy was a critical factor in their extension of membership beyond the bakery's white and middle-class foundations, the grocery's similar working-class membership makes it hard to accept CEO Herbert Gubbins's claim that participatory democratic management and governance disadvantages and excludes working-class people. Across class, members could indeed find the grocery's less streamlined processes frustrating, but they were just as likely to praise the freedom it gave them and the capacities it built. Where the bakery's formalization of managerialism masked the unequal treatment of bakery workers by race/ethnicity and gender, the grocery's formalization of participatory control weakened personal bias and promoted ethnoracial and gender diversity alongside working-class inclusion.

This chapter has questioned an overly neat division between bureaucratic and nonbureaucratic forms of organization—typically articulated as formalized managerialism versus informal democratic control—as well as claims regarding the ability of bureaucracy to create or redress inequality. Like others writing in this tradition (Adler and Borys 1996; Ashcraft 2001; Gouldner 1954), I argue for a conceptualization of bureaucracy as not merely "real world" versus "ideal type," but as a collection of identifiable variations with distinct inequality effects. In this study, *participatory* bureaucracy is contrasted with the taken-for-granted *managerial* version. Where managerial bureaucracy is inherently hierarchical—and entirely representative in any democratic aspect it may include—participatory bureaucracy is decentralized and largely direct in its management and governance. Participatory bureaucracy is explicitly formalized, more specialized than not, and entirely instrumental. In a worker cooperative, its instrumentality balances profits with workers' quality of life more than an entirely profit-oriented investor-owned firm, but it is an organizational means to an end. The two cooperatives in this study were both organizations developed to maximize individuals' ability to achieve ends-oriented goals.

But despite a shared instrumental bureaucratism, the two forms of bureaucracy have very different effects and benefits for workers. Contrasting the organization of authority at the bakery and the grocery illustrates a central insight of inequality regimes theory: greater hierarchy is associated with greater inequality (Acker 2006a). It does not suggest the same, however, about bureaucratic formalization, and instead supports the stream of scholarship claiming the egalitarian benefits of bureaucracy. But by proposing bureaucratic variations, this study offers a way out of the debate about whether bureaucracy increases or reduces inequality. Formalization may offer some protection to members of socially marginalized groups, but when combined with hierarchy those advantages are transformed into disadvantages; decentralization may open space for empowerment, but it similarly undermines that opportunity when combined with informality. Participatory bureaucracy, at once decentralized and formalized, protects empowerment processes without whitewashing the reproduction of social privilege.

Such an analysis still begs the question of how two originally very similar groups of people united for similar purposes would develop such very different bureaucracies. Bakery employees—particularly upper management—were not blind to class, ethnoracial, or gender inequality, and indeed prided themselves on providing a good livelihood to working-class people, including a disproportionately large number of Latinx workers. Nor was it inevitable that the white, middle-class founders of the grocery would have developed practices that disrupted their privileges: studies of other countercultural collectivist era alternative organizations found very different outcomes (Kleinman 1996; Ostrander 1999; Scott 2005; Sirianni 1993). Indeed, both support for and criticism of organizational practices and policies were common among bakery and grocery workers. Why would these similar groups develop and maintain such different structures?

Some parts of the answer lie in the cooperatives' 1980s crises and the subsequent divergence that resulted from their solutions to those crises. The success each found solidified their members' sense of what was and was not feasible and wise for a cooperative business in the twenty-first century. One important difference in such understanding that emerged was about the address of social inequalities: how much workplaces could or should try to reduce inequality, and which inequalities were the legitimate target(s) of workplaces. The bakery and the grocery's expectations about their organizational address of inequalities shaped distinct understandings of what it meant to be a worker, constituting a distinct "worker identity" at each cooperative. Chapter 7 explores the content of these identity projects, the diversity regimes each organization developed to address and manage these constructions, and the way these identities affected the bureaucratic structures that reproduced and interrupted inequality.

WORKER IDENTITIES
Making Inequality Regimes Meaningful

> **We did go through a period of time where we felt we needed to be more affirmative and just letting people *be* who they are. You know, 'cause it doesn't have anything to do with business. . . . In an ideal world, if you were a gay person and you felt that you wanted to let people know that that's who you were, we feel that you should be able to do that without any retribution from a coworker. We certainly go to great extents to say that, you know, as far as management's concerned, you are who you are.**
>
> —Keith Assis, People's Daily Bread Bakery

> **He was Black and he was gay and they hired him because he had piercings. I talked to the hiring committee because one of my friends applied and I'm like, "Why didn't you hire my friend?" And they're like, "Well, we wanted to give this guy a chance because, first of all, we didn't feel like the job market was an easy place for him. And, you know, he seemed like he would kind of fit in here as far as creating diversity. And he seemed nice and everything." And . . . when they told me that, I was like, "Oh yeah, that's a good thing."**
>
> —Jennifer Ruud, One World Natural Grocery

Why did People's Daily Bread Bakery and One World Natural Grocery tolerate such different kinds and degrees of organizational inequality? In chapter 6 I explored the role of organizational structure in producing this difference. By formalizing hierarchy, the bakery's managerial bureaucracy increased working-class opportunities but also subordinated men of color, marginalized white women, and excluded women of color. At the grocery the formalization of distributed management into a participatory bureaucracy protectively shielded members of commonly marginalized and excluded social groups from such forms of unequal treatment or opportunity. But what accounts for the development of such different versions of the "inequality regimes" identified by Joan Acker (2006b) and described in the "Worker Control" section of chapter 1 of this volume? Why should there be such different outcomes from two worker-oriented firms that were, as chapter 3 outlined, founded by such similar groups of people in the same historical and cultural space, that weathered such similar challenges and changes, and that drew on the same local labor market? How did a category of inequality like sexuality come to be seen by bakery management as something that "doesn't have anything to do with business," as Keith put it, but as a legitimate hiring criteria by grocery members like Jennifer?

While the importance of practices within occupation or industrial sector—the difference between a service-oriented supermarket and industrial food production—cannot be entirely discounted (Charles and Grusky 2005), I argue that the different ways of understanding workplace inequality as an organizational matter result from the legitimacy of claims made in terms of locally produced *worker identities*. In this chapter, I use the term to mean an organizationally specific concept of a self that operates at the individual and organizational levels. Worker identities exist, I will argue, in all workplaces but are particularly salient in worker cooperatives, where support to workers is the central rather than peripheral or concessionary motivation for action. The way in which class, race/ethnicity, gender and other social characteristics figure in the construction and articulation of worker identity is therefore consequential for the organization's reproduction or interruption of inequalities. While workers can certainly change worker identities through concerted actions, in all workplaces the contours and content of worker identity affect and are affected by the structure of the organization.

I first explore the pitfalls and possibilities in the use of "identity" as a concept different from that of social or developmental psychological literatures. I then flesh out the distinct worker identities manifest in workers' individual-level descriptions of themselves and others, and follow this with an exploration of the organizational processes and practices each cooperative used to regulate the social meaning of these identities, entrenching class as the primary characteristic of bakery worker identity and a shifting set of social categories as that of grocery worker identity. These identity differences, I then show, reinforced bureaucratic variation at the bakery and the grocery. While the class-focused bakery worker identity and the more protean grocery worker identity might seem to indicate stronger and weaker connections to organized labor given the labor movement's own historic class primacy, a different insight into relationships between worker identity and solidarity is offered in the account in the second to last section of the chapter that describes the two cooperatives' reactions to a grocery workers' strike in 2003. If organizations are where the sense of self and broader social categories are connected (Parker 2000; Tomaskovic-Devey and Avent-Holt 2019), this chapter proposes worker identities as a critical organizational technology to forge those linkages.

Monist and Pluralist Identities: Real in Their Consequences

By *worker identity* I do not refer to an organization's public or collective self-representation or its "personality" (e.g., Albert and Whetten 2004; Brown 2006; Hatch and Schultz 2002), nor the degree to which workers view their concerns and selves as aligned with those of their work, workplace, or employers (e.g., Ashforth and Schinoff 2016; Kunda 2006; Tajfel and Turner 1979). Instead I propose to think of worker identity as the consequential and locally emergent expression of self in a given organizational context.[1] Worker identity is articulated both directly (by organizational members) and indirectly (through organizational processes), and draws on social and local narratives of class, race/ethnicity, gender, sexuality, nationality, physical dis/ability, and the like: the industrial worker, for instance, is arguably implicitly masculine (Collinson 1992; Halle 1984; Willis 1990). Defining worker identity in this way draws on a field of study now coalescing as "relational inequality theory" (Tomaskovic-Devey and Avent-Holt 2019) that connects individuals' self-understanding to the emergence and transformation or maintenance of collectivities over time, as well as to the production and reproduction of stratified social categories that affect a person's or group's life chances (e.g., Fernandes 1997; Kasmir 1996; Kondo 1990; Lee 1998; Otis and Wu 2018; Salzinger 2003; Vallas 2003).

Before speaking of *worker* identity, however, it is necessary to address the theoretical project of identity itself. Since at least the 1960s a vast literature on the social, political, and economic uses of and issues with identity has developed (see Brubaker and Cooper 2000; Du Gay 2007; see also the "Worker Identity" section of chapter 1 of the present volume). Identity is messy; it has been criticized as imprecise and internally contradictory, invoking both sameness (as a perceived class, ethnoracial, or gender group) and uniqueness (of the self), the self-determination of subjects and their regulation by inherited systems of power (Wetherell and Mohanty 2010). As a noun, *identity* gets reified as a thing (Althusser 1971), a quality inherent in people rather than a process that is only meaningful in relation to others. It has been argued that such reification has led both social scientists and the identified subjects to treat identities as more durable than they are over time and across space (Brubaker and Cooper 2000; Du Gay 2007; Scott 1988), and as more cohesive and delimited—for instance, class identity versus gender identity versus ethnoracial identity—than lived experience of intersecting and intertwined categories suggests (Crenshaw 1991; Swidler 2001), and has lent weight to a range of oppressive social projects (see, e.g., Arvidsson 1999; Foucault 1980; Leyva 2017).

Some social scientists have proposed alternative concepts to dissuade the identified from thinking of identity as a thing and to instead grasp a particular function or action that the use of identity invokes: its *processual* quality (Brubaker and Cooper 2000), its *discursive* enactment (Somers 1994), and its *regulatory* use in specific times and places (Du Gay 2007; Foucault 2012). Others attempt to deal with the messily overlapping work identity does using different terms for different functions: Leslie Salzinger (2003) distinguishes the explicit categorization inherent in "identities" from the process of evoking a historically specific "subject/subjectivity" from the disciplinary "interpellation" process of being delimited as an actor. In all cases, these alternatives aim at more analytic distinction among the people, processes, times, and spaces that produce (or fail to produce) what gets commonly lumped together as "identity."

Yet this analytic distinction does not always advance our understanding of how the social world works. It is precisely identity's imprecision that makes it so potent: when people comply with interpellation, they do so because the identity used feels resonant with their subjectivity. This lightning-fast process of moving from an individual-level belief to the social structural level and back again is what is at stake. Just as foundational intersectional critique (e.g. Collins 1990; Combahee River Collective 1979; Crenshaw 1991; Hull, Scott, and Smith 2015) contends that the effort to analytically distinguish class from race/ethnicity from gender obscures those structures' simultaneity, their fluid shifts in effect, and their mutual reinforcement, this chapter claims that the conceptual messiness of identity captures what analytical distinction cannot. The attempts to resolve such tensions cannot get at the experiential quality of unresolved contradictions. As Julie Bettie puts it, despite the fact that "race, class, sexuality, and gender are not properties of individuals but axes of social organization that are shifting and fluid . . . these identities are routinely embraced as real by social actors . . . and are real in their consequences" (2003, 53).

Thus, following Stuart Hall's point that "there are no other, entirely different concepts" (1996, 1) to use instead, in this chapter, I "think with" the concept of identity to make the argument that it is a site where people accept, resist, or articulate claims made on them that then have consequences for the resources and rewards they get. Very simply, because so many people and organizations identify, it is valuable to understand how the beliefs, practices, and structures bundled together in "identity" connect. Worker identity illuminates how a belief in "who I am" becomes entangled with a belief in "who they are" in ways that motivate and restrict actions, connecting the individual to the organizational to the social structural.

But beyond the value of identity as a concept, this chapter shows how the local content of worker identities does not merely arise from but also acts to produce organizations' inequality regimes. I argue that the bakery developed a *monist* identity—one claiming a particular form of domination as originary and all others as derivative and likely to disappear after resolving the primary oppression (Albert et al. 1986)—that was overtly working class and covertly white and masculine. In contrast, the grocery's genuinely *pluralist* identity[2]—one that allowed for multiple iterations of self and others and explicitly resisted a hierarchy of primacy—encompassed a wider (although not complete) range of workplace inequalities.

In this analysis of the interplay of individual, organizational, and social structural inequalities, I take part in a relational inequality conversation that has engaged feminist (Acker 1990; Ferguson 1984; Ridgeway 2011), critical race (Berrey 2015; Castilla 2008; Wingfield 2009), and other liberationist organizational scholarship (Lareau 2003; Schilt 2010; Vallas 2003). This field of study "focus[es] on how categorical distinctions, when wed to organizational divisions of labor, become the interactional bases for more evaluation, inclusion and exclusion from opportunities, and the exploitation of effort and value" (Tomaskovic-Devey and Avent-Holt 2019, 3). Yet although much of this scholarship is relational in that it argues that organizations should be viewed as bundles of relationships rather than individuals (Tomaskovic-Devey and Avent-Holt 2019), there has been a curious willingness to treat the people in these organizational relationships as self-evident categories of actors: women, people of color, the working class. A concept of worker identity challenges this use of categorical difference as inherent or static. How people come to see themselves within particular categories in particular workplaces is, I argue, an organizational process. The difference between how bakery and grocery workers viewed themselves and others as workers was interactive, both shaping and shaped by their organization's practices. That is, I argue that organizations do not simply produce relationships that mediate inequality between categories of actors but that they also make meaningful the categorization of actors within those relationships.

Self and Others: Individual Expressions of Worker Identities

How did worker identities differ between the bakery and the grocery? In this section, I first explore workers' explicit identifications of themselves and of others. The differences in how bakery and grocery workers saw themselves and others *as workers* was not a mere reflection of history or material conditions but rather what Dorinne Kondo (1990) describes as a complex "crafting" of selves in relation to the organization and each other. As I will show, style and dress became an important arena for such crafting.

Bread Bakers and Breadwinners: Identifying at the Bakery

Self-representation. When I asked bakery workers to tell me a bit about themselves, they almost uniformly used traditional class narratives to do. Sales and delivery driver Dutch Henry was perhaps the most direct in his self-representation as a "fiercely proud" member of the working class. He described how his father lost his job of thirty years in the 1980s, which "weren't good for many people except the top two percent! Yeah, working-class people suffered terribly." This overt class consciousness helped to explain his materialist focus. Recall, for example, how in chapter 4 Dutch described the sole benefit of the cooperative aspect of the bakery as the return of profits to those who made the "widgets" in their "widget factory." He framed pursuit of his bakery job as an entirely economic decision by comparing it to similar jobs elsewhere: "Ran routes [on a competitor's bakery truck] next to two People's [Daily Bread Bakery] people, noticed that they got paid every time, their trucks ran, and stuck it out. One guy got me in to see the boss [the work group manager] and about six months later I got hired." Yet after some time in the field, I discovered that the cooperative was the source of most of Dutch's social network. He had regularly taken part in bakery social events, and had met his romantic partner through a coworker. He also used cultural descriptions of himself as working class. "Whatever happens to me, I will always be that same, will always be! If I'm the Sultan of Brunei someday, I will, you know?" he grinned. Then he taught me an Appalachian maxim from his childhood: "You can never *get above your raisin'*, no, you cannot." Although Dutch's class rhetoric was expressed in materialist terms and he described his choices as emanating from those material conditions, his self-representation was much more cultural and personal—albeit also a resolute articulation of class.

This was not only the case for white men at the bakery. Production "lead man" Valentín Rios, who helped me as I struggled on the bread line, had his own version of this narrative. He had left the city in which he had grown up and moved north in search of a more legitimate life than the semi-gangster past he alluded to. He told me that white, middle-class Herbert Gubbins, the bakery CEO, would tease him, calling him "barrio boy" in reference to the Chicanx neighborhood of his youth. Now, though, Valentín's role in the bakery allowed him to drop the curtains on this past, and he focused his self-representation on his role as a family provider whose earnings allowed him to support his son through college—an option he had never had himself. The working-class provider narrative (Halle 1984; Sennett and Cobb 1972) overtly connected masculinity to earning power and to familial nurturance (Bettie 2003; Collinson 1992). More covertly, however, it referenced a worker identity racially coded as white over the one racialized as Latinx in the word *barrio* (Roediger 1999; Weis 2004). The ambivalence with which Valentín described Herbert's term—a light tone but a raised eyebrow—suggested a discomfort as much to do with Herbert's racialization of his past as with any moralization about criminality (Lamont 2000). To be a working-class bakery member was to assume masculinity and to minimize deviations from whiteness.

This masculine and white version of the working-class self was, notably, also commonly used by the women who did not work in the office. Leslie Johnson, the white woman who had initially facilitated my entrée to the bakery (see chapter 1, "A Tale of Two Cooperatives" section), described herself as a sales and delivery driver whose good job allowed her to support her family despite only having achieved a high school diploma. Months later, though, I discovered that her family included her lesbian partner (and coworker), Laura Marks. It was equally long before she talked to me about how much of her job enjoyment came from the fact that she was free of managerial oversight as she drove her route. That is, despite being an out lesbian in a workplace that supported her relationship, and despite having a job that provided her with more autonomy than most bakery workers, Leslie chose the same provider narrative as heterosexual men with far less autonomy. Off-site she was happy to discuss the way the bakery had been a great place to raise children, grinning as she described how she or Laura would bring them along in their vans when they had a day off from school (at least before insurance regulations had forced a change in bakery policies). But, like Valentín, Leslie did not invoke the parts of her life that were outside normative working-class narratives when asked to represent her working self.

The exception to these self-representations was among the women of the office work group. Although they also described previous work experiences that led them to the bakery, like Dutch, or how work allowed them to provide for their children, like Valentín or Leslie, they were all far more likely to directly invoke nonearnings advantages of cooperative work to explain why they worked at the bakery. Pam Jorgeson, the office manager, favorably compared the bakery's respect for limiting working hours with her previous positions. Peggy Printz, a fairly new hire, noted that she had been able to change her hours to accommodate her daughter's school start time. Morning receptionist Mercedes Delgado insisted that her part-time schedule was chosen to allow her to chauffeur her daughter to after-school activities. In these ways, women in the office work group narratively asserted that being a bakery worker was not merely about providing earnings for their families but about work/life balance—something that seemed to be supported by the company in its symbols (individual family pictures on desks, family images in advertising) and certain practices (regular inclusion of family members at biannual parties, childcare provision at quarterly membership meetings). Yet this sense of family interaction as central to the working self did not travel beyond the walls of the all-woman office—indeed, almost tower-like, high above and far from the spaces of manual labor. The difference in worker identity articulated by office workers was part of what increasingly separated them from the others.

Representing others. The bakery's worker identity, however, was constituted not only in self-representations but also in descriptions of others: a process of drawing boundaries between who could and could not be considered as a worker. The abstract worker identity of the bakery was articulated as masculine and working class—sometimes as discrete categories, but often as overlapping. An example of the discretely masculine character of the bakery's worker identity could be seen in how bakery members—men and women, managers and managed alike—referred to production work as "hot and dirty" and to women as disliking "hot and dirty" work. The production work group's masculinity was also expressed as an issue of "language": who cursed, and around whom. Men and women across work groups expressed concern about whether the production shift crews had "watched their language" while I was there, or if the work group was too "salty." Surprisingly, despite their overt attention to me as a woman, no one seemed to notice how regularly *I* myself swore. When I misfed bread through the slicer or dropped packaged loaves, my habitual tendency to curse would (loudly) emerge. But rather than speak of how I might have been fitting in, Mark Costa, the graveyard assistant manager in production who had once warned "girls" off from applying for bakery work, said he was hopeful about the possibility of hiring women now because his crew had "cleaned up their language" during my week with them. Earlier, Charlie Navarro, the production manager, had warned me, "It's not the most professional environment there," and when I pressed him to explain his meaning, he said, "The language. When and if we do bring women in, we're going to have to watch the language." Any contradiction between my embodied professional femininity and its demonstrated profanity were irrelevant to the constitution of the bakery's worker identity as explicitly masculine and implicitly working class.[3]

Charlie's comments also signaled the more common intertwining of masculinity with class and race/ethnicity. In Charlie's contrast between production and a "professional environment," masculinity was collapsed with its working-class iteration. A similar logic emerged in the contrast drawn between manual and administrative work by Dutch when I rode his route with him, as he offered me genuine condolences for having spent the previous week shadowing workers in the office: "Ugh! Who'd want to work there?" This seemed an uncanny echo of the attitude observed by a grocery office worker, that such "paper pushing" was "gross."

But in Dutch's cultural rejection of the office as something distinct from what he described as the "hardworking Mexican men" who he claimed formed the "core group" of the bakery, he also linked a valorized *working-class* labor to masculinity and separated it from "ugh"-worthy white-collar labor and femininity.

Nor was he the only one to do this. Deploying the Marxian concept of unproductive labor, Herbert recalled the rare times when, helping to create a formula for a new product, he would spend part of his day on the production floor: "We make jokes: managers just sit on their asses and do nothing. I mean, I've committed that sin myself. . . . I [worked in production] a year ago, it nearly killed me! But I would go home . . . and if I had actually done production work, I would say [to my wife], 'I worked today.' Well, what the hell else did I do here!" Although he was aware of how he minimized the value of his administrative labor as CEO—most of his time at the bakery—compared to the "work" of manual labor, he seemed less aware of how this articulation collapsed "unproductive" administrative work with feminized office jobs, the others who "sit on their asses." Herbert thus consigned the most common form of women's work at the bakery to a nonwork status. Rather than being a subordinated form of masculinity (Connell 1995), at the bakery working-class masculinity was defiantly hegemonic.

While class and gender occupied fairly clear dimensions of the bakery's worker identity, race and ethnicity had a stealthy effect as well. Production, whose labor was at the heart of the bakery's worker identity, was not only reserved for men but also overwhelmingly ethnoracially marked men: not only the "hardworking Mexican men" described by Dutch, but in fact, a mix of immigrants from the Spanish-speaking Americas, nonimmigrants whose roots were in the once-Spanish parts of California, and a few who were African American or mixed race). Indeed, this comment followed his own self-description as culturally working class, and led him to ask, "Would you call [a group of employees who immigrated from a rural area] working-class? Probably not, weren't a lot of jobs where they came from. So they're working class *now*." In Dutch's explanation, then, the cooperative both generated what Karl Marx (1976) would call the "relations of production" that removed these immigrant men from less stratified agricultural roles and ensconced them as subordinated wage earners, but also afforded them the dignity of hard work and the economic rights to their share of profits. Despite a socially marginalized ethnoracial status, the working-class masculinity that contoured the bakery's worker identity allowed for their inclusion.

At the same time, however, it also suggested subtle limits on inclusion or even overt exclusion. When asked why most men of color were located in the production work group, white workers in and out of that work group used one of three narrative strategies to explain this concentration: first, that the local area had actively functioning networks connecting migrants from the Mexican state of Jalisco (a fact that might have accounted for half the Latinx workers, but not those from other regions, nor the nonimmigrants); second, a shared church membership (something I found little support for when I inquired); and third, a purported "*jefe* mentality," or a culturally linked willingness to defer to bosses (a claim that, even if it had not ignored a centuries-long history of resistance, could not be squared with the observable constancy of bakery production workers' complaints and noncompliance, as well as their impressive self-management skills during the frequent long stretches when assistant managers were doing paperwork off the production floor). The organizational stories told by white workers about Brown production workers were not only weakly connected to empirically observable social life; they also limited Brown workers' ability to fully inhabit the bakery's worker identity or make claims through it.

Monist identity. Both in terms of oneself or others, the bakery's worker identity drew strongly on an appraisal of the working class as powerful, hardworking, and essential to bakery success—a fairly traditional socialist and communist narrative dating from the nineteenth century (Scott 1988). Although it was a monist conception of class as the primary force shaping selves and others, masculinity was also embedded in this conceptualization of the working class, which made it more difficult to include women in this identity construction (although, if they were willing to accept masculinization, not impossible). These traditionally classed narratives also implicitly conflated a working-class identity with whiteness in the ways they positioned nonwhite working-class members of the bakery as Other, following an established American pattern of class discourse (Weis 2004). Whiteness, masculinity, and a working-class self were, it could be said, baked into the worker identity.

Many Flavors and Many Facets: Identifying at the Grocery

Self-representation. Class did not manifest in the grocery's worker identity in the way it did at the bakery despite the highly similar backgrounds of workers at both cooperatives. Only two grocery workers explicitly described themselves to me as "working class," and one of them was from England, a place where overt class categorization of self and others is a cultural constant (Sutcliffe-Braithwaite 2018). Although a few grocery workers did use the typically masculine and working-class provider narrative to present themselves, most used a mix of other frameworks to construct their worker identity: lifelong learners, freedom seekers, artists or musicians, and political or food activists. For instance, Jennifer, who claimed that she "liked to play boss" in the "Gender" section of chapter 5, was initially silent about her earnings (later described as "excellent" when directly asked). Instead she described her interest in learning about organic and vegetarian food after a childhood of being "raised pretty white trash, you know, macaroni and cheese, Hamburger Helper." As I described in the "Participatory Bureaucracy and Inequality at One World Natural Grocery" section of chapter 6, the grocery as university was a common trope used by grocery workers to me, their academic listener. But as grocery workers like Jennifer translated their sense of working-class roots similar to those of bakery driver Dutch Henry into a different language, they nevertheless articulated a working-class worker identity—albeit one articulated through different categories and narratives.

Jennifer also explained who she was in terms of personal freedom. "The whole idea [of a worker cooperative] to me *blew my mind*. Like 'Wow, no boss?' 'Cause I'm not one of the top good luck with bosses!" The ways in which the distributed management of the grocery was superior to managerial workplaces was another common thread among grocery workers' self-representations, despite the many ways it seemed as if floor workers' autonomy was severely curtailed by customers (see chapter 5, "Political Rights" section). Yet the ability to express a complex and particular combination of class, race/ethnicity, and gender expression seemed precious to Jennifer when she described her eclectic mix of styles:

> I do kind of keep pride in my trashy, white—I mean, I listen to [a modern country radio station] in the cooler and everybody gives me shit: "How do you listen to this?" I'm like, "Ah, you know, I don't have time, I'm too busy to put in all my CDs all the time." And I mean, I'm kind of different that way. And I'm, [*makes air quotes*] you know, [a] *"straight girl,"* which—I mean, I don't know, everybody thinks I'm a *queer straight girl.* . . . Working-related, I feel like I fit in really well. And I don't really feel any kind of separation with anybody.

Although Jennifer was aware of ways in which aspects of herself that she brought to work seemed different from or even bizarre to her coworkers—like her love of a type of music embraced by lower-class whites—she also felt that workplace practices allowed these differences to easily coexist, to minimize "separation with anybody." With multiple piercings in her face and ears, a number of tattoos visible on her arms, and hair in variable but always brightly colored shades, a desire for freedom from bosses was not surprising. But her outward appearance also allowed her to take on a *queer* modifier for the *straight* label that matched her typical romantic pattern of heterosexual relationships with cisgender men. The seeming dichotomy of *queer* and *straight* was presented as harmonized, and harmonized in a way I came to see was commonplace in grocery worker identity narratives.

Grocery workers typically would tell me about ways in which they saw themselves as different from their coworkers before telling me about how they saw themselves fitting in. Even before I heard Juanita Cole, an African American woman in her thirties, being teased as "the drill sergeant" for her strict work ethic, she had introduced herself to me as second-generation military and noted that it made her a little different from others at the grocery. Indeed, there seemed to be fewer veterans at the grocery than might be expected among such a large working-class membership (Lutz 2008). Juanita, though, focused on her military past as entrée to the grocery: her military forklift training had made her application stand out. As she saw it, "every job I had, I just used the military skills." Her military service was both a distinctive quality she used to individuate and a characteristic connecting her to the grocery as a whole.

In addition to the military, Juanita also focused on what she saw as the grocery's guarantee of freedom. Taking a grocery job had meant a pay cut, and retail seemed like a step back on any career ladder. But what made her choose the job, she explained, was the ability to be "honest" with customers, to dress and speak on the shop floor without censure, to enjoy the overlap of social and work life (her roommate a coworker, and her girlfriend in a band with another coworker), and to autonomously claim vacation time or switch shifts as needed to accommodate her band's practice and touring schedule. All of this, she concluded, came with earnings and benefits that now far outpaced what she would have been making if she had stayed at her last job.

Juanita's worker identity narrative was like Jennifer's in that it started with difference (a military past or being a fan of working-class musical culture) on its way to emphasizing similarity (developing an autonomous life, embracing an oppositional view of her sexuality). For another floor worker, Diego Degas, in the household goods work group, the different-but-included narrative revolved around his greater idealism that, as he saw it, could be a gift for improving the store. Diego, a fast-talking, Caribbean Latinx man in his twenties, described himself as having a "very idealistic self-identity," unlike most grocery workers who were more "into selling stuff." Diego had once tried to do social work with disabled adults, but found it too emotionally draining. For him the grocery could help make a better world in a different way: by curating a collection of "okay" products that did not add to social or environmental problems, and allowing customers to shop without having to make such determinations on the fly. He had successfully lobbied his work group's buyer to discontinue a household cleanser produced by a subsidiary of Monsanto, as I discovered shortly after we met when he was asked for it by a middle-aged African American customer in a FedEx uniform. When Diego explained why it was no longer stocked, the customer seemed to take his inability to buy the product he had been seeking in stride:

"That's cool," he said, comparing Monsanto to Nike, which was being targeted by activists at the time over its sweatshop production (Greenberg and Knight 2004). "It's globalization. They're exploiting the Third World." Diego's assessment of customer desires thus seemed accurate.

At the same time, while Diego had been able to direct his own work group's offerings, a vegetarian meat substitute produced by a Philip Morris subsidiary was still being sold two aisles away: he had no influence over another work group or its buyers' choices. Yet if I had thought this would provoke a sense of separation from the grocery in Diego, I was mistaken. Diego explained the different sales decisions as the valuable result of work groups' autonomy and a democratic cooperative. His individuation of himself as "very idealistic" was not about setting himself entirely apart from others only interested in "selling stuff" but a way to articulate his inclusion in the shared process of workplace democracy.

For all three grocery workers, self-representation as distinctive but incorporated created a complex worker identity. Rather than promoting a single characteristic that automatically limited coverage to certain kinds of workers, as the bakery's worker identity did, grocery workers' kaleidoscope of identifying narratives posited "mixture" as the grocery's worker identity.

Representing others. Like bakery workers, grocery workers fleshed out their worker identity not only in self-descriptions but in descriptions of others. Yet in the same way that their self-representations evoked a collected set of differences in place of an internally cohesive figure, their articulation of an abstract worker seemed less bounded and indeed less consistent than the bakery's. Chris Badger, the white, middle-class member of the packaged food work group who felt that knowing a worker gave job applicants more of an advantage than cooperative experience (see chapter 5, "Class" section), said, "I guess that when I started there [in the early 1990s], it still largely felt hippie-flavored with a good solid punk edge . . . and, of course, you know, more diverse than that, but . . . that kind of seems like where it was, but now the overall flavoring is much more complex." Indeed, it was often difficult for me to find times or places where boundaries were drawn. Unlike the bakery, where women were perceived to reject "hot and dirty" work and Latinx workers were characterized as subservient or having a "*jefe* mentality," the collectively imagined worker identity seemed encompassing.

The limits of this broad worker identity were visible, however, in workers' references to "hard work." A "hard worker" was one of the highest of compliments; to be described as "not a hard worker" was to have one's political and social standing—and perhaps even one's employment—threatened. Juanita Cole, "the drill sergeant," was explicitly identified as a hard worker by her work group member Sarah Drum; together, Juanita and Sarah used a coworker's persistent refusal to "pull his own weight" to justify firing him. Hard work could refer to the dedication assumed in someone who worked many hours. Jennifer Ruud used the term for a hospitalized coworker with pneumonia who called her to make sure a product demonstration was scheduled. Hard work could also mean the capacity for physical labor: a white, middle-class household goods worker, Susan Wells, who had been at the grocery for over a decade, claimed that floor work was a "horrible job" because it was primarily just tidying shelves, unlike the physically demanding work of unpacking and stocking new shipments that she performed in her capacity as a buyer. "It takes a kind of lazy person to stay in the [household goods floor worker] job," she said, and compared a newly hired young man who had taken a weekend morning receiving shift as "a hard worker" compared to another "lazy" one who had not. Although physical labor was strongly associated with masculinity at the bakery, it was not the case at the grocery: grocery women seemed as proud of their physical strength and stamina as grocery men did. Indeed, I observed two women cheese workers laughing at a middle-aged woman customer who had criticized them for "reversing" the "natural" gender order by lifting massive wheels of aged Parmesan from a dolly into the cooler while a man coworker, nursing a back injury, stood behind the counter distributing thin slices of Spanish sheep cheese to customers. If anything, the grocery seemed to provide a space in which women could take pleasure in their physical prowess, and men could acknowledge physical limits without fear of stigma.

Yet the term "hard work" was not simply code for physically demanding work. Andrew Jefferson, a white, middle-class produce worker, said, "There are two standards [of hard work]: how emotionally available you are to coworkers (which is kind of high school, but also political—you should know that One World is a very political place), but also how hard you work," which he described as being on time, being thorough, and taking on extra tasks, like helping someone find some herbs in the vegetable display even if your shift was on the fruit side. That the scope of hard work included relational aspects of the workplace seemed fairly accurate, particularly in terms of the recent firing of a member of his work group. Hired away from another work group in part due to his size and strength, this white, working-class man had been appreciated for agreeing to work several undesirable late-night shifts. While such hard work could have cemented his place in the work group, his refusal to respond to coworker criticism of his performance during these shifts undermined his physical contributions—confirming Andrew's assessment of the need to perform emotionally as well as physically to be seen as hardworking. Worker identity hinged, therefore, on the ability to relate to others.

Cashiers also grappled with this complex definition of hard work. Twenty-year-old Sara High, the mixed-race daughter of an older white man in another work group, was like many other cashiers in expressing an almost perverse pride in her work group. "Cashiering," she told me, is "so much harder than anything else. . . . You're stuck out there, you can't always go to the bathroom when you want to, customers are nastiest at the registers, it's physically tiring to stand in one place all day, and there's the repetitive injury issue." Others echoed the sense of hard work as a cashier, but primarily in terms of customers. One night, waiting for cashiers to finish counting up their cash drawers before the start of a membership meeting, a refrigerated food worker shook her head, saying, "I wouldn't want to be a cashier. They take money!" "They take *lip!*" shot back a packaged goods worker next to her, upping the ante by pointing out the verbal abuse directed at cashiers. Indeed, members of the cashiers work group complained that the same customers who rudely talked on their cell phones as their purchases were being rung up would snap at cashiers who took a call of their own. Customers picked fights, freaked out if someone tried to help them bag their groceries, freaked out if no one tried to help them. As in other work groups, customers were described as "needy": wanting to share too much about love lives, housing difficulties, or gut health. For cashiers (as well as many floor workers), "hard work" meant trying to find a balance between the physical and emotional demands of customer service and their own emotional autonomy.

Although hard work was not explicitly gendered—the more masculinized aspects of on-the-job face time and physically arduous labor were at least somewhat offset by the more feminized relational aspect—the need for at least some physical effort layered moral judgement onto differences of physical strength and stamina that were often connected to physical dis/ability and even more to age. Diana Flores, who had joined the store in the late 1970s after rising housing expenses required her to find a job to fund her countercultural life, had noticed this. When I asked her how welcoming the grocery was to a diverse population, she said, "I'd like to see more older workers. Once in a while we do hire an older worker, but I think that there are still problems, there's different levels of discrimination." To some extent, this centrality of physical effort to hard work resulted from the unusual mixture of governance, management, and manual labor that were part of most grocery positions. Unlike traditional supermarkets' sharper delineations between cognitive managerial work and physical floor work, few jobs at One World Natural Grocery were free of physical requirements. But the association of hard work with physical exertion shaped the grocery's worker identity and undermined workers who were unable to complete physically demanding labor.

For instance, Diana and two other older white women petitioned for discussion of their distress over a gory Halloween display at a Cooperative Concerns session, or CoCo (see chapter 5, "Political Rights" section). After the CoCo a younger worker claimed that only Diana, the oldest of the three at sixty-five, was being taken seriously because "people respect Diana on a conscience level and listen to her on that level"; as for the others, "none of them work hard, none of them work much, and that is a real bottom-line thing." Like Diana, the other two older women had scheduled themselves for workweeks that averaged twenty-four hours, the minimum necessary to preserve their health insurance and store discount. Because none of these women's jobs involved physically strenuous labor, because two of them were members of customer service (a work group generally viewed as a dumping ground for workers who were unable to perform the physically demanding labor of other work groups), and because all three had cut back their hours as a form of gradual retirement, they were not able to leverage the moral weight of "hard work" in favor of their cause. Whether as a motivator or a disciplinary tool, "hard work" was a key component of what it meant to be a worker at the cooperative, and effectively limited older and physically dis/abled people's access to the grocery's worker identity.

Pluralist identity. The grocery's worker identity did not link class to race/ethnicity or gender, and was far less cohesive or linear than the bakery's. At times this could seem like a class consciousness was simply missing: Jennifer's description of herself as "white trash" could not simply be read as a coded way of saying "working class," because its imprecision often generated misunderstanding (I overheard an older white woman from the Deep South call herself "white trash" and get scolded by an older white man from the same region, who tried unsuccessfully to convince her that she could not describe herself that way because "your parents went to college!"). Yet in positing the cooperative as a place of learning or freedom from being bossed around, the grocery's worker identity not only put key aspects of working-class experience at its center but simultaneously expressed other kinds of marginalized self-descriptions. In this the grocery worker identity was pluralist. Yet, even within in this pluralism, options were not limitless: while the description of the "overall flavoring" of the grocery's worker identity was "complex," as Chris put it, youth and normative physical ability were implicit requirements of inclusion.

Style and Worker Identity

Differences between the bakery's monist working-class identity and the grocery's pluralist complexity was, literally, visible in how bakery and grocery workers sartorially arrayed themselves as well as in their interpretations of their own (and each others') style. At the bakery, workers' "ordinary" form of dress cemented the whiteness and masculinity of an overt working-class identification, while the grocery's intentional (but alternative) flair refused this articulation of what it meant to be working class.

If bakery workers could be said to have a style, it would be "unobtrusive." Clothing was generally conventional in cut (not baggy, but not particularly revealing of the body) and in color (khaki, gray, navy, burgundy, hunter green, and white predominated). While office workers' clothes were more likely to require dry cleaning and production workers' more likely to be worn or stained, clean and neat clothes were generally the rule. Most workers wore pants, and the only skirts or dresses were worn by women. While there were some deviations—more masculine dress and styling among many women in delivery and shipping, production manager Charlie's long hair, Herbert's commonly worn dangling earrings, and what seemed a Halloween ritual of male managers in drag—such deviations underscored the bakery's routine gender normativity. Only sales and delivery drivers were required to wear shirts or jackets with the company logo, but throughout my years of observation I never observed another work group without at least one member wearing clothing with a bakery logo. All workers seemed to have acquired bakery-branded items through promotions, contests, team-building activities, or awards for accomplishments, and Herbert almost always wore logo-embroidered shirt. In general, the bakery style seemed to try to minimize individuality. If hair was dyed, it was to disguise graying. No workers had visible piercings other than in their ears, which was partly because jewelry could not be worn on the production floor but also because it was seen as peculiar: when, at a board meeting, transit driver and board member Adam Delaney was awarded a commemorative pin for his twenty-year service mark, his joke about pairing it with the one from his ten-year anniversary as nipple rings was met with exclamations of "Ugh!" and uncomfortable laughter. Overall, bakery workers seemed to reach for the kind of studied "ordinariness" that Florence Sutcliffe-Braithwaite (2018) argues has become a way of constituting a working-class self.

Many grocery workers, by contrast, were conspicuously styled. "There's this sense," explained Juanita, "like, 'Don't dress dowdy. Dress sexy!'" Juanita—on this day sporting vintage "menswear" purple pants, a "womenswear" cropped brown T-shirt that showed off her pierced belly button, and a black cap into which she had tucked her long dreadlocks—claimed workers were not hired for their looks but *were* exhorted by each other to dress "cute" for work. Across workers and work areas, grocery members were more likely to wear formfitting than loose clothes and seemed to be dressing for each other at least as much as for customers, regularly exchanging compliments that seemed to give genuine pleasure. While some grocery workers were, like bakery workers, consciously "ordinary"—clean and off-brand jeans, plain button-down shirts or T-shirts—many more seemed to engage creatively in their self-representation. Some revealed numerous piercings of a range of body parts, dramatic tattoos, unnatural hair colors, and T-shirts with overtly political messages attacking capitalism, colonialism, racism, or sexism or extolling the virtues of alternative sexualities or cultures. Others sported the crisply ironed chinos and pressed top-buttoned shirts or tight jeans and shiny fabric blouses popular among local Chicanx youth of the time, while still others rocked the oversize gold jewelry and baggy branded jeans of hip-hop culture. There were even some whose peacock feathers and colorful fabrics brought the hippie days of the 1960s and 1970s into the present. In addition, there seemed to be an overall rejection of normative gender presentation: it was not uncommon to see men as well as women in dresses or skirts; unshaved legs and armpits could be seen on women as well as men; and many workers could not easily be identified within a gender binary. Grocery workers were conscious of being on display to their two hundred coworkers as well as the hundreds of customers streaming through the store each day, and both pandered to and questioned their imagined public.

The contrast between bakery and grocery style norms was noticed by the bakery's sales and delivery drivers, some of whom had daily contact with grocery workers. Over an after-work drink with Dutch and another white, working-class man, Matt Koslowski, I asked for their impressions of grocery workers. Matt, in a green bakery-logo polo and dark blue jeans, shrugged, but Dutch, in a red logo polo and cargo shorts, gave a sharp bark of laughter and pronounced them "pretentious." He called out their habit of "dressing in rags"—the punk subcultural outfit of torn pants, ancient T-shirts, and faded hoodies—and thus reframed grocery workers' "cute" style as the affectation of middle-class kids. In this assessment, Dutch engaged with dress as the kind of communication of class and status described by Pierre Bourdieu as "opportunities to experience or assert one's position in social space, as a rank to be upheld or a distance to be kept" (1984, 57). By calling this style "pretentious" Dutch proposed that either the grocery workers were working-class people trying to disguise their class status by taking on the trappings of a more socially advantaged class, or they were middle-class "tourists" to a less privileged strata of society—what some have described as "poor chic" (Halnon 2002). In either case, though, the issue was that their style revealed what Erving Goffman describes as a "self-conscious attention to affect" (1951, 300) that signals, paradoxically, distance from rather than inclusion in a class to which one was not born. As Dutch continued, it was clear that he read this style as "poor chic" when he specifically named as a prime offender Joe Peterson, the young white safety coordinator described in the "Participatory Bureaucracy and Inequality at One World Natural Grocery" section of chapter 6, who had joined the grocery after dropping out of high school. As Bourdieu points out, "Men especially are forbidden every sort of 'pretension' in matters of culture, language or clothing" because such interest violates the construction of specifically working-class masculinity (1984, 382). Dutch mimed surprise and doubt when I told him he had identified someone as materially and militantly working-class as himself. I wondered if he had focused solely on Joe's ratty T-shirts and counterculturally chic black-line tattoos, or if he had noticed the costly and immaculately kept steel-toed Caterpillar boots and Ben Davis work pants that were far more common signs and practicalities of blue-collar labor. In his class militancy, Dutch used the terrain of style to stake a claim for what it meant to work as a member of the working class and what was excluded from that definition. Whereas working-class labor style was masculine and "realistic or, one might say, functionalist" (Bourdieu 1984, 200), that of grocery workers was suspiciously nonfunctional and deliberately aesthetic.

This is not to say that bakery workers had no aesthetic, but in the positive sanction of function over form and negative sanction of not "getting above your raisin'," it was quite a different aesthetic from grocery workers' expression of multiple urban Chicanx cholo/a, African American hip-hop, and urban/suburban punk and hippie styles. While Dutch was right that grocery workers were largely rejecting the style conventions of the historically American working-class habitus—one characterized by white and masculine forms of self-representation— he was *not* necessarily right that this meant they were asserting an identity that was not working class. Instead they were expanding the notion of working class to reincorporate explicitly anti-capitalist punk and hippie styles and ethnoracially distinctive cholo/a and hip-hop ones. In doing so they offered a gender and ethnoracial critique of the term *working class* and its historical exclusions.

Similar Demographics, Different Identities

The bakery and the grocery each had developed distinctive worker identities: deep abstractions of what it meant to be a worker at each cooperative that evoked both demographic and relational categories like class, race/ethnicity, gender, and a conceptualization of work and workers. At the bakery, a monist working-class identity corralled the self-conceptions of people of color and white women into a narrower range of positions than did the grocery's pluralist identity, which invoked multiple ways to be a worker and multiple ideas of what constituted work. And this was more than abstraction: worker identities were both legitimated by and legitimating factors in organizational processes. As the next section shows, worker identities were consequential for the organizational distribution of resources and rewards throughout the workforce.

Diversity Regimes: The Organization of Worker Identities

Inequality regimes function by linking organizational practices to organizational meanings. This section reveals how worker identities limited and mobilized the ability of each cooperative to address inequality through explicit processes like so-called diversity training and through more implicit ones like pay and personnel policies. As a constellation of organizational actions, these explicit and implicit practices function as diversity regimes, what Steven Vallas and I have theorized as the "formal provisions that firms develop in order to regulate differences among different categories of employees" (2016, 105). Diversity regimes can be seen as sets of processes within inequality regimes that specify which types of inequality are to be addressed and rationales for doing so. These include the administration of overt diversity, equity, and inclusion practices aimed at the *direct* interruption of inequality ranging from affirmative action to sensitivity training to mentor brokering, as well as more oblique practices such as dependent care provision, flexible scheduling, health care benefit policies, or the distribution of profits that have indirect but no less substantial effects. As part of inequality regimes, diversity regimes adjudicate between competing claims workers may make on the organization administratively, supporting or undermining worker identities.

The Bakery

Explicit address of inequality. The bakery's diversity regime was most overtly expressed in its diversity training. This was a response to the social identity-related conflicts in the early 1990s described in the "People's Daily Bread Bakery" section of chapter 3: accusations of sexual harassment and racism were exchanged between a white woman and an African American man, and an out white lesbian received targeted death threats from a homophobic white man coworker. While managers dealt directly with the people involved, they also felt that these incidences indicated a need for cultural change to address the increasing class, ethnoracial, and gender heterogeneity of the cooperative, and hired consultants for an intensive week with the entire workforce. These diversity trainers facilitated a series of whole-group and paired discussions using psychotherapeutic techniques aimed at identifying common humanity and thus promoting better interactions. Keith, the Latinx personnel director who described "letting people be who they are" in the first epigraph to this chapter, explained their reasoning:

You want to give everybody a chance to express—as long as they're respectful—express themselves as human beings. And that was very helpful to everybody! And it was very open and honest and private. . . . We certainly go to great extents to say that, as far as management's concerned, you are who you are. And there's a freedom of speech that involves politics, it involves philosophies, it involves sexual orientation, and anything else that human beings can think of. . . . As we got to know our coworkers . . . we found that lot of the barriers were kind of thrown off to the side and we could just accept that person as *that person* rather than thinking of them as a [*air quotes*]—you know, some type of label that each person makes up in their own mind.

Keith believed that workers could at least tolerate difference by allowing each other "freedom of speech." This approach to worker diversity has been termed a "discrimination-and-fairness perspective" that "is characterized by a belief in a culturally diverse workforce as a moral imperative to ensure justice and the fair treatment of all members of society" (Ely and Thomas 2001, 245). While these goals seem virtuous, the bakery's diversity training approach required simultaneously positing a common "human being" bond as more consequential than an individual's "type of label"; positing the individual apart from gender, sexuality, or race/ethnicity; and eliminating sites of conflict that might activate these "type of label" characteristics. This diversity training model posited ethnoracial and gender (and sexuality) characteristics as aspects of the larger society that had unfortunately leaked into the cooperative in this moment, and that needed to be neutralized for the good of the working-class subject whose struggles within capitalism were at the heart of the organization's reason for existence. Indeed, almost ten years later, no further formal diversity, equity, and inclusion programs had been introduced and there were no formally sanctioned discussions of how race/ethnicity, gender, and/or sexuality affected working conditions. Organizationally, the bakery had delimited race/ethnicity and gender as *external, irregular*, and *individual*, and its worker identity as something that preexisted such conditions.

That is not to say that there were no other explicit practices aimed at regulating inequalities. The membership strictly adhered to a bylaws requirement from the time of the managerial transition that the nine-member board of directors must include at least two women and at least two men, and to a well-publicized and strongly enforced anti-fraternization policy intended to protect women subordinates from men supervisors. Unlike the diversity training, these policies asserted gender inequalities as internal to the workplace, a continuous condition of work, and produced or maintained by organizational structures. Yet they were largely ineffective in creating an inclusive workplace. The board's gender representation requirement was disparaged by Herbert in membership meetings and by Keith in orientations as a wrongheaded leftover from collectivist times that directed attention away from board candidates' substantive merits, and potentially allowed unqualified candidates to make key bakery decisions. The anti-fraternization policies were widely (and incorrectly) construed literally as an injunction against friendships among workers regardless of rank in the managerial hierarchy, chilling off-site social relations. For instance, after being constantly invited to grocery gatherings during my observation period there, I wondered what I was doing wrong when no bakery workers extended any similar invitations. When I made a joke about this to the sales and delivery driver I was shadowing, Matt Koslowski, a white man in his fifties, he immediately invited me to come with him and Dutch to a locally infamous "redneck" bar that very afternoon. Two weeks later, when I brought up this excursion with a small knot of women drivers during the membership meeting break, four-year veteran Jackie Merchant griped, "Hey, I've never been invited!" and Sylvia Weedon, with more than twelve years' seniority, snorted, "Or me!" Despite being intended to reduce gender inequalities, the anti-fraternization policy had the unintended consequence of driving ethnoracialized and gendered informal networks underground, where they could proliferate without collective oversight or intervention.

In both cases the enactment of practices intended to explicitly address inequalities revealed some of the ways in which the monist working-class worker identity shaped the diversity and thus the inequality regimes of the bakery. The invocation of class as the primary determinant of a bakery worker's workplace self-relegated race/ethnicity and gender to the sidelines, undermining even those practices that had once been intended to address heterogeneity and any existing inequalities within or across class lines. In this way the diversity regime continued to minimize the importance of nonclass characteristics as central to a worker's being. That minimization also carried over into human resources and other processes, practices, and actions that were not intended to reduce or produce inequality but nevertheless had those effects.

Implicit address of inequality. In addition to policies and procedures that were explicitly designed and recognized as attempts to right social wrongs, others acted similarly but without being recognized as doing so. The least contested of these implicit addresses, which was also in many ways the most direct expression of working-class primacy in the bakery's worker identity, was its distribution of the wealth. Like most cooperatives, the bakery returned profits to its members based on labor contribution (see the "How Worker Cooperatives Work" section of chapter 2). But approximately a quarter of the bakery's annual profits were distributed to all workers—members or not—as bonuses for meeting work group goals. As I noted in chapter 3, this unusual practice was originally intended to help retain newer workers and increase worker solidarity, but its continuation elevated the value of *labor* to at least that of *ownership*. This appraisal of bakery labor's value helped to explain why the bakery equated on-the-job experience with academic certification, noticeable in the internal promotion of most managers from either the bakery's own floor (as with Charlie, the production manager, or Sherry Ferrar, the shipping manager), or from the floor of other bakeries (as with Pete MacCraig, the sales and delivery manager). The only one with the formal credentials typically associated with management—and the middle and upper middle classes—was Pam Jorgeson, the office manager. The working-class core of the bakery's worker identity provided moral legitimation for policies that defied routine corporate practices that reproduced class inequality, and reinforced the bakery's articulation of its members as working-class people.

In contrast, the bakery's approach to ethnoracial inequalities was more ambivalent, particularly in terms of integrating its primary Spanish-speaking workers. On one hand, the bakery sought to increase these workers' democratic participation in membership meetings by offering simultaneous interpretation through wireless headsets and cluster seating around an interpreter who could speak for them. But, on the other hand, the bakery limited such interpretation to governance functions, and managers offered no translation of documents into Spanish other than a few safety signs mandated by the state, expressing a fear that translation of only a portion of operational documents would leave them open to litigation in areas where they had not done so. While two of the production crews had adapted to the prevalence of primary Spanish speakers by using spoken Spanish to share information (see chapter 6), their processes were not institutionalized within the bakery. The ambivalence also extended to responsibility for communication: upper management hired an on-site Spanish instructor to train all levels of management during their working hours, but quickly ended the program when production assistant manager John Costa offended the instructor by refusing to fully engage with the classes and by insisting that English, not Spanish, was required of all workers. Indeed, the bakery continued to mandate that, if deemed necessary by their managers, its primary Spanish speakers take English as a Second Language courses at the local community college—with course fees paid by the bakery but the time not counted as working hours. The bakery's deflection of responsibility for the workplace communication to external providers seemed to suggest that linguistic divides—and the deep social inequality embedded in the English/Spanish divide of early twenty-first century California—were external to its worker identity. Unlike the bakery's atypical class-egalitarian promotion practices, its treatment of ethno-racialized language barriers articulated its ideal worker as English speaking, and Spanish as a deficiency of the worker self.

The ambivalence about gender inequality was even more pronounced and even less effective. The bakery had instituted a practice of combining vacation and sick paid time off into a "personal" category that could be used by workers at will. This combined personal time category reflected a 1990s human resources trend nationally promoted as particularly beneficial for women workers, who are more likely than men to feel the "time bind" (Hochschild 1997) of balancing family care responsibility and paid work. Yet while personal time seemed to protect women by combining sick days' unplanned flexibility with vacation days' freedom to use the time as desired, its potential for promoting gender equality at the bakery was undermined by another bakery policy offering incentives to trade excess personal time for cash. Most men I asked had cashed theirs out, while most women used theirs. No one I asked saw any problem with that: the twin policies offered legitimate excuses for time away but kept production and distribution going. That is, the bakery's class-focused worker identity prioritized workers' productive capacities over all other parts of their lives to the extent that none of the workers could see how this both relied on and reinforced the man as provider/woman as nurturer social binary—a social schema that has undermined the careers of those who are fantasized as loyal to family above workplace (Kennelly 1999; Stone 2007)—let alone why that reinforcement could be a workplace concern. The idea that a cooperative workplace might have a legitimate stake in encouraging men's provision of domestic care was made almost unimaginable due to the restrictive lens of the bakery's monist worker identity.

Managerial bureaucracy and worker identity. The bakery's monist worker identity was crucial to its organizational structure. As chronicled in the "People's Daily Bakery" section of chapter 3, the bakery's path from collective self-management to managerial bureaucracy had been a rocky one: even during the time of my study, more than a decade later, workers pushed back on managerial control in the name of "the cooperative." But the bakery's class-primary worker identity eased that process and in turn was reinforced by its managerial bureaucracy in two ways. First, its organizational transition was motivated by a desire to adapt cooperative practice to the capitalist world for the good of its workers. It relied on the assumption voiced by Herbert, the bakery's first and only CEO at the time of my study, that bakery workers' principal interests were safe and enduring jobs that provided enough income to sustain life—a "breadwinner" assumption similar to what had animated the labor movement for more than a century, and relegated to the sidelines gendered and ethnoracial concerns about relations between economic production and family and community well-being

(Acker 2006a; Gordon Nembhard 2014). For instance, Herbert waved off discussion of shipping manager Sherry's difficulties with her work group, attributing workers' criticisms to a general resentment of being told what to do. "What do working-class people *begrudgingly* accept?" he growled. "Management!" As he saw it, complaint was an inevitable part of profitability: management, and the accompanying curtailment of total individual freedom, was essential to the bakery's ability to support a working-class membership.

Second, the typical class tensions between upper-class management and working-class labor had been mitigated by hiring managers from the floor, which Herbert, as CEO, been instrumental in normalizing. That managers also were far more likely than nonmanagers to be elected to the board of directors—the only site at the bakery where workers could exercise authority over managers—was eased both by the real class parity between them and also by the class primacy of the bakery's worker identity. By constructing not only a *principally* but *unitarily* working-class worker identity, bakery managers could be workers' working-class proxy to the board of directors rather than the kinds of actors with different and opposing interests found in typical managerial workplaces. This worker identity provided congruence between the bakery's liberatory goals of working-class empowerment and its unequal distribution of power and autonomy. In doing so, it reinforced class as explanatory for workplace relations while minimizing gender and race/ethnicity as central structures of workplace power.

The organization of monist worker identity. In terms of explicit diversity training, implicit practices to formally regulate access to resources and rewards, and organizational structure, the bakery's diversity regime not only reflected but reinforced its monist worker identity as one constituted entirely by class structures. Positing processes historically associated with class (such as the extraction of value from labor) as universal to workers but processes associated with race/ethnicity and gender (such as language use or work/home balance) as particular and individual—and only needing an occasional check to keep such external forces from overwhelming the cooperative—the bakery's diversity regime reinforced the masculinity and whiteness that inhered in its working-class worker identity.

The Grocery

Explicit address of inequality. Like the bakery, the grocery began its direct address of inequalities as a response to conflict—in this case one that Jennifer Ruud, then a member of the Intracooperative Coordinating Committee (ICC), described as a "nightmare." A white, working-class, bisexual woman and two white, gay men lobbed accusations of homophobia and sexism at each other, leading to a series of appeals first to the ICC, and to their review by almost the entire membership in a multihour meeting recalled by Jennifer in the "Political Rights" section of chapter 5 as "a huge pile of money that was blowing out the window." Although the work group's terminations and the ICC's confirmation of them were upheld at the membership meeting, and while this seemed to strengthen trust in the cooperative's distributed management, the process also appeared to unearth a range of tensions regarding workers' prejudices and workplace inequalities. Diana, the white woman who also noted the store's ageism earlier, was vocal in her observation of manifestations of racism at the grocery:

> In my work group, I've seen a lot of people of color come and go. . . . And I think what's happening with a lot of them is we're impolite, we're not nice to them. . . . I think that they are less likely to, as one worker put it a long time ago, "eat shit." [My work group has] a worker now who's Black. And she does *not* want to be disrespected. I've been through many meetings where *very* disrespectful things were said about me and nobody said anything about it, although *she* does now. . . . That's an important thing in her life, and I think that led her into getting into that serious fight that we were talking about recently, but when I was talking to the other party in the fight, and I tried to raise the issue about discrimination with One World . . . [the white worker] said, *"Here?* At *One World?"* But a person of color would have a different point of view.

Between the ICC crisis and the conflicts Diana recalled, an ad hoc collection of grocery members requested and were granted funded hours from the board to look into a formal, structured way to address inequality in the cooperative. Animated by the grocery's characteristic do-it-yourself ethos, they rejected the diversity training model of external experts periodically conducting interventions, and instead solicited bids from consultants willing to train an internal grocery committee that came to be called the Anti-Oppression Task Force (AOTF). The AOTF's first mandate was to conduct an application-based, weeklong workshop for fourteen cooperative members each year. The workshop covered race/ethnicity, gender, and sexuality (although not class) and their interconnections, as well as strategies to remedy their inequalities in the workplace and beyond. Sally Helms, a white, middle-class AOTF member, explained that the committee tried to keep its work from becoming "more of a sensitivity training than an anti-oppression training" by focusing on the structural and cultural organizational factors that foster unequal outcomes rather than on members' emotional reactions or individual conflicts—those they delegated to informal postworkshop breaks or other organizational bodies like the ICC or the Successful Participation Committee's mediation team. Like AOTF members' committee participation, workshop participants were paid their normal hourly wage for the weeklong sessions. While only a small percentage of the grocery's workforce had taken part in one of the workshops at the time of my study, a robust language had seemed to develop: a former AOTF member described "stepping back," or taking herself out of the running for reelection to the Public Relations Committee in order to allow people of color to control the grocery's philanthropic focus; and a workshop participant described learning language to challenge coworkers' claims of "colorblindness."

The grocery's explicit approach to worker diversity had elements of the "discrimination-and-fairness perspective" taken by the bakery in that it connected its workforce diversity to larger socially egalitarian goals. But by insisting on addressing inequalities with an ongoing and paid committee, the grocery articulated a vision of diversity as central to its operations and of inequality as an abiding condition with potential remedy in the workplace—more like an "integration-and-learning" perspective, which puts diversity at the center and aims to reconfigure the organization and the social world around it (Ely and Thomas 2001). In proposing a bidirectional causal link between organizational practices and the social world, rejecting individualizing psychotherapeutic frameworks, and institutionalizing its activities, the grocery incorporated ethnoracial and gender concerns as *internal, structural,* and *continuous,* and as constitutive of its worker identity as pluralist and encompassing of internal difference.

This did not mean that the grocery's pluralist worker identity always translated into organizational reconfiguration. While the AOTF, in its secondary capacity as a weekly review of active or potential areas of organizational inequality, had helped to institutionalize specific policies making harassment or attack based on race/ethnicity, gender, or sexuality fireable offenses, it had not supported attempts by Diana and others to institute proportional representation on the board of directors (which was often disproportionately composed of white men and women) and the ICC (which was typically disproportionately composed of women of color and white women). AOTF members seemed to echo bakery leadership's disparagement of such policies when they claimed proportional representation policies would lead to more stigmatization than power redistribution. But they also claimed that trying to codify the parameters of proportional representation was problematic: If they specified gender, what would be the place of trans workers (of whom, at the time, there were only three self-identified this way)? Was legal ethnoracial category more important than skin color within populations of color? How should the fluidity of their workers' sexuality and relationships be translated into policy? Should class also be a matter of proportional representation and, if so, what measures would be used to determine it? The grocery's focus on *acts* (the relational process of what people think about or do to each other) over *essences* (the assignment of meaning and range of outcome based on static characteristics) asserted not only its members' fluctuations across social categories but also the mobile and inclusive quality of the grocery's worker identity. This sense of *being* as *doing* also translated into policies that less explicitly but no less practically defined what being a worker meant at the grocery.

Implicit address of inequality. Like the bakery, there were policies at the grocery that were not created with the intent of reducing social inequalities but that nevertheless had social inequality effects. Some of these were detailed in the "Political Rights" section of chapter 5, like the work group-based scheduling that gave those with dependent care responsibilities not only the ability to keep their job but also the kind of full legitimacy necessary to successfully run for positions in the distributed governance and management system. Other practices, like thinking about hiring as a way to level the broader playing field, as Jennifer noted in the second chapter epigraph, helped to articulate what it meant to be a grocery worker, prismatically refracting race/ethnicity, gender, and sexuality with its worker identity. The grocery's decisions about childcare benefits exhibited this kind of refraction. The benefit policy was unusual: parents could claim a taxable wage supplement of a dollar per hour per dependent child to offset childcare costs. A white man in the office work group proposed replacing this benefit, which barely made a dent in local hourly childcare costs, with a more commonplace pretax dependent care account that offered greater potential savings. Yet a small group of immigrant Central American men successfully defended the preservation of the original benefit, arguing that it allowed them to hire their immigrant community members who did not have state authorization to work. The membership voted to allow workers to choose between the benefits. That is, although childcare is often viewed as a gender issue in that it created a greater barrier to women's than to men's employment (Clawson and Gerstel 2014; Gornick and Meyers 2009), these grocery workers were able to get their coworkers to also view it through the lens of what were then highly ethnoracialized issues of migration and legal status (Sáenz and Douglas 2015). In creating these two benefit options, the grocery noted and addressed both the gendered and ethnoracialized constraints of its workers and in doing so legitimated the different facets of its worker identity. The preservation of the original policy surprised the bakery's personnel manager, Keith, who had overseen conversion of a similar policy to pretax accounts at the bakery: "How do people feel about that? I mean, you're doing the same work as the guy standing next to you and he's getting paid more because he has kids?" In this statement, Keith not only proposed the worker as a masculine "guy" but also assumed that these men would not see parental need as a legitimate aspect of being a worker. Yet it was the dollar-per-hour-per-child benefit that grocery workers—several of them men, most of them childless—told me about with pride when describing the benefits of their cooperative. Rather than a net loss to grocery workers' profits, it was a valued addition to their construction of worker identity.

Another practice that connected symbolic practices to the material ones shaping the grocery's worker identity were the choice of holidays observed with a store closing. The grocery stayed open on bank holidays like Presidents Day and Memorial Day, but closed to honor the birthday of Chicanx labor leader César Chávez more than a decade before it was designated a federal holiday by President Barack Obama, and both the global May Day and US Labor Day celebrations of workers. In this way it asserted not only a working-class dimension to its worker identity, but one that encompassed more than the typical hegemonic whiteness associated with labor (Roediger 1999). More complicated was the "Gay Day" closing for the local Sunday LGBTQ+ parade in June, which many work groups had come to use for annual inventory because it came right before the close of the fiscal year. A queer, white, working-class woman wrote a letter asking the board to ban inventory during this weekend, arguing that it stuck LGBTQ+ workers between the rock of informal work group pressure and the hard place of alienation from their local queer community. A straight, African American, working-class woman dissented, saying that the voluntary nature of work group inventories allowed members to embrace or retreat from LGBTQ+ events. The board, however, leaned on the grocery's commitment to distributed management and returned the issue to the work groups, albeit affirming the voluntary nature of inventory and the right to community participation for members of the LGBTQ+ community. In this way the board knitted together symbolic and material practices—holidays and work requirements—as part of worker identity encompassing of its workers' differing commitments.

Material practices and policies of communication also took on symbolic meaning regarding worker identity. English-to-Spanish and Spanish-to-English interpretation via wireless headsets were not only standard at membership meetings but also available to grocery work group meetings. Customer-facing signs, posters, and bulletins were almost always in both Spanish and English. Using in-house labor, English-language employment documents and weekly board and ICC meeting minutes were translated and transcribed into Spanish. And, in addition to standard English and Spanish, other ethnoracial language conventions were part of normal business communications. For instance, an African American ICC member's use of then-popular African American slang in her statement, "Don't be a hater, we're ballerz," provided an official exhortation to the membership not to complain about an ICC decision because the grocery was doing fine financially. By having such statements transcribed into weekly meeting minutes, which were disseminated with the expectation that all workers would use paid time to read them, worker identity was stretched across the racialized language differences of California to decenter Eurocentric "standard" English as its all-encompassing expressive medium.

Participatory bureaucracy and worker identity. Grocery workers were increasingly diverse *by* demographic categories like race and ethnicity, but also diverse *within* those categories. Yet the grocery's pluralist worker identity was, like the bakery's, a key factor in the maintenance of its organizational structure. For instance, although former enemy combatants from the civil wars and struggles in both Nicaragua and El Salvador continued their opposition on a different front at the grocery (see the "One World Natural Grocery" section of chapter 3), the grocery's conception of its workers as inherently nonidentical—its worker identity as plural at its essence—provided a narrative structure in which coexistence could continue. The development of participatory bureaucracy with the multiple nodes of power, the delegation of hiring to the work groups, and the recognition of variation in leadership practices described in chapter 6 all protected this plurality by providing numerous sites for workers to come together—*as some* if not *as one*. The grocery's internally heterogeneous worker identity demanded policies to protect decentralized and distributed power; the distribution of power then not only permitted but helped proliferate this pluralism by allowing multiple facets of the worker identity to grow and solidify.

The organization of pluralist worker identity. Like the bakery, the grocery's explicit and implicit policies that regulated access to resources and rewards formed a diversity regime (Meyers and Vallas 2016), a set of interlocking processes and policies that made concrete claims about who the grocery perceived its workers to be—that is, its worker identity. Like the bakery, the grocery did not make a "business case" for diversity (Herring 2009), or what Robin Ely and David Thomas (2001) characterize as an "access-and-legitimacy" approach: it did not claim that its hiring or worker reward programs helped it serve a Spanish-speaking community (although that did seem to be the case) or better interface with the women who constituted a majority of their customers. Yet the grocery differed from the entirely morals-based commitment that seemed to animate the bakery by focusing on the *pleasure* of diversity: the ability to have more enjoyable meetings, or relieve parents' burden, or connect with one's coworkers across language difference. That is, the grocery's diversity regime mitigated a *range* of social inequalities as organizational facts rather than abstractions—inequalities of class but *also* of race/ethnicity and gender. These differences drew on the grocery's conception of its workforce as contained within its encompassing worker identity, and reinforced its pluralism.

Organizational Outcomes: The Legitimation of Monist and Pluralist Worker Identities

Despite similar histories and objective demographics, the two cooperatives' diversity regimes were not similar. At the bakery, organizational policies and practices referenced class but not other social structures as the legitimate force constituting its members, and their policies and practices were most consistently used to alleviate inequalities of class. The grocery's diversity regime legitimated a range of social structures as constitutive of its members, and also as targets of organizational policies and practices. In both cases these diversity regimes helped to produce monist or pluralist worker identities by protecting, refraining from protecting, or even subordinating aspects of workers' selves.

Solidarities: Relationships between Worker and Social Identities

Do worker identities affect workers' ability to act in solidarity with each other across workplaces? Thus far, this chapter has mapped out the two cooperatives' different worker identity contents and the diversity regimes that made consequential these messy connections between individual perceptions and social categories. At both the bakery and the grocery, organizational articulations of workers were consistent with individual ones. Bakery workers used class as a consistent reference to make claims about themselves and each other as workers, and their policies supported this monist worker identity. Indeed, it seemed as if they had integrated an organizational and individual level of "class-conflict consciousness" (Zingraff and Schulman 1984) and removed what some class-oriented scholars have seen as barriers to the achievement of working-class power (Bookchin 1995; Gitlin 1995; Ollman 1972). In this view, the grocery's individual and organizational citation of race/ethnicity and gender as consequential and built into the workplace might appear to undermine the ability of workers to mobilize as a "class for itself" (Marx 2006), to view itself as a structurally constituted and bounded group capable of achieving collective power. That is, is a pluralist worker identity like that of the grocery too diffuse to make these kinds of claims? Does solidarity with the noncooperative working class require a class-focused worker identity?

The 2003 United Food and Commercial Workers Strike

This question was no longer abstract in the fall of 2003, when the United Food and Commercial Workers (UFCW) union organized a strike of more than seventy thousand frontline grocery workers in over nine hundred locations of four of the major supermarket chains in Southern California (Wilson 2008). The union's pickets took a significant economic toll: customers stayed away not only in Southern California but often, sympathetically, in Northern California. The strike's success made it seem as if pickets might spread to Northern California. How would this affect the bakery and the grocery?

The bakery. When I asked bakery managers and sales and delivery drivers how they were going to deal with the strike if it came north, my question was interpreted as a logistical rather than philosophical or emotional one: bakery workers described how they had previously gotten product around picket lines by wearing large "worker-owned" badges to distinguish themselves from unionized delivery drivers, or by coordinating with (presumably strikebreaker) loading dock receivers to minimize contact with picket lines. I must have showed my surprise at being misinterpreted: bakery drivers reacted angrily when they realized I had assumed they would not cross a picket line. Frankie Ricci, a white, working-class man, snapped, "We're nonunion, and the last time [there was a grocery strike] the Teamsters told us to deliver if you can." Sylvia, the white, working-class woman who had never been invited to the bar with her men co-workers, chimed in, "It's aimed at consumers, not vendors." Although it was absolutely true that the bakery (like the grocery) was not unionized, I became aware that I had confused the regularity of its working-class references for a robust class consciousness. But the bakery's monist worker identity did not appear to mobilize a sense of shared class interests beyond the bakery walls, or at least not the kind that led to solidarity with striking UFCW grocery workers. In this case, bakery worker-owners seemed to embody the projected fears of earlier decades of workers' revolutions: acting more from the "owner" than the "worker" half of their status, they primarily expressed interest in getting their products to (super)market.

The grocery. Because grocery workers tended to use their worker discount to shop on-site and rarely patronized the local supermarkets, I did not anticipate any collective action on their part. But, again, I was surprised: at the instigation of a worker active in the local labor council, a voluntary automatic payroll deduction was immediately set up to support the UFCW strike fund. In the December holiday season, at the height of the strike, approximately 20 percent of the grocery's workers were contributing.[4] When I asked about their motivations, some fund participants used class terms in their statements like, "We're all workers," but most framed it differently. Many described increased sales at the cooperative because their customers were staying away from one of the targeted supermarkets, and said they did not want to profit from the struggles of "people like me," as one Latina cashier put it. When I asked what that meant, One World Natural Grocery workers described Southern California grocery workers as women with children, people on a tight budget, or people of color.[5] What emerged were materially supportive, class-solidaristic actions based on identifications through race/ethnicity, gender, and consumer power. In these ways the grocery reconfigured the meaning of class by reinterpreting class as inherently lodged within gendered and ethnoracial relations of power.

Solidarities: Monist Limitations and Pluralist Possibilities

Although the labor movement has been actively grappling with its troubled history of domination by whites and men (Fantasia and Voss 2004; Leymon 2011; Lipsitz 1994; Milkman 1987, 2006; Roediger 1999), it has not fully overcome the persistent narrative that at best relegates ethnoracial and gender concerns to the periphery (Alimahomed-Wilson 2016; Avendaño 2019), and at times has posited diversity as a threat (Iverson and Kuruvilla 1995). The bakery and the grocery, however, undermine such a logic: the bakery by its disconnection of class narratives from class solidarity, and the grocery by its class-solidaristic actions without narratives of working-class unity. Indeed, a study of the active picket lines in the 2003 grocery workers' strike found that the language and action from the union and its locals produced a far more ethnoracially exclusionary practice (Wilson 2008) than One World Natural Grocery's "people like me" approach.

It seems an increasingly dangerous mistake to assume that the self-professed achievement of class consciousness produces class solidarity. Indeed, as Julie Bettie points out, all that we can really ascertain is a classed *identity*, and "such an identity may not necessarily be a politicized one" (2003, 43). Identities may be resources from which solidarity can be generated, but solidarity does not simply arise from them. As contemporary political organizers Astra Taylor and Leah Hunt-Hendrix note, "Solidarity isn't a feeling or affect, a fuzzy sense of connection or unity; nor is it a preexisting bond within an established and stable group. . . . Solidarity is not something you have, it is something you do—a set of actions taken toward a common goal . . . it must be made, not found" (2019, 26–27). The grocery's pluralist worker identity did not inherently produce solidarity with other workers, but in its broadness it *permitted* more kinds of attachment across differences of space and ownership than the bakery's monist worker identity. Far from being a dangerous distraction or even an alternative path to solidarity, overt race/ethnicity and gender identifications may be necessary to create the conceptions of class that can generate class solidarity.

Summary: The Consequences of Worker Identity

The insight that we act in accordance with who we believe ourselves to be has long animated sociology (e.g., Denzin 2008; Mead 1962), including studies of organizations and work scholarship. It is no less true that others' beliefs about who we are shapes the actions that are taken towards us; our access to power and other resources often depends on how we are assigned to one category or another, generating dense and local patterns of allocation that can be described as "inequality regimes" (Acker 2006b). Our identities—these consequential fictions "produced in specific historical and institutional sites within specific discursive formations and practices, by specific enunciative strategies" (Hall 1996, 3)—both emerge from and affect what happens in these organizational inequality regimes and the social worlds in which they are embedded. Identity may not be real in the sense of inherent, permanent, or even necessary, but it is routinely experienced as such—and is therefore no less mobilizing than other social forces. As this chapter has shown, worker identities articulate categorical differences between and among self and others, enact or dissolve boundaries, and help to allocate rewards and restrictions along lines that often echo and almost always reinforce broader social patterns of inequality.

The way worker identities link individual self-perception to external events and meanings is illustrative of a key insight from inequality regime scholarship: that the inequalities of workplace organization affect the larger social world. This is not a deterministic claim; workers regularly resist interpellations and transform identification processes (Bank Muñoz 2008; Hossfeld 1990; Lee 1998; Salzinger 2003). But more often they do not, and that is because the organizational processes that link external social meanings to internal and individual articulations of selves tend to seem natural, normal, and unchanging. Identities may be the most tenacious part of normative control because they so rarely seem separable from the workers they articulate.

The consequences of People's Daily Bread Bakery and One World Natural Grocery workers' beliefs about who they were and the actions that resulted from those beliefs were experienced at the level of individual interaction, in the construction and reproduction of their organizations, and in social structures of meaning and empowerment. Interactionally, bakery and grocery workers viewed themselves and others in very different ways despite their demographic similarities: through a monist "breadwinner" lens at the bakery that focused on class but disguised the presumed whiteness and masculinity of its subject, and through a pluralist prism of "many flavors" refracting class, race/ethnicity, gender, and other social categories at the grocery. These differences became resources that could be organizationally deployed to question or legitimate policies and practices.

Organizationally, the cooperatives' diversity regimes were simultaneously being informed by their respective worker identities and acting to reinforce them. Each diversity regime adjudicated between competing claims workers might make, supporting and tailoring the organizational worker identities. Where bakery workers mostly drew on class discourses of material rewards and refused consideration of workers as constituted through ethnoracial and gender narratives, grocery workers more readily linked ethnoracial and gender discourses to ones of freedom in explaining their rewards as workers. Further, these diversity regimes were administered and mediated through a particular structure of authority each bureaucracy provided that affected participation in such tailoring. The monist construction of the bakery's worker identity invoked and legitimated hierarchical management, and that in turn narrowed the range of workers whose voices counted in articulating their worker identity or the legitimacy of claims that could be made in the name of workers. The grocery's pluralist worker identity, on the other hand, not only allowed a wider range of voices into that process but also required multiple sites and kinds of formalized authority to protect a wider range of legitimate inhabitations of that identity. The embrace of managerial bureaucracy that accompanied the bakery's economic empowerment of its working-class membership fostered an embrace of divisions of power more generally, and of the legitimacy of inequality, as well as practically constraining women's opportunities. The grocery's novel participatory bureaucracy symbolically reduced the legitimacy of inequality and practically opened more doors to jobs and power. Each organization's worker identity established a basis for the kinds of claims could be made by, for, and on its worker-owner members.[6]

Finally, these local worker identities were both *invested with* and *reproductive of* external social meanings. This was evident in ways that were hard to see, such as what was considered a proper hiring criteria or the internal distribution of power, and also in more conspicuous incidents like the 2003 UFCW strike. The bakery's restrictive worker identity helped to connect external beliefs about how race/ethnicity and gender affected workers' desires and abilities to internal practices like hiring and promotion, as well as limiting the connections workers could make to those outside the bakery—and thus to the larger labor movement. On the other hand, the grocery's more expansive notion of a worker offered a place to question external social meanings and proposed a new way of thinking about alliances between workers across different arrangements of work and labor.

The argument I have made here has two parts: first, that there was nothing fated or necessary about the divergence of these cooperatives, including the divergence of their worker identities; and, second, that the divergence of worker identities was consequential for the degree and steepness of each organization's inequality regime. The two worker identities were not *determined* by the workforce composition, the organizational policies and structures of authority, or external social meanings. Instead, the accretions of interactions among people, organizations, and social meanings produced subject positions that animated further actions. The bakery's focus on class was not the natural outcome of a white-majority workforce or the occupational concentration of men, nor even a form of manipulation by white men for their benefit. Nevertheless, the bakery's monist worker identity had the unintended consequence of benefiting white men through processes that were shielded by the monist conception of workers and their legitimate claims. Similarly, the grocery's pluralist worker identity was neither reflective of a heterogeneous workforce nor particularly intended to produce one; like the bakery, the grocery's worker identity and many of its consequences were not planned or foreseen. Nevertheless, there were far more opportunities to make claims across race/ethnicity and gender due to the pluralist and prismatic quality of the grocery's worker identity. The types and meanings of the categories that translated into inequalities were produced at—not reflected by—each cooperative organization. That is, identifying the local character of a worker identity, connecting it to the organizational processes that construct and maintain it, and delineating the organizational actions it authorizes is as critical to developing worker empowerment as a similar inventory of worker ownership and control.

BUREAUCRACIES, DEMOCRACIES, AND ECONOMIES

A Future of Work

> **We're in *low* tech. We're making bread and making crazy dollars for what we're doing. . . . People stay because they're treated well and because they're compensated well. There's a great deal of trust here also in that workers trust that management is leading them down the right path.**
>
> —Stuart White, People's Daily Bread Bakery

> **God bless the unions, but we've gone beyond the unions. We are worker owned and worker run. We don't need the union because we have taken our business and made it work for the workers. We get the profits.**
>
> —Jon Kaplan, One World Natural Grocery

What do workers want? On the surface, People's Daily Bread Bakery's "crazy dollars" and One World Natural Grocery's claim of profit being how the cooperative was made to "work for the workers" seem to suggest a similar focus on pay. But underneath, they had very different approaches to the diversity of worker interests, such as job security, workplace safety, respect and dignity, equal opportunities and just treatment, voice, and participation in day-to-day operations and long-term strategy. That is, the issues facing worker cooperatives—how to ascertain and fulfill goals, which organizational structures facilitate such goals, and what it means to live within any given configuration of capitalism—are not new challenges. Democratic worker-owned businesses embody long-standing hopes for and conflicts over the meaning of worker empowerment. In this book I have tried to portray the challenges faced by worker owners, the different ways they met these challenges, and the intended and unintended outcomes of their efforts.

In this final chapter, I take a look at the bakery and the grocery of the 2020s, both still in business as this book goes to press. These cooperatives not only persisted past the 1970s countercultural collectivist era but, as I will describe, weathered the Great Recession of 2007–9 and its long recovery period (Allegretto and Byambaa 2018). Both now show all signs of surviving the economic crisis generated by the global COVID-19 pandemic and continuing to support their increasingly Black and Brown working-class members (Cimen et al. 2021). The strength of the worker cooperative enterprise is underscored by the continued ability of these cooperatives to support their workers at a time when so many other businesses closed for good, but still leaves open the question of what labor means in the present day. How can worker ownership and worker control be organizationally manifested, and what does it mean to mobilize "as a worker" within capitalist society in the present moment? The current state of the bakery and grocery raises key questions about what work can look like, what role workplaces have in reproducing or reducing social inequalities, and what workers might be able to achieve collectively. As this chapter contends, these cooperatives' experiences offer potential lessons not only for other cooperatives, but noncooperative workers and even labor writ large.

The Bakery and the Grocery Today

Between 2007 and 2009 the global economy went into near collapse as a result of financialization, or the relatively unchecked influence of globally-aligned finance capital on daily economic life (Davis and Kim 2015; Tomaskovic-Devey and Lin 2011)—particularly homeownership (Fligstein and Goldstein 2011)—combined with a rising neoliberal morality sanctifying profit above all else (Mizruchi 2010; Van der Zwan 2014). Seemingly overnight, as California became the ground zero of the burst housing bubble (Bardhan and Walker 2011), homeowners in the bakery's town of Colina and the grocery's city of Edgefield were "underwater," owing more to the bank than the resale value of their homes. Bakery and grocery workers' 401k accounts—the main retirement vehicles for members of both cooperatives—were devalued on average by one-third (Wolff, Owens, and Burak 2011), with some cooperative members reporting losses of up to 50 percent in 2008. In a short time, the individual wealth amassed by cooperative members I had studied was severely compromised.

But—as was *not* the case for hundreds of thousands of Americans—bakery and grocery workers' jobs remained secure. Both cooperatives found the immediate postcrash years just as good as or better than previous years. Consumers still made sandwiches with the bakery's bread and filled their carts at the grocery. Indeed, workers at both sites theorized that sales were up because the financial squeeze led their customers to skip restaurants and prepare more food at home. Neither cooperative laid workers off or involuntarily cut hours during the Great Recession, and within a few years both used increased profits to begin ambitious remodeling projects: photovoltaic panels for the bakery's recently purchased new plant, and more parking and a more appealing interior footprint for the grocery. Housing prices rose again, and 401ks regained ground. The global financial crisis was not only experienced as somewhat of a financial boon by both businesses but also seemed to confirm the possibility of rejecting neoliberal morality and practicing human-scaled and human-focused economic life.

"Nobody Moves Out, Nobody Leaves"

The bakery had already committed to giving up its leased Colina plant and renovating one purchased in a town fifteen miles north when the impact of the Great Recession began to be felt, and so it plowed ahead. Its new production floor, collaboratively designed by production workers and the maintenance work group manager, included an expansion of the "racetrack" cooling system installed after I had last been to the old plant: baked goods just out of the ovens rose on a series of overhead conveyor belts circling the entire production area until dropping back down, ready to be sliced, to the packaging area. A wonder of efficient continuous production, it eliminated the dangerous and unpleasant job of depanning hot baked goods straight from the ovens—and thus eliminated the bakery's need for temporary workers. It also meant that control over the production process was now entirely in the mixer's hands. Unlike the old noncontinuous system I observed in 2003, workers could no longer adjust timing at various stages along the way, but were instead controlled by the automated production process. But this did not seem particularly concerning to the membership. CEO Herbert Gubbins proposed the racetrack and the membership voted in favor of its implementation with none of the contentious quality engendered by the change from weekly to biweekly pay described in the "Inequality and Inclusion" section of chapter 4. Although there had been some anger following layoffs among the production crews when the racetrack was introduced to adjust for the reduced labor needs, it had markedly increased efficiency and production—leading to earnings of "crazy dollars."

The biggest change at the bakery was Herbert's retirement shortly before I returned to check in. The bakery used his exit as an opportunity to shake things up by hiring a new CEO from outside—a white man with food industry management experience—at double Herbert's old salary. "It's really different around here now," claimed the white marketing manager, Stuart White, in 2015. "Herbert, love him for all he's accomplished, and he got us to this point, but bringing in somebody new from the outside was the best thing for this bakery." The bakery's workforce had by this time contracted from 120 workers to eighty-five, partly after a second round of production layoffs following the move to the new plant. And by 2015 the mostly white local route delivery work groups were eliminated in favor of outsourcing all delivery to the national contracts. While many of the drivers were initially retrained in the marketing work group, they left in a third round of layoffs a few years before the COVID-19 pandemic hit. Although the new CEO had moved on a few years later and been replaced via the internal promotion of a white man who had formerly managed the plant maintenance work group, his changes continued to affect the bakery. In news articles, bakery leadership spoke compassionately about the hardships of layoffs, but emphasized the increasing need for competitive efficiency in a growing organic market.

Nevertheless, most of the faces on the production line were familiar to me when I returned for a visit in 2015. Tom Rowe, the ambitious former board member who had learned Spanish on his own dime in hopes of developing managerial skills capable of leading a crew at a projected second Midwestern plant, was hard at work on the bread line. I wondered if Stuart had been referring to him when he ruefully noted, "I can think of one person in particular who's been packaging bread for over twenty years, college educated, would love to move up, but nobody moves out, nobody leaves, so opportunities don't present themselves." It was not only the general face of production workers that seemed to have changed little—all men, mostly Latinx—but indeed many of the specific workers' faces.[1] The increasing length of tenure at the bakery—now across class and ethnicity/race—seemed a clear result of the high bakery earnings in a region where jobs were quickly polarizing along a "good" high-paid/"bad" low-paid axis. And this level of material reward was generally attributed to the managers' vision and the efficiency of a managerial bureaucracy.

"We Were the Collective That Survived"

Things at the grocery were more mixed in 2015. For one thing, although several workers complained that they could not get as many hours as they wanted, no one had been laid off or forced to drop hours. It was visibly apparent that there were more workers of color and fewer white men. The grocery had been prescient in its purchase of a number of properties adjacent to the store during the first two decades of the century, and this made its displacement by the chain stores going in around it less likely. But although the Great Recession had initially brought more shoppers into the store, the national economic recovery seemed to do the opposite. Workers reported that a tech-fueled round of gentrification had displaced loyal customers to towns now too far (or separated by too much tech-worker traffic) for them to shop at the grocery. They speculated that the new tech workers ate for free on their corporate campuses or in restaurants: they seemed not to cook for themselves. In 2014 and 2015, worker profit-sharing distributions were in the low hundreds of dollars where they had once averaged about $10,000 annually, and cash dividends were minimized to preserve the grocery's working capital. In 2015 the grocery instituted a hiring freeze and voted to reduce free health care benefits for dependents.

Jon Kaplan, one of a small cohort of grocery members old enough to remember the years of hiring freezes and benefit cuts in the 1980s, felt that while the grocery had "taken our business and made it work for the workers," this success had, paradoxically, led to practices that were now hurting the grocery's bottom line. "It used to be that there was the fat of One World that always kept things going. It didn't really matter that we were inefficient, that we were not too nice to the customers, that we didn't have the cleanest store, that we were badly run—whatever the case was—because there was endless supply of customers. *We were cool*. For whatever reason, we were the collective that survived." Although I disagreed with some of his assessment (for instance, the widely used online review website Yelp had more praise than criticism of the grocery's customer service in 2015), there was indeed little fat to live on. "We're working more for less money," said another long-term worker with a grim set to her jaw.

These local economic changes affected workers too: like the grocery's customers, many workers now lived in far-flung locations, commuting more than an hour in each direction. This made them less able to drop in for a membership or committee meeting, let alone socialize after work. And members now more openly discussed an issue that had previously been taboo: reducing participative governance and management. Jon told me, "I want to start having *managers*. I would call them 'shift coordinators' to appease the idiots." Although no proposals had convinced the pro-direct democracy "idiot" majority to create either managers or "shift coordinators," it was equally true that no one reported shouts of "Go work somewhere else!" at the introduction of such proposals, such as those I had heard in response to similar proposals in 2003. Whether economic hardship had undermined confidence in the grocery's participatory bureaucracy, or if it had instead undermined grocery workers' solidarity and the trust it generated in each other's ability to collectively run a multimillion-dollar business, 2015 was a low point for the grocery's participatory bureaucracy.

But despite the general gloom in 2015, the grocery found a way forward. It recovered its sales through more targeted advertisement and through contracting with freelance shopper services like Instacart, which outsourced the problems of traffic and parking to gig workers. By the time of the 2020 COVID-19 pandemic, shoppers seemed to willingly line up, six feet apart, awaiting their chance to be one of the small number of customers allowed into the grocery at a time. Grocery workers still relied heavily on its participatory bureaucracy to make decisions including those to allocate worker hours to the production of masks, to shorten shopping hours, to increase taxi funds for workers whose public transportation options were reduced or eliminated, and to continue medical benefits for workers whose individual or family member medical status required an indefinite leave of absence. The use of this formalized democratic hybrid management and control system seemed to re-cement workers' commitment to the cooperative. Despite their struggles, the grocery continued to affirm its participatory bureaucracy.

Worker Cooperatives in the Golden Valley and the World

Much of what the cooperatives experienced had to do with changes in the Golden Valley that were both social structural and cultural. The flows of capital through new technical enterprises disrupted established communities across most of the economic spectrum, consumer ties to nonchain establishments, and the stability of working people. Less materially, the once-alluring glow of camaraderie within the Golden Valley was diminished more and more by the increasing visibility of homeless adults and families in places where the ultrarich indulged in extravagant clothes, cars, food, and other luxuries (Côté, House, and Willer 2015; Piff et al. 2010). Perhaps Jon was right in saying that the grocery had "gone beyond the unions" by owning and having democratic control over the workplace, and perhaps Stuart was right that the bakery's management was thus far "leading them down the right path," but neither cooperative had separately or jointly developed the kind of political power once held by unions to protect working communities against the encroachment of corporate firms or investment-oriented homeownership (Domhoff 2013; Freeman and Medoff 1984; Western 1997). Both were imperiled by regional changes, and neither offered unambiguous proof that alternative organizations could shelter workers without a larger "ecosystem" of similar organizations (Pinto 2018).

Pandemic Economies

As this book goes to press in 2021, is still too early to know how the pandemic—and recovery—will affect the bakery and the grocery. It is certainly possible that, as happened during the Great Recession, the sudden shift from restaurant and pre-made meal consumption to household food preparation initially benefited both cooperatives but will not produce a lasting increase in their customers or revenues. Both cooperatives may face problems in their supply chains if the firms on which they rely don't survive the pandemic. An increase in remote work and schooling may undermine the ubiquity of portable lunches on the bakery's sandwich bread, and the discovery of Instacart's convenience may cut into the grocery's profit margin if employees of high-tech firms continue to hire people to stock their kitchens instead of doing it themselves—or if they even stay in the high-priced Golden Valley now that remote work has been tried and tested.

Yet if the previous crisis is any indication, both the bakery and the grocery are better poised to weather major shifts in the economy than are their noncooperative competitors. Their prioritization of their workers instead of ever-increasing profits for external shareholders shifts the logic of operations to a manageable terrain. While the Great Recession significantly reduced bakery employment and grocery earnings, it neither decimated nor impoverished either workforce—which is quite different from what is facing employees of the "vanishing" corporation (Davis 2016) or recently devastated small businesses (Bartik et al. 2020; Bloom, Fletcher, and Yeh 2021). The long history of worker cooperative expansion during economic crisis recounted in chapter 2 suggests that, rather than threatening either cooperative, the current moment may build on growth from the previous decade (Palmer 2017) to generate a new mass generation of worker ownership and control. Indeed, whatever damage the pandemic inflicts on corporations and housing speculation could open a space for worker cooperatives to gain a previously impossible footing.

Implications: Other Economies

In chapter 1, I asked what future possibilities worker cooperatives might *prefigure*, or enact in the present with the goal of a very different economy and society than we have now. For researchers, viewing worker cooperatives as compositions of "practices, processes, actions, and meanings that result in and maintain class, gender, and racial inequalities" (Acker 2006b, 443) points to a very practical use of the inequality regimes approach within the growing field of relational inequality theory (Tomaskovic-Devey and Avent-Holt 2019). This book has offered two conceptual frameworks with which to do that: bureaucratic variation and worker identity. But it also offers three kinds of lessons about what is possible and useful: how labor can be coordinated in different ways, how egalitarian working conditions can be created, and how a broader movement for worker rights and possibilities, a "solidarity economy," can be gleaned from worker cooperatives.

Transforming Work

Workers can run their own businesses. Let them. This book joins a body of scholarship showing that working people are interested in and capable of managing their own businesses, and that such businesses are just as likely to be financially successful as any other small business (Davis 2017; Jones 2012). In-house managerial training in conjunction with opportunities for participative self-management or promotions from the floor allows workers to connect tacit to strategic knowledge and successfully run businesses. This research adds to the conclusion drawn by Corey Rosen, John Case, and Martin Staubus (2005) that formalized training and information sharing are critical to the ability of firms to realize the productivity benefits of worker ownership (whether democratic or not). Crucially, this must be supported with pay: self-managing workers need to be compensated for performing what are typically managerial functions. That workers are far more likely to participate when their participation is literally valued as work is a lesson not just for worker-owned cooperatives but also for nondemocratically worker-owned or non-worker-owned firms that want high employee participation. The noted difficulty of eliciting tacit knowledge from workers may stem from their resistance to donating their knowledge and skill without any benefits of pay or positional status. As worker cooperative developers increasingly urge conversions of existing businesses over start-ups (Abell 2014; Olsen 2013), such changes to organizational culture may be critical to their success.

Job and time autonomy are central concerns for workers. Address them. When workers manage their own labor, scheduling is different than in managerial regimes. From academic survey answers repeated across decades (Blauner 1966; Freeman and Rogers 2006; Gouldner 1954; Turco 2016) to the hopeful—if perhaps misinformed (Kalleberg and Vallas 2017; Pichault and McKeown 2019)—embrace of schedule control through "gig economy" jobs at Uber and the like, it is clear that working people are willing to make significant material concessions in order to have some control over when, where, and how they work. This choice is not a misunderstanding of "real interests" narrowly read as wealth; even Karl Marx understood such a singular goal as merely "better payment for the slave" (Marx 1964, 188). Grocery workers' repeated trade-in of income for "hours for what we will" echoes a key demand of industrial workers and the early labor movement (Roediger 1999; Rosenzweig 1983). Pushing back against a neoliberal morality, which articulates anything other than wealth as "pragmatically" suspect, cooperatives as well as unions can unapologetically make the case for job and time autonomy. Corporations may find themselves ignoring such demands at their peril.

Workers can cooperate across difference. Facilitate coordination. Despite studies from the 1980s through the early 2000s claiming that worker cooperatives are most successful when their population is homogeneous along some key social characteristic—class, race/ethnicity, or gender (Bernstein 1982; Pencavel 2001; Rothschild and Whitt 1986; Russell 1984)—both the bakery and the grocery show that the formal codification of egalitarian principles in organizational practices (whether managerial or democratic) creates viable and diverse worker ownership. This opens up new possibilities for worker cooperative formation and transformation. Indeed, using new legislation, partnerships, and municipal development funding (DePasquale, Sarang, and Vena 2018; Ifateyo 2014; Lo and Koenig 2017; Rose et al. 2021), the post-2008 generation of cooperatives has been intentionally and successfully rooted in low-income communities and among workers of color, including household service cooperatives such as EcoMundo Cleaning in the Bronx and Cooperative Janitorial Services in Cincinnati; childcare cooperatives like NannyBee in New York City; and grocery stores like Mandela Food Cooperative in Oakland, California, and Ujamaa Freedom Market in Asheville, North Carolina. In an attempt to get past the racialized and gendered barrier of building enough initial capital to start up a new cooperative enterprise, cooperative development organizations such as the Cooperative Fund of New England, the Democracy at Work Institute, the ICA Group, the Ohio Employee Ownership Center, Project Equity, and the Sustainable Economies Law Center have been turning their attention to succession strategies, or pathways for retiring firm owners to pass the torch to their workers. Of course, it is still an open question whether the current white men business owners will sell their firms to cooperatives that are led—in whole or in part—by people of color and white women; historically, noncooperative succession has largely been a process of white men passing their firms to white men (Byrne, Fattoum, and Thébaud 2019; Ferguson and Koning 2018; Tomaskovic-Devey and Avent-Holt 2019). It is possible that, without careful attention to the gender and ethnoracial dynamics of succession strategies, worker cooperatives may unwittingly preserve white men's wealth accumulation (Oliver and Shapiro 1997). For this and many other reasons, the historical association of worker-owner homogeneity with worker cooperative success should be taken as a challenge to do better, not as organizational strategy.

Dismantling Inequality Regimes

Bureaucracy does not inevitably produce inequality. Reconsider bureaucracy. Bureaucracy varies (Gouldner 1954) and, despite the pendulum swing away from its deployment, it can be highly beneficial for worker cooperatives. At the

moment bureaucracy seems to either be disparaged as weighing down freedom
and innovation with its rules and regulations (Heckscher and Donnellon 1994)
or sacralized in its Weberian ideal type, its priests pronouncing heresy on any
who would dare try to bend its meaning to encompass the type of change experienced by all social forms over time (Du Gay 2000). But bureaucracy should not
be defined by hierarchy any more than by the now-defunct lifetime career.
More useful is an understanding of bureaucracy as an organizational form that
enshrines power in a mesh of *explicit and documented rules* that *govern and rationalize actors' behavior* and *create accountability and predictability* for their
actions. An organization that is missing or weak in certain characteristics proposed by a European academic scholar a century ago may be no less bureaucratic if, on the whole, it embodies and advances these bureaucratic logics and
discourses. But it may be more likely to advance the goal of egalitarian worker
ownership and control without some of those characteristics blocking the way.
Understanding bureaucracy as *varied* may provide a new approach to the noted
lack of empirical correspondence between "bureaucratic" organizations and inequalities (Britton 2000). Organizations with social justice aims should reconsider the potential of bureaucracy in its participatory form as a way to coordinate
successful and egalitarian economic action.

**Inequality congeals in centralized management. Develop participatory
control.** Despite the way power and resources have tended to collect around more
socially privileged members (Mansbridge 1980) under conditions of structurelessness (Freeman 1984), the grocery shows how this tendency can be averted.
By integrating direct democratic control into its bureaucracy, the grocery both
preserved a crucial degree of worker autonomy and allowed the organization to
function as a profitable business for more than thirty years. In this the grocery
aligns with the formalized but nonhierarchical social movements that have
emerged in the past twenty years (Polletta 2002; Polletta and Hoban 2016). One
key to just participatory democracy, it seems, is the formalization of bureaucratic
processes and logics. That the formalized and broadly democratic practices of
the grocery's participatory bureaucracy reduced occupational segregation and
exclusions more than the bakery's managerial bureaucracy, however, expands
options beyond worker-owned firms. It suggests that the formalization of participatory management—not only training but also documentation of practices
and policies that make management visible and accessible—can harmonize the
internal and external calls for corporate diversity, inclusion, and equity with productive goals. That is, strategies to produce more democracy also produce better conditions for working together across perceived difference.

Inequality is central to organizational processes. Address it directly. In line
with decades of research on diversity management (Bell and Hartmann 2007;

Thomas and Ely 1996) that has shown how "colorblind" (Ray and Purifoy 2019) or "power evasive" (Frankenberg 1993) approaches to ethnoracial inequality undermine organizations' ability to reduce it, the bakery's monist construction of an implicitly white (man) "breadwinner" worker subject wove inequality into organizational processes: its hiring, firing, and promotion practices favored whites and men. If the bakery's survival resulted from its managerial decision to jettison certain parts of the organization (the mostly Latinx production work group; the mostly white sales and delivery work group), the cost of such survival was increased naturalization of a divide between so-called skilled and unskilled labor and the associated earnings and prestige that typically accompanies this divide. In contrast, the grocery's overt recognition of ethnoracial inequalities among its workers allowed it to identify and change organizational practices that were perpetuating those inequalities. Its participatory bureaucracy may have been less effective at planning for the future as it unfolded, but relatively equal parceling out of suffering across race/ethnicity, gender, and economic background preserved an important aspect of egalitarianism that increased workers' commitment to the cooperative—and produced intersectional understandings that generated solidaristic action with noncooperative workers.

Reimagining Labor

Labor is under attack. It needs worker cooperatives. At minimum, democratically controlled and worker-owned firms represent a potential new base of membership for a labor movement that has been bled to the edge of death. Despite significant vulnerabilities of worker cooperatives—historic and contemporary class, ethnoracial, and gender exclusions; overidentification with the "owner" half of their character and subsequent replacement of human- with profit-centered practices; and dependence on unstable or undermining economic support from the state and/or local businesses—they must be part of any collective action to improve the lives and fortunes of working people. The dream of shared labor/corporate governance failed to materialize (Freeman and Medoff 1984; Western 1997), and the sustained corporate and state attack on unions (Kalleberg 2011) has not only reduced union membership but driven wages down across industries and occupations (Western and Rosenfeld 2011). Despite the relatively recent uptick in some sectors and among people of color and white women (Cobble 2007; Milkman and Ott 2014), and despite growing desire for unionization among unorganized workers (Kochan et al. 2019), the labor movement's historical singular focus on collective bargaining (Greene 1998) now reveals its weakness: even a mighty entity can be crushed if there is one target. But a new worker movement is developing: labor and worker ownership are already coming together. From the Black and Brown women of the Bronx worker-owned union Cooperative Home Care Associates (Huertas-Noble 2016; Pinto 2021), to the ethnoracially diverse low-income members of the Mondragón/United Steel-workers Evergreen cooperatives in Cincinnati (Schlachter 2017); to the post-pandemic and city hall-supported drive by Chinese American workers in New York City to take ownership of their historic and unionized banquet hall, Jing Fong (Chang 2021), we are seeing the rise of a more broadly conceived worker mobilization of unions and worker cooperatives, worker centers and nonprofit job developers, immigration activists and community anti-poverty initiatives (Abell 2014; Berry 2013; Fine 2005; Hoover, Harris, and Johnson 2012). Such wide-ranging labor movement can shift tactics and spaces as needed, collaborate and provide solidarity, develop new alliances, and imagine new ways to work.

Worker cooperatives are prone to isolation and moralizing. They need labor. If worker cooperatives represent potential new blood, the labor movement is the body to be reinvigorated—to act and to wield political power. One World Natural Grocery member Jon Kaplan might believe, as his quote in the second epigraph to this chapter indicates, that worker cooperative members "don't need" unions, but it's unclear if the current state of the grocery confirms that belief. Without the kind of encompassing movement that once created neighborhoods full of people who would not set foot in an establishment that failed to display a union card, single-organization economic justice efforts may be lost. It takes a movement that is diverse by social characteristics, organizations, and strategies to build institutions and societies that can provide reasonably supportive, safe, and intellectually and creatively engaging work, as well as protect non-work time for meaningful connection with others. And it takes material benefit. To disrupt inequality regimes, worker cooperatives need to see a path to economic success under current conditions. A worker cooperative that is incapable of providing material support winds up bestowing an unearned mantle of moral superiority on its financially privileged members and will be unable to recruit and retain members across wealth inequality. Particularly—but not only—in the areas identified by cooperative developers as ripe for empowerment of marginalized communities, business plans will be at least as important as social mission statements. "Bread and roses" means that movements must include "soft" benefits like autonomy, creativity, joy, and beauty—but not at the expense of bread.

The worker we imagine shapes the problems we try to solve. Think intersectionally. For too long the productive "worker" subject has been narrowly constructed as industrial, masculine, and white. Deviations from these qualities have required a modifier: the "woman worker," the "Asian worker," the "service worker," and so on. The monist worker identity does labor no favors. The seemingly inherent class character of work is inevitably shaped by the meanings and effects of race/ethnicity, gender, sexuality, and other social characteristics. For labor to leverage the power of worker ownership and control, it must decenter industrial work as normative and instead conceptualize work as varied and changing. It must decenter masculinity and whiteness—and indeed gender and ethnoracial hierarchies—if it is ever to resist settling for the meager dividends of masculinity and whiteness within capitalism when so much more is possible. Bringing the process of worker identity formation into view allows us to rethink the meaning of labor as an activity and as a social movement, allows a more pluralist understanding of work and workers, and allows a broader labor horizon to emerge.

"The Future is Dark": Worker Cooperatives and Other Worlds

If worker cooperatives prefigure any of the futures I suggested in chapter 1, they do so, as scholar of Latin American worker movements Ana Dinerstein (2015) insists, as hopefulness. Worker cooperatives show that workers are fully capable of self-management—hierarchically or laterally—across differences of class, race/ethnicity, and gender; that worker movements are far from dead; that workplace democracy is a natural fit for a thriving sustainable, locally rooted economy (Gunn 2004; Myers and Sbicca 2015). If worker cooperation is utopian, it is as the kind of "real utopia" articulated by the late visionary Erik Olin Wright (2010). The members of People's Daily Bread Bakery and One World Natural Grocery did not believe they could create a perfect world through their cooperatives. But they believed dehumanization and intense stratification were not necessary for their economic survival, that the struggle for "people before profits" was feasible in the here and now. Workers at both cooperatives were proud of leveling inequity, of extending benefits across class and race/ethnicity and, where successful, gender. Worker cooperatives offer hope.

Prefiguration is not necessarily an individual characteristic. Worker cooperatives do not seem to transform their members into more socially progressive voters or into community activists. In fact, studies of the labor republican, self-help, and countercultural collectivist eras suggest that members tend to be or become more conservative through their experience in worker cooperatives (Greenberg 1986; Kasmir 1996; Martin 2013; Sobering, Thomas, and Williams 2014). Yet individual worker-owners may be the wrong unit of analysis; it is less at the level of persons and more at the level of organizations that worker cooperatives matter. Worker cooperatives have innovated democratic practices that have been carried into other workplaces, helped to change laws that have bene-fited B Corporations, and opened a pathway for recent immigrants to have eco-nomic stability (Abell 2014; Gordon Nembhard 2014; Hale and Carolan 2018; Wilson 2010; Yorra 2019). That is, worker cooperatives enrich the fields of eco-nomic and democratic institutions.

Because even if participation in a worker cooperative does not change its members into more socially progressive voters or community participants, new relational categories are generated through worker cooperatives: *worker* and *owner* are no longer set in binary opposition. While this can be puzzling within the dominant labor framework—what does it mean to be a worker absent the exploitation of labor by owners of capital?—it creates an incentive for alterna-tive labor theorization of relations such as the community or friendship rela-tions of the self-help and countercultural collectivist era cooperatives described in chapter 2. Today worker cooperatives prefigure an understanding of "work-ing class" as a "*distributive class process*, where appropriated surplus labor is dis-tributed to a variety of social destinations" (Gibson-Graham 2006, 54, emphasis in original).

What are these social destinations? Worker cooperatives are famously local in their economic benefit through the circulation of workers' incomes in their communities, hiring local services, and often directing grants and support to local community organizations (Kennelly and Odekon 2016; Gordon Nembhard 2014). From the multiple housecleaning cooperatives that developed with the support of Prospera in Oakland, California, to the caterers of Centro de Traba-jadores Unidos's Las Visionarias Cooperativa in Chicago, to the Home Care As-sociates cooperative in Philadelphia, worker cooperatives provide necessary services within low-income communities of color and are more and more the face of the US cooperative sector (Berry and Bell 2018; Gutiérrez 2019). This is due, at least in part, to the newly targeted efforts of cooperative developers and the expansion of capital investment funds for cooperatives (Abello 2021; Rose et al. 2021), drawing on inequality research increasingly circulating in worker ownership circles.

But worker cooperatives are only one among many alternative economic in-stitutions that, drawing on innovations from Indigenous movements of the Global South (Dinerstein 2015; Gibson-Graham 2006), are sometimes collec-tively called the *solidarity economy* (Dacheux and Goujon 2011; Utting et al. 2015). The solidarity economy encompasses practices and organizations marry-ing concepts of social justice and environmental sustainability that include food-oriented organizing such as consumer cooperatives in "food deserts" or community gardens that supply food banks (Alkon and Guthman 2017); worker centers that balance labor policy activism with direct support for marginalized workers (Fine 2006); credit unions and community-based insurance agencies (Schneiberg 2011); and time banks, land trusts, and community-supported agriculture programs (Pinto 2018). And this solidarity economy is not *only* local but becomes global through the networking and distribution of just and sustainable goods and services (Gibson-Graham et al. 2017; Kennelly and Odekon 2016), arcing perhaps towards an entirely different "mode of exchange" from the capitalism we know (Karatani 2014). While, as J. K. Gibson-Graham caution, this should not be seen as a "ready-made alternative economy," it does begin to map out "diverse organizations and practices as powerful constituents of an enlivened noncapitalist politics of place" (2006, xii).

Of course, in the present moment, it can be hard to believe that workers can collectively control their day-to-day working lives, particularly when working conditions seem to be getting worse for so many and the extraction of wealth is impoverishing more and more people for the benefit of fewer and fewer. It can be hard to believe in prefiguration when the future seems ever more bleak: the rapid pace of destruction of the planet's ability to sustain vigorous human life, the unending state of wars, the rise of authoritarian political regimes around the world. It can be hard to believe that worker cooperatives offer more than temporary shelter.

And even if human societies survive, it is legitimate to wonder if workers will not become possessive, fiercely guarding their gates against those perceived as invaders and outsiders. One could fairly easily imagine cooperative members taking up "the master's tools" (Lorde 1984) if they are left lying around and reconstructing relations of exclusion, exploitation, and stratification among the economic pyramids of wealth and opportunity.

But this volume has put the spotlight on sites where worker cooperatives were able to resist the naturalization of inequality. There are conditions under which working people will choose to share rather than hoard, to recognize rather than pave over differences and divisions, to address rather than exploit privilege and disadvantage. Workers develop new identities that position solidarity not merely as morally superior but as fiscally and socially wise, and interpersonal differences as pleasures to be enjoyed. Workers create organizations that limit individual accumulation but offer financial support on a scale that allows time for engagement with community, friendship, artistic production, family, the natural world, and the many other parts of life that exist beyond the workplace.

The worker cooperatives in this book are, like the nightly news, a snapshot of a particular time and place. They promise neither a way out nor doom. The social critic Rebecca Solnit (2015) quotes a fragment from Virginia Woolf's diary to remind us that "the future is dark," that there are various possible outcomes, beautiful and horrifying, of what we see around us today. That does not mean we simply walk into an unknown future; rather, we create it through our choices. Without the active participation of all working people, those choices will likely be for continued exploitation. But another world—cooperative and egalitarian— is indeed possible.

Appendix A

A DISCUSSION OF METHODS

In the fall of 2000, I was a second-year graduate student, frustrated—like many who embark on their first research project—with roadblocks to what I had thought would be my doctoral research. My romantic partner at the time was employed at a worker-owned cooperative grocery store, and I had become so accustomed to his descriptions of its decentralized management that I had come to view participatory democratic control as a bedrock feature of worker cooperatives. I was therefore surprised when, one night over dinner with friends, he described a driver he had come to know on her delivery rounds to his store complaining about "bosses" and unfavorably comparing her employment with his as "not cooperative" despite the fact that it was also a democratic worker-owned cooperative. Those of us around the table who knew a bit about One World Natural Grocery asked him to tell us what she meant, and he explained that People's Daily Bread Bakery, like most other bakeries of its size, used hierarchical management for its day-to-day operations, unlike the shared, group-level decision-making we all associated with the grocery and "co-ops" more generally. But here was a co-op with managers. How had that happened? As I asked more questions, I began to realize how my view of worker cooperatives had been narrowed by the generation of countercultural worker "collectives" I had encountered, and that there were many other forms worker ownership could take.

I initially set out to understand why and under what conditions members of a worker cooperative would preserve or hand over control to others, and how those choices might affect their work experiences. At the turn of the twenty-first century there was no large worker cooperative movement in the United States as there is today. Although there were some studies of larger organizations in Europe (Bartlett et al. 1992; Comisso 1979; Whyte and Whyte 1991; 1988) and the Pacific Northwest (Berman 1982; Gunn 1984; Pencavel 2001), most available research on worker cooperatives in North America had been conducted in the 1970s and 1980s, and almost all of it on cooperatives small enough to use all-worker, face-to-face and friendship-based participatory management (Jackall and Levin 1984; Lindenfeld and Rothschild-Whitt 1982; Mellor, Hannah, and Stirling 1988; Rothschild-Whitt 1979; Rothschild and Whitt 1986). But these were local cooperatives with between one and two hundred members. This was a size at which I assumed at least some delegation of power was being made, and at which they were navigating some level of internal social difference. I embarked on a crash course in bureaucratic theory, workplace participation, and worker cooperative history, and by the following year had begun the pilot phase of what would become this book.

Research Design

This book is based on qualitative and archival research that evolved over nearly fifteen years into a mixed methods longitudinal study. My research process can be broken down into five phases: (1) a pilot study to assess the field of large-scale worker cooperatives in the United States, sensitize myself to the concerns and issues among contemporary worker cooperatives on the West Coast, and select my case studies; (2) an organizational ethnography of the two worker cooperatives; (3) collection of archival and financial data from both sites, along with regional occupational and earnings data from public sources; (4) dedicated data analysis; and (5) follow-up interviews and visits. I focused on the West Coast partly for feasibility reasons (my location and limited travel funds as a graduate student at the time), but also, as I describe in chapter 2, because the majority of worker cooperatives that had grown past the face-to-face size were on the West Coast.

Because there were so few of these large worker cooperatives, I did all I could to preserve the confidentiality of those who participated in my research. In addition to changing the bakery's and grocery's names, the name of the region, city and town names, and the names of every worker in the two cooperatives, I also attributed possibly contentious statements to unspecified research subjects where possible. I also changed some identifiable organizational details: not only products made or sold, or other organizations that were central to the cooperatives' histories, but I also adjusted some Googleable dates. While such changes mean that this text is not an absolutely accurate historical document of these two cooperatives, my ability to explain organizational processes and individuals' experiences of those processes while protecting the privacy of those individuals and organizations seemed a worthwhile sociological trade-off. Historians may beg to differ.

My approach was fundamentally one of a qualitative researcher, as I attempted to discern the local meanings embedded in "worker ownership" and "worker control," and how those concepts might be locally classed, ethnoracialized, and/or gendered. Yet although I approached the research from a critical theory perspective that there is no objective place from which any researcher can study or write, nor a singular and fixed reality that can be translated onto the page that is fairly typical of qualitative research (Lincoln, Lynham, and Guba 2011), I chose a mixed methods approach that combined content and historical analysis with ethnographic data in aid of enriching qualitative understanding (Hesse-Biber 2010). While a mixed methods approach such as this may be less able to elicit or portray the complexity of any individual cooperative member compared to a smaller-scale and purely ethnographic study, its qualitative orientation preserves the focus on how individuals act as nodes of power in the interpretation and instantiation of power.

The qualitative research included both interview and observation in order to understand the relationship between cooperative members' "saying" and "doing" (Khan and Jerolmack 2013): it is not only that the way people describe and perform their actions differs but that the difference itself often reveals values or practices that can be hard to assess by listening or observing alone. Comparing the difference between what people said and did at each cooperative in this study allowed me, for instance, to understand how "working-class" identification motivates different actions, as I discuss in chapter 7.

Although I did not center myself in the research or this text in an autoethnographic fashion (Adams, Jones, and Ellis 2015), I also did not minimize or evade the effect of myself as an embodied researcher. I treated my "ethnographic self" (Coffey 1999) as one research instrument in the array I used. In my field notes I interrogated my reactions to what I observed and heard (and discussed); at several points within this text I have consciously included myself as speaker in interviews and as agent in actions—college-educated and university-credentialed, white-presenting, urban, relatively normatively gendered. For instance, when bakery production managers and workers consistently claimed a need to change their behaviors due to my imputed feminine presence, as I describe in the "Bread Bakers and Breadwinners" section of chapter 7, I am able to empirically discuss the gendered organizational and interpersonal processes that would not otherwise have been available given the all-men production workforce at the time. But my mindfulness that the methods I used for research were inherently embodied in myself also meant that I needed to use caution regarding the meaning behind the speech directed at me: the repeated metaphoric use of the cooperative as a "university" by grocery workers, as I noted in the "Participatory Worker Democracy" section of chapter 6, seems more likely to be a translation for my particular benefit as a researcher engaged in academic study than a way of asserting a superior status as "educated" in comparison to noncooperative occupational peers. That is, while my research approach has been to continuously ask how my positionality informs the research I produce, this is done mostly in relation to the background process of research than the foreground process of narration.

As other white women doing qualitative studies have found (e.g., Britton 2003), research participants did not seem to view their researcher's gender as restraint on the expression of sexist ideas. But it is possible that those ideas were even more developed than what was recounted to me. Similarly, it could be that a researcher whose speech patterns and credentials did not announce them as part of the middle class might have heard deeper or more nuanced class theorization; a Black or Brown researcher might have been privy to critical analyses of how ethnicity and race play out in ways that I was not. Certainly a researcher who was a bilingual/bicultural Spanish speaker could have had much greater access to the observations and theorizations of the cooperatives' primary Spanish speakers (roughly 5 percent of the workers at each site) than I did: my limited Spanish left me unable to conduct interviews with these members in either cooperative, and I tried but failed at each site to recruit enough participants for a four- to eight-person interpreted focus group. Given the significant proportion of Spanish-speaking immigrants in US cooperative workplaces (Gutiérrez 2019), many of whom were well-acquainted with the thriving Mexican cooperative movement (Hernandez 2006) prior to immigration, this is a key area where future research is needed.

Phase I: Pilot Study

The first research phase took place between October 2001 and March 2003. To get a sense of worker cooperatives in the moment and the potential of larger-scale operations, my research included attendance at a conference for worker cooperative members and developers; one-day observations (site visits) at the four largest West Coast worker cooperatives (including the bakery and the grocery), which were selected for their inability to coordinate work in the face-to-face style that had been the signature of the small, friendship-based countercultural collectivist cooperatives of the 1970s and 1980s (see chapter 2); twelve semistructured one-on-one interviews; and observation of a bakery governance meeting, a bakery membership meeting, a grocery membership meeting, and a grocery party. I then coded and analyzed the data, and produced a preliminary analysis as a conference paper. In all, I spent about 125 hours in the field during this process, and about twice as many hours analyzing the data.

Observation. In October 2001, I introduced myself at the then-annual Western Worker Cooperative Conference as an academic observer, explained my interests, and solicited informational interviews from members of the bakery and grocery as well as from members of a sexual products retail/wholesale business in California and a bicycle manufacturer in Oregon. These contacts helped grant me access to site visits and semistructured interviews with members of all four of the larger West Coast cooperatives.

Interviews. In the first phase of the project, I cast a wide net. The interviews were recruited as a convenience sample of those members of these cooperatives who responded to my conference solicitations, workplace flyers, and announcements made at the four sites. As I narrowed my focus on the bakery and the grocery, I attended membership meetings at both sites, introduced myself and my interest in discovering what working conditions were like in a worker-owned business, and put up interview sign-up sheets and contact information. At the grocery, six people used the public sign-up sheet, but only one contacted me directly; at the bakery, two people contacted me directly and only one (a manager) used the public sign-up sheet. Finally, and only at the bakery, I directly solicited work group managers and asked them to make announcements at work group meetings with a short paragraph about me and my research. Most of those who agreed to let me interview or observe them expressed both a desire to have a larger public understanding of what worker ownership looked like and a desire to spice up the routine of their typical working day. (For interview questions, see appendix B.) I also used snowball sampling, asking those who had talked to me to refer me to others who they thought might offer new insights or different angles on things or who were "key players," but I did not specify social characteristics like class, race/ethnicity, or gender. With the aim of ensuring privacy and confidentiality, most interviews were conducted in my home or theirs, but three were conducted in worksite conference rooms or private offices with closed doors, and two interviewees requested the public (and noisy) space of a café, despite my discouragement of such public spaces for both privacy and sound quality reasons. Interviews lasted between 75 and 135 minutes. In this phase of the project, snowball sampling skewed my sample towards white workers, but not by gender self-identification, rough markers of class such as parents' education or occupation, or by the type of work done within each cooperative.

Recruitment and access. While my romantic relationship with the grocery member had faded by the time I began my project, my friendship with him, the coworkers he had introduced me to, and people I had met through the Western

Worker Cooperative Conference no doubt helped to vouch for me when I was asking permission to visit and interview. As I describe in chapter 1, however, this potential entrée did not stop me from making initial mistakes in approaching both the grocery and the bakery. Luckily, these were not fatal errors, and I was eventually directed towards the appropriate members and governing bodies, who then gave me permissions and much helpful guidance and support in conducting the research.

Reflections in the field. I recorded all interviews, and transcribed them myself or had them professionally transcribed (as funds allowed) within a month of the interview in order to be sure that I would have an accurate record of our discussions. In all cases I listened to the interviews one to three times within a week of conducting them, and "open coded" them, making notes of what stood out to me for later "focused coding" and analysis (Emerson, Fretz, and Shaw 1995). Through the transcription, open coding, and thematic memo-writing on these interviews and observational field notes—that is, beginning to systematically address the aspects of these interviews that singly and together stood out to me—as well as the production of a summary conference paper, this pilot phase helped me map out each organization's basic structure and history, its overt conflicts, and some of its internal tensions.

Phase II: Organizational Ethnography

I conceived of the second phase of the project as an organizational ethnography, shifting from my pilot phase unit of analysis of individuals within an organization to the organization itself (Neyland 2007). Although the second phase only lasted from July 2003 to November 2004, this data make up a significant portion of what I describe in this book. Research during this phase included twelve weeks of intensive observation (six weeks at each site), primarily conducted over July, August, and the first half of September 2003; two further orientation sessions at the bakery in October and December 2003; membership meetings (quarterly at the bakery and monthly at the grocery) through May 2004; one committee meeting at the bakery and four at the grocery; one production work group meeting at the bakery and one produce work group meeting at the grocery; official parties (three at the bakery, two at the grocery); informal social gatherings (two at the bakery, four at the grocery); and a second Western Worker Cooperative Conference in October 2003, where I presented and gathered feedback on preliminary findings to a primarily cooperative-member audience.

At this time I definitively narrowed my focus to the bakery and the grocery, as it had become apparent that they made for the kind of "natural experiment" fashionable in social science research at the time (Dunning 2012): founded at a similar time and with a similar demographic, both natural foods-focused, both located in the same geographic region. Although I felt regret in dropping the other two cooperatives, by odd coincidence both converted to noncooperative ownership over the following five years. My access was facilitated by physical proximity to both sites: I realized early on that living within a couple miles of the grocery allowed me to easily accommodate last-minute schedule changes or invitations for interviews, observations, and social events with grocery workers. To ensure similar opportunities at the bakery, I temporarily moved to a town near the bakery for eight weeks in August–September 2003.

The pilot study had sensitized me to potential differences that might make comparison between production and retail firms difficult, particularly in terms of understanding the class, race/ethnicity, and gender concerns of job opportunities and workplace participation. Factory work is associated with masculinity and retail sales with femininity (despite the association of femininity with food preparation, or the fact that men were the majority of Californian grocery workers at the time); natural foods retail has been historically associated with whiteness while food production in California is increasingly associated with Brownness. I drew on comparative-historical sociological strategies (Mahoney 2004) to first examine organizational differences "within-case" between (1) the most white collar, (2) manual, (3) customer-oriented, and (4) conflictual work groups in each cooperative; and then conduct "across-case" comparisons between (1) the office work group at both sites, (2) the production work group at the bakery and the produce work group at the grocery, (3) the sales and delivery work group at the bakery and the cashiers work group at the grocery, and (4) shipping at the bakery and housewares at the grocery. This two-step process has the benefit of not glossing over the specific conditions of each organization, but also allowing some degree of comparison and generalizability outside a single case study (Ayres, Kavanaugh, and Knafl 2003).

Observation. I did not try to conduct participant observation as an employee or intern in the tradition of many other workplace ethnographic scholars (e.g., Kunda 2006; Otis and Wu 2018; Salzinger 2003; Sobering 2019b, Williams 2006). This was, in large part, because worker cooperative "good jobs" (Kalleberg 2009) have little turnover, and neither the grocery nor the bakery had the kind of unpaid internship programs that others have used for immersive involvement (Sobering 2019a). Indeed, the most typical response to my offers to pitch in ranged from mild to intense offense, with comments that suggested I was trying to find out information they did not want to share, or that I was insinuating that their tasks required no training and I could just pick them up. Yet being forced into a position of nonparticipant observation sensitized me to the way ethnographers tend to rank participant observation as *inherently* superior to the nonparticipant variety. While the studies I just noted are characterized by clear ethnographic advantages—internalized and embodied understandings of normative nuances, the ability to distinguish managerial ideology from what happens in practice, direct access to workplace "gossip," and insights into uncodified but nevertheless standard workplace practices—participant observation can also introduce irresolvable distortions of meaning. It is not only that researchers may be treated as potential spies for management (e.g., Milkman 1997), but also that writing as a participant observer may efface key differences of experience: those who will shortly be returning to their academic jobs may perceive and interpret their day-to-day actions and long-term work trajectories quite differently than those who will not. As a nonparticipant observer, the distinction between myself as researcher and those I observed as workers was sharply drawn, preventing any possible appropriation of cooperative workers' narratives. That is, the purported weakness of nonparticipant observation (the inability to stand in the shoes of another) may also be its strength: to underline the fact that no scholarship can ever fully capture others' workplace experiences, and to remind researchers to be humble in the face of competing accounts (Stacey 1988).

Four work groups at each cooperative allowed me to shadow volunteers: thirty-six members in all. I was with them from the moment they entered the workplace until they went home, which sometimes meant going off-site on delivery, buying, or print runs. On only three days did I do anything other than nonparticipant observation: one bakery manager, Charlie Navarro in production, gave me a "tryout" on the bread slicing and packaging line; one member of the grocery's produce work group, Juanita Cole, happily handed me a broom to help out at the end of the night; and one member of the grocery's housewares work group, Susan Wells, gave me a pricing gun to help process a new shipment of drinking glasses. Most often, though, my offers to help were refused. Instead I would usually locate myself near the person whose shift I was shadowing, notebook and ballpoint pen in hand, and use rapid scrawl and an improvised shorthand—what Robert Emerson, Rachel Fretz, and Linda Shaw (1995) call "jottings"—to record comments verbatim or summarize discussions and actions. In the few instances in which I was unable to do this because my hands were occupied with the task I had been given or, as with the grocery's cashier work group, I was told that my notebook would make customers uncomfortable, I took breaks in a private space at least once per hour to write up what I had observed. I did not position myself as the silent "family dog" in the manner of Arlie Hochschild and Anne Machung (1989), but rather asked numerous questions about what people were doing and why they were doing it, as well as questions about their backgrounds and previous work experience (see appendix C).

Interviews. Although the primary focus at this time was on the larger organizations rather than individuals, I also conducted nine follow-up interviews with current members. With the exception of the bakery CEO, which took place in person in the bakery's café and lasted almost two hours, follow-up interviews were conducted by telephone for fifteen to thirty minutes. To supplement the historical material I was starting to collect, I also interviewed three former members of both cooperatives (one from the grocery and two from the bakery) who were referred to me by current members; each interview took between two and three hours.

Access and recruitment. Getting access to organizations and their members is not as simple as choosing a site and showing up. Luckily, as other organizational ethnographers have found (Chen 2009; Ferguson 1991; Ho 2009; Turco 2016), existing relations helped to facilitate organizational access, including the ten interviews I had by this time conducted with grocery and bakery workers. At the bakery, I do not know if the advice of the bakery driver I met to "start at the top" was the *only* way I would have had such great access, but certainly the CEO's formal direction to managers to allow me to attend meetings, observe workers, and interview people on the clock sped up my ability to start talking to people.

To elicit volunteers for observation, I used the convenience and snowball methods I have described for interviews but also directly solicited Black and Brown members of the four work groups I studied with the goal of having a less ethnoracially homogenous sample. Because of the overrepresentation of whites in the first-phase interviews, I strove to get a rough demographic picture of the work groups I observed. Race/ethnicity and gender could be found in the demographic records shared with me for the entire workforce, but neither a worker's educational attainment nor a self-selected or imputed class category was part of such records. I was, however, able to query not only those I shadowed but also approximately three-fourths of their fellow work group members either on the floor or before or after work group meetings, regarding markers of class (see appendix C). With the exception of the office work groups at both sites—where, as I discuss in chapters 4 and 5, there were many more people with college degrees, professional parents, and/or childhoods in family-owned homes—the mostly working-class markers were consistent among the six other work groups I observed at the bakery and the grocery. Other than the grocery's cheese work group (which seemed to have more members with middle-class markers than any other), nothing suggested that class composition of the work groups I surveyed differed from those of their coworkers in other work groups.

Almost everyone I approached allowed me to shadow them. Only one person turned down my request: an immigrant Latinx grocery worker who explained that despite our years-long acquaintance in social justice organizing, he opposed and would not personally participate in what he saw as the inherent exploitation of less powerful social actors by academic researchers—what we social scientists problematize as the practice of "studying down" (Schwartzman 1993). While I felt morally and intellectually compelled by his argument, I was also compelled by my academic program's time line for dissertation completion: already slowed by a lack of funding requiring me to teach almost every term I was a graduate student, I could not stop and redesign a study in collaboration with those I wanted to study as participatory action research approaches suggest (Kemmis, McTaggart, and Nixon 2014). His critique, however, does point not only to the value of designing research in collaboration with those researched but also to the increasing need to do so among populations who are aware of and engaged with the political debates among researchers.

No one at the bakery turned down my requests to observe, but when, on my third day of observation, I discovered that at least some workers interpreted their managers' "encouragement" to let me shadow and talk with them as more of a directive to do so, I realized my potential to coerce information. I therefore asked fewer questions about their personal backgrounds and experiences outside the workplace to avoid harm and ensure that consent was indeed given (NCPHSBBR 1978). Because I no longer directly asked about family class background, I used workers' own education as a back-up proxy for class at the bakery, and noted any spontaneous self-identifications of race/ethnicity, gender, and sexuality. Almost without exception I got into fairly deep and mutual discussions at the bakery about our family backgrounds and work experiences, however, and was thus able to collect roughly similar data on class, race/ethnicity, and gender at each site.

Reflections in the field. At the end of each day I either turned my rough jottings into more narrative and detailed field notes or literally filled in gaps on the page with more detail than I had been able to add on the floor. As Emerson, Fretz, and Shaw (1995) suggest, this practice of capturing actions, dialogue, and researcher insights in real time both supplemented my insufficient memory and helped sensitize me to the range and variety of social life I observed. Fleshing out field notes afterwards ensured that I kept track of important nuances—a tone of voice or specific body language, the spatial relationship between workers and customers—and allowed me to notice patterns across a day that went unseen at the time. At each site I spent an average of nine hours per day and five days per week engaged in this kind of observation, attending work group and committee meetings, participating in new worker orientations, and/or taking part in company-sponsored and informal social events, followed up with at least one and up to two hours of field note review and revision after each day of fieldwork. I spent approximately 540 hours doing fieldwork in the summer of 2003, and approximately 20 further hours of follow-up interviews.

Phase III: Contexts

The third phase, from January 2004 through May 2005, involved the collection of nonethnographic data: archival and financial data from the two cooperatives and publicly available occupational and earnings data on local and national labor markets. Although ethnographic data uniquely provides both a sense of what people do and why they believe they do it (Emerson, Fretz, and Shaw 1995), key material details such as earnings or working hours, as well as broader social and economic contexts like local occupational opportunities and earnings, provide a critical context for those actions and beliefs about them (Morrill and Fine 1997).

My archival process was to sit at a table in a public lounge with my laptop and carefully spread out a set of the material collected by each cooperative, review it, take notes on it in an Excel spreadsheet and then return it to its guardian or replace it where I found it. The material consisted of historical meeting agendas and minutes, organizational manuals, orientation handouts, news clippings, photo albums, and video recordings on VHS tape. While neither cooperative's archive was complete or always in a consistent order, both provided a rich, continuous, and often narrative sense of the cooperatives' histories.

In addition to historical materials, both sites emailed me complete financial data on all regular employees for 2003 in Excel spreadsheets with names redacted, including demographic characteristics, length of tenure and membership, annual pay, benefits, and earnings from various forms of profit sharing. Much of this I was able to triangulate, or test agreement with (Hesse-Biber 2010), using available quantitative data on local communities and labor markets. The public data were accessed online, and included local and regional US Census and American Community Survey data on community earnings from the US Census Bureau's now-defunct American FactFinder; labor market and occupational data from the Bureau of Labor Statistics; and news items in local papers and regional websites. An example of this triangulation process can be found in the comparison I draw in chapter 5 between grocery workers' claims about not being able to afford to buy land, their actual earnings in the wage statements I was able to analyze, and the county-level earnings data against which I compare grocery data.

Phase IV: Analysis

The majority of the analysis took place during the fourth phase, from August 2005 to August 2007. As common to most qualitative researchers, new patterns and meanings emerged once I "exited the field," and stopped actively interviewing, observing, or studying archives at the two cooperatives. That is, this degree of analysis was quite different from the exploratory analysis I did while in the field.

A critical part of analysis is "coding," or systematically combing through collected data to identify key aspects and themes (Saldaña 2011). This was a process I started at the end of phase I, but now had to do for phase II and phase III data. I retyped handwritten field notes, reformatted interview transcripts and memos, and transferred all the data into a qualitative data analysis software program, HyperRESEARCH. This program allowed me to comprehensively recode the data, focusing not only on the intersectional qualities of class, race/ethnicity, and gender at the sites but also on the decidedly bureaucratic characteristics of the grocery. I used a mix of inductive and deductive analysis to develop a total of sixty-one codes organized into seven themes. These inductive and deductive processes echo—although do not fully map onto—the problem of what John Van Maanen (1979) has described as "first order" versus "second order" data, or the local meanings of participants versus those a researcher inevitably brings with them to a project. For instance, an "accountability and responsibility" code inductively emerged within the "authority" theme I had created deductively—an in vivo code drawn from words used repeatedly by bakery and grocery members to discuss the development and operation of workplace authority, and alerted me to the ways in which authority was similarly, not differently, invested across the two seemingly distinct organizational forms. In contrast, a "gender" code I created within my "social characteristics" theme was entirely deductive: an intellectual interest and concern I brought with me about how the ubiquitous femininity/masculinity binary informed the construction and maintenance of the workplace. Both kinds of analysis were critical in this study, and—more importantly—they each shaped the other: my interest in gender led me to problematize "accountability and responsibility" in terms of "gender" (among other social characteristics).

The issue of "first order" and "second order" meanings and inductive and deductive analysis was perhaps most pressing when it came to demographic labeling in comparisons among and between bakery and grocery workers. The categories I use here did not always correspond to their self-identifications, and outwardly similar workers might not use similar labels across the two organizations. That is, similar wealth and educational backgrounds were claimed as "lower middle class" or "working class" depending (mostly) on the organizational context; gender was recognized and discussed as binary at the bakery and multiple at the grocery; workers were sorted into four racial categories by the personnel work group at the bakery, but into many more by self-selection at the grocery. That is not to say that researchers should not inquire about self-identifications by class, race/ethnicity, and/or gender. Indeed, I theorize reasons for the lack of consistency in identification processes at length in chapter 7 and argue that, when it comes to motivations for the actions of workers *as* workers, identification *processes* are as significant as static conditions like material wealth or legal ethnoracial and gender designation. Yet it was impossible to elicit or describe the relationship between each worker's multiplicity of social markers and self-identifications, and to even try to do so would be to ignore the way that class, race/ethnicity, and gender function as *systems of power* in intersecting ways to shape individual lives (McCall 2005). That is, social categorization inevitably does epistemic violence to individuals by distorting self-definitions (Spivak 1999), but the obliteration of social categories removes potent forms of analysis and remedies for historic, society-wide, and increasing patterns of unjust reward and deprivation. I chose in this book to use these broad and at times deceptively discrete class, ethnoracial, and gender categories in order to speak to similar constraints and conditions across individual lives and organizational clusters—and particularly in terms of the ones that have a demonstrated bearing on individual opportunities (Avent-Holt and Tomaskovic-Devey 2019; Ridgeway 2011; Weeden et al. 2007). In doing so I am no doubt forcing some people into boxes they would not have put themselves and obscuring other, possibly more effective, identity formations that might open up further avenues of workplace and social change. I have chosen to err on the side of being able to speak about the interaction of organizational forms and collectivities.

Phase V: Follow-Up

The fifth part of this research, which lasted almost until the time of publication, began during phase II: the experience of examining each cooperative's archives also involved a degree of "revisit" observation (Burawoy 2003), of returning to the original sites with a comparative eye. Because I examined the archival materials in spaces through which cooperative members passed for about five hours on one day each month for about six months, I would inevitably exchange greetings and catch up with workers I had observed or interviewed, also learning about what was new or changing at that cooperative. I recorded these observations as field notes and added them to the data I analyzed in phase IV.

But although I formally "exited the field" in 2005, I kept in contact with several cooperative workers I met during my research during the analysis phase and at least annually through 2011. This involved phone calls, emails, or in-person meetings to check my understandings of specific documented policies, observed procedures, or outcomes of votes that had been in process, or simply asking how things were going at each site—particularly but not only in relation to the 2007–09 Great Recession and its years of lingering unemployment and loss of wealth. As

I analyzed my data, wrote and revised what I first submitted as a doctoral dissertation, and then developed into this book, I continued to follow the fortunes of each cooperative through both documented sources (the news and, later, social media; and the occasional mention in academic papers and documentary films), and through the informal grapevine of worker ownership researchers, educators, and support service organizers. Through these direct and indirect channels of information I continued to have a fairly strong sense of the changes and continuities at each site.

In June 2015, I conducted a more systematic follow-up that included site visits at both the grocery and the bakery, email and phone check-ins with several of those I had interviewed in the previous decade, and two semistructured interviews with longtime members who had been in leadership roles in the past five years (the president of the board of directors at the bakery, and someone with multiple terms on the board of directors and the Intracooperative Coordinating Committee at the grocery). These latter interviews focused on changes and continuities since the Great Recession and subsequent recovery, specifically in regard to organizational formalization, authority distribution, and workforce demographic composition and distribution. As I note in chapter 8, the COVID-19 pandemic presents new challenges, but my informal check-ins and media review suggest no reason to believe that the effect of the pandemic will be dramatically different from that of the Great Recession.

I did not originally intend to follow the lives of workers and organizations over nearly fifteen years, but the unfolding of my project over this period led to the new insights I have outlined here regarding the relationships between worker ownership and control and workplace inequality. By starting my study at a moment of economic expansion in 2001 (Hall et al. 2001) and continuing through the peaks and valleys of the early 2000s to the Great Recession and its recovery, I was able to identify continuities in these cooperatives' "practices, processes, actions, and meanings" (Acker 2006b) that were able—or unable—to attenuate the heightened inequalities of the Great Recession and its recovery period (Redbird and Grusky 2016). Certainly it is rarely practical for doctoral research to attempt such a longitudinal study; I would advise against it! And yet I think we underestimate the value of the relationship building inherent to interviews and ethnography as a basis for further longitudinal study. Had I undertaken a mass survey or only conducted archival research as a graduate student, I think few workers would have found the time to talk to me ten years later. The strong relationships I developed through qualitative research allowed me to return to the same sites over time, to see how members of the two cooperatives were faring, and to better assess the explanatory value of monist managerial bureaucracy and pluralist participatory bureaucracy.

INTERVIEW SCHEDULE

Introductions

- Discussant background
- How did discussant come to work at co-op?

Timeline

- Structure, size, diversity, and other changes or continuities

Formal Structure

- What is the structure of the co-op?
- How do people (not) become managers? How is this seen/discussed in the co-op? Benefit?
- Committee management: Why do people run? What is the benefit? Is it different by class, race/ethnicity, gender, and/or sexuality?
- Is there a trade-off between participation and efficiency?
- (Feelings about structure? Agree or disagree? How does it work? Improvements?)

Informal Structure

- Other than formal structure, how is power exerted? Who has it? How does it change hands? Official versus unofficial? Are there "indispensable" people? What does/doesn't membership vote on?
- Is there a difference in what is seen as work between the office and other parts of the business?
- Do the various work groups get along? Is there rivalry? What sort?
- Are there strong friendships among workers?

Staying/Leaving

- How do discussants know work is valued by the organization or fellow worker-owners?
- What sort of people have stayed? What sort have left? Why?
- What are the pay and benefits?
- How are external hires done? Co-op "fit" vs. diversity?
- Internal hiring: How are decisions made and received? How integrated are work groups with each other?
- How are people fired? Are there alternatives to firing (making life unpleasant, retraining, transferring)?
- Difference between co-op-oriented people vs. paycheck-oriented people?

Identity

- How do discussants identify selves? (What forms of identification practices do they use?)
- What problems are there? How are problems in the co-op dealt with (structurally and informally)?
- Specific problems: Gender? Race/ethnicity? Sexuality? Power tripping? Fights? Discipline?

Diversity

- How is co-op welcoming to various populations (class, race/ethnicity, gender, sexuality, ability)?
- Diversity training at co-op: At all? How? Who initiated, and why?

- How diverse are the various departments or managerial strata or committees?

Other

- What advantages or disadvantages are there to working in a co-op?
- How/is the job connected to participant vision of how the world could or should be?

OBSERVATION QUESTIONS

Firm/work group:
Chosen name for study (if any):
Job title/responsibilities:
Years in work group:
Years at cooperative:
Previous job (outside cooperative):
Previous work group(s), if any:
Gender:
Age:
Racial/ethnic identity:
First language:
Sexual identity:
Class identity:
Education:
Parents' education:
Parents' occupation(s):
Childhood area (rural, urban, suburban):
Childhood home owned or rented:
Immigrant/US-born?

1. WORKER COOPERATIVES

1. Unless otherwise indicated, all quoted statements by grocery and bakery employees are drawn from observations, interviews, and discussions with the author between 1999 and 2004.

2. The names of the companies and the people I observed and interviewed, identifying details, and the names of locations within (and descriptions of) the Golden Valley geographic area in which the pseudonymous One World Natural Grocery and People's Daily Bread Bakery are situated have been changed to disguise the actual businesses, although details that are crucial to the meaning of this work have been retained. This has sometimes made it difficult to capture the subtlety of affection and critique, as often these were expressed by playing on the names of people, places, or elected bodies. But it was not impossible. For instance, the pointed joke made by bakery workers in chapter 4 about the relative power of the CEO was not expressed as "coopHERBERTive" but as a different pun playing on the CEO's real name.

3. For more specific details on each of the companies' employment practices and their finances, see chapters 4 and 5.

4. For a more detailed description of the development of the grocery's workforce, see chapter 5.

5. This figure is somewhat of an underrepresentation. Unlike the grocery, the bakery contracted with temporary employment agencies and the production division had a small but regular cadre of temporary employees—almost all of whom were observed to be Latinx during my study—but contingent employment was not tracked in the way permanent employment was at the bakery.

6. For a more detailed description of the development of the bakery's workforce, see chapter 4.

7. Some firms that meet this criteria are legally structured as limited liability corporations or ESOPs, but that choice is often based on perceived tax or other legal benefits; the social structure of these firms follows the worker cooperative model (Palmer 2017).

8. In some rare cases, worker cooperatives combine member bases, forging a partnership with consumers or the state.

9. There is somewhat more variety of economic organization than table 1.3 can capture. Corporations may organize as B Corporations that specify social as well as economic outcomes in their charters (Kurland 2018); some ESOPs adopt other forms of employee profit sharing, as well as broader democratic control (Blasi, Freeman, and Kruse 2013; Kruse et al. 2004); and community, nonprofit, and family-owned organizations are often an important part of the universe inhabited by worker cooperatives (Ben-Ner 2018; Gordon Nembhard 2014; Pinto 2018; Rothschild and Stephenson 2009). These, however, are the most common types of organizations with which worker cooperatives are confused.

10. Although there is evidence that employee ownership that is not formally democratic tends to increase employee participation and autonomy (Logue and Yates 1999),

it seems to be much more likely to be the case where the ESOP owns the majority of stock (Cheney et al. 2014; Rosen, Case, and Staubus 2005).

2. "BY DEED INSTEAD OF BY ARGUMENT"

1. Theoretically, cooperative members are also liable for *losses* in proportion to their contribution to total annual hours.

2. Some scholars have argued that worker cooperatives are inherently born of economic crisis (Ben-Ner 1988, Dickstein 1991), although a meta-analysis of cooperative formation studies around the world suggests this is not the case (Staber 1993).

3. Steve Leikin sees the era's origins in the pre–Civil War efforts of these "practical utopians," but notes that most of these enterprises did not survive the war (2004).

4. There were also a variety of attempts to create alternative residential communities from not only labor and agrarian movements (Leikin 1999), but also feminist socialists and Christians (Taylor 1983), who found cooperative enterprise a useful anchor for their new towns (Curl 2009).

5. The so-called Haymarket Riot of 1886 occurred in Chicago, IL, at an anarchist-led rally that was part of a broad labor general strike. A bomb was thrown—either by a rallying striker or a police agent—and the police attacked the demonstrators, resulting in the official deaths of seven police officers and one civilian. This led to the state crackdown on the eight-hour day movement and labor in general, culminating in a speedy trial and death sentences for eight radical labor activists, and a shift in popular support away from socialism and anarchism (Avrich 1984, Green 2007).

6. In some places, a cynical "labor capitalism" arose, in which capital was supplied by—and directly returned to—individual local labor leaders (Frank 1994, 66).

7. As Clark Kerr (1939) notes, cooperative participation was on the basis of the family rather than the individual. Thus, while "active membership" denoted labor exchange (on farms, in transportation, in depot coordination, or otherwise), active members' families were included as cooperative beneficiaries.

8. This shift continued into the 1970s among most white farming cooperatives, but Jessica Gordon Nembhard (2014) argues that this was far from the case with the Black farming cooperatives, which maintained a strong social justice narrative.

9. Joyce Rothschild and J. Allen Whitt have estimated that in the mid-1970s there were over five thousand such worker-owned collectives (1986, 11). This is, however, such a vastly larger number than any others found at that time or later that it seems likely that they are including "free stores" and other enterprises that operated on unpaid labor. Indeed, in a later work, Rothschild included social enterprises and nongovernmental organizations that were not worker owned within her definition of "egalitarian cooperation" (2009, 1028).

10. As a comparison, see Rivera (2012) for a discussion of how cultural knowledges are foregrounded in elite professional services firms.

11. Some college-educated children of the middle class did join the labor movement—often explicitly to promote more socially egalitarian and anticapitalist action within the labor movement (Olney 2011)—but they were the exception that tended to prove the rule.

12. This account relies entirely on Robert Jackall's (1984) ethnographic study of the cooperative, and the Cheese Board's own history in its cookbook (Cheese Board Collective 2003).

13. In 1996 the Cheese Board joined with local cooperative developers to spin off a series of "incubator" cooperatives named for Father José María Arizmendiarrieta, founder of the Mondragón cooperatives in the Basque region of Spain. By using the day the bakery is normally closed—first at the Cheese Board, and then at each successive Arizmendi site—to teach the new Arizmendi Bakery cooperatives the Cheese Board's

pizza and baking recipes, a small chain of cooperative retail bakeries was spawned that are still in business as this book goes to press.

14. This point is similarly made by Steven Vallas (1999) regarding Michael Piore and Charles Sabel's (1984) analysis of the rise of Fordist production versus craft-based industries.

3. METAMORPHOSES

1. As Wini Breines (2001) notes, numerous scholars have focused on how postwar middle-class youth felt unusual confidence about their future—if also, as C. Wright Mills puts it, "uneasiness and indifference" (1959, 11). For many working-class Americans, this period was also one of inclusion in a future of advantage, as this was when Jews and southern Europeans migrated into the economically privileged racial category of whiteness (Aronowitz 1992; Brodkin 1998); for Black and Brown working-class Americans, it was a politically contradictory time when barriers were articulated in national conversations, when some movement was made towards tearing those barriers down, and when they were also reinforced and rearticulated (Lipsitz 1998).

2. Not all long-term members agreed that former workers had gone on to make "twice the money." When I brought up this rationale for the change in organizational structure, Greybo ran down a list of former members and listed other trajectories: a woman who had gone into construction, a man who was the photo lab manager for a local Walmart store, another who had moved to Oregon, and another who had started his own small distribution company. "I don't know of anybody that got such great skills and they're gone [to make 'twice the money']" she countered.

3. This incident is described in a publication by the consultants in which the name of the cooperative is clearly identified, so I have not cited it here.

4. See the section "How Worker Cooperatives Work" in chapter 2 for a discussion of how worker shares are determined. To keep the Internal Revenue Service at bay, the bakery almost always erred on the side of caution and held as much as possible as working capital until the worker separated from the company. Rolling payouts solved the problem described in chapter 2 of satisfying workers' desire to access the value of their productive efforts and the IRS's suspicion that worker cooperatives were simply shirking payroll taxes by transferring earnings from wages to profit sharing.

5. As is the case with most other people and organizations in this book, the Shire is a pseudonym for a real organization that existed at the time.

6. During my period of observation, only the produce work group had simultaneous interpretation at its primarily English-language meetings.

7. It is beyond the scope of this research to explain how these cooperatives were able to gain and hold their market share, although some of their success is surely due to the lack of large-scale competition until the early 2000s.

8. There were, of course, exceptions, such as the Cheese Board Collective that remained purposefully small. Its disproportionately white and middle-class workforce continued to extract a reasonably supportive living in its upper-middle-class Gourmet Ghetto neighborhood of Berkeley, California.

4. PEOPLE'S DAILY BREAD BAKERY

1. Although I primarily use the term *Latinx* to describe people who are racialized through a purported historical, cultural, or ancestral relationship to Spanish and/or Portuguese rather than Northern European colonization of the Americas, I follow the lead of workers at both sites and use their ethnoracial self-descriptions (e.g., *Hispanic*) where such self-identifications were made.

2. Internally, work group managers were known as area coordinators and the CEO as the general coordinator, but I have used the more standard firm position terms for ease of reading.

3. This information comes from the US Census Bureau's 2003 American Community Survey summary tables; the county name has been concealed to protect confidentiality.

4. Earnings encompass wages, gainsharing, profit sharing, and dividends, but exclude health and other external benefits, paid time off, and the employee discount.

5. The bakery also used a small number of short-term temporary workers—particularly in production, and particularly in the summer to help produce seasonal hamburger and hot dog buns—and these workers were not eligible for membership or any form of profit sharing. Part-time permanent workers would take longer to achieve the required minimum hours worked, but were eligible for membership. Indeed, the only two permanent part-time workers were both members.

6. While both the bakery and the grocery collected data on workers' race/ethnicity and gender as required by law for employers of their size, neither collected data on class. I have estimated socioeconomic class broadly—as working, middle, or upper class—based on worker responses about their own and their parents' education, where they grew up, what their parents did for a living, and if they owned or rented a home growing up. I then extrapolated from those people I interacted with to estimates of the population as a whole. Most of those I interviewed or observed had no college degrees, nor did their parents, and their parents held positions that would be considered working-class (hired farmhand, waitress, construction worker, etc.). Few, however, were poor; many grew up in homes their parents owned. Some had gone to college, and some had grown up in rural settings with parents in working-class jobs, but they or their parents had gone to exclusive colleges: they were some version of the countercultural 1970s and 1980s "drop outs" from middle-class society described by Tim Miller (1991). The ones I classified as upper middle class mostly self-described as such and confirmed this with names of colleges they and their parents had attended, the towns in which they grew up, or their parents' occupations. No one self-identified as or described being from a truly upper-class background.

7. While the term *people of color* mostly meant Latinx workers at the bakery, there were also two African Americans and one mixed-race person.

8. In addition to the Bureau of Labor Statistics data, I rely here on the 2005 American Community Survey data from the US Census Bureau on adult median earnings by what they call "sex," work experience, and ethnicity/race, accessed in December 2006, but cannot cite specific tables without disclosing the cooperative's location.

9. At the bakery, gender was identified by the personnel director using only the terms of the *he* or *she* gender binary common at the time (although workers who felt they belonged in the other category would, in theory, have been able to correct their records). I do not know if there were workers who identified as transgender or nonbinary and were unable to use these other categories, or if there simply were no transgender or nonbinary bakery workers.

5. ONE WORLD NATURAL GROCERY

1. See chapter 4, note 1, regarding terms used for ethnoracial identification of workers in this study.

2. This information comes from the US Census Bureau's 2003 American Community Survey summary tables; the county name has been concealed to protect confidentiality.

3. Although the grocery had 214 workers on its books in 2003, I excluded those who were terminated part of the way through the year or were scheduled to work less than five hours per week, resulting in a sample of 187 that the following figures are based on.

4. As with the bakery, earnings includes wages, profit sharing, and dividends but excludes benefits, paid time off, and the employee discount.

5. I did not discover what proportion of bakery or grocery workers owned their homes. At the bakery, it seemed that many of the sales and delivery and office workers—and most managers—did. But a member of the bakery production work group also requested that I not talk too loudly about his homeownership for fear of creating a division between himself and the majority of production workers, who rented their homes. At the grocery, however, homeownership was clearly the exception rather than the rule.

6. I always followed up with the dissenter, and in all cases but one the issue was wanting to know more about the project and not having an "abstain" option, as would have been the case in a formal vote.

7. It should be noted that because workers were paid well but nowhere near at the rates of management in typical corporations, it would still be cheaper to have even a hundred workers paid at the cooperative average hourly earnings of twenty-eight dollars for five hours of such managerial work ($140,000) every decade or so than to hire a cohort of managers at annual market rates to make the same decisions.

8. For a discussion of how class status was interpreted and assigned, see chapter 4, note 6.

9. The office, by contrast, primarily hired internally—perhaps because external office workers' starting wage expectations exceeded what the grocery paid.

10. In this the grocery was similar to other large California supermarkets, where 91 percent of employees topped out at a high school diploma or less (Dube and Lantsberg 2004).

11. The numbers of men and women of color and white women whose management positions are truly powerful may be even lower, as research has found gender—and, one might presume, ethnoracial—disparities in the actual power of those with managerial titles (Cohen and Huffman 2007).

12. As with race and ethnicity, grocery workers self-identified their gender, and the grocery offered a "transgender" category that was not accepted by the state at the time. Yet because, only two workers self-identified as transgender during my study—and contributed less than 1 percent of the cooperative's annual labor—this analysis primarily treats gender as a binary category at the grocery. It is important to realize, however, that workers' self-identifications varied, and the categories of *woman* and *man* were not exclusively used by those who were assigned those categories at birth regardless of whether they self-identified as transgender.

13. I have excluded those with work schedules of fewer than five hours per week from my sample (well below the twenty-four hours required to be eligible for health benefits)—a work group almost entirely composed of women. That is, there were even more women officially employed at the grocery, but none were politically active and most rarely even attended their work group meetings. Their membership was "special," at the work group's discretion, and was largely a way for these workers to keep their 20 percent shopping discount. See also note 12 regarding how workers were categorized by gender.

14. Both transgender grocery workers were in this ethnoracial category.

6. MANAGERIAL AND PARTICIPATORY BUREAUCRACIES

1. My analysis overlaps with Paul Adler and Bryan Borys's (1996) "enabling" and "coercive" bureaucracies in arguing that formalization is not independent of how it is linked to control. Where they assume a universal worker to focus more on organizational innovation and individual experiences of autonomy and satisfaction, however, I am interested in how formalization may produce different organizational effects depending on workers' social status.

2. Here I am developing a concept that differs from two earlier uses: Harry Kranz's (1976) notion of the need for the populations of corporate and state bureaucracies to reflect the gender and ethnoracial characteristics of national populations; and Susan Moffitt's (2014) conception of the need for more transparency and more generative than fixed notions of expertise in existing bureaucratic structures. My version is most closely aligned with David Rosenbloom's (1975) usage—which focuses on employee inclusion in the organization of labor, middle-management inclusion in top-level organizational decisions, and ethnoracial and gender inclusiveness—but I explicitly describe a distributed form of management as well as governance, and problematize inclusion.

3. For a description of the grocery's jurisdictional allocation, see the "Political Rights" section of chapter 5.

4. See chapter 4, note 1, regarding terms used for ethnoracial identification of workers in this study.

7. WORKER IDENTITIES

1. Eileen Otis and Tongyu Wu (2018) have a similar formulation of the "deficient worker" as organizationally produced and generative of inequality.

2. Although Michael Albert and colleagues (1986) define "eclectic pluralism" as a sequential shifting between categories to address particular spheres of social life (class for work, gender for family, etc.), my use of the term *pluralist* assumes simultaneity and is closer to their "holist" proposition. I argue here, however, that simultaneity is not necessarily total or totalizing, and thus avoid holism's contention that each part always represents and is always contained within a larger whole.

3. It may be that former women production workers had complained about production floor profanity. Indeed, when I shadowed Mercedes at her reception desk, she told me that she would sometimes have to call up to Herbert to stop cursing, telling me, "We're a business! Plus, I don't like that language." That is, bakery management may have had an empirical basis for its focus on "language." In its address of this perceived problem, however, it seems to have landed squarely in the "equality-versus-difference" dilemma identified by feminists in the 1990s: either women are inherently equal and thus cannot be extended affirmative action, or they are disadvantaged and thus may be subject to various kinds of protective—and exclusionary—legislation (Scott 1988).

4. This percentage was reported to me by the office worker who was in charge of the payroll deductions; I did not independently corroborate this figure, although it seemed to map onto what I found while talking to workers.

5. The fund originator was a white, middle-class grocery worker, but the office worker administering the fund corroborated my anecdotal observation that Latinx workers were the majority of those who signed up.

6. That a reciprocal relationship existed between the organizational structures and each organization's worker identity does not imply that it was an automatic or inevitable outcome. Leslie Salzinger (2003), for instance, shows how conflicts between the two could undermine workplace authority.

8. BUREAUCRACIES, DEMOCRACIES, AND ECONOMIES

1. By 2018 there were at least two Latinx women working a smaller production line at the bakery, according to news and social media reports.

Bibliography

Aalbers, Rick, and Wilfred Dolfsma. 2015. *Innovation Networks: Managing the Networked Organization*. Oxon, UK: Routledge.

Abell, Hilary. 2014. *Worker Cooperatives: Pathways to Scale*. Tacoma Park, MD: Democracy Collaborative.

Abello, Oscar Perry. 2021. "Worker-Owned Cooperatives Are Creating Their Own Funding Networks." *YES!*, February 22, 2021. https://www.yesmagazine.org/economy/2021/02/22/worker-owned-cooperatives-investment-network.

Acker, Joan. 1990. "Hierarchies, Jobs, Bodies: A Theory of Gendered Organizations." *Gender & Society* 4 (2): 139–58.

——. 2006a. *Class Questions: Feminist Answers*. Lanham, MD: Rowman and Littlefield.

——. 2006b. "Inequality Regimes: Gender, Class, and Race in Organizations." *Gender & Society* 20 (4): 441–64.

Adams, Tony E., Stacy Holman Jones, and Carolyn Ellis. 2015. *Autoethnography*. Oxford: Oxford University Press.

Adler, Paul S. 2012. "The Sociological Ambivalence of Bureaucracy: From Weber via Gouldner to Marx." *Organization Science* 23 (1): 244–66.

Adler, Paul S., and Bryan Borys. 1996. "Two Types of Bureaucracy: Enabling and Coercive." *Administrative Science Quarterly* 41 (1): 61–89.

AFL-CIO (American Federation of Labor and Congress of Industrial Organizations). 2019. "AFL-CIO Releases 2019 Executive Paywatch Report." Press release, June 25, 2019. https://aflcio.org/press/releases/afl-cio-releases-2019-executive-paywatch-report.

Albert, Michael, Mel King, Leslie Cagan, Robin Hahnel, Holly Sklar, Noam Chomsky, and Lydia Sargent. 1986. *Liberating Theory*. Cambridge, MA: South End.

Albert, Stuart, and David A. Whetten. 2004. "Organizational Identity." In *Organizational Identity: A Reader*, edited by Mary Jo Hatch and Majken Schultz, 89–118. Oxford: Oxford University Press.

Ali, Tariq. 1984. *The Stalinist Legacy: Its Impact on Twentieth-Century World Politics*. New York: Penguin.

Alimahomed-Wilson, Jake. 2016. *Solidarity Forever? Race, Gender, and Unionism in the Ports of Southern California*. Lanham, MD: Lexington Books.

Alkon, Alison Hope. 2008. "From Value to Values: Sustainable Consumption at Farmers Markets." *Agriculture and Human Values* 25 (4): 487–98.

——. 2012. *Black, White, and Green: Farmers Markets, Race, and the Green Economy*. Athens: University of Georgia Press.

Alkon, Alison Hope, and Julie Guthman. 2017. "Introduction." In *The New Food Activism*, edited by Alison Hope Alkon and Julie Guthman, 1–28. Berkeley: University of California Press.

Allegretto, Sylvia A., and Uyanga Byambaa. 2018. *A Post-Great Recession Overview of Labor Market Trends in the United States and California*. Berkeley: Institute for Research on Labor and Employment, University of California.

Alperovitz, Gar, Ted Howard, and Thad Williamson. 2010. "The Cleveland Model." *Nation*, March 2010, 21–24.

Alter, Catherine. 1998. "Bureaucracy and Democracy in Organizations: Revisiting Feminist Organizations." In *Private Action and the Public Good*, edited by Walter W. Powell and Elisabeth S. Clemens, 258–71. New Haven, CT: Yale University Press.

Ames, Lynda J. 1995. "When Sense Is Not Common: Alternatives to Hierarchy at Work." *Economic and Industrial Democracy* 16 (4): 553–76.

Anderson, Sarah, John Cavanaugh, Chuck Collins, Sam Pizzigati, and Mike Lapham. 2007. *Executive Excess: The Staggering Social Cost of U.S. Business Leadership*. Washington, DC: Institute for Policy Studies / United for a Fair Economy.

Appelbaum, Eileen, Thomas Bailey, Peter Berg, and Arne L. Kalleberg. 2000. *Manufacturing Advantage: Why High-Performance Work Systems Pay Off*. Ithaca, NY: ILR Press, an imprint of Cornell University Press.

Aronowitz, Stanley. 1992. *The Politics of Identity: Class, Culture, Social Movements*. New York: Routledge.

Arvidsson, Stefan. 1999. "Aryan Mythology as Science and Ideology." *Journal of the American Academy of Religion* 67 (2): 327–54.

Aschemann, Jessica, Ulrich Hamm, Simona Naspetti, and Raffele Zanoli. 2007. "The Organic Market." In *Organic Farming: An International History*, edited by William Lockeretz, 123–51. Cambridge: Center for Agriculture and Bioscience International.

Ashcraft, Karen Lee. 2001. "Organized Dissonance: Feminist Bureaucracy as Hybrid Form." *Academy of Management Journal* 44 (6): 1301–22.

Ashforth, Blake E., and Beth S. Schinoff. 2016. "Identity under Construction: How Individuals Come to Define Themselves in Organizations." *Annual Review of Organizational Psychology and Organizational Behavior* 3 (1): 111–37.

Avendaño, Ana. 2019. "#Metoo inside the Labor Movement." *New Labor Forum* 28 (1): 66–75.

Avent-Holt, Dustin, and Donald Tomaskovic-Devey. 2019. "Organizations as the Building Blocks of Social Inequalities." *Sociology Compass* 13 (2).

Avrich, Paul. 1984. *The Haymarket Tragedy*. Princeton, NJ: Princeton University Press.

Ayres, Lioness, Karen Kavanaugh, and Kathleen A. Knafl. 2003. "Within-Case and Across-Case Approaches to Qualitative Data Analysis." *Qualitative Health Research* 13 (6): 871–83.

Bank Muñoz, Carolina. 2008. *Transnational Tortillas: Race, Gender, and Shop-Floor Politics in Mexico and the United States*. Ithaca, NY: ILR Press, an imprint of Cornell University Press.

Barber, Kathleen L. 2000. *A Right to Representation: Proportional Election Systems for the Twenty-First Century*. Columbus: Ohio State University Press.

Bardhan, Ashok, and Richard Walker. 2011. "California Shrugged: Fountainhead of the Great Recession." *Cambridge Journal of Regions, Economy and Society* 4 (3): 303–22.

Baron, James N., Michael T. Hannan, and M. Diane Burton. 1999. "Building the Iron Cage: Determinants of Managerial Intensity in the Early Years of Organizations." *American Sociological Review* 64 (4): 527–47.

Baron, James N., Michael T. Hannan, Greta Hsu, and Özgecan Koçak. 2007. "In the Company of Women: Gender Inequality and the Logic of Bureaucracy in Start-up Firms." *Work and Occupations* 34 (1): 35–66.

Barrow, Frederica H. 2007. "Forrester Blanchard Washington and His Advocacy for African Americans in the New Deal." *Social Work* 52 (3): 201–8.

Bart, Pauline B., and Melinda Bart Schlesinger. 1982. "Collective Work and Self Identity: The Effect of Working in a Feminist Illegal Abortion Collective." In *Workplace *Democracy and Social Change*, edited by Frank Lindenfeld and Joyce Rothschild-Whitt, 139–53. Boston: Porter Sargent.

Bartik, Alexander W., Marianne Bertrand, Zoë B. Cullen, Edward L. Glaeser, Michael Luca, and Christopher T. Stanton. 2020. *How Are Small Businesses Adjusting to COVID-19? Early Evidence from a Survey.* Cambridge, MA: National Bureau of Economic Research.

Bartlett, Will, John Cable, Saul Estrin, Derek C. Jones, and Stephen C. Smith. 1992. "Labor-Managed Cooperatives and Private Firms in North Central Italy: An Empirical Comparison." *Industrial and Labor Relations Review* 46 (1): 103–18.

Bathmaker, Ann-Marie, Nicola Ingram, and Richard Waller. 2013. "Higher Education, Social Class and the Mobilisation of Capitals: Recognising and Playing the Game." *British Journal of Sociology of Education* 34 (5–6): 723–43.

Baum, Dale, and Robert A. Calvert. 1989. "Texas Patrons of Husbandry: Geography, Social Contexts, and Voting Behavior." *Agricultural History* 63 (4): 36–55.

Belasco, Warren James. 1989. *Appetite for Change: How the Counterculture Took on the Food Industry, 1966–1988.* New York: Pantheon Books.

Bell, Joyce M., and Douglas Hartmann. 2007. "Diversity in Everyday Discourse: The Cultural Ambiguities and Consequences of 'Happy Talk.'" *American Sociological Review* 72 (6): 895–914.

Bell, Myrtle P., Joy Leopold, Daphne Berry, and Alison V. Hall. 2018. "Diversity, Discrimination, and Persistent Inequality: Hope for the Future through the Solidarity Economy Movement." *Journal of Social Issues* 74 (2): 224–43.

Ben-Ner, Avner. 1988. "The Life Cycle of Worker-Owned Firms in Market Economies: A Theoretical Analysis." *Journal of Economic Behavior and Organization* 10 (3): 287–313.

——. 2018. "Reflections on the Future Evolution of the Social, Nonprofit and Cooperative Enterprise." *Annals of Public and Cooperative Economics* 89 (1): 109–24.

Berman, Katrina V. 1982. "The Worker-Owned Plywood Collectives." In *Workplace Democracy and Social Change*, edited by Frank Lindenfeld and Joyce Rothschild-Whitt, 161–75. Boston: Porter Sargent.

Bernstein, Paul. 1982. "Necessary Elements for Effective Worker Participation in Decision-Making." In *Workplace Democracy and Social Change*, edited by Frank Lindenfeld and Joyce Rothschild-Whitt, 51–81. Boston: Porter Sargent.

Bernstein, Shana. 2011. *Bridges of Reform: Interracial Civil Rights Activism in Twentieth-Century Los Angeles.* New York: Oxford University Press.

Berrey, Ellen. 2015. *The Enigma of Diversity: The Language of Race and the Limits of Racial Justice.* Chicago: University of Chicago Press.

Berry, Daphne P. 2013. "Effects of Cooperative Membership and Participation in Decision Making on Job Satisfaction of Home Health Aides." In *Sharing Ownership, Profits, and Decision-Making in the 21st Century*, edited by Douglas Kruse, 3–25. Bingley, UK: Emerald.

Berry, Daphne P., and Myrtle P. Bell. 2018. "Worker Cooperatives: Alternative Governance for Caring and Precarious Work." *Equality, Diversity and Inclusion: An International Journal* 37 (4): 376–91.

Berry, Daphne P., and Stu Schneider. 2011. "Improving the Quality of Home Health Aide Jobs: A Collaboration between Organized Labor and a Worker Cooperative." In *Employee Ownership and Shared Capitalism: New Directions in Research*, edited by Edward J. Carberry, 59–89. Champaign, IL: Labor and Employment Relations Association.

Bettie, Julie. 2003. *Women without Class: Girls, Race and Identity.* Berkeley: University of California Press.

Blake, Fay M., and H. Morton Newman. 1984. "Upton Sinclair's Epic Campaign." *California History* 63 (4): 305–12.

Blasi, Joseph R., Richard B. Freeman, and Douglas L. Kruse. 2013. *The Citizen's Share: Putting Ownership Back into Democracy*. New Haven, CT: Yale University Press.

Blasi, Joseph R., Douglas L. Kruse, and Aaron Bernstein. 2003. *In the Company of Owners: The Truth about Stock Options (and Why Every Employee Should Have Them)*. New York: Basic Books.

Blau, Peter M. 1956. *Bureaucracy in Modern Society*. New York: Crown.

Blauner, Robert. 1966. *Alienation and Freedom: The Factory Worker and His Industry*. Chicago: University of Chicago Press.

——. 1972. *Racial Oppression in America*. New York: Harper and Row.

Block, Fred. 1990. *Postindustrial Possibilities: A Critique of Economic Discourse*. Berkeley: University of California Press.

——. 2012. "Varieties of What? Should We Still Be Using the Concept of Capitalism?" In *Political Power and Social Theory*, edited by Julian Go, 269–91. Bingley, UK: Emerald.

Bloom, Nicholas, Robert S. Fletcher, and Ethan Yeh. 2021. *The Impact of COVID-19 on US Firms*. Cambridge, MA: National Bureau of Economic Research.

Blum, Linda. 1991. *Between Feminism and Labor: The Significance of the Comparable Worth Movement*. Berkeley: University of California Press.

Bonilla-Silva, Eduardo. 2014. *Racism without Racists: Color-Blind Racism and the Persistence of Racial Inequality in the United States*. 4th ed. Lanham, MD: Rowman and Littlefield.

Bookchin, Murray. 1995. *Social Anarchism or Lifestyle Anarchism: An Unbridgeable Chasm*. Edinburgh: AK Press.

Borowiak, Craig, Maliha Safri, Stephen Healy, and Marianna Pavlovskaya. 2017. "Navigating the Fault Lines: Race and Class in Philadelphia's Solidarity Economy." *Antipode* 50 (3): 577–603.

Bourdieu, Pierre. 1984. *Distinction: A Social Critique of the Judgment of Taste*. Translated by Richard Nice. Cambridge, MA: Harvard University Press.

——. 1986. "The Forms of Capital," translated by Richard Nice. In *Handbook of Theory and Research for the Sociology of Education*, edited by John G. Richardson, 241–58. New York: Greenwood.

Branch, Enobong Hannah, and Caroline Hanley. 2014. "Upgraded to Bad Jobs: Low-Wage Black Women's Relative Status since 1970." *Sociological Quarterly* 55 (2): 366–95.

Brandow, Karen, Jim McDonnell, and Vocations for Social Change. 1981. *No Bosses Here! A Manual on Working Collectively and Cooperatively*. 2nd ed. Boston: Alyson.

Breines, Wini. 1989. *Community and Organization in the New Left, 1962–1968: The Great Refusal*. New Brunswick, NJ: Rutgers University Press.

——. 2001. *Young, White, and Miserable: Growing up Female in the Fifties*. Chicago: University of Chicago Press.

Brenner, Aaron, Robert Brenner, and Calvin Winslow, eds. 2010. *Rebel Rank and File: Labor Militancy and Revolt from Below during the Long 1970s*. London: Verso.

Britton, Dana M. 2000. "The Epistemology of the Gendered Organization." *Gender & Society* 14 (3): 418–34.

——. 2003. *At Work in the Iron Cage*. New York: New York University Press.

Brodkin, Karen. 1998. *How Jews Became White Folks and What That Says about Race in America*. New Brunswick, NJ: Rutgers University Press.

Brown, Andrew D. 2006. "A Narrative Approach to Collective Identities." *Journal of Management Studies* 43 (4): 731–53.

Brubaker, Rogers, and Frederick Cooper. 2000. "Beyond 'Identity.'" *Theory and Society* 29: 1–47.

Buck, Solon Justus. 1913. *The Granger Movement: A Study of Agricultural Organization and Its Political, Economic and Social Manifestations, 1870–1880.* Cambridge, MA: Harvard University Press.

Burawoy, Michael. 2003. "Revisits: An Outline of a Theory of Reflexive Ethnography." *American Sociological Review* 68 (6): 645–79.

Bureau of Labor Statistics. US Department of Labor, Occupational Employment Statistics, Metropolitan Area, May 2003. Retrieved September 25, 2018. http://www.bls .gov/oes/tables.htm.

Byrne, Janice, Salma Fattoum, and Sarah Thébaud. 2019. "A Suitable Boy? Gendered Roles and Hierarchies in Family Business Succession." *European Management Review* 16 (3): 579–96.

Carberry, Edward J. 2010. "Who Benefits from Shared Capitalism? The Social Stratification of Wealth and Power in Companies with Employee Ownership." In *Shared Capitalism at Work: Employee Ownership, Profit and Gain Sharing, and Broad-Based Stock Options*, edited by Douglas L. Kruse, Richard B. Freeman, and Joseph R. Blasi, 317–49. Chicago: University of Chicago Press.

Castilla, Emilio J. 2008. "Gender, Race, and Meritocracy in Organizational Careers." *American Journal of Sociology* 113 (6): 1479–1526.

Cerny, George. 1963. "Cooperation in the Midwest in the Granger Era, 1869–1875." *Agricultural History* 37 (4): 187–205.

Chambers, Clarke A. 1962. "The Cooperative League of the United States of America, 1916–1961: A Study of Social Theory and Social Action." *Agricultural History* 36 (2): 59–81.

Chang, Mariko Lin. 2006. "Women and Wealth." In *Wealth Accumulation and Communities of Color in the United States: Current Issues*, edited by Jessica Gordon Nembhard and Ngina Chiteji, 112–30. Ann Arbor: University of Michigan Press.

Chang, Sophia. 2021. "Chinatown Banquet Hall's Workers and Supporters Propose Collective Ownership Plan to Launch New Restaurant." *Gothamist*, March 13, 2021. https://gothamist.com/food/chinatown-banquet-halls-workers-and-supporters -propose-collective-ownership-plan-launch-new-restaurant.

Charles, Maria, and David B. Grusky. 2005. *Occupational Ghettos: The Worldwide Segregation of Women and Men.* Stanford, CA: Stanford University Press.

Chatman, Jennifer A. 2010. "Norms in Mixed Sex and Mixed Race Work Groups." *Academy of Management Annals* 4 (1): 447–84.

Cheese Board Collective. 2003. *The Cheese Board: Collective Works; Bread, Pastry, Cheese, Pizza.* Berkeley: Ten Speed Press.

Chen, Katherine K. 2009. *Enabling Creative Chaos: The Organization Behind the Burning Man Event.* Chicago: University of Chicago Press.

Cheney, George, Iñaki Santa Cruz, Ana Maria Peredo, and Elías Nazareno. 2014. "Worker Cooperatives as an Organizational Alternative: Challenges, Achievements and Promise in Business Governance and Ownership." *Organization* 21 (5): 591–603.

Cimen, Sabiha, Lovia Gyarkye, Maggie Jones, Jamie Lauren Keiles, Jody Rosen, Kim Tingley, Marcela Valdes, and Carvell Wallace. 2021. "Workers on the Edge." *New York Times Magazine*, February 17, 2021, https://www.nytimes.com/interactive/2021/02 /17/magazine/remote-work-return-to-office.html?searchResultPosition=1.

Clawson, Dan, and Mary Ann Clawson. 1999. "What Has Happened to the US Labor Movement? Union Decline and Renewal." *Annual Review of Sociology* 25 (1): 95–119.

Clawson, Dan, and Naomi Gerstel. 2014. *Unequal Time: Gender, Class, and Family in Employment Schedules.* New York: Russell Sage Foundation.

Cobb, J. Adam. 2016. "How Firms Shape Income Inequality: Stakeholder Power, Executive Decision Making, and the Structuring of Employment Relationships." *Academy of Management Review* 41 (2): 324–48.

Cobble, Dorothy Sue. 2007. *The Sex of Class: Women Transforming American Labor.* Ithaca, NY: ILR Press, an imprint of Cornell University Press.

Coffey, Amanda. 1999. *The Ethnographic Self: Fieldwork and the Representation of Identity.* London: Sage.

Cohen, Jean L. 1983. "Rethinking Social Movements." *Berkeley Journal of Sociology* 28: 97–113.

Cohen, Philip N. 2013. "The Persistence of Workplace Gender Segregation in the US." *Sociology Compass* 7 (11): 889–99.

Cohen, Philip N., and Matthew Huffman. 2007. "Working for the Woman? Female Managers and the Gender Wage Gap." *American Sociological Review* 72 (5): 681–704.

Collins, Patricia Hill. 1990. *Black Feminist Thought: Knowledge, Consciousness, and the Politics of Empowerment.* Boston: Unwin Hyman.

Collins, Sharon M. 1997. "Black Mobility in White Corporations: Up the Corporate Ladder but out on a Limb." *Social Problems* 44 (1): 55–67.

Collinson, David L. 1992. *Managing the Shopfloor: Subjectivity, Masculinity, and Workplace Culture.* Berlin: Walter de Gruyter.

Collinson, David L., and Jeff Hearn. 1994. "Naming Men as Men: Implications for Work, Organization and Management." *Gender, Work and Organization* 1 (1): 2–22.

Combahee River Collective. 1979. "The Combahee River Collective: A Black Feminist Statement." In *Capitalist Patriarchy and the Case for Socialist Feminism*, edited by Zillah R. Eisenstein, 362–72. New York: Monthly Review Press.

Comisso, Ellen. 1979. *Workers' Control under Plan and Market: Implications of Yugoslav Self-Management.* New Haven, CT: Yale University Press.

Connell, R. W. 1995. *Masculinities.* Berkeley: University of California Press.

Cook, Michael L. 1995. "The Future of U.S. Agricultural Cooperatives: A Neo-institutional Approach." *American Journal of Agricultural Economics* 77 (5): 1153–59.

Correll, Shelley J., and Stephen Bernard. 2010. "Normative Discrimination and the Motherhood Penalty." *Gender & Society* 24 (5): 616–46.

Côté, Stéphane, Julian House, and Robb Willer. 2015. "High Economic Inequality Leads Higher-Income Individuals to Be Less Generous." *Proceedings of the National Academy of Sciences* 112 (52): 15838–43.

Cotter, David A., Joan M. Hermsen, and Reeve Vanneman. 2004. *Gender and Work: The Continuity of Change.* New York: Russell Sage Foundation.

Cotterill, Ronald W. 1978. "Declining Competition in Food Retailing: An Opportunity for Consumer Food Cooperatives?" *Journal of Consumer Affairs* 12 (2): 250–65.

Courpasson, David, and Stewart Clegg. 2006. "Dissolving the Iron Cages? Tocqueville, Michels, Bureaucracy and the Perpetuation of Elite Power." *Organization* 13 (3): 319–43.

Cowie, Jefferson. 2012. *Stayin' Alive: The 1970s and the Last Days of the Working Class.* New York: New Press.

Crenshaw, Kimberlé W. 1991. "Mapping the Margins: Intersectionality, Identity Politics, and Violence against Women of Color." *Stanford Law Review* 43 (6): 1241–99.

Crowley, Jocelyn Elise, and Theda Skocpol. 2001. "The Rush to Organize: Explaining Associational Formation in the United States, 1860s–1920s." *American Journal of Political Science* 45 (4): 813–29.

Curl, John. 2009. *For All the People: Uncovering the Hidden History of Cooperation, Co-operative Movements, and Communalism in America.* Oakland, CA: PM.

Dacheux, Eric, and Daniel Goujon. 2011. "The Solidarity Economy: An Alternative Development Strategy?" *International Social Science Journal* 62 (203–4): 205–15.

Dalla Costa, Mariarosa, and Selma James. 1973. *The Power of Women and the Subversion of the Community.* Bristol, UK: Falling Wall.

Davis, Flora. 1991. *Moving the Mountain: The Women's Movement in America since 1960.* New York: Simon and Schuster.

Davis, Gerald F. 2016. *The Vanishing American Corporation: Navigating the Hazards of a New Economy.* Oakland, CA: Berrett-Koehler.

Davis, Gerald F., and Suntae Kim. 2015. "Financialization of the Economy." *Annual Review of Sociology* 41 (1): 203–21.

Davis, Joshua Clark. 2017. *From Head Shops to Whole Foods: The Rise and Fall of Activist Entrepreneurs.* New York: Columbia University Press.

Davis, Mike. 1997. "Sunshine and the Open Shop: Ford and Darwin in 1920s Los Angeles." *Antipode* 29 (4): 356–82.

DeHart-Davis, Leisha. 2009. "Can Bureaucracy Benefit Organizational Women? An Exploratory Study." *Administration and Society* 41 (3): 340–63.

De Leon, Cedric. 2016. "Black from White: How the Rights of White and Black Workers Became 'Labor' and 'Civil' Rights after the U.S. Civil War." *Labor Studies Journal* 42 (1): 10–26.

Deller, Steven, Ann Hoyt, Brent Hueth, and Reka Sundaram-Stukel. 2009. *Research on the Economic Impact of Cooperatives.* Madison: University of Wisconsin Center for Cooperatives.

Denzin, Norman K. 2008. *Symbolic Interactionism and Cultural Studies: The Politics of Interpretation.* New York: John Wiley and Sons.

DePasquale, Dan, Surbhi Sarang, and Natalie Bump Vena. 2018. "Forging Food Justice through Cooperatives in New York City." *Fordham Urban Law Journal* 45 (4): 909–50.

Dickstein, Carla. 1991. "The Promise and Problem of Worker Cooperatives." *Journal of Planning Literature* 6 (1): 16–33.

Diefenbach, Thomas, and John A. A. Sillince. 2011. "Formal and Informal Hierarchy in Different Types of Organization." *Organization Studies* 32 (11): 1515–37.

DiMaggio, Paul J., and Walter W. Powell. 1983. "The Iron Cage Revisited: Institutional Isomorphism and Collective Rationality in Organizational Fields." *American Sociological Review* 48 (2): 147–60.

Dinerstein, Ana Cecilia. 2007. "Workers' Factory Takeovers and New State Policies in Argentina: Towards an 'Institutionalisation' of Non-governmental Public Action?" *Policy and Politics* 35 (3): 529–50.

——. 2015. "Autonomy in the Key of Hope: Understanding Prefiguration." In *The Politics of Autonomy in Latin America: The Art of Organising Hope*, edited by Ana Cecilia Dinerstein, 58–75. London: Palgrave Macmillan.

Domhoff, G. William. 2013. "Power in America: The Rise and Fall of Labor Unions in the U.S." Who Rules America" (blog), February 2013. https://whorulesamerica.ucsc.edu/power/history_of_labor_unions.html.

Drew, Jesse. 1998. "Call Any Vegetable: The Politics of Food in San Francisco." In *Reclaiming San Francisco: History, Politics, Culture*, edited by James Brook, Chris Carlsson, and Nancy J. Peters, 317–32. San Francisco: City Lights.

Dube, Arindrajit, and Alex Lantsberg. 2004. *Wage and Health Benefit Restructuring in California's Grocery Industry: Public Costs and Policy Implications.* Berkeley: UC Berkeley Center for Labor Research and Education.

Du Bois, W. E. B. 1907. *Economic Co-operation among Negro Americans*. Atlanta: Atlanta University Press.

——. 1935. *Black Reconstruction: An Essay toward a History of the Part Which Black Folk Played in the Attempt to Reconstruct Democracy in America, 1860–1880*. New York: Harcourt Brace and Company.

Du Gay, Paul. 2000. *In Praise of Bureaucracy: Weber, Organization, Ethics*. London: Sage.

——. 2007. *Organizing Identity: Persons and Organizations "After Theory."* London: Sage.

Dunning, Thad. 2012. *Natural Experiments in the Social Sciences: A Design-Based Approach*. Cambridge: Cambridge University Press.

Echols, Alice. 1989. *Daring to be Bad: Radical Feminism in America, 1967–1975*. Minneapolis: University of Minnesota Press.

Eisenstein, Hester. 1995. "The Australian Femocrat Experiment: A Feminist Case for Bureaucracy." In *Feminist Organizations: Harvest of the Women's Movement*, edited by Myra Marx Ferree and Patricia Yancey Martin, 69–83. Philadelphia: Temple University Press.

Ellerman, David. 1990. *The Democratic Worker-Owned Firm: A New Model for the East and for the West*. London: Routledge.

Elliot, James R., and Ryan A. Smith. 2004. "Race, Gender, and Workplace Power." *American Sociological Review* 69 (3): 365–86.

Elvins, Sarah. 2012. "Selling Scrip to America: Ideology, Self-Help and the Experiments of the Great Depression." *International Journal of Community Currency Research* 16: 14–21.

Ely, Robin J., and David A. Thomas. 2001. "Cultural Diversity at Work: The Effects of Diversity Perspectives on Work Group Processes and Outcomes." *Administrative Science Quarterly* 46 (2): 229–73.

Emerson, Robert M., Rachel I. Fretz, and Linda L. Shaw. 1995. *Writing Ethnographic Fieldnotes*. Chicago: University of Chicago Press.

Engberg, George B. 1941. "The Knights of Labor in Minnesota." *Minnesota History* 22 (4): 367–90.

England, Paula, George Farkas, Barbara Stanek Kilbourne, and Thomas Dou. 1988. "Explaining Occupational Sex Segregation and Wages: Findings from a Model with Fixed Effects." *American Sociological Review* 53 (4): 544–58.

Epstein, Barbara. 1991. *Political Protest and Cultural Revolution: Nonviolent Direct Action in the 1970s and 1980s*. Berkeley: University of California Press.

Evan, William M. 1957. "Social Structure, Trade Unionism, and Consumer Cooperation." *ILR Review* 10 (3): 440–47.

Fantasia, Rick, and Kim Voss. 2004. *Hard Work: Remaking the American Labor Movement*. Berkeley: University of California Press.

Faue, Elizabeth. 2017. *Rethinking the American Labor Movement*. New York: Routledge.

Federici, Silvia. 1975. *Wages against Housework*. Bristol, UK: Falling Wall.

——. 2004. *Caliban and the Witch: Women, the Body and Primitive Accumulation*. Brooklyn, NY: Autonomedia.

Ferguson, Ann Arnett. 1991. "Managing without Managers: Crisis and Resolution in a Collective Bakery." In *Ethnography Unbound: Power and Resistance in the Modern Metropolis*, edited by Michael Burawoy, 108–32. Berkeley: University of California Press.

Ferguson, John-Paul, and Rembrand Koning. 2018. "Firm Turnover and the Return of Racial Establishment Segregation." *American Sociological Review* 83 (3): 445–74.

Ferguson, Kathy E. 1984. *The Feminist Case against Bureaucracy*. Philadelphia: Temple University Press.

Fernandes, Leela. 1997. *Producing Workers: The Politics of Gender, Class, and Culture in the Calcutta Jute Mills*. Philadelphia: University of Pennsylvania Press.

Fine, Janice. 2005. "Community Unions and the Revival of the American Labor Movement." *Politics and Society* 33 (1): 153–99.

——. 2006. *Worker Centers: Organizing Communities at the Edge of the Dream*. Ithaca, NY: ILR Press, an imprint of Cornell University Press.

Fink, Leon. 1983. *Workingmen's Democracy: The Knights of Labor and American Politics*. Urbana: University of Illinois Press.

Flacks, Richard, and Nelson Lichtenstein. 2015. *The Port Huron Statement: Sources and Legacies of the New Left's Founding Manifesto*. Philadelphia: University of Pennsylvania Press.

Fligstein, Neil, and Adam Goldstein. 2011. "The Roots of the Great Recession." In *The Consequences of the Great Recession*, edited by David B. Grusky, Bruce Western, and Christopher Wimer, 21–55. New York: Russell Sage Foundation.

Foner, Philip Sheldon. 1977. *History of the Labor Movement in the United States*. Vol. 3, *The Policies and Practices of the American Federation of Labor 1900–1909*. New York: International.

Foucault, Michel. 1973. *Madness and Civilization: A History of Insanity in the Age of Reason*. Translated by Richard Howard. New York: Vintage Books.

——. 1980. *The History of Sexuality*. Vol. 1: *An Introduction*. Translated by Robert Hurley. New York: Vintage Books.

——. 2012. *Discipline and Punish: The Birth of the Prison*. Translated by Alan Sheridan. New York: Vintage Books.

Frank, Dana. 1994. *Purchasing Power: Consumer Organizing, Gender, and the Seattle Labor Movement, 1919–1929*. Cambridge: Cambridge University Press.

Frankenberg, Ruth. 1993. *White Women, Race Matters: The Social Construction of Whiteness*. Minneapolis: University of Minnesota Press.

Freeman, Jo. 1984. "The Tyranny of Structurelessness." In Jo Freeman and Cathy Levine, *Untying the Knot: Feminism, Anarchism, and Organisation*, 5–16. London: Dark Star/Rebel.

Freeman, Richard B., and James L. Medoff. 1984. *What Do Unions Do?* New York: Basic Books.

Freeman, Richard B., and Joel Rogers. 2006. *What Workers Want*. Ithaca, NY: ILR Press, an imprint of Cornell University Press.

Friedland, Roger, and Robert R. Alford. 1991. "Bringing Society Back In: Symbols, Practices and Institutional Contradictions." In *The New Institutionalism in Organizational Analysis*, edited by Walter W. Powell and Paul J. DiMaggio, 232–63. Chicago: University of Chicago Press.

Fullerton, Michael, ed. 1992. *What Happened to the Berkeley Co-Op? A Collection of Opinions*. Davis, CA: Center for Cooperatives.

Fung, Archon, and Erik Olin Wright. 2001. "Deepening Democracy: Innovations in Empowered Participatory Governance." *Politics and Society* 29 (1): 5–41.

Funkhouser, Edward. 1995. "Remittances from International Migration: A Comparison of El Salvador and Nicaragua." *Review of Economics and Statistics* 77 (1): 137–46.

Gamson, Zelda F., and Henry M. Levin. 1984. "Obstacles to the Survival of Democratic Workplaces." In *Worker Cooperatives in America*, edited by Robert Jackall and Henry M. Levin, 219–44. Berkeley: University of California Press.

Gerteis, Joseph. 2002. "The Possession of Civic Virtue: Movement Narratives of Race and Class in the Knights of Labor." *American Journal of Sociology* 108 (3): 580–615.

Gibson-Graham, J. K. 2003. "Enabling Ethical Economies: Cooperativism and Class." *Critical Sociology* 29 (2): 123–61.

———. 2006. *The End of Capitalism (as We Knew It): A Feminist Critique of Political Economy*. Minneapolis: University of Minnesota Press.

Gibson-Graham, J. K., Jenny Cameron, Kelly Dombroski, Stephen Healy, and Ethan Miller. 2017. *Cultivating Community Economies: Tools for Building a Liveable World*. Washington, DC: Next System Project. https://thenextsystem.org/sites /default/files/2017-08/JKGibsonGraham-1-1.pdf.

Gitlin, Todd. 1993. *The Sixties: Years of Hope, Days of Rage*. New York: Bantam Books.

———. 1995. *The Twilight of Common Dreams: Why America Is Wracked by Culture Wars*. New York: Metropolitan.

Goffman, Erving. 1951. "Symbols of Class Status." *British Journal of Sociology* 2 (4): 294–304.

———. 1999. *The Presentation of Self in Everyday Life*. N.p.: Peter Smith.

Goldman, Emma. 2011. *Living My Life*. New York: Cosimo.

Goodwyn, Lawrence. 1976. *Democratic Promise: The Populist Moment in America*. Oxford: Oxford University Press.

———. 1981. *The Populist Movement: A Short History of the Agrarian Revolution in America*. Oxford: Oxford University Press.

Gordon Nembhard, Jessica. 2014. *Collective Courage: A History of African American Cooperative Economic Thought and Practice*. University Park: Pennsylvania State University Press.

———. 2018. "African American Cooperatives and Sabotage: The Case for Reparations." *Journal of African American History* 103 (1–2): 65–90.

Gornick, Janet C., and Marcia Meyers. 2009. *Gender Equality: Transforming Family Divisions of Labor*. London: Verso.

Gouldner, Alvin W. 1954. *Patterns of Industrial Bureaucracy: A Case Study of Modern Factory Administration*. New York: Free Press.

Gourevitch, Alex 2013. "Labor Republicanism and the Transformation of Work." *Political Theory* 41 (4): 591–617.

Gramsci, Antonio. 1971. *Selections from the Prison Notebooks*. Translated by Quintin Hoare and Geoffrey Nowell Smith. New York: International Publishers.

Green, James. 2007. *Death in the Haymarket: A Story of Chicago, the First Labor Movement and the Bombing That Divided Gilded Age America*. Toronto: Anchor Canada.

Greenberg, Edward S. 1986. *Workplace Democracy: The Political Effects of Participation*. Ithaca, NY: Cornell University Press.

Greenberg, Josh, and Graham Knight. 2004. "Framing Sweatshops: Nike, Global Production, and the American News Media." *Communication and Critical/Cultural Studies* 1 (2): 151–75.

Greene, Julie. 1998. *Pure and Simple Politics: The American Federation of Labor and Political Activism, 1881–1917*. Cambridge: Cambridge University Press.

Greenwald, Anthony G., and Linda Hamilton Krieger. 2006. "Implicit Bias: Scientific Foundations." *California Law Review* 94 (4): 945–67.

Gregor, Gall. 2013. "An Agency of Their Own: Sex Worker Union Organising." *Gender in Management: An International Journal* 28 (4): 247–50.

Guinier, Lani, and Martha Minow. 2007. "Dynamism, Not Just Diversity." *Harvard Journal of Law and Gender* 30: 269–78.

Gunn, Christopher Eaton. 1984. *Workers' Self-Management in the United States*. Ithaca, NY: Cornell University Press.

———. 2004. *Third-Sector Development: Making up for the Market*. Ithaca, NY: Cornell University Press.

Guthman, Julie. 2004. *Agrarian Dreams: The Paradox of Organic Farming in California*. Berkeley: University of California Press.

Gutiérrez, Kateri. 2019. "Latinas Are Equipped for the Cooperative Movement." *Harvard Journal of Hispanic Policy* 31: 85–88.

Hacker, Sally. 1989. *Pleasure, Power and Technology.* London: Unwin Hyman.

Haedicke, Michael A. 2016. *Organizing Organic: Conflict and Compromise in an Emerging Market.* Stanford, CA: Stanford University Press.

Hale, James, and Michael Carolan. 2018. "Cooperative or Uncooperative Cooperatives? Digging into the Process of Cooperation in Food and Agriculture Cooperatives." *Journal of Agriculture, Food Systems, and Community Development* 8 (1): 113–32.

Hales, Colin. 2002. "'Bureaucracy-Lite' and Continuities in Managerial Work." *British Journal of Management* 13 (1): 51–66.

Hall, Robert, Martin Feldstein, Ben Bernanke, Jeffrey Frankel, Robert Gordon, and Victor Zarnowitz. 2001. *The Business-Cycle Peak of March 2001.* Cambridge, MA: National Bureau of Economic Research.

Hall, Stuart. 1996. "Introduction: Who Needs 'Identity'?" In *Questions of Cultural Identity*, edited by Stuart Hall and Paul du Gay, 1–17. London: Sage.

Halle, David. 1984. *American's Working Man: Work, Home, and Politics among Blue Collar Property Owners.* Chicago: University of Chicago Press.

Hallett, Tim, and Marc J. Ventresca. 2006. "Inhabited Institutions: Social Interactions and Organizational Forms in Gouldner's Patterns of Industrial Bureaucracy." *Theory and Society* 35 (2): 213–36.

Halnon, Karen Bettez. 2002. "Poor Chic: The Rational Consumption of Poverty." *Current Sociology* 50 (4): 501–16.

Hannan, Michael T., M. Diane Burton, and James N. Baron. 1996. "Inertia and Change in the Early Years: Employment Relations in Young, High Technology Firms." *Industrial and Corporate Change* 5 (2): 503–36.

Harrington, Austin, Barbara L. Marshall, and Hans-Peter Müller. 2006. *Encyclopedia of Social Theory.* London: Routledge.

Hartman, Heidi. 1981. "The Unhappy Marriage of Marxism and Feminism: Towards a More Progressive Union." In *Women and Revolution: A Discussion of the Unhappy Marriage of Marxism and Feminism*, edited by Lydia Sargent, 1–41. Boston: South End.

Harvey, David. 1989. *The Condition of Postmodernity: An Enquiry into the Origins of Cultural Change.* Malden, MA: Blackwell.

Hatch, Mary Jo, and Majken Schultz. 2002. "The Dynamics of Organizational Identity." *Human Relations* 55 (8): 989–1018.

Heckscher, Charles C., and Anne Donnellon. 1994. *The Post-bureaucratic Organization: New Perspectives on Organizational Change.* Thousand Oaks, CA: Sage.

Hernandez, Sarah. 2006. "Striving for Control: Democracy and Oligarchy at a Mexican Cooperative." *Economic and Industrial Democracy* 27 (1): 105–35.

Herring, Cedric. 2009. "Does Diversity Pay? Race, Gender, and the Business Case for Diversity." *American Sociological Review* 74 (2): 208–24.

Herrmann, Robert O. 1970. "Consumerism: Its Goals, Organizations and Future." *Journal of Marketing* 34 (4): 55–60.

Hesse-Biber, Sharlene Nagy. 2010. *Mixed Methods Research: Merging Theory with Practice.* New York: Guilford.

Hirsch, Barry T., and David A. Macpherson, eds. 2004. *Union Membership and Earnings Data Book: Compilations from the Current Population Survey.* Washington, DC: Bureau of National Affairs.

Ho, Karen Zouwen. 2009. *Liquidated: An Ethnography of Wall Street.* Durham, NC: Duke University Press.

Hochschild, Arlie Russell. 1983. *The Managed Heart: Commercialization of Human Feeling.* Berkeley: University of California Press.

——. 1997. *The Time Bind: When Work Becomes Home and Home Becomes Work.* New York: Metropolitan Books.

Hochschild, Arlie Russell, and Anne Machung. 1989. *The Second Shift: Working Parents and the Revolution at Home.* New York: Viking Penguin.

Hodson, Randy. 2001. *Dignity at Work.* Cambridge: Cambridge University Press.

Hoffmann, Elizabeth A. 2001. "Confrontations and Compromise: Dispute Resolution at a Worker Cooperative Coal Mine." *Law and Social Inquiry* 26 (3): 555–96.

——. 2005. "Dispute Resolution in a Worker Cooperative: Formal Procedures and Procedural Justice." *Law and Society Review* 39 (1): 51–82.

Hogeland, Julie A. 2006. "The Economic Culture of US Agricultural Cooperatives." *Culture, Agriculture, Food and Environment* 28 (2): 67–79.

Hondagneu-Sotelo, Pierrette. 2007. *Doméstica: Immigrant Workers Cleaning and Caring in the Shadows of Affluence.* Berkeley: University of California Press.

Hoover, Melissa. 2008. "Another Workplace Is Possible: Co-Ops and Workplace Democracy." In *Solidarity Economy: Building Alternatives for People and the Planet: Papers and Reports from the U.S. Social Forum 2007,* edited by Jenna Allard, Carl Davidson, and Julie Matthaei, 239–56. Chicago: ChangeMaker.

Hoover, Melissa, Logan Harris, and Amy Johnson. 2012. *Preliminary Census of Worker Cooperatives in the United States.* San Francisco: Democracy at Work Institute.

Hossfeld, Karen J. 1990. "'Their Logic against Them': Contradictions in Sex, Race, and Class in Silicon Valley." In *Women Workers and Global Restructuring,* edited by Kathryn Ward, 149–78. Ithaca, NY: ILR Press, an imprint of Cornell University Press.

Howard, John Robert. 1969. "The Flowering of the Hippie Movement." *Annals of the American Academy of Political and Social Science* 382: 43–55.

Hoyer, Mary. 2015. "The Power of Collaboration: Labor Unions and Worker Co-ops in the U.S." Slide presentation at the Cooperatives and the World of Work Research Conference, Antalya, Turkey, November 9–10, 2015.

Huertas-Noble, Carmen. 2016. "Worker-Owned and Unionized Worker-Owned Cooperatives: Two Tools to Address Income Inequality." *Clinical Law Review* 22 (2): 325–58.

Hull, Akasha (Gloria T.), Patricia Bell Scott, and Barbara Smith. 2015. *But Some of Us Are Brave: All the Women Are White, All the Blacks Are Men: Black Women's Studies, 2nd ed.* New York: Feminist Press.

Hunt, Gerald, and Monica Bielski Boris. 2007. "The Lesbian, Gay, Bisexual and Transgender Challenge to American Labor." In *The Sex of Class: Women Transforming American Labor,* edited by Dorothy Sue Cobble, 81–98. Ithaca, NY: ILR Press, an imprint of Cornell University Press.

Iannello, Kathleen P. 1992. *Decisions without Hierarchy: Feminist Interventions in Organization Theory and Practice.* New York: Routledge.

Ifateyo, Ajowa Nzinga 2014. "A Co-op State of Mind: New York City Jumpstarts Worker Cooperatives." *In These Times,* August 18, 2014. http://inthesetimes.com/article/17061/a_co_op_state_of_mind.

Ignatiev, Noel. 1995. *How the Irish Became White.* London: Routledge.

International Cooperative Alliance. N.d. "Cooperative Identity, Values & Principles." Web page, accessed June 28, 2021. https://www.ica.coop/en/cooperatives/cooperative-identity.

Iverson, Roderick D., and Sarosh Kuruvilla. 1995. "Antecedents of Union Loyalty: The Influence of Individual Dispositions and Organizational Context." *Journal of Organizational Behavior* 16 (6): 557–82.

Jackall, Robert. 1984. "Paradoxes of Collective Work: A Study of the Cheeseboard, Berkeley, California." In *Worker Cooperatives in America,* edited by Robert Jackall and Henry M. Levin, 109–35. Berkeley: University of California Press.

Jackall, Robert, and Joyce Crain. 1984. "The Shape of the Small Worker Cooperative Movement." In *Worker Cooperatives in America*, edited by Robert Jackall and Henry M. Levin, 88–104. Berkeley: University of California Press.

Jackall, Robert, and Henry M. Levin. 1984. *Worker Cooperatives in America*. Berkeley: University of California Press.

Jacobs, Jerry A., and Kathleen Gerson. 2004. *The Time Divide: Work, Family, and Gender Inequality*. Cambridge, MA: Harvard University Press, 2004.

John, Sarah, Haley Smith, and Elizabeth Zack. 2018. "The Alternative Vote: Do Changes in Single-Member Voting Systems Affect Descriptive Representation of Women and Minorities?" *Electoral Studies* 54: 90–102.

Johnston, Josée, and Shyon Baumann. 2014. *Foodies: Democracy and Distinction in the Gourmet Foodscape*. New York: Routledge.

Johnston, Josée, Andrew Biro, and Norah MacKendrick. 2009. "Lost in the Supermarket: The Corporate-Organic Foodscape and the Struggle for Food Democracy." *Antipode* 41 (3): 509–32.

Jones, Derek C. 1979. "U.S. Producer Cooperatives: The Record to Date." *Industrial Relations* 18 (3): 342–57.

——. 1984. "American Producer Cooperatives and Employee-Owned Firms: A Historical Perspective." In *Worker Cooperatives in America*, edited by Robert Jackall and Henry M. Levin, 37–56. Berkeley: University of California Press.

Jones, Derek C., and Panu Kalmi. 2012. "Economies of Scale Versus Participation: A Co-Operative Dilemma?" *Journal of Entrepreneurial and Organizational Diversity* 1 (1): 37–64.

Jones, Derek C., and Donald J. Schneider. 1984. "Self-Help Production Cooperatives: Government Administered Cooperatives During the Depression." In *Worker Cooperatives in America*, edited by Robert Jackall and Henry M. Levin, 57–84. Berkeley: University of California Press.

Kalev, Alexandra. 2009. "Cracking the Glass Cages? Restructuring and Ascriptive Inequality at Work." *American Journal of Sociology* 114 (6): 1591–1643.

Kalev, Alexandra, Frank Dobbin, and Erin Kelly. 2006. "Best Practices or Best Guesses? Assessing the Efficacy of Corporate Affirmative Action and Diversity Programs." *American Sociological Review* 71: 589–617.

Kalev, Alexandra, and Vincent J. Roscigno. 2016. "Interview: Bureaucracy, Bias, and Diversity—Structural Constraints and Opportunities in Organizations." In *Rethinking Diversity*, edited by Cordula Braedel-Kühner and Andreas Müller, 111–20. Wiesbaden, Germany: Springer.

Kalleberg, Arne L. 2011. *Good Jobs, Bad Jobs: The Rise of Polarized and Precarious Employment Systems in the United States, 1970s to 2000s*. New York: Russell Sage Foundation.

Kalleberg, Arne L., and Steven P. Vallas. 2017. "Probing Precarious Work: Theory, Research, and Politics." *Research in the Sociology of Work* 31: 1–30.

Kallinikos, Jannis. 2004. "The Social Foundations of the Bureaucratic Order." *Organization* 11 (1): 13–36.

Kalmi, Panu. 2007. "The Disappearance of Cooperatives from Economics Textbooks." *Cambridge Journal of Economics* 31 (4): 625–47.

Kanter, Rosabeth Moss. 1977. *Men and Women of the Corporation*. New York: Basic Books.

Kantrowitz, Stephen. 2000. "Ben Tillman and Hendrix McLane, Agrarian Rebels: White Manhood, "The Farmers," and the Limits of Southern Populism." *Journal of Southern History* 66 (3): 497–524.

Kao, Grace, Kara Joyner, and Kelly Stamper Balistreri. 2019. *The Company We Keep: Interracial Friendships and Romantic Relationships from Adolescence to Adulthood.* New York: Russell Sage Foundation.

Karatani, Kojin. 2014. *The Structure of World History: From Modes of Production to Modes of Exchange.* Translated by Michael K. Bourdaghs. Durham, NC: Duke University Press.

Kasmir, Sharryn. 1996. *The Myth of Mondragón: Cooperatives, Politics, and Working-Class Life in a Basque Town.* Albany: State University of New York Press.

Kautsky, Karl, and W. H. Kerridge. 1920. *Terrorism and Communism: A Contribution to the Natural History of Revolution.* London: National Labour Press.

Kellogg, Katherine C. 2009. "Operating Room: Relational Spaces and Microinstitutional Change in Surgery." *American Journal of Sociology* 115 (3): 657–711.

——. 2011. *Challenging Operations: Medical Reform and Resistance in Surgery.* Chicago: University of Chicago Press.

Kelly, Erin L., Samantha K. Ammons, Kelly Chermack, and Phyllis Moen. 2010. "Gendered Challenge, Gendered Response: Confronting the Ideal Worker Norm in a White-Collar Organization." *Gender & Society* 24 (3): 281–303.

Kelly, Erin L., and Frank Dobbin. 1998. "Employer Response to Antidiscrimination Law, 1961 to 1996." *American Behavioral Scientist* 41 (7): 960–84.

Kemmis, Stephen, Robin McTaggart, and Rhonda Nixon. 2014. *The Action Research Planner: Doing Critical Participatory Action Research.* Singapore: Springer.

Kennelly, Ivy. 1999. "'That Single Mother Element': How White Employers Typify Black Women." *Gender & Society* 13 (2): 168–92.

Kennelly, James J., and Mehmet Odekon. 2016. "Worker Cooperatives in the United States, Redux." *WorkingUSA* 19 (2): 163–85.

Kerber, Linda K. 1988. "Separate Spheres, Female Worlds, Woman's Place: The Rhetoric of Women's History." *Journal of American History* 75 (1): 9–39.

Kerr, Clark. 1939. "Productive Enterprises of the Unemployed: 1931–1938." PhD diss., University of California.

Kerr, Clark, and Paul S. Taylor. 1935. *The Self-Help Cooperatives in California.* Berkeley: University of California Press.

Kessler-Harris, Alice. 2003. *Out to Work: A History of Wage-Earning Women in the United States.* New York: Oxford University Press.

Khan, Shamus, and Colin Jerolmack. 2013. "Saying Meritocracy and Doing Privilege." *Sociological Quarterly* 54 (1): 9–19.

King, Deborah. 1988. "Multiple Jeopardy, Multiple Consciousness: The Context of a Black Feminist Ideology." *Signs: Journal of Women in Culture and Society* 14 (1): 46–73.

Kleinman, Sherryl. 1996. *Opposing Ambitions: Gender and Identity in an Alternative Organization.* Chicago: University of Chicago Press.

Kmec, Julie A. 2003. "Minority Job Concentration and Wages." *Social Problems* 50 (1): 38–59.

——. 2005. "Setting Occupational Sex Segregation in Motion: Demand-Side Explanations of Sex Traditional Employment." *Work and Occupations* 32 (3): 322–54.

Kochan, Thomas A., Duanyi Yang, William T. Kimball, and Erin L. Kelly. 2019. "Worker Voice in America: Is There a Gap between What Workers Expect and What They Experience?" *ILR Review* 72 (1): 3–38.

Kondo, Dorinne K. 1990. *Crafting Selves: Power, Gender, and Discourses of Identity in a Japanese Workplace.* Chicago: University of Chicago Press.

Kranz, Harry. 1976. *The Participatory Bureaucracy: Women and Minorities in a More Representative Public Service.* Lexington, MA: Lexington Books.

Kruse, Douglas L., Richard B. Freeman, and Joseph R. Blasi. 2010. "Do Workers Gain by Sharing? Employee Outcomes under Employee Ownership, Profit Sharing, and Broad-Based Stock Options." In *Shared Capitalism at Work: Employee Ownership, Profit and Gain Sharing, and Broad-Based Stock Options*, edited by Douglas Kruse, Richard Freeman, and Joseph R. Blasi, 257–89. Chicago: University of Chicago Press.

——, eds. 2010. *Shared Capitalism at Work: Employee Ownership, Profit and Gain Sharing, and Broad-Based Stock Options*. Chicago: University of Chicago Press.

Kruse, Douglas L., Richard B. Freeman, Joseph R. Blasi, Robert Buchele, Adria Scharf, Loren Rodgers, and Chris Mackin. 2004. "Motivating Employee-Owners in ESOP Firms: Human Resource Policies and Company Performance." In *Employee Participation, Firm Performance and Survival*, edited by Virginie Perotin and Andrew Robinson, 101–27. Bingley, UK: Emerald.

Kunda, Gideon. 2006. *Engineering Culture: Control and Commitment in a High-Tech Culture*. Rev. ed. Philadelphia: Temple University Press.

Kurland, Nancy. 2018. "ESOP Plus Benefit Corporation: Ownership Culture with Benefit Accountability." *California Management Review* 60 (4): 51–73.

Lamont, Michèle. 1992. *Money, Morals, and Manners: The Culture of the French and American Upper-Middle Class*. Chicago: University of Chicago Press.

——. 2000. *The Dignity of Working Men: Morality and the Boundaries of Race, Class, and Immigration*. New York: Russell Sage Foundation / Cambridge, MA: Harvard University Press.

Lareau, Annette. 2003. *Unequal Childhoods: Class, Race, and Family Life*. Berkeley: University of California Press.

Larrabure, Manuel, Marcelo Vieta, and Daniel Schugurensky. 2011. "The 'New Cooperativism' in Latin America: Worker-Recuperated Enterprises and Socialist Production Units." *Studies in the Education of Adults* 43 (2): 181–96.

Leab, Daniel J. 1966. "Barter and Self-Help Groups 1932–33." *Midcontinent American Studies Journal* 7 (1): 15–24.

Lee, Ching Kwan. 1998. *Gender and the South China Miracle: Two Worlds of Factory Women*. Berkeley: University of California Press.

Leidner, Robin. 1999. "Emotional Labor in Service Work." *Annals of the American Academy of Political and Social Science* 561 (1): 81–95.

Leikin, Steven Bernard. 1999. "The Citizen Producer: The Rise and Fall of Working-Class Cooperatives in the United States." In *Consumers against Capitalism: Consumer Cooperation in Europe and North America, 1840–1990*, edited by Ellen Furlough and Carl Strikwerda, 93–112. New York: Rowman and Littlefield.

——. 2001. "The Cooperative Coopers of Minneapolis." *Minnesota History* 57 (8): 386–405.

——. 2004. *The Practical Utopians: American Workers and the Cooperative Movement in the Gilded Age*. Detroit: Wayne State University Press.

Lenin, Vladimir Ilyich. 1987. *Essential Works of Lenin: "What Is to Be Done?" and Other Writings*. New York: Dover.

Levine, Susan. 1983. "Labor's True Woman: Domesticity and Equal Rights in the Knights of Labor." *Journal of American History* 70 (2): 323–39.

Levinson, Marc. 2011. *The Great A&P and the Struggle for Small Business in America*. New York: Hill and Wang.

Lewis, Penny W. 2013. *Hardhats, Hippies, and Hawks: The Vietnam Antiwar Movement as Myth and Memory*. Ithaca, NY: ILR Press, an imprint of Cornell University Press.

Leymon, Ann Shirley. 2011. "Unions and Social Inclusiveness: A Comparison of Changes in Union Member Attitudes." *Labor Studies Journal* 36 (3): 388–407.

Leyva, Luis A. 2017. "Unpacking the Male Superiority Myth and Masculinization of Mathematics at the Intersections: A Review of Research on Gender in Mathematics Education." *Journal for Research in Mathematics Education* 48 (4): 397–433.

Lichtenstein, Nelson. 2009. *The Retail Revolution: How Wal-Mart Created a Brave New World of Business*. New York: Henry Holt.

Lima, Jacob Carlos. 2007. "Workers' Cooperatives in Brazil: Autonomy vs Precariousness." *Economic and Industrial Democracy* 28 (4): 589–621.

Lincoln, Yvonna S., Susan A. Lynham, and Egon G. Guba. 2011. "Paradigmatic Controversies, Contradictions, and Emerging Confluences, Revisited." In *The Sage Handbook of Qualitative Research*, edited by Norman K. Denzin, 97–128. Thousand Oaks, CA: Sage.

Lindenfeld, Frank, and Joyce Rothschild-Whitt, eds. 1982. *Workplace Democracy and Social Change*. Boston: Porter Sargent.

Lindquist, Evert A., John Restakis, and the Institute of Public Administration of Canada. 2001. *The Co-op Alternative: Civil Society and the Future of Public Services*. Toronto: Institute of Public Administration of Canada.

Lipset, Seymour Martin, Martin A. Trow, and James Samuel Coleman. 1956. *Union Democracy: The Internal Politics of the International Typographical Union*. New York: Free Press.

Lipsitz, George. 1994. *Rainbow at Midnight: Labor and Culture in the 1940s*. Urbana: University of Illinois Press.

——. 1998. *The Possessive Investment in Whiteness: How White People Profit from Identity Politics*. Philadelphia: Temple University Press.

Lo, Joann, and Biko Koenig. 2017. "Food Workers and Consumers Organizing Together for Food Justice." In *The New Food Activism*, edited by Alison Hope Alkon and Julie Guthman, 133–56. Berkeley: University of California Press.

Logue, John, and Jacquelyn S. Yates. 1999. "Worker Ownership American Style: Pluralism, Participation and Performance." *Economic and Industrial Democracy* 20 (2): 225–52.

Lorde, Audre. 1984. *Sister Outsider: Essays and Speeches*. Trumansburg, NY: Crossing Press.

Lucas, Michael D. 1997. "Salting and Other Union Tactics: A Unionist's Perspective." *Journal of Labor Research* 18 (1): 55–64.

Lurie, Jonathan. 1974. "Commodities Exchanges, Agrarian 'Political Power,' and the Antioption Battle, 1890–1894." *Agricultural History* 48 (1): 115–25.

Lutz, Amy. 2008. "Who Joins the Military? A Look at Race, Class, and Immigration Status." *Journal of Political and Military Sociology* 36 (2): 167–88.

Luxemburg, Rosa. 2006. *Reform or Revolution and Other Writings*. Translated by Integer. Mineola, NY: Dover.

Mahoney, James. 2000. "Path Dependence in Historical Sociology." *Theory and Society* 29 (4): 507–48.

——. 2004. "Comparative-Historical Methodology." *Annual Review of Sociology* 30: 81–101.

Mansbridge, Jane J. 1980. *Beyond Adversary Democracy*. New York: Basic Books.

Marti, Donald B. 1984. "Sisters of the Grange: Rural Feminism in the Late Nineteenth Century." *Agricultural History* 58 (3): 247–61.

Martin, Laura Renata. 2013. "'California's Unemployed Feed Themselves': Conservative Intervention in the Los Angeles Cooperative Movement, 1931–1934." *Pacific Historical Review* 82 (1): 33–62.

Martin, Patricia Yancey. 2003. "'Said and Done' versus 'Saying and Doing': Gendering Practices, Practicing Gender at Work." *Gender & Society* 17 (3): 342–66.

Marx, Karl. 1964. *Economic and Philosophic Manuscripts of 1844.* Translated by Martin Milligant. New York: International Publishers.

——. 1976. *Capital: A Critique of Political Economy.* Translated by David Fernbach. New York: Random House.

——. 1985. "Inaugural Address of the International Working Men's Association" (1864). In Karl Marx and Frederick Engels, *Marx and Engels Collected Works*, vol. 20, *Marx and Engels 1864–68*, 5–16. London: Lawrence and Wishart.

Marx, Karl, and Freidrich Engels. 2006. *The Communist Manifesto.* Translated by Samuel Moore. New York: Penguin.

Massey, Douglas S., and Nancy A. Denton. 1993. *American Apartheid: Segregation and the Making of the Underclass.* Cambridge, MA: Harvard University Press.

McCall, Leslie. 2005. "The Complexity of Intersectionality." *Signs: Journal of Women in Culture and Society* 30 (3): 1771–1800.

McMath, Robert C., Peter H. Argersinger, Connie L. Lester, Michael F. Magliari, Walter Nugent, and David B. Danbom. 2008. "'Agricultural History' Roundtable on Populism: Robert C. McMath Jr., Peter H. Argersinger, Connie L. Lester, Michael F. Magliari, and Walter Nugent." *Agricultural History* 82 (1): 1–35.

McMillian, John Campbell, and Paul Buhle. 2003. *The New Left Revisited.* Philadelphia: Temple University Press.

McPherson, Miller, Lynn Smith-Lovin, and James M. Cook. 2001. "Birds of a Feather: Homophily in Social Networks." *Annual Review of Sociology* 27: 415–44.

Mead, George Herbert. 1962. *Mind, Self, and Society: From the Standpoint of a Social Behaviorist.* Edited by Charles W. Morris. Chicago: University of Chicago Press.

Mellor, Mary, Janet Hannah, and John Stirling. 1988. *Worker Cooperatives in Theory and Practice.* Milton Keynes, UK: Open University Press.

Meyers, Joan S. M., and Steven Peter Vallas. 2016. "Diversity Regimes in Worker Cooperatives: Workplace Inequality under Conditions of Worker Control." *Sociological Quarterly* 57 (1): 98–128.

Michels, Robert. 1959. *Political Parties.* New York: Dover.

Milkman, Ruth. 1987. *Gender at Work: The Dynamics of Job Segregation by Sex during World War II.* Urbana: University of Illinois Press.

——. 1997. *Farewell to the Factory: Auto Workers in the Late Twentieth Century.* Berkeley: University of California Press.

——. 2006. *L.A. Story: Immigrant Workers and the Future of the U.S. Labor Movement.* New York: Russell Sage Foundation.

——. 2007. "Two Worlds of Unionism: Women and the New Labor Movement." In *The Sex of Class: Women Transforming American Labor*, edited by Dorothy Sue Cobble, 63–80. Ithaca, NY: ILR Press, an imprint of Cornell University Press.

Milkman, Ruth, and Ed Ott. 2014. *New Labor in New York: Precarious Workers and the Future of the Labor Movement.* Ithaca, NY: ILR Press, an imprint of Cornell University Press.

Milkman, Ruth, and Kim Voss. 2004. *Rebuilding Labor: Organizing and Organizers in the New Union Movement.* Ithaca, NY: ILR Press, an imprint of Cornell University Press.

Miller, Genna R. 2011. "Gender and Participation in Decision-Making in Labor-Managed Firms: The Context of the USA." *Economic and Industrial Democracy* 32 (1): 87–113.

Miller, Timothy. 1991. *The Hippies and American Values.* Knoxville: University of Tennessee Press.

——. 1999. *The 60s Communes: Hippies and Beyond.* Syracuse, NY: Syracuse University Press.

Mills, C. Wright. 1959. *The Sociological Imagination.* New York: Oxford University Press.

Mitchell, H. L. 1973. "The Founding and Early History of the Southern Tenant Farmers Union." *Arkansas Historical Quarterly* 32 (4): 342–69.

Mizruchi, Mark S. 2010. "The American Corporate Elite and the Historical Roots of the Financial Crisis of 2008." In *Markets on Trial: The Economic Sociology of the U.S. Financial Crisis,* part B, edited by Michael Lounsbury and Paul M. Hirsch, 103–39. Bingley, UK: Emerald.

Moffitt, Susan L. 2014. *Making Policy Public: Participatory Bureaucracy in American Democracy.* New York: Cambridge University Press.

Monaco, Marina, and Luca Pastorelli. 2013. "Trade Unions and Worker Cooperatives in Europe: A Win-Win Relationship; Maximizing Social and Economic Potential in Worker Cooperatives." *International Journal of Labour Research* 5 (2): 227–50.

Morrill, Calvin, and Gary Alan Fine. 1997. "Ethnographic Contributions to Organizational Sociology." *Sociological Methods and Research* 25 (4): 424–51.

Moss, Philip, and Chris Tilly. 1996. "'Soft' Skills and Race: An Investigation of Black Men's Employment Problems." *Work and Occupations* 23 (1): 252–76.

Mullen, Ann L. 2010. *Degrees of Inequality: Culture, Class, and Gender in American Higher Education.* Baltimore: Johns Hopkins University Press.

Murray, Robert K. 1955. *Red Scare: A Study in National Hysteria, 1919–1920.* Minneapolis: University of Minnesota Press.

Myers, Justin Sean, and Joshua Sbicca. 2015. "Bridging Good Food and Good Jobs: From Secession to Confrontation within Alternative Food Movement Politics." *Geoforum* 61: 17–26.

Naison, Mark. 1968. "The Southern Tenants' Farmers' Union and the CIO." *Radical America* 2 (5): 36–54.

National Center for Employee Ownership. 2020. "How an Employee Stock Ownership Plan (ESOP) Works." Web page, August 24, 2020. https://www.nceo.org/articles/esop-employee-stock-ownership-plan.

National Cooperative Bank. N.d. "Community Impact." Web page, accessed July 20, 2021. https://www.ncb.coop/about-us/community-impact.

NCPHSBBR (National Commission for the Protection of Human Subjects of Biomedical and Behavioral Research). 1978. *The Belmont Report: Ethical Principles for the Protection of Human Subjects of Research.* Washington, DC: US Government Printing Office.

Nelson, Arthur C., and Kenneth J. Dueker. 1990. "The Exurbanization of America and Its Planning Policy Implications." *Journal of Planning Education and Research* 9 (2): 91–100.

Nestle, Marion, and Sally Guttmacher. 1992. "Hunger in the United States: Rationale, Methods, and Policy Implications of State Hunger Surveys." *Journal of Nutrition Education* 24 (1): 18S–22S.

Neyland, Daniel. 2007. *Organizational Ethnography.* London: Sage.

Nicolaides, Becky M. 2002. *My Blue Heaven: Life and Politics in the Working-Class Suburbs of Los Angeles, 1920–1965.* Chicago: University of Chicago Press.

Nishii, Lisa H. 2013. "The Benefits of Climate for Inclusion for Gender-Diverse Groups." *Academy of Management Journal* 56 (6): 1754–74.

Nussbaum, Karen. 2007. "Working Women's Insurgent Consciousness." In *The Sex of Class: Women Transforming American Labor,* edited by Dorothy Sue Cobble, 159–76. Ithaca, NY: ILR Press, an imprint of Cornell University Press.

Oerton, Sarah. 1994. "Exploring Women Workers' Motives for Employment in Cooperative and Collective Organizations." *Journal of Gender Studies* 3 (3): 289–97.

Offe, Claus. 1985. "New Social Movements: Challenging the Boundaries of Institutional Politics." *Social Research* 52 (4): 817–68.

Okun, Arthur M. 1975. *Equality and Efficiency: The Big Tradeoff.* Washington: Brookings Institution Press.

Oliver, Melvin L., and Thomas M. Shapiro. 1997. *Black Wealth/White Wealth: A New Perspective on Racial Inequality.* New York: Routledge.

Ollman, Bertell. 1972. "Toward Class Consciousness Next Time: Marx and the Working Class." *Politics and Society* 3 (1): 1–24.

Olney, Peter. 2011. "Rebel Rank and File: Learning from the 1970s." Labor Notes (blog), April 26, 2011. http://labornotes.org/blogs/2011/04/rebel-rank-and-file-learning-1970s?language=en.

Olsen, Erik K. 2013. "The Relative Survival of Worker Cooperatives and Barriers to Their Creation." In *Sharing Ownership, Profits, and Decision-Making in the 21st Century,* edited by Douglas Kruse, 83–107. Bingley, UK: Emerald.

Omi, Michael, and Howard Winant. 1994. *Racial Formation in the United States: From the 1960s to the 1990s.* 2nd ed. New York: Routledge.

Osterud, Nancy Grey. 1993. "Gender and the Transition to Capitalism in Rural America." *Agricultural History* 67 (2): 14–29.

Ostrander, Susan A. 1999. "Gender and Race in a Pro-feminist, Progressive, Mixed-Gender, Mixed-Race Organization." *Gender & Society* 13 (5): 628–42.

Otis, Eileen, and Tongyu Wu. 2018. "The Deficient Worker: Skills, Identity, and Inequality in Service Employment." *Sociological Perspectives* 61 (5): 787–807.

Padavic, Irene. 1992. "White-Collar Work Values and Women's Interest in Blue-Collar Jobs." *Gender & Society* 6 (2): 215–30.

Palmer, Timothy C. 2014. *Democratic Workplace Ownership after the Great Recession: An Economic Overview of US Worker Cooperatives in 2013.* San Francisco: Democracy at Work Institute.

——. 2017. *Worker Cooperatives in the U.S.: 2015 State of the Sector.* Oakland, CA: Democracy at Work Institute.

Paranque, Bernard, and Hugh Willmott. 2014. "Cooperatives—Saviours or Gravediggers of Capitalism? Critical Performativity and the John Lewis Partnership." *Organization* 21 (5): 604–25.

Parker, Florence Evelyn. 1956. *The First 125 Years: A History of Distributive and Service Cooperation in the United States, 1829–1954.* Chicago: Cooperative League of the USA.

Parker, Martin. 2000. *Organizational Culture and Identity: Unity and Division at Work.* London: Sage.

——. 2008. "Managerialism and Its Discontents." In *The Sage Handbook of Organizational Behavior,* vol. 2, edited by Stewart R. Clegg and Cary L. Cooper, 85–98. London: Sage.

Parsons, Stanley B., Karen Toombs Parsons, Walter Killilae, and Beverly Borgers. 1983. "The Role of Cooperatives in the Development of the Movement Culture of Populism." *Journal of American History* 69 (4): 866–85.

Pasha, Abdurrahman. 2014. "The Self-Help Cooperative Movement in Los Angeles, 1931–1940." PhD diss., University of Oregon.

Pateman, Carole. 1970. *Participation and Democratic Theory.* Cambridge: Cambridge University Press.

Pencavel, John. 2001. *Worker Participation: Lessons from the Worker Co-ops of the Pacific Northwest.* New York: Russell Sage Foundation.

——. 2012. *Worker Cooperatives and Democratic Governance*. Bonn, Germany: Forschungsinstitut zur Zukunft der Arbeit.

Pichault, François, and Tui McKeown. 2019. "Autonomy at Work in the Gig Economy: Analysing Work Status, Work Content and Working Conditions of Independent Professionals." *New Technology, Work and Employment* 34 (1): 59–72.

Pierce, Jennifer L. 1995. *Gender Trials: Emotional Lives in Contemporary Law Firms*. Berkeley: University of California Press.

Piff, Paul K., Michael W. Kraus, Stéphane Côté, Bonnie Hayden Cheng, and Dacher Keltner. 2010. "Having Less, Giving More: The Influence of Social Class on Prosocial Behavior." *Journal of Personality and Social Psychology* 99 (5): 771–84.

Piketty, Thomas. 2014. *Capital in the Twenty-First Century*. Translated by Arthur Goldhammer. Cambridge, MA: Harvard University Press.

Pinto, Sanjay. 2018. "Worker Co-operatives and Other Alternative Forms of Business Organization." In *Handbook of the International Political Economy of the Corporation*, edited by Andreas Nölke and Christian May, 76–92. Cheltenham, UK: Edward Elgar.

——. 2021. "Economic Democracy, Embodied: A Union Co-op Strategy for the Long-Term Care Sector." In *Organizational Imaginaries: Tempering Capitalism and Tending to Communities through Cooperatives and Collectivist Democracy*, edited by Katherine K. Chen and Victor T. Chen, 163–84. Bingley, UK: Emerald.

Piore, Michael J. 1986. "The Decline of Mass Production and the Challenge to Union Survival." *Industrial Relations Journal* 17 (3): 207–13.

Piore, Michael J., and Charles F. Sabel. 1984. *The Second Industrial Divide: Possibilities for Prosperity*. New York: Basic Books.

Pollan, Michael. 2006. *The Omnivore's Dilemma: A Natural History of Four Meals*. New York: Penguin.

Polletta, Francesca. 2002. *Freedom Is an Endless Meeting: Democracy in American Social Movements*. Chicago: University of Chicago Press.

Polletta, Francesca, and Katt Hoban. 2016. "Why Consensus? Prefiguration in Three Activist Eras." *Journal of Social and Political Psychology* 4 (1): 286–301.

Radicalesbians. 1970. *The Woman Identified Woman*. Boston: New England Free Press.

Ray, Raka. 1999. *Fields of Protest: Women's Movements in India*. Minneapolis: University of Minnesota Press.

Ray, Victor. 2019. "A Theory of Racialized Organizations." *American Sociological Review* 84 (1): 26–53.

Ray, Victor, and Danielle Purifoy. 2019. "The Colorblind Organization." In *Race, Organizations, and the Organizing Process*, edited by Melissa E. Wooten, 131–50. Bingley, UK: Emerald.

Redbird, Beth, and David B. Grusky. 2016. "Distributional Effects of the Great Recession: Where Has All the Sociology Gone?" *Annual Review of Sociology* 42 (1): 185–215.

Reinelt, Claire. 1995. "Moving onto the Terrain of the State: The Battered Women's Movement and the Politics of Engagement." In *Feminist Organizations: Harvest of the New Women's Movement*, edited by Myra Marx Ferree and Patricia Yancey Martin, 84–104. Philadelphia: Temple University Press.

Reskin, Barbara F. 2000. "The Proximate Causes of Employment Discrimination." *Contemporary Sociology* 29 (2): 319–28.

Reskin, Barbara F., and Patricia Roos. 1990. *Job Queues, Gender Queues: Explaining Women's Inroads into Male Occupations*. Philadelphia: Temple University Press.

Rhode, Paul W. 2001. *The Evolution of California Manufacturing*. San Francisco: Public Policy Institute of California.

Ridgeway, Cecilia L. 2011. *Framed by Gender: How Gender Inequality Persists in the Modern World*. New York: Oxford University Press.

Rivera, Lauren A. 2012. "Hiring as Cultural Matching: The Case of Elite Professional Service Firms." *American Sociological Review* 77 (6): 999–1022.

Roediger, David R. 1999. *The Wages of Whiteness*. Rev. ed. London: Verso.

Roediger, David R., and Philip S. Foner. 1989. *Our Own Time: A History of American Labor and the Working Day*. New York: Verso.

Roof, Wade Clark. 1999. *Spiritual Marketplace: Baby Boomers and the Remaking of American Religion*. Princeton, NJ: Princeton University Press.

Rose, Jessica, Marjorie Kelly, Sarah Stranahan, Michelle Camou, and Karen Kahn. 2021. *Opportunity Knocking: Impact Capital as the Transformative Agent to Take Employee Ownership to Scale*. Washington, DC: Democracy Collaborative.

Rose, Nancy E. 1988. "Production-for-Use or Production-for-Profit? The Contradictions of Consumer Goods Production in 1930s Work Relief." *Review of Radical Political Economics* 20 (1): 46–61.

——. 1990. "Discrimination against Women in New Deal Work Programs." *Affilia* 5 (2): 25–45.

Rose, Sonya. 1992. *Limited Livelihoods: Gender and Class in Nineteenth-Century England*. Berkeley: University of California Press.

Rosen, Corey, John Case, and Martin Staubus. 2005. *Equity: Why Employee Ownership Is Good for Business*. Boston: Harvard Business Press.

Rosenbloom, David H. 1975. "The Rise of 'Participatory Bureaucracy' in the United States Federal Service." *Philippine Journal of Public Administration* 19: 293–305.

Rosenzweig, Roy. 1983. *Eight Hours for What We Will: Workers and Leisure in an Industrial City, 1870–1920*. Cambridge: Cambridge University Press.

Roszak, Theodore. 1995. *The Making of a Counter Culture: Reflections on the Technocratic Society and Its Youthful Opposition*. Berkeley: University of California Press.

Roth, Matthew. 2011. "Coming Together: The Communal Option." In *Ten Years That Shook the City: San Francisco 1968–1978*, edited by Chris Carlsson, 192–208. San Francisco: City Lights Books.

Roth, Wendy D., and Gerhard Sonnert. 2011. "The Costs and Benefits of 'Red Tape': Antibureaucratic Structure and Gender Inequity in a Science Research Organization." *Social Studies of Science* 41 (3): 385–409.

Rothschild, Joyce. 2009. "Workers' Cooperatives and Social Enterprise: A Forgotten Route to Social Equity and Democracy." *American Behavioral Scientist* 52 (7): 1023–41.

Rothschild, Joyce, and Max Stephenson Jr. 2009. "The Meaning of Democracy in Nonprofit and Community Organizations: Charting the Currents of Change." *American Behavioral Scientist* 52 (6): 800–806.

Rothschild, Joyce, and J. Allen Whitt. 1986. *The Cooperative Workplace: Potentials and Dilemmas of Organizational Democracy and Participation*. Cambridge: Cambridge University Press.

Rothschild-Whitt, Joyce. 1979. "The Collectivist Organization: An Alternative to Rational-Bureaucratic Models." *American Sociological Review* 44 (4): 509–27.

Rothschild-Whitt, Joyce, and J. Allen Whitt. 1986. "Worker-Owners as an Emergent Class: Effects of Cooperative Work on Job Satisfaction, Alienation and Stress." *Economic and Industrial Democracy* 7 (3): 297–317.

Rowan, Brian. 1982. "Organizational Structure and the Institutional Environment: The Case of Public Schools." *Administrative Science Quarterly* 27 (2): 259–79.

Russell, Raymond. 1984. "The Role of Culture and Ethnicity in the Degeneration of Democratic Firms." *Economic and Industrial Democracy* 5: 73–96.

Sáenz, Rogelio, and Karen Manges Douglas. 2015. "A Call for the Racialization of Immigration Studies: On the Transition of Ethnic Immigrants to Racialized Immigrants." *Sociology of Race and Ethnicity* 1 (1): 166–80.

Saldaña, Johnny. 2011. "Writing and Presenting Qualitative Research." In *Fundamentals of Qualitative Research*, 139–65. New York: Oxford University Press.

Sallaz, Jeffrey J. 2002. "The House Rules: Autonomy and Interests among Service Workers in the Contemporary Casino Industry." *Work and Occupations* 29 (4): 394–427.

Saloutos, Theodore. 1953. "The Grange in the South, 1870–1877." *Journal of Southern History* 19 (4): 473–87.

Salzinger, Leslie. 2003. *Genders in Production: Making Workers in Mexico's Global Factories*. Berkeley: University of California Press.

Santa Barbara Legal Collective. 1982. "Is Anybody There? Notes on Collective Practice." In *Workplace Democracy and Social Change*, edited by Frank Lindenfeld and Joyce Rothschild-Whitt, 247–56. Boston: Porter Sargent.

Saxenian, AnnaLee. 1983. "The Urban Contradictions of Silicon Valley: Regional Growth and the Restructuring of the Semiconductor Industry." *International Journal of Urban and Regional Research* 7 (2): 237–62.

Saxton, Alexander. 1995. *The Indispensable Enemy: Labor and the Anti-Chinese Movement in California*. Berkeley: University of California Press.

Sazama, Gerald W. 2000. "Lessons from the History of Affordable Housing Cooperatives in the United States: A Case Study in American Affordable Housing Policy." *American Journal of Economics and Sociology* 59 (4): 573–608.

Schilt, Kristen. 2010. *Just One of the Guys? Transgender Men and the Persistence of Gender Inequality*. Chicago: University of Chicago Press.

Schlachter, Laura Hanson. 2017. "Stronger Together? The USW-Mondragon Union Co-op Model." *Labor Studies Journal* 42 (2): 124–47.

Schneiberg, Marc. 2011. "Toward an Organizationally Diverse American Capitalism? Cooperative, Mutual, and Local, State-Owned Enterprise." *Seattle University Law Review* 34 (4): 1409–34.

Schneiberg, Marc, Marissa King, and Thomas Smith. 2008. "Social Movements and Organizational Form: Cooperative Alternatives to Corporations in the American Insurance, Dairy, and Grain Industries." *American Sociological Review* 73 (4): 635–67.

Schneider, Daniel, Kristen Harknett, Josh Choper, Sigrid Luhr, and Adam Storer. 2019. *It's About Time: How Work Schedule Instability Matters for Workers, Families, and Racial Inequality*. Berkeley: Institute for Research on Labor and Employment, University of California, Berkeley.

Schoening, Joel. 2006. "Cooperative Entrepreneurialism: Reconciling Democratic Values with Business Demands at a Worker-Owned Firm." In *Worker Participation: Current Research and Future Trends*, edited by Vicki Smith, 293–315. Bingley, UK: Emerald.

Schumacher, Ernst Friedrich. 1973. *Small Is Beautiful: Economics as if People Mattered*. New York: Harper and Row.

Schwartzman, Helen B. 1993. *Ethnography in Organizations*. Newbury Park, CA: Sage.

Scott, Ellen K. 2005. "Beyond Tokenism: The Making of Racially Diverse Feminist Organizations." *Social Problems* 52 (2): 232–54.

Scott, Joan Wallach. 1988. *Gender and the Politics of History*. New York: Columbia University Press.

——. 1991. "The Evidence of Experience." *Critical Inquiry* 17 (4): 773–97.

Selznick, Philip. 1949. *TVA and the Grass Roots: A Study in the Sociology of Formal Organization*. Berkeley: University of California Press.

Sennett, Richard, and Jonathan Cobb. 1972. *The Hidden Injuries of Class*. New York: Alfred A. Knopf.

Shafer, David A. 2005. *The Paris Commune: French Politics, Culture, and Society at the Crossroads of the Revolutionary Tradition and Revolutionary Socialism*. New York: Palgrave Macmillan.

Sirianni, Carmen. 1993. "Learning Pluralism: Democracy and Diversity in Feminist Organizations." In *Critical Studies in Organization and Bureaucracy*, edited by Frank Fischer and Carmen Sirianni, 554–76. Philadelphia: Temple University Press.

Sirianni, Carmen, and Cynthia Negrey. 2000. "Working Time as Gendered Time." *Feminist Economics* 6 (1): 59–76.

Skaggs, Sheryl. 2008. "Producing Change or Bagging Opportunity? The Effects of Discrimination Litigation on Women in Supermarket Management." *American Journal of Sociology* 113 (4): 1148–82.

Skeggs, Beverley. 1997. *Formations of Class and Gender: Becoming Respectable*. London: Sage.

——. 2011. "Imagining Personhood Differently: Person Value and Autonomist Working-Class Value Practices." *The Sociological Review* 59 (3): 496–513.

Smith, Adam. 1994. *The Wealth of Nations*. New York: Modern Library.

Smith, Vicki. 2001. *Crossing the Great Divide: Worker Risk and Opportunity in the New Economy*. Ithaca, NY: ILR Press, an imprint of Cornell University Press.

Sobering, Katherine. 2016. "Producing and Reducing Gender Inequality in a Worker-Recovered Cooperative." *Sociological Quarterly* 57 (1): 129–51.

——. 2019a. "The Relational Production of Workplace Equality: The Case of Worker-Recuperated Businesses in Argentina." *Qualitative Sociology* 42 (4): 543–65.

——. 2019b. "Watercooler Democracy: Rumors and Transparency in a Cooperative Workplace." *Work and Occupations* 46 (4): 411–440.

Sobering, Katherine, Jessica Thomas, and Christine L. Williams. 2014. "Gender In/Equality in Worker-Owned Businesses." *Sociology Compass* 8 (11): 1242–55.

Solnit, Rebecca. 2015. *Men Explain Things to Me*. Updated ed. Chicago: Haymarket Books.

Somer, Margaret R. 1994. "The Narrative Constitution of Identity: A Relational and Network Approach." *Theory and Society* 23 (5): 605–49.

Sommer, Robert, and Carla Fjeld. 1983. "Consumer Protection Programs in Food Cooperatives." *Policy Studies Review* 2 (3): 455–64.

Sousa, Jorge. 2015. "Realizing the Cooperative Advantage at the Atkinson Housing Cooperative: The Role of Community Development to Improve Public Housing." *Journal of Entrepreneurial and Organizational Diversity* 4 (1): 52–74.

Spellman, Susan V. 2016. *Cornering the Market: Independent Grocers and Innovation in American Small Business*. New York: Oxford University Press.

Spivak, Gayatri Chakravorty. 1999. *A Critique of Postcolonial Reason: Toward a History of the Vanishing Present*. Cambridge, MA: Harvard University Press.

Staber, Udo. 1993. "Worker Cooperatives and the Business Cycle: Are Cooperatives the Answer to Unemployment?" *American Journal of Economics and Sociology* 52 (2): 129–43.

Stacey, Clare L. 2011. *The Caring Self: The Work Experiences of Home Care Aides*. Ithaca, NY: ILR Press, an imprint of Cornell University Press.

Stacey, Judith. 1988. "Can There Be a Feminist Ethnography?" *Women's Studies International Forum* 11 (1): 21–27.

Stainback, Kevin, and Donald Tomaskovic-Devey. 2012. *Documenting Desegregation: Racial and Gender Segregation in Private-Sector Employment since the Civil Rights Act*. New York: Russell Sage Foundation.

Stark, David. 2009. "Heterarchy: The Organization of Dissonance." In *The Sense of Dissonance: Accounts of Worth in Economic Life*, 1–34. Princeton, NJ: Princeton University Press.

Steinberg, Ronnie J. 1995. "Gendered Instructions: Cultural Lag and Gender Bias in the Hay System of Job Evaluation." In *Gender Inequality at Work*, edited by Jerry Jacobs, 57–92. Thousand Oaks, CA: Sage.

Stevenson, Lois A. 1986. "Against All Odds: The Entrepreneurship of Women." *Journal of Small Business Management* 24 (4): 30–36.

Stinchcombe, Arthur. 1965. "Social Structure and Organizations." In *Handbook of Organizations*, edited by J. G. March, 142–93. Chicago: Rand McNally.

Stone, Pamela. 2007. *Opting Out? Why Women Really Quit Careers and Head Home*. Berkeley: University of California Press.

Storey, John, Imanol Basterretxea, and Graeme Salaman. 2014. "Managing and Resisting 'Degeneration' in Employee-Owned Businesses: A Comparative Study of Two Large Retailers in Spain and the United Kingdom." *Organization* 21 (5): 626–44.

Storrs, Landon R. Y. 2006. "Left-Feminism, the Consumer Movement, and Red Scare Politics in the United States, 1935–1960." *Journal of Women's History* 18 (3): 40–67.

Stuber, Jenny M. 2011. *Inside the College Gates: How Class and Culture Matter in Higher Education*. Lanham, MD: Lexington Books.

Sutcliffe-Braithwaite, Florence. 2018. *Class, Politics, and the Decline of Deference in England, 1968–2000*. Oxford: Oxford University Press.

Swidler, Ann. 1973. "The Concept of Rationality in the Work of Max Weber." *Sociological Inquiry* 43 (1): 35–42.

——. 1979. *Organization without Authority: Dilemmas of Social Control in Free Schools*. Cambridge, MA: Harvard University Press.

——. 2001. *Talk of Love: How Culture Matters*. Chicago: University of Chicago Press.

Tajfel, Henri, and John C. Turner. 1979. "An Integrative Theory of Intergroup Relations." In *The Social Psychology of Intergroup Relations*, edited by Stephen Worchel and William G. Austin, 33–47. Monterey: Brooks-Cole.

Taylor, Astra, and Leah Hunt-Hendrix. 2019. "One for All." *New Republic*, September 2019, 24–29.

Taylor, Barbara. 1983. *Eve and the New Jerusalem: Socialism and Feminism in the Nineteenth Century*. New York: Pantheon Books.

Taylor, Keeanga-Yamahtta. 2016. *From #Blacklivesmatter to Black Liberation*. Chicago: Haymarket Books.

Taylor, Kieran. 2010. "American Petrograd: Detroit and the League of Revolutionary Black Workers." In *Rebel Rank and File: Labor Militancy and Revolt from Below during the Long 1970s*, edited by Aaron Brenner, Robert Brenner and Calvin Winslow, 311–33. London: Verso.

Taylor, Peter Leigh. 1994. "The Rhetorical Construction of Efficiency: Restructuring and Industrial Democracy in Mondragón, Spain." *Sociological Forum* 9 (3): 459–89.

Thomas, David A., and Robin J. Ely. 1996. "Making Differences Matter: A New Paradigm for Managing Diversity." *Harvard Business Review* 74 (5): 79–90.

Thompson, David J. 1992. "What's Next for California's Consumer Co-Ops?" In *What Happened to the Berkeley Co-Op? A Collection of Opinions*, edited by Michael Fullerton, 87–92. Davis, CA: Center for Cooperatives.

Tilly, Charles. 1998. *Durable Inequality*. Berkeley: University of California Press.

Tilly, Chris. 1997. "Arresting the Decline of Good Jobs in the USA?" *Industrial Relations Journal* 28 (4): 269–74.

Tomaskovic-Devey, Donald, and Dustin Avent-Holt. 2019. *Relational Inequalities: An Organizational Approach*. New York: Oxford University Press.

Tomaskovic-Devey, Donald, and Ken-Hou Lin. 2011. "Income Dynamics, Economic Rents, and the Financialization of the U.S. Economy." *American Sociological Review* 76 (4): 538–59.

Tonnesen, Sara. 2012. "Stronger Together: Worker Cooperatives as a Community Economic Development Strategy." *Georgetown Journal on Poverty Law and Policy* 20: 187–209.

Tontz, Robert L. 1964. "Memberships of General Farmers' Organizations, United States, 1874–1960." *Agricultural History* 38 (3): 143–56.

Trotsky, Leon. 1922. *Dictatorship vs. Democracy (Terrorism and Communism): A Reply to Karl Kautsky, by Leon Trotsky [Pseud.].* New York: Workers Party of America.

Tselos, George. 1977. "Self-Help and Sauerkraut: The Organized Unemployed, Inc., of Minneapolis." *Minnesota History* 45 (8): 306–20.

Turco, Catherine. 2016. *The Conversational Firm: Rethinking Bureaucracy in the Age of Social Media.* New York: Columbia University Press.

US Census Bureau. 2004. *2004 County Business Patterns: Geography Area Series; County Business Patterns by Employment Size.* Washington, DC: US Census Bureau.

Utting, Peter, Cecilia Rossel, Suzanne Bergeron, Stephen Healy, Carina Millstone, Bénédicte Fonteneau, Georgina Gómez, Marguerite Mendell, Paul Nelson, and John-Justin McMurtry. 2015. *Social and Solidarity Economy: Beyond the Fringe.* London: Zed Books.

Vallas, Steven P. 1999. "Rethinking Post-Fordism: The Meaning of Workplace Flexibility." *Sociological Theory* 17 (1): 68–101.

——. 2003. "Rediscovering the Color Line within Work Organizations: The 'Knitting of Racial Groups' Revisited." *Work and Occupations* 30 (4): 379–400.

Valocchi, Steve. 1990. "The Unemployed Workers Movement of the 1930s: A Reexamination of the Piven and Cloward Thesis." *Social Problems* 37 (2): 191–205.

Van der Zwan, Natascha. 2014. "Making Sense of Financialization." *Socio-Economic Review* 12 (1): 99–129.

Van Maanen, John. 1979. "The Fact of Fiction in Organizational Ethnography." *Administrative Science Quarterly* 24 (4): 539–50.

Vieta, Marcelo. 2009. "The Social Innovations of Autogestión in Argentina's Worker-Recuperated Enterprises: Cooperatively Reorganizing Productive Life in Hard Times." *Labor Studies Journal* 35 (3): 295–321.

Viggiani, Frances A. 1997. "Democratic Hierarchies in the Workplace: Structural Dilemmas and Organizational Action." *Economic and Industrial Democracy* 18 (2): 231–60.

——. 1999. "'Doing the Right Thing' Organisational Structure and Process for Democratic Governance in the Firm." *Industrial Relations Journal* 30 (3): 229–42.

——. 2011. "Phoenix Trucking—'I Believe in Democracy up to a Point': Democratizing Management Hierarchies." *International Journal of Management and Innovation* 3 (1): 1–31.

Virtue, G. O. 1905. "The Co-operative Coopers of Minneapolis." *Quarterly Journal of Economics* 19 (4): 527–44.

——. 1932. "The End of the Cooperative Coopers." *Quarterly Journal of Economics* 46 (3): 541–45.

Vogel, Lise. 1983. *Marxism and the Oppression of Women: Toward a Unitary Theory.* New Brunswick, NJ: Rutgers University Press.

Voss, Kim. 1993. *The Making of American Exceptionalism: The Knights of Labor and Class Formation in the Nineteenth Century.* Ithaca, NY: Cornell University Press.

Walsh, James P., and Robert D. Dewar. 1987. "Formalization and the Organizational Life Cycle." *Journal of Management Studies* 24 (3): 215–31.

Ward, Colin. 2011. *Autonomy, Solidarity, Possibility: The Colin Ward Reader.* Edited by Chris Wilbert and Damian F. White. Oakland, CA: AK Press.

Ward, Jane. 2008. *Respectably Queer: Diversity Culture in LGBT Activist Organizations.* Nashville: Vanderbilt University Press.

WCIRB (Workers' Compensation Insurance Rating Bureau of California). 2019. "Experience Modification." Web page. https://www.wcirb.com/guide-to-workers-compensation/experience-rating/experience-modification.

Webb, Sidney, and Beatrice Potter Webb. 1897. *Industrial Democracy.* London: Longmans, Green.

——. 1920. *A Constitution for the Socialist Commonwealth of Great Britain.* London: Longmans, Green.

Weber, Max. 1946. *From Max Weber: Essays in Sociology.* Translated by Hans H. Gerth and C. Wright Mills. New York: Oxford University Press.

——. 1978. *Economy and Society.* Berkeley: University of California Press.

Weeden, Kim A., Young-Mi Kim, Matthew Di Carlo, and David B. Grusky. 2007. "Social Class and Earnings Inequality." *American Behavioral Scientist* 50 (5): 702–36.

Weeks, Kathi. 2011. *The Problem with Work: Feminism, Marxism, Antiwork Politics, and Postwork Imaginaries.* Durham, NC: Duke University Press.

Weis, Lois. 2004. *Class Reunion: The Remaking of the American White Working Class.* New York: Routledge.

Wells, Miriam J. 1996. *Strawberry Fields: Politics, Class, and Work in California Agriculture.* Ithaca, NY: Cornell University Press.

Western, Bruce. 1997. *Between Class and Market: Postwar Unionization in the Capitalist Democracies.* Princeton, NJ: Princeton University Press.

Western, Bruce, and Jake Rosenfeld. 2011. "Unions, Norms, and the Rise in U.S. Wage Inequality." *American Sociological Review* 76 (4): 513–37.

Wetherell, Margaret, and Chandra Talpade Mohanty. 2010. "Introduction." In *The Sage Handbook of Identities,* edited by Margaret Wetherell and Chandra Talpade Mohanty, 2–26. London: Sage.

Whyte, William Foote, and Kathleen King Whyte. 1991. *Making Mondragón: The Growth and Dynamics of the Worker Cooperative Complex.* 2nd ed. Ithaca, NY: ILR Press, an imprint of Cornell University Press.

Wickham, James, Gráinne Collins, Lidia Greco, and Josephine Browne. 2008. "Individualization and Equality: Women's Careers and Organizational Form." *Organization* 15 (2): 211–31.

Wilensky, Harold L. 1961. "The Trade Union as a Bureaucracy." In *Complex Organizations: A Sociological Reader,* edited by Amitai Etzioni, 221–34. New York: Holt, Rinehart and Winston.

Williams, Christine L. 2006. *Inside Toyland: Working, Shopping, and Social Inequality.* Berkeley: University of California Press.

Willis, Paul. 1977. *Learning to Labor.* New York: Columbia University Press.

——. 1990. "Masculinity and Factory Labor." In *Culture and Society: Contemporary Debates,* edited by Jeffrey A. Alexander and Steven Seidman, 183–95. Cambridge: Cambridge University Press.

Wilson, Amanda. 2010. "Co-opting Precariousness: Can Worker Cooperatives Be Alternatives to Precarious Employment for Marginalized Populations? A Case Study of Immigrant and Refugee Worker Cooperatives in Canada." *Just Labour: A Canadian Journal of Work and Society* 16: 59–75.

Wilson, Jake B. 2008. "The Racialized Picket Line: White Workers and Racism in the Southern California Supermarket Strike." *Critical Sociology* 34 (3): 349–67.

Wilson, William Julius. 1987. *The Truly Disadvantaged: The Inner City, the Underclass, and Public Policy*. Chicago: University of Chicago Press.

——. 1996. *When Work Disappears: The World of the New Urban Poor*. New York: Alfred A. Knopf.

Wingfield, Adia Harvey. 2009. "Racializing the Glass Escalator: Reconsidering Men's Experiences with Women's Work." *Gender & Society* 23 (1): 5–26.

Witherell, Rob. 2013. "An Emerging Solidarity: Worker Cooperatives, Unions, and the New Union Cooperative Model in the United States." *International Journal of Labour Research* 5 (2): 251–68.

Wolff, Edward N., Lindsay A. Owens, and Esra Burak. 2011. "How Much Wealth Was Destroyed in the Great Recession?" In *The Consequences of the Great Recession*, edited by David B. Grusky, Bruce Western, and Christopher Wimer, 127–58. New York: Russell Sage Foundation.

Wood, Elisabeth Jean. 2003. *Insurgent Collective Action and Civil War in El Salvador*. Cambridge: Cambridge University Press.

Wright, Erik Olin. 2006. "Compass Points: Toward a Socialist Alternative." *New Left Review* 41: 93–141.

——. 2010. *Envisioning Real Utopias*. London: Verso.

——. 2011. "Real Utopias." *Contexts* 10 (2): 36–42.

Yasukochi, George. 1992. "The Berkeley Co-op—Anatomy of a Noble Experiment." In *What Happened to the Berkeley Co-Op? A Collection of Opinions*, edited by Michael Fullerton, 23–32. Davis, CA: Center for Cooperatives.

Yinger, J. Milton. 1960. "Contraculture and Subculture." *American Sociological Review* 25 (5): 625–35.

Yorra, Emma. 2019. "Scaling Social Justice: A Latinx Immigrant Worker Co-Op Franchise Model." *Nonprofit Quarterly*, February 14, 2019. https://nonprofitquarterly.org/2019/02/14/scaling-social-justice-a-latinx-immigrant-worker-co-op-franchise-model/.

Zingraff, Rhonda, and Michael D. Schulman. 1984. "Social Bases of Class Consciousness: A Study of Southern Textile Workers with a Comparison by Race." *Social Forces* 63 (1): 98–116.

Zinn, Howard. 2003. *A People's History of the United States, 1492–Present*. New York: Harper Perennial.

Index

Page numbers in *italics* indicate figures and tables.